THE

AUTOBIOGRAPHY OF LEIGH HUNT.

"Most men when drawn to speak about themselves,
Are moved by little and little to say more
Than they first dreamt; until at last they blush,
And can but hope to find secret excuse
In the self-knowledge of their auditors."

WALTER SCOTT'S Old Play.

A NEW EDITION, REVISED BY THE AUTHOR.

LONDON:
SMITH, ELDER & CO., 15, WATERLOO PLACE.
1870.

CONTENTS.

INTRODUCTION

BY THE AUTHOR'S ELDEST SON.

THIS edition of the *Autobiography* was revised by Mr. Leigh Hunt, and brought down to the present year by his own hand. He had almost completed the passages which he intended to add; but he had left some portions which were marked for omission in a state of doubt. From the manner in which the work was written, points of interest here and there were passed over indistinctly or omitted altogether, and some inaccuracies were overlooked in the re-perusal. In a further revision by the writer's eldest son, several obscurities have been cleared away, inaccuracies have been corrected, and omissions have been supplied. The interpolated passages, whether in the text or in notes, are distinguished by being included in brackets.

In the Preface to the earlier edition, the Author avowed that he felt a difficulty in having to retrace a life which was marked by comparatively little incident, and was necessarily, therefore, mainly a retrospect of his own writings. Another difficulty, of which he was evidently conscious only through its effect in cramping his pen, lay in an excess of scruple when he approached personal matters. In the revisal of this second edition, however, the lapse of time had in some degree freed him from restraint; and while the curtailments necessary to compress the bulk of the volume have been made principally in the more detailed portions of the literary retrospect, the additions have tended to increase the personal interest of the text. The work is relieved of some other portions, because they may be found in his collected writings, or because the subject-matter to which they refer is out of date. The result of the alterations is, that the biographical part of the volume is brought more closely together, while it is presented with greater fulness and distinctness.

The reader of this Autobiography will find it less a relation of the events which happened to the writer, than of their impression on himself, and the feelings which they excited, or the ideas which they prompted. This characteristic of the writing is in a great degree a characteristic of the man, and thus the book reflects his own life more than on a first judgment it might be supposed to do. His whole existence and his habit of mind, were essentially literary. If it were possible to form any computation of the hours which he expended severally in literary labour and in recreation, after the manner of statistical comparisons, it would be found that the largest portion of his hours was devoted to hard work in the seclusion of the study, and that by far the larger portion of the allotted "recreation" was devoted to reading, either in the study or in the society of his family. Those who knew him best will picture him to themselves clothed in a dressing-gown, and bending his head over a book or over the desk. At some periods of his life he rose early, in order that he might get to work early; in other periods he rose late, because he sat over the desk very late. For the most part, however, he habitually came down "too late" to breakfast, and was no sooner seated sideways at the table than he began to read. After breakfast he repaired to his study, where he remained until he went out to take his walk. He sometimes read at dinner, though not always. At some periods of his life he would sleep after dinner; but usually he retired from the table to read. He read at tea time, and all the evening read or wrote. In early life his profession led him, as a critic, to the theatres, and the same employment took him there at later dates. In the earlier half of his existence he mixed somewhat in society, and his own house was noted, amongst a truly selected circle of friends, for the tasteful ease of its conversation and recreation, music usually forming a staple in both the talk and the diversion. It was at this period of his life that his appearance was most characteristic, and none of the portraits of him adequately conveyed the idea of it. One of the best, a half-length chalk drawing, by an artist named Wildman, perished. The miniature by Severn was only a sketch on a small scale, but it suggested the kindness and animation of his countenance. In other cases, the artists knew too little of their sitter to catch the most familiar traits of his aspect. He was rather tall, as straight as an arrow, and looked slenderer than he really was. His hair was black and shining, and slightly inclined to wave; his head was high, his forehead straight and white, his eyes black and sparkling, his general complexion dark. There was in his whole carriage and manner an extraordinary degree of life. Years and trouble had obscured that brilliancy when the drawing was made of which a copy is prefixed to the present volume; but it is a faithful portrait, in which the reader will see much of the reflection, the earnestness, and the affectionate thought that were such leading elements in his character.

As life advanced, as his family increased faster than his means, his range of visiting became more contracted, his devotion to labour more continuous, and his friends reduced to the small number of those who came only to steal for conversation the time that he otherwise would have given to his books. Such friends he welcomed heartily, and seldom allowed them to feel the tax which they made him pay for the time thus consumed.

Even at seasons of the greatest depression in his fortunes, he always attracted many visitors, but still not so much for any repute that attended him as for his personal qualities. Few men were more attractive "in society," whether in a large company or over the fireside. His manners were peculiarly animated; his conversation, varied, ranging over a great field of subjects, was moved and called forth by the response of his companion, be that companion philosopher or student, sage or boy, man or woman ; and he was equally ready for the most lively topics or for the gravest reflections—his expression easily adapting itself to the tone of his companion's mind. With much freedom of manners, he combined a spontaneous courtesy that never failed, and a considerateness derived from a ceaseless kindness of heart that invariably fascinated even strangers. In the course of his newspaper career, more than one enemy has come to his house with the determination to extort disavowals or to chastise, and has gone away with loud expressions of his personal esteem and liking.

This tendency to seclusion in the study had a very large and serious influence upon Leigh Hunt's life. It arose, as we have seen, from no dislike to society; on the contrary, from youth to his very latest days, he preferred to have companions with him ; but it was necessary to be surrounded by his books. He used to ascribe this propensity to his two years' seclusion in prison; and it is probable that that circumstance did contribute to fasten upon his character what must still have been an inborn tendency; for it continued through all changes of position. His natural faculties conduced to make him regard all things that came before him chiefly from the intellectual or imaginative point of view. He had no aptitude for material science, and always retained a very precarious grasp of mere dry facts; which, indeed, in proportion as they tended to the material or the hard, he almost disliked: the result was, that he viewed all things as in a mirror, and chiefly as they were reflected in books or illuminated by literary commentary.

It is a necessary consequence of such a habit of mind that he often failed to see realities directly as they were; and a further result was, that false ideas which were industriously circulated of him, in the first instance by political enemies, were confirmed, or even strengthened, by false conceptions which he formed of himself, and did not conceal. At a very early date, he felt bound to avow his liberal opinions on the subject of religion: in those days it was a common and an easy retort for an opponent to insinuate, that the man who was not sound in the most important opinions of all, must be wicked at heart, and therefore immoral in conduct; and, accordingly, Leigh Hunt has been accused of lax morality in his personal life. To him the shocking part of these accusals lay in their uncharitableness, their disingenuousness, or their malignity. In reply, he pointed to the charity enjoined by the Divine Author of Christianity, and qualified even his antagonism to such charges by appeals to charitable constructions, and admissions of the foibles of human nature, which suggested that there might be some foundation of truth for the charge. He was accused of improvidence, and he admitted incapacities for computation in matters of money, or anything else, which sounded very like a reluctant confession. Stern critics discerned, in the pleasurable traits of his gayer poems, proofs of effeminacy and weakness; and throughout Leigh Hunt's writings will be found admissions, or even spontaneous announcements, of personal timidity. If there were not numbers

disposed to accept the best construction of the man, it
would be difficult indeed to make them easily understand how utterly unfounded are these apparent confir-
mations and admissions.

Such foibles as Leigh Hunt had lay altogether in
different directions. In early life he had no very profound respect for appearances, but his conduct was
guided by a rigour of propriety that might shame many
of his accusers; and in later life he entertained a
growing respect for appearances from the sense of the
mischief which misconstrued example might do. His
so-called improvidence resulted partly from actual disappointment in professional undertakings, partly from
a real incapacity to understand any subjects when they
were reduced to figures, and partly also from a readiness
of self-sacrifice, which was the less to be guessed by
any who knew him, since he seldom alluded to it, and
never, except in the vaguest and most unintelligible
terms, hinted at its real nature or extent. His personal
timidity was simply an intellectual hallucination, in some
degree founded upon what he supposed ought to be the
utterly unmoved feelings of " a brave man." I have
seen him in many situations calculated to try the nerves,
and never saw him moved by personal fear. He has
been in a carriage of which the horses ran away, and
seemed only to enjoy the rapidity of the motion; in
fact, I believe he could scarcely present to his mind the
chances of personal mischief that were before us. I
have seen him threatened, more than once, by brutal
and brawny rustics, whom he instantly approached with
an animated and convincing remonstrance. I have seen
him in a carriage nearly carried away by a flooded
river, his whole anxiety being centred in one of his
children whom he thought to be more exposed than
himself. I have seen him for weeks together, each hour
of the day, in imminent danger of shipwreck, and never

observed the slightest solicitude, except for those about him. On the occasion which he mentions, when the drunken steward endangered our being run down by two large ships that passed us like vast clouds astern, the lanterns were relit and handed up by Leigh Hunt with the coolness of a practised seaman. But there *was* a species of fear which beset him in every situation of life—it was, lest he might not do quite what was right; lest some terrible evil should be inflicted upon somebody else; and this thought, if he reflected, did sometimes paralyse his action and provoke evident emotion.

Perhaps the mastering trait in his character was a conscientiousness which was carried even to extremes. While he possessed the uncertain grasp of material facts which I have mentioned, and viewed things most distinctly when they were presented to his mind in the mirror of some abstraction, he never was able to rest with a final confidence in his own judgment. The anxiety to recognise the right of others, the tendency to " refine," which was noticed by an early school companion, and the propensity to elaborate every thought, made him, along with the direct argument by which he sustained his own conviction, recognise and almost admit all that might be said on the opposite side. If, indeed, the facts upon which he had to rely had become matter of literary record, he would collect them with an unwearied industry of research; but in the action of life these resources did not always avail him; and the excessive anxiety to take into account all that might be advanced on every side, with the no less excessive wish to do what was right, to avoid every chance of wrong, and, if possible, to abstain from causing any pain, begot an uncertainty of purpose for which I can find no known prototype except in the character of Hamlet.

The ultra-conscientiousness has affected even his

biography. With an unbounded frankness in speaking of himself, he soon paused in speaking of others, from the habit of questioning whether he had " any right" to do so ; and thus an habitual frankness was accompanied by an habitual and unconquerable reserve. His Autobiography is characteristically pronounced in its silence. He has nowhere related the most obvious family incidents. The silence is broken almost in an inverse proportion to the intimacy of his relations. He scarcely mentions his own marriage ; excepting the faintest possible allusions, the only one of his children to whom he alludes has been to a certain extent before the public ; and even where his personal friends gave him, in their own recognition by the public, the right to speak of them openly, he has faithfully used the right in the peculiar ratio which has been pointed out,—freely mentioning those with whom he held intercourse chiefly in literary matters or in society, sparingly those whose intercourse powerfully affected his own life. A conspicuous instance is afforded by the friend who ultimately became his successor in maintaining the general independence of the *Examiner*, who has placed in the library immortal contributions to the political history of the English Commonwealth, who endeared himself to Leigh Hunt even less by most valuable and laborious services than by kindness of heart and generosity of mind, and who retained his strongly expressed affection to the last. It was not that he did not respond to the warmest affection which he could so well inspire ; but in proportion as it was strongly felt and personal he seemed to regard it as unfitted for public allusion.

It would ill become a son gratuitously to reveal " the faults " of his father ; though he himself taught me to speak out the truth as I believe it. If I differ with him, it is in *not* being ready to see " faults " in any character, since I know of no abstract or ideal measure by which the shortcoming could be established. But in his case it is most desirable that his qualities should be known as they were; for such deficiencies as he had are the honest explanation of his mistakes; while, as the reader may see from his writing and his conduct, they are not, as the faults of which he was accused would be, incompatible with the noblest faculties both of head and heart. To know Leigh Hunt as he was, was to hold him in reverence and love.

The likeness to Hamlet was not lost even in a sort of aggressive conscientiousness. It affected his appreciation of character, which was, of course, modified also by the oblique sense of facts. Hence, some incidents in his life which had the most serious consequences to others, and therefore to himself. When he first became acquainted with a new friend whom he liked, he noticed with all his vivacity of ready and intense admiration the traits which he thought to be chiefly prominent in the aspect and bearing of the other; constructed a character inferentially, and esteemed his friend accordingly. This constructive appreciation would survive the test of years. Then he would discover that in regard to some quality or other which he had ascribed to his friend " he was mistaken;" the whole conception of the admired character at once fell to the ground; and his own disappointment recoiled with bitterness and grief on the perplexed and grieved friend. He never knew the pain he thus caused to some of the most loving hearts, which continued unchanged to him.

If, indeed, he knew it, the simple knowledge was enough to cure the evil. No man ever lived who was more prepared to make thorough work with the practice of his own precepts—and his precepts were always noble in their spirit, charitable in their construction. No injury done to him, however inexcusable, however unceasing, or however painful in its consequences, could exhaust his power of forgiveness. His animation, his sympathy with what was gay and pleasurable, his avowed doctrine of cultivating cheerfulness, were manifest on the surface, and could be appreciated by those who knew him in society, most probably even exaggerated as salient traits, on which he himself insisted with a sort of gay and ostentatious wilfulness. In the spirit which made him disposed to enjoy "anything that was going forward," he would even assume for the evening a convivial aspect, and urge a liberal measure of the wine with the gusto of a *bon vivant*. Few that knew him so could be aware, not only of the simple and uncostly sources from which he habitually drew his enjoyments, but of his singularly plain life, extended even to a rule of self-denial. Excepting at intervals when wine was recommended to him, or came to him as a gift of friendship, his customary drink was water, which he would drink with the almost daily repetition of Dr. Armstrong's line, "Nought like the simple element dilutes." For, a trick of playing with a certain round of quotations was among the traits of his character most conspicuous even to casual visitors. In the routine of life, it may be said, he almost thought in a slang of the library. His dress was always plain and studiously economical. He would *excuse* the extreme plainness of his diet, by ascribing it to a delicacy of health, which he overrated. His food was often nothing but bread and meat at dinner, bread and tea for two meals of the day, bread alone for luncheon or for supper. His liberal constructions were shown to others, his strictness to himself. If he heard that a friend was in trouble, his house was offered as a "home;" and it was literally so, many times in his life. Sometimes this generosity was repaid with outrageous ingratitude—with scandal-mongering, and even calumnious inventions: he excused the wrong, as the consequence of deficient sense, of early training, or of congenital fault; "for," he would remark, "it is impossible to say what share, now, X.'s father and mother may have had in his doing so, or what ancestor of X.'s may not have been *really* the author of my suffering—and his." When he was once reminded of his sacrifices for others, he answered, as if it dismissed the subject, " It was only for my own relations;" but his memory deceived him extravagantly. It was not that his kindness was undiscriminating; for he " drew the line" with much clearness between what he "could" do for the mere sake of helping the unfortunate, and the willingness to share whatever he might have with those he really esteemed and loved—not a few. The tenderness of his affection was excessive : it disarmed some of the most reckless ; it made him throw a veil of impenetrable reserve over weaknesses of others, from which he suffered in ways most calculated to mortify and pain him, but which he suffered with never-failing kindness, and with silence absolutely unbroken.

It must not be supposed, however, that with all his disposition to refine, his love of the pleasurable, and his tenderness, he was a mere easy sentimentalist. If he may be compared to Hamlet, it was Hamlet buckling himself to hard work, and performing with vigour and conscientious completeness. Seldom have writers so conscientiously verified all their statements of fact. His constant industry has been mentioned : he could work from early morning till far into midnight, every day, for months together ; and he had been a hard-working man all his life. For the greater part, even his recreation was auxiliary to his work. He had thus acquired a knowledge of authorities most unusual, and had heaps of information " at his fingers' ends ;" yet he habitually verified even what he knew already, though it should be only for some parenthetical use. No tenderness could shake him from sternly rebuking or opposing where duty bade him do so; and for a principle he was prepared to sacrifice everything, as he had sacrificed money and liberty. For all his excessive desire not to withhold his sympathy, not to hurt others' feelings, or not to overlook any possible excuse for infirmity, moral as well as physical, he never paltered with his own sincerity. He never swerved from what he believed to be the truth.

In the course of his long life as a public writer, political and polemical animosities died away, and were succeeded by a broader recognition of common purposes and common endeavours, to which he had not a little contributed. Although some strange misconceptions of Leigh Hunt's character still remained,—strange, though, as we have seen, not difficult to explain,—the acknowment of his genuine qualities had widely extended. There had been great changes, some liberals had become conservative, more conservatives had become liberal, all had become less dogmatic and uncharitable. His personal friendships embraced every party; but through all, the spirit of his opinions, the qualities of his character, the unweariedness of his industry, continued the same. To promote the happiness of his kind, to minister to the more educated appreciation of order and beauty, to open more widely the door of the library, and more widely the window of the library looking out upon nature,—these were the purposes that guided his studies and animated his labour to the very last.

AUTOBIOGRAPHY OF LEIGH HUNT.

CHAPTER I.

THE AUTHOR'S PROGENITORS.

THE circumstances that led to this Autobiography will transpire in the course of it. Suffice it to say for the present, that a more involuntary production it would be difficult to conceive ; though I trust it will not be found destitute of the entertainment which any true account of experiences in the life of a human being must of necessity, perhaps, contain.

I claim no importance for anything which I have done or undergone, but on grounds common to the interests of all, and to the willing sympathy of my brother-lovers of books. Should I be led at any time into egotisms of a nature that make me seem to think otherwise, I blush beforehand for the mischance, and beg it to be considered as alien from my habits of reflection. I have had vanities enough in my day ; and, as the reader will see, became aware of them. If I have any remaining, I hope they are only such as nature kindly allows to most of us, in order to comfort us in our regrets and infirmities. And the more we could look even into these, the less ground we should find in them for self-complacency, apart from considerations that respect the whole human race.

There is a phrase, for instance, of "fetching a man's mind from his cradle." But does the mind begin at that point of time? Does it begin even with his parents? I was looking once, in company with Mr. Hazlitt, at an exhibition of pictures in the British Institution, when casting my eyes on the portrait of an officer in the dress of the time of Charles the Second, I exclaimed, "What a likeness to Basil Montagu!" (a friend of ours). It turned out to be his ancestor, Lord Sandwich. Mr. Hazlitt took me across the room, and showed

me the portrait of a celebrated judge, who lived at the same
period. "This," said he, "is Judge So-and-so; and his
living representative (he is now dead) has the same face and
the same passions." The Hazlitt then of the same age might
have been the same Hazlitt that was standing with me before
the picture ; and the same may have been the case with the
writer of these pages. There is a famous historical bit of
transmission called the "Austrian lip ;" and faces, which we
consider peculiar to individuals, are said to be common in
districts : such as the Boccaccio face in one part of Tuscany,
and the Dante face in another. I myself have seen, in the
Genoese territory, which is not far from Corsica, many a face
like that of the Bonapartes; and where a race has strong
blood in it, or whatever may constitute the requisite vital
tendency, it is probable that the family likeness might
be found to prevail in the humblest as well as highest
quarters. There are families, indeed, of yeomen, which are
said to have flourished like oaks, in one and the same spot,
since the times of the Anglo-Saxons. I am descended, both
by father's and mother's side, from adventurous people, who
left England for the New World, and whose descendants have
retained the spirit of adventure to this day. The chances are,
that in some respects I am identical with some half-dozen, or
perhaps twenty of these; and that the mind of some cavalier
of the days of the Stuarts, or some gentleman or yeoman, or
"roving blade," of those of the Edwards and Henrys—perhaps the gallant merchant-man, "Henry Hunt" of the old
ballad—mixed, alas ! with a sedentary difference—is now
writing these lines, ignorant of his former earthly self and of
his present ! I say earthly, for I speak it with no disparagement to the existence of an individual "soul"—a point in
which I am a firm believer ; nor would it be difficult to
reconcile one opinion with the other, in ears accustomed to
such arguments ; but I must not enter upon them here.*

* "Then Henrye Hunt, with vigour hott,
  Came bravely on the other side,
  Soon he drove downe his foremast tree,
    (*Sir Andrew Barton's, to wit*)
  And killèd fourscore men beside.
 'Nowe, out alas!' Sir Andrewe cryed,
  'What may a man now think, or say?
  Yonder merchant theefe, that pierceth mee,
  He was my prisoner yesterday.'"
   Ballad of Sir Andrew Barton, in Percy's Reliques, vol. 2.
             [Barton

The name of Hunt is found among the gentry, but I suspect it is oftener a plebeian name. Indeed it must be so, like almost all others, from the superabundance of population on the plebeian side. But it has also a superabundance of its own; for in the list of sixty of the commonest names in England, given by Mr. Lower in his *Essay on Family Nomenclature*, it stands fifty-fourth. On the other hand, offsets from aristocratic trees wander into such remote branches, that the same name is found among those of the few families that have a right to quarter the royal arms. I should be very proud to be discovered to be a nine hundred and fiftieth cousin of Queen Victoria; the more so, inasmuch as I could, patiently enough, have let the claim lie dormant in the case of some of her Majesty's predecessors. My immediate progenitors were clergymen; and Bryan Edwards's *History of the West Indies* contains a map of Barbados (their native place) with one of the residences designated by it—apparently a minor estate— yet the name of Hunt does not appear either in the old map in the *History of Barbados* by Ligon, or in the lists of influential or other persons in that by Sir Robert Schomburgck. There is a "Richard Hunt, Esq." in the list of subscribers to Hughes's *Natural History of Barbados*, which contains also the name of Dr. Hunt, who was Hebrew and Arabic professor at Oxford, and whose genealogy the biographer cannot discover. Perhaps the good old oriental scholar belongs to our stock, and originated my love of the Arabian Nights! The tradition in the family is that we descend from Tory cavaliers (a wide designation), who fled to the West Indies from the ascendancy of Cromwell; and on a female side, amidst a curious mixture of quakers and soldiers, we derive ourselves not only from gentry, but from kings—that is to say, *Irish* kings!—personages (not to say it disrespectfully to the wit and misfortunes of the sister-island) who rank pretty much on a par with the negro chief, surrounded by half a dozen lords in ragged shirts, who asked

Barton, a kind of "Scottish rover on the seas" (as the ballad calls him), worried the English navigation in the time of Henry the Eighth, and was killed in the engagement here noticed, in which the two ships under his command were captured by two English ships under the command of Sir Thomas, and Sir Edward Howard. Hunt was captain of a merchantman, of Newcastle, which traded to Bordeaux, and which had been one of Barton's prizes. I hope the gallant seaman's Bordeaux claret was ancestor of that which my progenitors drank in Barbados.

the traveller what his brother kings thought of him in
Europe. A learned and friendly investigator into the matter
thinks the Cromwell tradition a mistake, and brings us from
a clergyman of the name of Isaac Hunt (my father's name),
who left Exeter for Barbados in the time of James the First.
He connects us also with a partner in the mercantile firm of
Hunt and Lascelles in that island, one of which latter persons
came into England during the first half of the last century,
and gave rise to the noble family of Harewood. In the
British Museum is a manuscript journal that was kept in
this year by a Hunt of the same Christian name of Isaac.
I take our paternal family stock to have been divided for
many generations between the clerical and mercantile professions.

The etymology, however, of the name is obvious; and very
unfit does it render it for its present owners. The pastime in
which their Saxon ancestors may have excelled, so as to derive
from it their very appellation, is contrary to the principles of
their descendants! But hunting was not merely a pastime
in old Saxon days. It was a business and a necessity; there
were children to feed, and wild beasts to be exterminated.
Besides, one must share and share alike in the reputation of
one's fellow-creatures. I dare say the Hunts were as ferocious
in those days as their name may have implied. They have
since hunted in other ways, not always without a spice of
fierceness ; and smarting have been the wounds which they
have both given and taken.

[The more probable etymology of the name traces it to the
geographical use of the word, designating a district used for
the chase. The tradition of Irish kings has probably been
introduced by a very doubtful connection with the Hunts of
Ireland, who have changed their name for that of De Vere,
which they also claim by inheritance. One of the family, in
a jocular way, claimed cousinship with Leigh Hunt ; but if
any relationship existed, it must have been before either
family left England for Barbados, or for Ireland. The Bickleys,
mentioned subsequently, were not of Irish origin, though Sir
William served in Ireland. The Hunts of Barbados were
among the very earliest settlers, and the name may be seen in
a list published in Barbados in 1612 ; but it is testimony
from which the autobiographer probably shrunk with dislike,
for it is an old list, perhaps the oldest existing list, of negro
slave-owners. There is reason to believe that members of the

family revisited their native country in the course of the seventeenth and eighteenth centuries.]

I have begun my book with my progenitors and with childhood, partly because " order gives all things view," partly because, whatever we may assume as we grow up respecting the " dignity of manhood," we all feel that childhood was a period of great importance to us. Most men recur to it with delight. They are in general very willing to dilate upon it, especially if they meet with an old schoolfellow; and therefore, on a principle of reciprocity, and as I have long considered myself a kind of playmate and fellow-disciple with persons of all times of life (for none of us, unless we are very silly or naughty boys indeed, ever leave off learning in some school or other), I shall suppose I have been listening to some other young gentleman of sixty or seventy years of age over his wine, and that I am now going to relate about half as much respecting my existence as he has told us of his own.

My grandfather, himself the son, I believe, of a clergyman, was Rector of St. Michael's, in Bridge Town, Barbados. He was a good-natured man, and recommended the famous Lauder to the mastership of the free school there; influenced, no doubt, partly by his pretended repentance, and partly by sympathy with his Toryism. Lauder is said to have been discharged for misconduct. I never heard that; but I have heard that his appearance was decent, and that he had a wooden leg: which is an anti-climax befitting his history.* My

---

* Since writing this passage, I find a more serious conclusion to his history in a book entitled *Creoliana ; or, Social and Domestic Scenes and Incidents in Barbados in Days of Yore,* by J. W. Orderson. He is there said to have failed in his school ; and to have set up a huckster's shop with the aid of an African woman whom he had purchased. After behaviour to a daughter by this woman which cannot be described, and her repulses of which he resented by ordering her to be scourged, he sold her to a naval captain, who rescued her from the infliction.

Let us hope that Lauder would have denied the paternity imputed to him. Perhaps, indeed, he would have denied more, or did deny it; for his answer of the charges yet remains to be heard. The poor girl afterwards became the fat and flourishing landlady of an hotel ; and is famous in Barbadian and nautical annals for having successfully drawn up a bill of damages to the amount of seven hundred pounds against his Royal Highness Prince William Henry, afterwards Duke of Clarence and King William the Fourth, who in a fit of ultra-joviality with the mess of the Forty-ninth Regiment, demolished all

grandfather was admired and beloved by his parishioners for
the manner in which he discharged his duties. He died at an
early age, in consequence of a fever taken in the hot and
damp air, while officiating incessantly at burials during a
mortality. His wife, who was an O'Brien, or rather Bryan,
very proud of her descent from the kings aforesaid (or of the
kings from *her*), was as good-natured and beloved as her
husband, and very assiduous in her attentions to the negroes
and to the poor, for whom she kept a set of medicines, like
my Lady Bountiful. They had two children besides my
father : Ann Courthope, who died unmarried ; and Elizabeth, wife of Thomas Dayrell, Esq., of Barbados, one of
the family of the Dayrells of Lillingstone, and father by a
first marriage of the late barrister of that name. I mention both of these ladies, because they will come among my
portraits.

To these their children, the worthy Rector and his wife
were a little too indulgent. When my father was to go to the
American continent to school, the latter dressed up her boy
in a fine suit of laced clothes, such as we see on the little gentlemen in Hogarth ; but so splendid and costly, that when the
good pastor beheld him, he was moved to utter an expostula-
tion. Objection, however, soon gave way before the pride of
all parties ; and my father set off for school, ready spoilt, with
plenty of money to spoil him more.

He went to college at Philadelphia, and became the scape-
grace who smuggled in the wine, and bore the brunt of the
tutors. My father took the degree of Master of Arts, both at
Philadelphia and New York. When he spoke the farewell
oration on leaving college, two young ladies fell in love with
him, one of whom he afterwards married. He was fair and
handsome, with delicate features, a small aquiline nose, and
blue eyes. To a graceful address he joined a remarkably fine
voice, which he modulated with great effect. It was in reading, with this voice, the poets and other classics of England,
that he completed the conquest of my mother's heart. He
used to spend the evenings in this manner with her and her
family,—a noble way of courtship ; and my grandmother
became so hearty in his cause, that she succeeded in carrying

the furniture in her house, to the very beds ; the cunning hostess
(whom he upset as he went away) refusing to interfere with the
vivacities of " Massa, the King's son," which she prudently concluded
he would pay for like a gentleman.

it against her husband, who wished his daughter to marry a wealthy neighbour. [The bride was Mary, the daughter of Stephen Shewell, a merchant of Philadelphia, a vehement man, both in public and in family matters. The other lady was Mary's aunt, although the girls were about the same age.]

My father was intended, I believe, to carry on the race of clergymen, as he afterwards did; but he went, in the first instance, into the law. The Americans united the practice of attorney and barrister. My father studied the law under articles to one of the chief persons in the profession; and afterwards practised with distinction himself. At this period (by which time all my brothers except one were born) the Revolution broke out; and he entered with so much zeal into the cause of the British Government, that, besides pleading for loyalists with great fervour at the bar, he wrote pamphlets equally full of party warmth, which drew on him the popular odium. His fortunes then came to a crisis in America. Early one morning, a great concourse of people appeared before his house. He came out,—or was brought. They put him into a cart prepared for the purpose (conceive the anxiety of his wife!), and, after parading him about the streets, were joined by a party of the revolutionary soldiers with drum and fife. The multitude, some days before, for the same purpose, had seized Dr. Kearsley, a staunch Tory, who on learning their intention had shut up the windows of his house, and endeavoured to prevent their getting in. The doctor had his hand pierced by a bayonet, as it entered between the shutters behind which he had planted himself. He was dragged out and put into the cart, dripping with blood; but he lost none of his intrepidity; for he answered their reproaches and outrage with vehement reprehensions; and, by way of retaliation on the "Rogue's March," struck up "God save the King." My father, who knew Kearsley, had endeavoured to persuade him not to add to their irritation; but to no purpose. The doctor continued infuriate, and more than once fainted from loss of blood and the violence of his feelings. My father comparatively softened the people with his gentler manners; yet he is understood, like Kearsley, to have had a narrow escape from tarring and feathering. A tub of tar, which had been set in a conspicuous place in one of the streets for that purpose, was overturned by an officer intimate with our family. The well-bred loyalist, however, did not escape entirely from

personal injury. One of the stones thrown by the mob gave
him such a severe blow on the head, as not only laid him
swooning in the cart, but dimmed his sight for life. At length,
after being carried through every street in Philadelphia, he
was deposited, as Dr. Kearsley had been, in a prison in
Market Street. The poor doctor went out of his mind, and
ended his days not long afterwards in confinement.* My
father, by means of a large sum of money given to the sen-
tinel who had charge of him, was enabled to escape at
midnight. He went immediately on board a ship in the
Delaware, that belonged to my grandfather, and was bound
for the West Indies. She dropped down the river that same
night; and my father went first to Barbados, and afterwards
to England, where he settled.

My mother was to follow my father as soon as possible,
which she was not able to do for many months. The last time
she had seen him, he was a lawyer and a partisan, going out
to meet an irritated populace. On her arrival in England, she
beheld him in a pulpit, a clergyman, preaching tranquillity.
When my father came over, he found it impossible to continue
his profession as a lawyer. Some actors, who heard him read,
advised him to go on the stage; but he was too proud for that,
and he went into the Church. He was ordained by the celebrated Lowth, then Bishop of London ; and he soon became
so popular that the Bishop sent for him and remonstrated
against his preaching so many charity sermons. His lordship
said that it was ostentatious in a clergyman, and that he saw
his name in too many advertisements. My father thought it
strange, but acquiesced. It is true he preached a great many
of these sermons. I am told that for a whole year he did
nothing else ; and perhaps there was something in his manner
a little startling to the simplicity of the Church of England.
I remember, when he came to that part of the Litany where

* I learn this particular respecting Dr. Kearsley from an amusing
and interesting book, entitled *Memoirs of a Life chiefly passed in
Pennsylvania*, the anonymous author of which is understood to have
been a Captain Graddon, or Graydon, an officer in the American
service. The same work has occasioned me to represent the treat-
ments of Kearsley and my father as occurring on two distinct days,
instead of simultaneously, as in the family tradition, the Captain
informing us that he was an eye-witness of both.

There appears to have been something constitutionally wild in the
temperament of Kearsley. The Captain describes him as having
ridden once, during a midnight frolic, into the parlour of a lodging-
house, mounted on horseback, and even up the stairs !

the reader prays for his deliverance " in the hour of death and at the day of judgment," he used to make a pause at the word " death," and drop his voice on the rest of the sentence. The effect was striking; but the repetition must have hurt it. I am afraid it was a little theatrical. His delivery, however, was so much admired by those who thought themselves the best judges, that Thomas Sheridan, father of the celebrated Sheridan, came up to him one day, after service, in the vestry, and complimented him on having profited so well from his *Treatise on Reading the Liturgy*. My father was obliged to tell him that he had never seen it.

I do not know whether it was Lowth, but it was some bishop, to whom my father one day, in the midst of a warm discussion, being asked, " Do you know who I am ?" replied, with a bow, " Yes, my lord ; dust and ashes." Doubtless the clergyman was warm and imprudent. In truth, he made a great mistake when he entered the profession. By the nature of the tenure, it was irretrievable ; and his whole life after was a series of errors, arising from the unsuitability of his position. He was fond of divinity ; but it was as a specu-lator, not as a dogmatist, or one who takes upon trust. He was ardent in the cause of Church and State ; but here he speculated too, and soon began to modify his opinions, which got him the ill-will of the Government. He delighted his audiences in the pulpit ; so much so, that he had crowds of carriages at the door. One of his congregations had an en-graving made of him ; and a lady of the name of Cooling, who was member of another, left him by will the sum of 500*l*., as a testimony of the pleasure and advantage she had derived from his discourses.

But unfortunately, after delighting his hearers in the pulpit, he would delight some of them a little too much over the table. He was extremely lively and agreeable ; was full of generous sentiments; could flatter without grossness ; had stories to tell of lords whom he knew ; and when the bottle was to circulate, it did not stand with him. All this was dangerous to a West Indian who had an increasing family, and who was to make his way in the Church. It was too much for him ; and he added another to the list of those who, though they might suffice equally for themselves and others in a more considerate and contented state of society, and seem to be the born delights of it, are only lost and thrown out in a system of things which, by going upon the ground of individual aggrandizement, compels dispositions of a more sociable and reasonable nature either to become parties concerned, or be ruined in the refusal. It is doubtless incumbent on a husband and father to be careful under all circumstances : and it is easy for most people to talk of the necessity of being so, and to recommend it to others, especially when they have been educated to the habit. Let those fling the first stone who, with the real inclination and talent for other things (for the inclination may not be what they take it for), confine themselves industriously to the duties prescribed them. There are more victims to errors committed by society itself than society supposes.

But I grant that a man is either bound to tell society so, or to do as others do. My father was always zealous, theoretically speaking, both for the good of the world, and for that of his family (I remember a printed proposal which he drew up for an academy, to be entitled the " Cosmopolitical Seminary "); but he had neither uneasiness enough in his blood, nor, perhaps, sufficient strength in his convictions, to bring his speculations to bear ; and as to the pride of cutting a figure above his neighbours, which so many men mistake for a better principle of action, he could dispense with that. As it was, he should have been kept at home in Barbados. He was a true exotic, and ought not to have been transplanted. He might have preached there, and quoted Horace, and been gentlemanly and generous, and drunk his claret, and no harm done. But in a bustling, commercial state of society, where the enjoyment, such as it is, consists in the bustle, he was neither very likely to succeed, nor to meet with a good construction, nor to end his pleasant ways with pleasing either the world or himself.

It was in the pulpit of Bentinck Chapel, Lisson Green, Paddington, that my mother found her husband officiating. He published a volume of sermons preached there, in which there is little but elegance of diction and a graceful morality. His delivery was the charm ; and, to say the truth, he charmed everybody but the owner of the chapel, who looked upon rent as by far the most eloquent production of the pulpit. The speculation ended with the preacher being horribly in debt. Friends, however, were lavish of their assistance. Three of my brothers were sent to school ; the other, at her earnest entreaty went to live (which he did for some years) with Mrs. Spencer, a sister (I think) of Sir Richard Worsley, and a delicious little old woman, the delight of all the children of her acquaintance. She occupied at one time a small house which belonged to her in the Paddington Road, and in the front garden of which, or in that of the house next to it (I forget which, but they were both her property), stood a beautiful almond-tree, not long since cut down. Never shall I forget the enchanting effect which the bright green rails of the gardens of these houses used to have upon me when I caught sight of them in going there with my mother. My father and mother took breath, in the meantime, under the friendly roof of Mr. West, the painter, who had married her aunt. The aunt and niece were much of an age, and both fond of books. Mrs. West, indeed, ultimately became a martyr to them; for the physician declared that she lost the use of her limbs by sitting in-doors.

From Newman Street my father went to live in Hampstead Square, whence he occasionally used to go and preach at Southgate. The then Duke of Chandos had a seat in the neighbourhood of Southgate. He heard my father preach, and was so pleased with him, that he requested him to become tutor to his nephew, Mr. Leigh, which the preacher did, and he remained with his Grace's family for several years. The Duke was Master of the Horse, and originated the famous epithet of " heaven-born minister," applied to Mr. Pitt. I have heard my father describe him as a man of great sweetness of nature and good breeding. He was the grandson of Pope and Swift's Duke of Chandos. He died in 1789, and left a widow, who survived him for several years in a state of mental alienation. I mention this circumstance, because I think I have heard it said in our family, that her derangement was owing to a piece of thoughtlessness, the notice of which may serve as a caution. She was a woman of great animal spirits; and happening to thrust aside the Duke's chair when he was going to sit down, the consequences were such, that being extremely attached to him, she could never forgive herself, but lost her husband and senses at once. The Duchess had already been married to a gentleman of the name of Elletson. She was daughter of Sir Richard Gamon, and mother of an heiress, who carried the title of Chandos into the Grenville family.

To be tutor in a ducal family is one of the roads to a bishopric. My father was thought to be in the highest way to it. He was tutor in the house, not only of a duke, but of a state officer, for whom the King had a personal regard. His

manners were of the highest order; his principles in Church
and State as orthodox, to all appearance, as could be wished;
and he had given up flourishing prospects in America for
their sake. But the same ardent and disinterested sense of
right which induced him to make that sacrifice in behalf of
what he thought due to his Sovereign, made him no less ready
to take the part of any one holding opposite opinions whom
he considered to be ill-used; and he had scarcely set his foot
in England, when he so distinguished himself among his brother loyalists for his zeal in behalf of a fellow-countryman
who had served in the republican armies, that he was given
to understand it was doing him no service at court.

This gentleman was the distinguished American artist,
Colonel Trumbull. Mr. Trumbull, at that time a young man,
had left the army to become a painter; to which end he had
crossed the Atlantic, and was studying under Mr. West. The
Government, suspecting him to be a spy, arrested him, and it
was not without exertions extremely creditable to Mr. West
himself, as well as to my father (for the future President of
the Academy was then commencing his own career under
regal patronage), that the supposed dangerous ex-officer was
set free. Mr. Trumbull, in his memoirs, has recorded his
obligations to both. Those on the part of my father, as a
loyalist, he pronounces to have been not only perilous but
unique. He says, in a letter to his father, Governor Trumbull :—

" Mr. West, who has been very much my friend, spoke
immediately both to the King and the American secretary,
and was encouraged by both to expect that as soon as the
noise should have subsided a little I should be discharged.
However, after waiting two months, I wrote to Lord George
Germaine, but received no answer. Mr. West, at the same
time, could not obtain a second interview with him. In February, a Mr. Hunt, a refugee from Philadelphia, formerly an
assistant to Mr. West" (this is a mistake, my father never
had anything to do with painting), " conversing with Mr. West
on the subject, was so far convinced of the absurdity and injustice of the treatment I had received, that he entered warmly
into my interest, and with great perseverance urged the other
refugees to assist him in undeceiving the ministry, and gain-
ing my discharge. Not one, however, joined him; and after
a fortnight's solicitation, he was told by Mr. Thompson, Lord
George Germaine's secretary, a Woburn lad, that he made

himself very busy in this affair, and very little to his own reputation ; that he had best stop, for all his applications in my behalf were useless."*

And again, in the Appendix to the same work, page 319 :—
" I had little left to hope, unless from some favourable turn of affairs in America.   An effort indeed was made through Mr. Hunt, a refugee from Philadelphia, upon the feelings of his fellows, which does honour to him, and was pushed so far as almost to endanger his own safety, but without any other effect than showing the detestable rancour which, with very few exceptions, is the common mark of their character."

Mr. Trumbull's opinion of the loyalists in general must be taken *cum grano ;* for though he appears to have been an estimable, he was also an irritable, man; but this does not diminish the honour due to my father's efforts.   There can be little doubt, however, that those efforts did him mischief with the King, who, not knowing him so well as he did Mr. West, being naturally given to dislike those who in any respect differed with him, and probably having been made acquainted with some indiscreet evidence of warmth in the prosecution of his endeavours for Mr. Trumbull, is very likely to have conceived an impression of him unfavourable to the future clergyman.   I know not how soon, too, but most likely before long, my father, as he became acquainted with the Government, began to doubt its perfections; and the King, whose minuteness of information respecting the personal affairs of his subjects is well known, was most likely prepared with questions, which the Duke of Chandos was not equally prepared to answer.

Meanwhile, the honest loyalist was getting more and more distressed.   He removed to Hampstead a second time : from Hampstead he crossed the water; and the first room I have any recollection of is one in a prison.   It was in the King's Bench.   Here was the game of rackets, giving the place a strange lively air in the midst of its distresses; here I first heard, to my astonishment and horror, a verse of a song, sung out, as he tottered along, by a drunken man, the words of which appeared to me unspeakably wicked : and here I remember well, as he walked up and down, the appearance of a

* *Autobiography, Reminiscences, and Letters of John Trumbull, from 1756 to 1841.*   New York and London, 1841.   The Thompson here contemptuously mentioned as "a Woburn lad," was afterwards the celebrated Count Rumford.

prisoner who was at that time making no little noise in the world, and who was veritably wicked enough. He was a tall thin man, in a cocked hat, had an aquiline nose, and altogether appeared to my childish eyes a strangely inconsistent-looking person for a man of his character, and much of a gentleman. I have an impression on my memory that I was told he had run a needle through his wife's tongue. This was Andrew Robinson Stoney Bowes, Esq., which last name he had assumed on his marriage with the Countess of Strathmore, for cruel treatment of whom in his attempt to extort her property he had been sentenced to an imprisonment of three years. His surgeon and biographer, Jesse Foot, in summing up his character, says of him, that he was " cowardly, insidious, hypocritical, tyrannic, mean, violent, selfish, deceitful, jealous, revengeful, inhuman, and savage, without a single countervailing quality." It is not improbable that Mr. Foot might have been one of the persons he deceived; but the known events of the man's life really go far to make him out this kind of monster; and Foot suppresses most of the particulars of his cruelty as too shocking to detail. He was one of those madmen who are too conventionally sane to be locked up, but who appear to be born what they are by some accident of nature.

Mr. West took the liberty of representing my father's circumstances to the king. It is well known that this artist enjoyed the confidence of his Majesty in no ordinary degree. The king would converse half a day at a time with him, while he was painting. His Majesty said he would speak to the bishops; and again, on a second application, he said my father should be provided for. My father himself also presented a petition ; but all that was ever done for him, was the putting his name on the Loyalist Pension List for a hundred a year, —a sum which he not only thought extremely inadequate for the loss of seven or eight times as much in America, a cheaper country, but which he felt to be a poor acknowledgment even for the active zeal which he had evinced, and the things which he had said and written ; especially as the pension came late, and his circumstances were already involved. Small as it was, he was obliged to mortgage it; and from this time till the arrival of some relations from the West Indies, several years afterwards, he underwent a series of mortifications and distresses, not always without reason for self-reproach. Unfortunately for others, it might be said of him, what Lady

Mary Wortley said of her kinsman, Henry Fielding, " that give him his leg of mutton and bottle of wine, and in the very thick of calamity he would be happy for the time being." Too well able to seize a passing moment of enjoyment, he was always scheming, never performing ; always looking forward with some romantic plan which was sure to succeed, and never put in practice. I believe he wrote more titles of non-existing books than Rabelais. At length he found his mistake. My poor father ! He grew deeply acquainted with arrests, and began to lose his graces and (from failures with creditors) his good name. He became irritable with the consequences, and almost took hope of better days out of the heart that loved him, and was too often glad to escape out of its society. Yet such an art had he of making his home comfortable when he chose, and of settling himself to the most tranquil pleasures, that if she could have ceased to look forward about her children, I believe, with all his defects, those evenings would have brought unmingled satisfaction to her, when, after brightening the fire and bringing out the coffee, my mother knew that her husband was going to read Saurin or Barrow to her, with his fine voice and unequivocal enjoyment.

We thus struggled on between quiet and disturbance, between placid readings and frightful knocks at the door, and sickness, and calamity, and hopes, which hardly ever forsook us. One of my brothers went to sea,—a great blow to my poor mother. The next was articled to an attorney. My brother Robert became pupil to an engraver, and my brother John was apprenticed to Mr. Reynell, the printer, whose kindly manner, and deep iron voice, I well remember and respect. I had also a regard for the speaking trumpet, which ran all the way up his tall house, and conveyed his rugged whispers to his men. And his goodly wife, proud of her husband's grandfather, the bishop; never shall I forget how much I loved her for her portly smiles and good dinners, and how often she used to make me measure heights with her fair daughter Caroline, and found me wanting ; which I thought not quite so hospitable.

As my father's misfortunes, both in America and England, were owing, in the first instance, to feelings the most worthy and disinterested, so they were never unaccompanied with manifestations of the same zeal for others in smaller, though not always equally justifiable ways, which he had shown in the greater. He hampered himself, for instance, by becoming security for other people. This, however, he could only have done out of his usual sanguine belief in the honesty of those whom he assisted; for of collusion with anything deliberately unworthy, he was as incapable as he was trusting. His pen, though irregular, or unprofitable to himself, was always at the service of those who required it for memorials or other helps. As to his children, he was healthy and sanguine, and always looked forward to being able to do something for them; and something for them he did, if it was only in grafting his animal spirits on the maternal stock, and setting them an example of independent thinking. But he did more. He really took care, considering his unbusinesslike habits, towards settling them in some line of life. It is our faults, not his, if we have not been all so successful as we might have been: at least it is no more his fault than that of the West Indian blood of which we all partake, and which has disposed all of us, more or less, to a certain aversion from business. And if it may be some vanity in us, at least it is no dishonour to our turn of mind, to hope, that we may have been the means of circulating more knowledge and entertainment in society, than if he had attained the bishopric he looked for, and left us ticketed and labelled among the acquiescent.

Towards the latter part of his life, my father's affairs were greatly retrieved by the help of his sister, Mrs. Dayrell, who came over with a property from Barbados. My aunt was generous; part of her property came among us also by a marriage [most probably of the author's eldest brother Stephen Shewell Hunt with Christiana Dayrell]. My father's West Indian sun was again warm upon him. On his sister's death, to be sure, his struggles recommenced, though not at all in comparison to what they had been. Recommence, however, they did; and yet so sanguine was he in his intentions to the last, and so accustomed had my mother been to try to believe in him, and to persuade herself she did, that not long before she died he made the most solemn promises of amendment, which by chance I could not help overhearing, and which she received with a tenderness and a tone of joy, the remembrance of which brings the tears into my eyes. My father had one taste well suited to his profession, and in him, I used to think, remarkable. He was very fond of sermons; which he was rarely tired of reading, or my mother of hearing. I have mentioned the effect which these used to have upon her. When she died, he could not bear to think she was dead; yet retaining, in the midst of his tears, his indestructible tendency to seize on a cheering reflection, he turned his very despair into consolation; and in saying, " She is not dead, but sleeps," I verily believe the image became almost a literal thing with him. Besides his fondness for sermons, he was a great reader of the Bible. His copy of it is scored with manuscript; and I believe he read a portion of it every morning to the last, let him have been as satisfied or dissatisfied with himself as he might for the rest of day. This was not hypocrisy; it was habit, and real fondness: though, while he was no hypo- crite, he was not, I must confess, remarkable for being explicit about himself; nor did he cease to dogmatize in a sort of official manner upon faith and virtue, lenient as he thought himself bound to be to particular instances of frailty. To young people, who had no secrets from him, he was especially indulgent, as I have good reason to know. He delighted to show his sense of a candour in others, which I believe he would always have practised himself, had he been taught it early. For many years before his death, he had greatly relaxed in the orthodoxy of his religious opinions. Both he and my mother had become Unitarians. They were also Universalists, and great admirers of Mr. Winchester, parti- cularly my mother.* My father was willing, however, to hear all sides of the question, and used to visit the chapels of the most popular preachers of all denominations. His favourite among them, I think, was Mr. Worthington, who preached at a chapel in Long Acre, and had a strong natural eloquence. Politics and divinity occupied almost all the conversation that I heard at our fire-side. It is a pity my father had been so spoilt a child, and had strayed so much out of his sphere; for he could be contented with little. He was one of the last of the gentry who retained the old fashion of smoking. He indulged in it every night before he went to bed, which he did at an early hour; and it was pleasant to see him sit, in his tranquil and gentlemanly manner, and

* " The Universalists cannot, properly speaking, be called a distinct sect, as they are frequently found scattered amongst various denomi- nations. They are so named from holding the benevolent opinion, that all mankind, nay, even the demons themselves, will be finally restored to happiness, through the mercy of Almighty God."—History of all Religions and Religious Ceremonies, p. 263. What an impiety towards "Almighty God," that anybody could ever have thought the reverse!

relate anecdotes of "my Lord North" and the Rockingham administration, interspersed with those mild puffs and urbane resumptions of the pipe. How often have I thought of him under this aspect, and longed for the state of society that might have encouraged him to be more successful! Had he lived twenty years longer he would have thought it was coming. He died in the year 1809, aged fifty-seven, and was buried in the churchyard in Bishopsgate Street. I remember they quarrelled over his coffin for the perquisites of the candles; which put me upon a great many reflections, both on him and on the world.

I bless and am grateful to his memory. One of the last sayings of the last surviving of his children but myself, was a tribute to it equally simple and sincere. "What a kind man," said my brother Robert, "he was!"

My grandfather, by my mother's side, was Stephen Shewell, merchant of Philadelphia, who sent out his "argosies." His mother was a quaker, and he, himself, I believe, descended from a quaker stock. He had ships trading to England, Holland, and the West Indies, and used to put his sons and nephews in them as captains. For sausages and "botargoes" (first authors, perhaps, of the jaundice in our blood), Friar John would have recommended him. As Chaucer says,

"It snewèd, in his house, of meat and drink."

On that side of the family we seem all sailors and rough subjects, with a mitigation (on the female part) of quakerism; as, on the father's side, we are creoles and claret-drinkers, very polite and clerical.

My grandmother's maiden name was Bickley. I believe her family came from Buckinghamshire. The coat of arms are three half-moons; which I happen to recollect, because of a tradition we had, that an honourable augmentation was made to them of three wheat-sheaves, in reward of some gallant achievement performed in cutting off a convoy of provisions [by Sir William Bickley, a partisan of the House of Orange, who was made a Banneret. He was reputed in the family to have been the last Englishman who received the title of a Knight Banneret, by receiving Knighthood from the royal hand, on the field]. My grandmother was an openhearted, cheerful woman, of a good healthy blood. The family consisted of five daughters and two sons. One of the daughters died unmarried: of the four others, three are dead also; the fourth still lives, as upright in her carriage as when she was young, and the intelligent mother of two intelligent daughters, one of whom, the wife of Dr. Swift, a physician, is distinguished for her talent in writing verses. One of my uncles died in England, a mild, excellent creature, more fit for solitude than the sea. The other, my uncle Stephen, a fine handsome fellow of great good nature and gallantry, was never heard of, after leaving the port of Philadelphia for the West Indies. He had a practice of crowding too much sail, which is supposed to have been his destruction. They said he did it "to get back to his ladies."

My uncle was the means of saving his namesake, my brother Stephen, from a singular destiny. Some Indians, who came into the city to traffic, had been observed to notice my brother a good deal. It is supposed they saw in his tall little person, dark face, and long black hair, a resemblance to themselves. One day they enticed him from my grandfather's house in Front Street, and taking him to the Delaware, which was close by, were carrying him off across the river, when his uncle descried them and gave the alarm. His threats induced them to come back; otherwise, it is thought, they intended to carry him into their own quarters, and bring him up as an Indian; so that, instead of a rare character of another sort,—an attorney who would rather compound a quarrel for his clients than get rich by it;—we might have had for a brother the Great Buffalo, Bloody Bear, or some such grim personage. I will indulge myself with the liberty of observing in this place, that with great diversity of character among us, with strong points of dispute even among ourselves, and with the usual amount, though not perhaps exactly the like nature, of infirmities common to other people,—some of us, may be, with greater,—we have all been persons who inherited the power of making sacrifices for the sake of a principle.

My grandfather, though intimate with Dr. Franklin, was secretly on the British side of the question when the American war broke out. He professed to be neutral, and to attend only to business; but his neutrality did not avail him. One of his most valuably laden ships was burnt in the Delaware by the Revolutionists, to prevent its getting into the hands of the British ; and besides making free with his botargoes, they despatched every now and then a file of soldiers to rifle his house of everything else that could be serviceable : linen, blankets, &c. And this, unfortunately, was only a taste of what he was to suffer; for, emptying his mercantile stores from time to time, they paid him with their continental currency, paper-money; the depreciation of which was so great as to leave him, at the close of the war, bankrupt of everything but some houses, which his wife brought him. They amounted to a sufficiency for the family support; and thus, after all his neutralities, he owed all that he retained to a generous and unspeculating woman. His saving grace, however, was not on all occasions confined to his money. He gave a strong instance of his partiality to the British cause, by secreting in his house a gentleman of the name of Slater, who commanded a small armed vessel on the Delaware, and who was not long since residing in London. Mr. Slater had been taken prisoner, and confined at some miles' distance from Philadelphia. He contrived to make his escape, and astonished my grandfather's family by appearing before them at night, drenched in the rain, which descends in torrents in that climate. They secreted him for several months in a room at the top of the house.

My mother at that time was a brunette with fine eyes, a tall lady-like person, and hair blacker than is seen of English growth. It was supposed that Anglo-Americans already began to exhibit the influence of climate in their appearance. The late Mr. West told me, that if he had met myself or any of my brothers in the streets, he should have pronounced, without knowing us, that we were Americans. My mother had no accomplishments but the two best of all, a love of nature and of books. Dr. Franklin offered to teach her the guitar; but she was too bashful to become his pupil. She regretted this afterwards, partly, no doubt, for having lost so illustrious a master. Her first child, who died, was named after him. I know not whether the anecdote is new; but I have heard, that when Dr. Franklin invented the Harmonica, he concealed it from his wife till the instrument was fit to play; and then woke her with it one night, when she took it for the music of angels. Among the visitors at my grandfather's house, besides Franklin, was Thomas Paine ; whom I have heard my mother speak of, as having a countenance that inspired her with terror. I believe his aspect was not capti-vating ; but most likely his political and religious opinions did it no good in the eyes of the fair loyalist.

My mother was diffident of her personal merit, but she

had great energy of principle. When the troubles broke out, and my father took that violent part in favour of the king, a letter was received by her from a person high in authority, stating, that if her husband would desist from opposition to the general wishes of the colonists, he should remain in security; but that if he thought fit to do otherwise, he must suffer the consequences which awaited him. The letter concluded with advising her, as she valued her husband's and family's happiness, to use her influence with him to act accordingly. To this, "in the spirit of old Rome and Greece," as one of her sons has proudly and justly observed (I will add, of Old England, and, though contrary to our royalist opinions, of New America, too,) my mother replied, that she knew her husband's mind too well to suppose for a moment that he would so degrade himself; and that the writer of the letter entirely mistook her, if he thought her capable of endeavouring to persuade him to an action contrary to the convictions of his heart, whatever the consequences threatened might be. Yet the heart of this excellent woman, strong as it was, was already beating with anxiety for what might occur; and on the day when my father was seized, she fell into a fit of the jaundice, so violent, as to affect her ever afterwards, and subject a previously fine constitution to every ill that came across it.

It was nearly two years before my mother could set off with her children for England. She embarked in the *Earl of Effingham* frigate, Captain Dempster, who, from the moment she was drawn up the sides of the vessel with her little boys, conceived a pity and respect for her, and paid her the most cordial attention. In truth, he felt more pity for her than he chose to express; for the vessel was old and battered, and he thought the voyage not without danger. Nor was it. They did very well till they came off the Scilly Islands, when a storm arose which threatened to sink them. The ship was with difficulty kept above water. Here my mother again showed how courageous her heart could be, by the very strength of its tenderness. There was a lady in the vessel who had betrayed weaknesses of various sorts during the voyage; and who even went so far as to resent the superior opinion which the gallant captain could not help entertaining of her fellow-passenger. My mother, instead of giving way to tears and lamentations, did all she could to keep up the spirits of her children. The lady in question did the reverse;

and my mother feeling the necessity of the case, and touched with pity for children in the same danger as her own, was at length moved to break through the delicacy she had observed, and expostulate strongly with her, to the increased admiration of the captain, who congratulated himself on having a female passenger so truly worthy of the name of woman. Many years afterwards, near the same spot, and during a similar danger, her son, the writer of this book, with a wife and seven children around him, had occasion to call her to mind; and the example was of service even to him, a man. It was thought a miracle that the *Earl of Effingham* was saved. It was driven into Swansea Bay, and borne along by the heaving might of the waves into a shallow, where no vessel of so large a size ever appeared before; nor could it ever have got there, but by so unwonted an over-lifting.

Having been born nine years later than the youngest of my brothers, I have no recollection of my mother's earlier aspect. Her eyes were always fine, and her person lady-like; her hair also retained its colour for a long period; but her brown complexion had been exchanged for a jaundiced one, which she retained through life; and her cheeks were sunken, and her mouth drawn down with sorrow at the corners. She retained the energy of her character on great occasions; but her spirit in ordinary was weakened, and she looked at the bustle and discord of the present state of society with a frightened aversion. My father's danger, and the war-whoops of the Indians which she heard in Philadelphia, had shaken her soul as well as frame. The sight of two men fighting in the streets would drive her in tears down another road; and I remember, when we lived near the park, she would take me a long circuit out of the way rather than hazard the spectacle of the soldiers. Little did she think of the timidity with which she was thus inoculating me, and what difficulty I should have, when I went to school, to sustain all those fine theories, and that unbending resistance to oppression, which she inculcated. However, perhaps it ultimately turned out for the best. One must feel more than usual for the sore places of humanity, even to fight properly in their behalf. Never shall I forget her face, as it used to appear to me coming up the cloisters, with that weary hang of the head on one side, and that melancholy smile!

One holiday, in a severe winter, as she was taking me

home, she was petitioned for charity by a woman sick and ill-clothed. It was in Blackfriars' Road, I think about midway. My mother, with the tears in her eyes, turned up a gateway, or some such place, and beckoning the woman to follow, took off her flannel petticoat, and gave it her. It is supposed that a cold which ensued, fixed the rheumatism upon her for life. Actions like these have doubtless been often performed, and do not of necessity imply any great virtue in the performer; but they do if they are of a piece with the rest of the character. Saints have been made for charities no greater.

The reader will allow me to quote a passage out of a poem of mine, because it was suggested by a recollection I had upon me of this excellent woman. It is almost the only passage in that poem worth repeating, which I mention, in order that he may lay the quotation to its right account, and not suppose I am anxious to repeat my verses because I fancy they must be good. In everything but the word " happy," the picture is from life. The bird spoken of is the nightingale—the

> " Bird of wakeful glow,
> Whose louder song is like the voice of life,
> Triumphant o'er death's image; but whose deep,
> Low, lovelier note is like a gentle wife,
> A poor, a pensive, yet a happy one,
> Stealing, when daylight's common tasks are done,
> An hour for mother's work; and singing low,
> While her tired husband and her children sleep."

I have spoken of my mother during my father's troubles in England. She stood by him through them all; and in everything did more honour to marriage, than marriage did good to either of them; for it brought little happiness to her, and too many children to both. Of his changes of opinion, as well as of fortune, she partook also. She became a Unitarian, a Universalist, perhaps a Republican; and in her new opinions, as in her old, was apt, I suspect, to be a little too peremptory, and to wonder at those who could be of the other side. It was her only fault. She would have mended it had she lived till now. Though not a republican myself, I have been thought, in my time, to speak too severely of kings and princes. I think I did, and that society is no longer to be bettered in that manner, but in a much calmer and nobler way. But I was a witness, in my childhood, to a great deal of suffering; I heard of more all over the world; and kings

and princes bore a great share in the causes to which they
were traced.

Some of those causes were not to be denied. It is now
understood, on all hands, that the continuation of the American war was owing to the personal stubbornness of the king.
My mother, in her indignation at him for being the cause of
so much unnecessary bloodshed, thought that the unfortunate
malady into which he fell was a judgment of Providence.

My mother's intolerance, after all, was only in theory.
When anything was to be done, charity in her always ran
before faith. If she could have served and benefited the king
himself personally, indignation would soon have given way to
humanity. She had a high opinion of everything that was
decorous and feminine on the part of a wife; yet when a poor
violent woman, the wife of an amiable and eloquent preacher,
went so far on one occasion as to bite his hand in a fit of
jealous rage as he was going to ascend his pulpit (and he
preached in great pain), my mother was the only female of her
acquaintance that continued to visit her; alleging that she
needed society and comfort so much the more. She had the
highest notions of chastity; yet when a servant came to her,
who could get no place because she had had an illegitimate
child, my mother took her into her family upon the strength
of her candour and her destitute condition, and was served
during the remainder of the mistress's life with affectionate
gratitude.

My mother's favourite books were Dr. Young's *Night
Thoughts* (which was a pity), and Mrs. Rowe's *Devout Exer-
cises of the Heart*. I remember also her expressing great
admiration of the novels of Mrs. Inchbald, especially the
Simple Story. She was very fond of poetry, and used to
hoard my verses in her pocket-book, and encourage me to
write, by showing them to the Wests and the Thorntons.
Her friends loved and honoured her to the last; and, I believe,
they retained their regard for the family.

My mother's last illness was long, and was tormented with
rheumatism. I envied my brother Robert the recollection of
the filial attentions he paid her; but they shall be as much
known as I can make them, not because he was my brother
(which is nothing), but because he was a good son, which is
much; and every good son and mother will be my warrant.
My other brothers, who were married, were away with their
families; and I, who ought to have attended more, was as

giddy as I was young, or rather a great deal more so. I attended, but not enough. How often have we occasion to wish that we could be older or younger than we are, according as we desire to have the benefit of gaiety or experience! Her greatest pleasure during her decay was to lie on a sofa, looking at the setting sun. She used to liken it to the door of heaven, and fancy her lost children there, waiting for her. She died in the fifty-third year of her age, in a little miniature house which stands in a row behind the church that has been since built in Somerstown; and she was buried, as she had always wished to be, in the churchyard of Hampstead.

CHAPTER II.
CHILDHOOD.

I HAVE spoken of the Duke of Chandos, to whose nephew, Mr. Leigh, my father became tutor. Mr. Leigh, who gave me his name, was son of the duke's sister, Lady Caroline, and died member of parliament. He was one of the kindest and gentlest of men, addicted to those tastes for poetry and sequestered pleasure, which were conspicuous in his son, Lord Leigh; for all which reasons it would seem, and contrary to the usurping qualities in such cases made and provided, he and his family were subjected to one of the most extraordinary charges that a defeated claim ever brought drunken witnesses to set up,—no less than the murder and burial of a set of masons, who were employed in building a bridge, and whose destruction in the act of so doing was to bury both them and a monument which they knew of for ever! To complete the romance of the tragedy, a lady, the wife of the usurper, presides over the catastrophe. She cries, "Let go!" while the poor wretches are raising a stone at night-time, amidst a scene of torches and seclusion; and down goes the stone, aided by this tremendous father and son, and crushes the victims of her ambition! She meant, as Cowley says Goliah did of David,

> "At once their murder and their monument."

If a charge of the most awful crimes could be dug up against the memories of such men as Thomson and Shenstone, or of Cowley, or Cowper, or the "Man of Ross," it could not have created more laughing astonishment in the minds of those who knew them, than such a charge against the family of the Leighs. Its late representative, in the notes to his volume of poems, printed some years ago, quoted the "following beautiful passage" out of Fielding:—

"It was the middle of May, and the morning was remarkably serene, when Mr. Allworthy walked forth on the terrace, where the dawn opened every minute that lovely prospect we have before described, to his eye. And now having sent forth streams of light which ascended to the firmament before him, as harbingers preceding his pomp, in the full blaze of his majesty up rose the sun; than which one object alone in this lower creation could be more glorious, and that Mr. Allworthy himself presented—a human being replete with benevolence, meditating in what manner he might render himself most acceptable to his Creator by doing most good to his creatures."

"This," adds the quoter, "is the portrait of a fictitious personage; but I see in it a close resemblance to one whose memory I shall never cease to venerate."

The allusion is to his father, Mr. Leigh.

But I must not anticipate the verdict of a court of justice.* Indeed, I should have begged pardon of my noble friend for speaking of this preposterous accusation, did not the very excess of it force the words from my pen, and were I not sure that my own father would have expected them from me, had he been alive to hear it. His lordship must accept them as an effusion of grateful sympathy from one father and son to another.

Lord Leigh has written many a tender and thoughtful verse, in which, next to the domestic affections and the progress of human kind, he shows that he loves above all things the beauties of external nature, and the tranquil pleasures they suggest.

So much do I agree with him, that it is a pleasure to me to know that I was even born in so sweet a village as Southgate. I first saw the light there on the 19th of October, 1784. It found me cradled, not only in the lap of the nature which I love, but in the midst of the truly English scenery which I love beyond all other. Middlesex in general, like my noble friend's county of Warwickshire, is a scene of trees and meadows, of "greenery" and nestling cottages ; and Southgate is a prime specimen of Middlesex. It is a place lying out of the way of

* The verdict was subsequently given. It almost seemed ridiculous, it was so unnecessary; except, indeed, as a caution to the like of those whom it punished.

innovation, therefore it has the pure, sweet air of antiquity about it ; and as I am fond of local researches in any quarter, it may be pardoned me if in this instance I would fain know even the meaning of its name. There is no Northgate, East-gate, or Westgate in Middlesex : what, then, is Southgate? No topographer tells us ; but an old map of the country twenty-five miles round London, drawn up some years pre-vious to my childhood, is now before me ; and on looking at the boundaries of Enfield Chase, I see that the "Chase-gate," the name most likely of the principal entrance, is on the north side of it, by North-Hall and Potter's Bar ; while Southgate, which has also the name of "South Street," is on the Chase's opposite border ; so that it seems evident that Southgate meant the southern entrance into the chase, and that the name became that of a village from the growth of a street. The street, in all probability, was the consequence of a fair held in a wood which ran on the western side of it, and which, in the map, is designated " Bush Fair." *Bush*, in old English, meant not only a hedge, but a wood ; as *Bois* or *Bosco* does in French and Italian. Moses and the "burning bush" is Moses and the " burning wood ; " which, by the way, presents a much grander idea than the modicum of hedge commonly assigned to the celestial apparition. There is a good deal more wood in the map than is now to be found. I wander in imagination through the spots marked in the neighbourhood, with their pleasant names—Woodside, Wood Green, Palmer Green, Nightingale Hall, &c., and fancy my father and mother listening to the nightingales, and loving the new little baby, who has now lived to see more years than they did.

Southgate lies in a cross-country road, running from Ed-monton through Enfield Chase into Hertfordshire. It is in the parish of Edmonton ; so that we may fancy the *Merry Devil* of that place still playing his pranks hereabouts, and helping innocent lovers to a wedding, as in the sweet little play attributed to Dryden. For as to any such devils going to a place less harmonious, it is not to be thought possible by good Christians. Furthermore, to show what classical ground is round about Southgate, and how it is associated with the best days of English genius, both old and new, Edmonton is the birthplace of Marlowe, the father of our drama, and of my friend Horne, his congenial celebrator. In Edmonton churchyard lies Charles Lamb ; in Highgate churchyard,

Coleridge; and in Hampstead have resided Shelley and Keats, to say nothing of Akenside before them, and of Steele, Arbuthnot, and others, before Akenside.

But the neighbourhood is dear to me on every account; for near Southgate is Colney Hatch, where my mother became acquainted with some of her dearest friends, whom I shall mention by-and-by. Near Colney Hatch is Finchley, where our family resided on quitting Southgate; and at no great distance from Finchley is Mill Hill, where lived excellent Dr. W. M. Trinder, Vicar of Hendon, who presented in his person the rare combination of clergyman and physician. He boasted that he had cured a little child (to wit, myself) of a dropsy in the head. The fact was contested, I believe, by the lay part of the profession; but it was believed in the family, and their love for the good doctor was boundless.

I may call myself, in every sense of the word, etymological not excepted, a son of mirth and melancholy; for my father's Christian name (as old students of onomancy would have heard with serious faces) was Isaac, which is Hebrew for "laughter," and my mother's was Mary, which comes from a word in the same language signifying "bitterness." And, indeed, as I do not remember to have ever seen my mother smile, except in sorrowful tenderness, so my father's shouts of laughter are now ringing in my ears. Not at any expense to her gravity, for he loved her, and thought her an angel on earth; but because his animal spirits were invincible. I inherit from my mother a tendency to jaundice, which at times has made me melancholy enough. I doubt, indeed, whether I have passed a day during half my life, without reflections, the first germs of which are traceable to sufferings which this tendency once cost me. My prevailing temperament, nevertheless, is my father's; and it has not only enabled me to turn those reflections into sources of tranquillity and exaltation, but helped my love of my mother's memory to take a sort of pride in the infirmity which she bequeathed me.

I forget whether it was Dr. Trinder—for some purpose of care and caution—but somebody told my mother (and she believed it), that if I survived to the age of fifteen I might turn out to possess a more than average amount of intellect; but that otherwise I stood a chance of dying an idiot. The reader may imagine the anxiety which this information would give to a tender mother. Not a syllable, of course, did she breathe to me on the subject till the danger was long past, and doubly did I then become sensible of all the marks of affection which I called to mind; of the unusual things which she had done for me; of the neglect, alas! which they had too often experienced from me, though not to her knowledge ; and of the mixture of tenderness and anxiety which I had always noted in her face. I was the youngest and least robust of her sons, and during early childhood I used hardly to recover from one illness before I was seized with another. The doctor said I must have gone through an extraordinary amount of suffering. I have sometimes been led to consider this as the first layer of that accumulated patience with which, in after life, I had occasion to fortify myself ; and the supposition has given rise to many consolatory reflections on the subject of endurance in general.

To assist my recovery from one of these illnesses, I was taken to the coast of France, where, as usual, I fell into another ; and one of my earliest recollections is of a good-natured French woman, the mistress of the lodging-house at Calais, who cried over the " poore littel boy," because I was a heretic. She thought I should go to the devil. Poor soul! What torments must the good-hearted woman have undergone; and what pleasant pastime it is for certain of her loud and learned inferiors to preach such doctrines, careless of the injuries they inflict, or even hoping to inflict them for the sake of some fine deity-degrading lesson, of which their sordid imaginations and splenetic itch of dictation assume the necessity. It was lucky for me that our hostess was a gentle, not a violent bigot, and susceptible at her heart of those better notions of God which are instinctive in the best natures. She might otherwise have treated me, as a late traveller says, infants have been treated by Catholic nurses, and murdered in order to save me.*

In returning from the coast of France, we stopped at Deal, and I found myself, one evening, standing with an elder brother on the beach, looking at a shoal of porpoises, creatures of which he had given me some tremendous, mysterious notion. I remember, as if it were yesterday, feeling the shades of evening, and the solemnity of the spectacle, with an awful intensity. There they were, tumbling along in the foam, what exactly I knew not, but fearful creatures of some sort. My brother spoke to me of them in an under tone of voice,

* *Letters from the Bye-ways of Italy.* By Mrs. Henry Stisted.

and I held my breath as I looked. The very word "porpoise" had an awful, mouthfilling sound.

This brother of mine, who is now no more, and who might have been a Marinell himself, for his notions of wealth and grandeur (to say nothing of his marrying, in succession, two ladies with dowries, from islands, whom ancient imagination could easily have exalted into sea-nymphs), was then a fine tall lad, of intrepid spirit, a little too much given to playing tricks on those who had less. He was a dozen years older than I was, and he had a good deal of the despot in a nature otherwise generous.

To give an instance of the lengths to which my brother Stephen carried his claims of ascendancy, he used to astonish the boys, at a day-school to which he went at Finchley, by appearing among them with clean shoes, when the bad state of the lanes rendered the phenomenon unaccountable. Reserve, on the one side, and shame on another, kept the mystery a secret for some time. At length it turned out that he was in the habit, on muddy days, of making one of his brothers carry him to school on his shoulders.

This brother (Robert), who used to laugh at the recollection, and who, as I have intimated, was quite as brave as the other, was at a disadvantage on such occasions, from his very bravery; since he knew what a horror my mother would have felt had there been any collision between them; so he used to content himself with an oratorical protest, and acquiesce. Being a brave, or at all events irritable little fellow enough myself, till illness, imagination, and an ultra tender and anxious rearing, conspired to render me fearful and patient, I had no such consequences to think of. When Stephen took me bodily in hand, I was only exasperated. I remember the furious struggles I used to make, and my endeavours to get at his shins, when he would hold me at arm's length, "aggravating" me (as the phrase is) by taunting speeches, and laughing like a goblin.

But on the "night-side of human nature," as Mrs. Crowe calls it, he "had me." I might confront him and endeavour to kick his shins by daylight, but with respect to ghosts, as the sailor said, I did not "understand their tackle." I had unfortunately let him see that I did not like to be in the dark, and that I had a horror of dreadful faces, even in books. I had found something particularly ghastly in the figure of an old man crawling on the ground, in some frontispiece—I think to a book called the *Looking-Glass;* and there was a fabulous wild-beast, a portrait of which, in some picture-book, unspeakably shocked me. It was called the Mantichora. It had the head of a man, grinning with rows of teeth, and the body of a wild-beast, brandishing a tail armed with stings. It was sometimes called by the ancients *Martichora.* But I did not know that. I took the word to be a horrible compound of *man* and *tiger.* The beast figures in Pliny and the old travellers. Apollonius had heard of him. He takes a fearful joy in describing him, even from report :—

"Apollonius asked 'if they had among them the Martichora.' 'What!' said Iarchas, 'have you heard of that animal; for if you have, you have probably heard something extraordinary of its figure.' 'Great and wonderful things have I heard of it,' replied Apollonius. 'It is of the number of quadrupeds, has a head like a man's, is as large as a lion with a tail from which bristles grow, of the length of a cubit, all as sharp as prickles, which it shoots forth like so many arrows against its pursuers.'" *

That sentence, beginning "Great and wonderful things," proves to me, that Apollonius must once have been a little boy, looking at the picture-books. The possibility of such "creatures" being "pursued" never occurred to me. Alexander, I thought, might have been encountered while crossing the Granicus, and elephants might be driven into the sea; but how could any one face a beast with a man's head? One look of its horrid countenance (which it always carried fronting you, as it went by—I never imagined it seen in profile) would have been enough, I concluded, to scare an army. Even full-grown dictionary makers have been frightened out of their propriety at the thought of him. "Mantichora," says old Morell—" *bestia horrenda* "—(a brute fit to give one the horrors).

In vain my brother played me repeated tricks with this frightful anomaly. I was always ready to be frightened again. At one time he would grin like the Mantichora; then he would roar like him; then call about him in the dark. I remember his asking me to come up to him one night at the top of the house. I ascended, and found the door shut. Suddenly a voice came through the key-hole, saying, in its hollowest tones, "The Mantichora's coming." Down I rushed to the parlour, fancying the terror at my heels.

* *Berwick's Translation*, p. 176.

I dwell the more on this seemingly petty circumstance, because such things are no petty ones to a sensitive child. My brother had no idea of the mischief they did me. Perhaps the mention of them will save mischief to others. They helped to morbidize all that was weak in my temperament, and cost me many a bitter night.*

Another time I was reading to him, while he was recovering in bed from an accident. He was reckless in his play; had once broken his leg on Hampstead Heath ; and was now getting well from a broken collar-bone. He gave me a volume to read to him, either of *Elegant Extracts* or *Aikin's Miscellanies* (I think the former), and selected the story of " Sir Bertrand." He did not betray by his face what was coming. I was enchanted with the commencement about the "dreary moors" and the " curfew ; " and I was reading on with breathless interest, when, at one of the most striking passages,— probably some analogous one about a noise,—he contrived, with some instrument or other, to give a tremendous knock

---

* Since this passage was written, I have met with one in Tod's *Travels in Western India*, p. 82, &c., in which the veritable origin of the idea of the Mantichora is, I have no doubt, set forth. India has ever been a land of extremes, both spiritual and bodily. At the moment when I write (September, 1857) it is a land of horrors. Here is one, existing five-and-thirty years ago, and in all probability existing still, which shows the outrageous tendency to excess on the side of mad superstition, and of brute contradiction to humanity, characteristic of the lower forms of Indian degradation. It is the sect of the Aghori, who, among other unspeakable viands, fed on dead bodies, and were first re-mentioned, after the ancient writers, by the celebrated traveller Thevenot, who says they were called *Merdi-coura*, or eaters of men. Colonel Tod observes, " It is a curious fact, as D'Anville adds, that ' this *espèce de bête*,' this *Merdi-cour*, or, properly, *Merdi-khor*, should have been noticed by Pliny, Aristotle, and Ctesias, under nearly the same name—*Marti-chora*, giving its synonym in their own language, Ἀνθρωποφάγος ; for *Merdi-khor* is a Persian compound, from *merd*, 'man,' and *khoordun* 'to eat.'"

" I passed," says the Colonel, " the *gopha*, or cave, of the most celebrated of the monsters of the present age, who was long the object of terror and loathing to Aboo and its neighbourhood. His name was Futteh Poori ; who, after having embowelled whatever came in his way, took the extraordinary resolution of immuring himself in his cell. The commands of maniacs generally meet with ready obedience ; and as he was regarded by many in this light, his desire was implicitly fulfilled. The mouth of the cave was built up ; and will remain so, till some mummy-hunting Frank shall re-open it, or till phrenology form a part of the modern education of a Hindu ; when, doubtless, the organ of destruction on the cranium of Futteh Poori will exhibit a high state of development."

on the wall. Up I jumped, aghast ; and the invalid lay rolling with laughter.

So healthily had I the good fortune to be brought up in point of religion, that (to anticipate a remark which might have come in at a less effective place) I remember kneeling one day at the school-church during the Litany, when the thought fell upon me—"Suppose eternal punishment should be true." An unusual sense of darkness and anxiety crossed me—but only for a moment. The next instant the extreme absurdity and impiety of the notion restored me to my ordinary feelings ; and from that moment to this,—respect the mystery of the past as I do, and attribute to it what final good out of fugitive evil I may,—I have never for one instant doubted the transitoriness of the doctrine and the unexclusive goodness of futurity. All those question-begging argumentations of the churches and schools, which are employed to reconcile the inflictions of the nursery to the gift of reason, and which would do quite as well for the absurdities of any one creed as another (indeed, they would be found to have done so, were we as deeply read in the religions of the East as of the West), come to nothing before the very modesty to which they appeal, provided it is a modesty healthy and loving. The more even of fugitive evil which it sees (and no ascertained evil suffered by any individual creature is otherwise), nay, the more which is disclosed to it in the very depths and concealments of nature, only the more convinces it that the great mystery of all things will allow of no lasting evil, visible or invisible ; and therefore it concludes that the evil which does exist is for some good purpose, and for the final blessing of all sentient beings, of whom it takes a care so remarkable.

I know not whether it was fortunate or unfortunate for me, humanly speaking, that my mother did not see as far into healthiness of training in other respects as in this. Some of the bad consequences to myself were indeed obvious, as the reader has seen; but it may have enabled me to save worse to others. If I could find any fault with her memory (speaking after an ordinary fashion), it would be that I was too delicately bred, except as to what is called good living. My parents were too poor for luxury. But she set me an example of such excessive care and anxiety for those about us, that I remember I could not see her bite off the ends of her thread while at work without being in pain till I was sure she would not swallow them. She used to be so agitated at the sight of

3

discord and quarrelling, particularly when it came to blows, and between the rudest or gayest combatants in the street, that, although it did not deprive her of courage and activity enough to interfere (which she would do if there was the slightest chance of effect, and which produced in myself a corresponding discrimination between sensibility and endeavour), it gave me an ultra-sympathy with the least show of pain and suffering; and she had produced in me such a horror, or rather such an intense idea of even violent words, and of the commonest trivial oath, that being led one day, perhaps by the very excess of it, to snatch a "fearful joy" in its utterance, it gave me so much remorse that for some time afterwards I could not receive a bit of praise, or a pat of encouragement on the head, without thinking to myself, " Ah! they little suspect that I am the boy who said, ' d—n it.' "

Dear mother! No one could surpass her in generosity; none be more willing to share, or to take the greatest portion of blame to themselves, of any evil consequences of mistake to a son; but if I have not swallowed very many camels in the course of my life, it has not been owing, perhaps, to this too great a straining at gnats. How happy shall I be (if I may) to laugh and compare notes with her on the subject in any humble corner of heaven; to recall to her the filial tenderness with which she was accustomed to speak of the mistakes of one of her own parents, and to think that her grandchildren will be as kind to the memory of their father.

I may here mention, as a ludicrous counterpart to this story, and a sample of the fantastical nature of scandal, that somebody having volunteered a defence of my character on some occasion to Mr. Wordsworth, as though the character had been questioned by him—the latter said he had never heard anything against it, except that I was "given to swearing."

I certainly think little of the habit of swearing, however idle, if it be carried no further than is done by many gallant and very good men, wise and great ones not excepted. I wish I had no worse faults to answer for. But the fact is, that however I may laugh at the puerile conscience of the anecdote just mentioned, an oath has not escaped my lips from that day to this.

I hope no " good fellow " will think ill of me for it. If he did, I should certainly be tempted to begin swearing immediately, purely to *vindicate* my character. But there was no swearing in our family; there was none in our school (Christ Hospital); and I seldom ever fell in the way of it anywhere except in books; so that the practice was not put into my head. I look upon Tom Jones, who swore, as an angel of light compared with Blifil, who, I am afraid, swore no more than myself. Steele, I suspect, occasionally rapped out an oath; which is not to be supposed of Addison. And this, again, might tempt me into a grudge against my nonjuring turn of colloquy; for I must own that I prefer open-hearted Steele with all his faults, to Addison with all his essays. But habit is habit, negative as well as positive. Let him that is without one, cast the first sarcasm.

After all, swearing was once seriously objected to me, and I had given cause for it. I must own, that I even begged hard to be allowed a few oaths. It was for an article in a magazine (the *New Monthly*), where I had to describe a fictitious person, whose character I thought required it; and I pleaded truth to nature, and the practice of the good old novelists; but in vain. The editor was not to be entreated. He was Mr. Theodore Hook. Perhaps this was what gave rise to the poet's impression.

But to return to my reminiscences. It may appear surprising to some, that a child brought up in such scruples of conscience, and particularly in such objections to pugnacity, should have ever found himself in possession of such toys as a drum and a sword. A distinguished economist, who was pleased the other day to call me the "spoiled child of the public" (a title which I should be proud to possess), expressed his astonishment that a person so "gentle" should have been a fighter in the thick of politics. But the "gentleness" was the reason. I mean, that under certain circumstances of training, the very love of peace and comfort, in begetting a desire to see those benefits partaken by others, begets a corresponding indignation at seeing them withheld.

I am aware of the perils of reaction to which this feeling tends; of the indulgence in bad passions which it may disguise; of the desirableness of quietly advocating whatever is quietly to be secured; of the perplexity occasioned to all these considerations by the example which appears to be set by nature herself in her employment of storm and tempest; and of the answer to be given to that perplexity by the modesty of human ignorance and its want of certainty of foresight. Nevertheless, till this question be settled (and the sooner the justice of the world can settle it the better), it renders the best natures liable to inconsistencies between theory and practice, and forces them into self-reconcilements of conscience, neither quite so easy in the result, nor so deducible from perfect reason as they would suppose. My mother, whose fortunes had been blighted, and feelings agonized, by the revolution in America, and who had conceived such a horror of war, that when we resided once near the Park, she would take a long circuit (as I have before mentioned), rather than go through it, in order to avoid seeing the soldiers, permitted me, nevertheless, to have the drum and the sword. Why? Because, if the sad necessity were to come, it would be her son's duty to war against war itself—to fight against those who oppressed the anti-fighters.

My father, entertaining these latter opinions without any misgiving (enforced, too, as they were by his classical education), and both my parents being great lovers of sermons, which he was in the habit of reading to us of an evening, I found myself at one time cultivating a perplexed ultra-conscientiousness with my mother; at another, laughing and being jovial with my father; and at a third, hearing from both of them stories of the Greek and Roman heroes, some of whom she admired as much as he did. The consequence was, that I one day presented to the astonished eyes of the maid-servant a combination that would have startled Dr. Trinder, and delighted the eyes of an old Puritan. To clap a sword by my side, and get the servant to pin up my hat into the likeness of the hat military, were symptoms of an ambition which she understood and applauded; but when I proceeded to append to this martial attire one of my father's bands, and, combining the military with the ecclesiastical authority, got upon a chair to preach to an imaginary audience over the back of it, she seemed to think the image realized of "heaven and earth coming together." However, she ended with enjoying, and even abetting, this new avatar of the church militant. Had I been a Mohammed, she would have been my first proselyte, and I should have called her the Maid-servant of the Faithful. She was a good, simple-hearted creature, who from not having been fortunate with the first orator in whom she believed, had stood a chance of ruin for life, till received into the only family that would admit her; and she lived and died in its service.

The desire thus childishly exhibited, of impressing some

religious doctrine, never afterwards quitted me; though, in consequence of the temperament which I inherited from one parent, and the opinions which I derived from both, it took a direction singularly cheerful. For a man is but his parents, or some other of his ancestors, drawn out. My father, though a clergyman of the Established Church, had settled, as well as my mother, into a Christian of the Universalist persuasion, which believes in the final restoration of all things. It was hence that I learned the impiety (as I have expressed it) of the doctrine of eternal punishment. In the present day, a sense of that impiety, in some way or other, whether of doubt or sophistication, is the secret feeling of nine-tenths of all churches; and every church will discover, before long, that it must rid itself of the doctrine, if it would not cease to exist. Love is the only creed destined to survive all others. They who think that no church can exist without a strong spice of terror, should watch the growth of education, and see which system of it is the most beloved. They should see also which system in the very nursery is growing the most ridiculous. The threat of the "black man and the coal-hole" has vanished from all decent infant training. What answer is the father, who would uphold the worst form of it, to give to the child whom he has spared the best?

How pleasant it is, in reviewing one's life, to look back on the circumstances that originated or encouraged any kindly tendency! I behold, at this moment, with lively distinctness, the handsome face of Miss C., who was the first person I remember seeing at a pianoforte; and I have something of a like impression of that of Miss M., mother, if I mistake not, or, at all events, near relation, of my distinguished friend Sheridan Knowles. My parents and his were acquainted. My mother, though fond of music, and a gentle singer in her way, had missed the advantage of a musical education, partly from her coming of a half-quaker stock, partly (as I have said before) from her having been too diffident to avail herself of the kindness of Dr. Franklin, who offered to teach her the guitar.

The reigning English composer at that time was " Mr. Hook," as he was styled at the head of his songs. He was the father of my punctilious editor of the magazine, and had a real, though small vein of genius, which was none the better for its being called upon to flow profusely for Ranelagh and Vauxhall. He was composer of the " Lass of Richmond

Hill" (an allusion to a *penchant* of George IV.), and of another popular song more lately remembered, "'Twas within a mile of Edinborough town." The songs of that day abounded in Strephons and Delias, and the music partook of the gentle inspiration. The association of early ideas with that kind of commonplace, has given me more than a toleration for it. I find something even touching in the endeavours of an innocent set of ladies and gentlemen, my fathers and mothers, to identify themselves with shepherds and shepherdesses, even in the most impossible hats and crooks. I think of the many heartfelt smiles that must have welcomed love letters and verses containing that sophisticate imagery, and of the no less genuine tears that were shed over the documents when faded; and criticism is swallowed up in those human drops. This is one of the reasons why I can read even the most faded part of the works of Shenstone, and why I can dip again and again into such correspondence as that of the Countesses of Hertford and Pomfret, and of my Lady Luxborough, who raises monuments in her garden to the united merits of Mr. Somerville and the god Pan. The feeling was true, though the expression was sophisticate and a fashion ; and they who cannot see the feeling for the mode, do the very thing which they think they scorn; that is, sacrifice the greater consideration for the less.

But Hook was not the only, far less the most fashionable composer. There were (if not all personally, yet popularly contemporaneous) Mr. Lampe, Mr. Oswald, Dr. Boyce, Linley, Jackson, Shield, and Storace, with Paesiello, Sacchini, and others at the King's Theatre, whose delightful airs wandered into the streets out of the English operas that borrowed them, and became confounded with English property. I have often, in the course of my life, heard "Whither, my love?" and "For tenderness formed," boasted of, as specimens of English melody. For many years I took them for such myself, in common with the rest of our family, with whom they were great favourites. The first, which Stephen Storace adapted to some words in the *Haunted Tower*, is the air of "La Rachelina" in Paesiello's opera *La Molinara*. The second, which was put by General Burgoyne to a song in his comedy of the *Heiress*, is "Io sono Lindoro," in the same enchanting composer's *Barbiere di Siviglia*. The once popular English songs and duets, &c., "How imperfect is expression;" "For me, my fair a wreath has wove;" "Henry cull'd the flow'ret's bloom;" "Oh, thou wert born to please me;" "Here's a health to all good lasses;" "Youth's the season made for joys;" "Gently touch the warbling lyre;" "No, 'twas neither shape nor feature;" "Pray, Goody, please to moderate;" "Hope told a flattering tale;" and a hundred others, were all foreign compositions, chiefly Italian. Every burlesque or *buffo* song, of any pretension, was pretty sure to be Italian.

When Edwin, Fawcett, and others, were rattling away in the happy comic songs of O'Keeffe, with his triple rhymes and illustrative jargon, the audience little suspected that they were listening to some of the finest animal spirits of the south —to Piccini, Paesiello, and Cimarosa. Even the wild Irishman thought himself bound to go to Naples, before he could get a proper dance for his gaiety. The only genuine English compositions worth anything at that time, were almost confined to Shield, Dibdin, and Storace, the last of whom, the author of "Lullaby," who was an Italian born in England, formed the golden link between the music of the two countries, the only one, perhaps, in which English accentuation and Italian flow were ever truly amalgamated; though I must own that I am heretic enough (if present fashion is orthodoxy) to believe, that Arne was a real musical genius, of a very pure, albeit not of the very first water. He has set, indeed, two songs of Shakspeare's (the "Cuckoo song," and "Where the bee sucks,") in a spirit of perfect analogy to the words, as well as of the liveliest musical invention; and his air of "Water parted," in *Artaxerxes*, winds about the feelings with an earnest and graceful tenderness of regret, worthy in the highest degree of the affecting beauty of the sentiment.*

All the favourite poetry of the day, however, was of one cast. I have now before me a *Select Collection of English Songs*, by Ritson, published in the year 1783, in three volumes octavo, the last of which contains the musical airs. The style is of the following description:—

> Almeria's face, her shape, her air,
> *With charms resistless wound the heart*, &c. p. 2.

---

* "Dr. Haydn was delighted with *Artaxerxes*; and he told my dear mother (for he was frequently with us at Vauxhall) that he had not an idea we had such an opera in the English language."—Letter of Mrs. Henslow in Cradock's *Literary and Miscellaneous Memoirs*. Vol. iv. p. 133.

(I should not wonder if dear Almeria Thornton, whose tender affection for my mother will appear in another chapter, was christened out of this song.)

> Say, Myra, why is gentle love, &c.
> *Which racks the amorous breast,*

by Lord Lyttelton, the most admired poet, perhaps, of the age.

> *When Delia on the plain appears;*

also by his lordship.

> *In vain, Philander, at my feet.*
> Ah, *Damon, dear shepherd,* adieu.

> Come, thou rosy dimpled boy,
> Source of every heartfelt joy,
> Leave the blissful bowers a while,
> *Paphos and the Cyprian isle.*

This was a favourite song in our house. So was " Come, now, all ye social powers," and

> Come, let us dance and sing,
> While all Barbados bells shall ring;

probably on account of its mention of my father's native place. The latter song is not in Ritson. It was the finale in Colman's *Inkle and Yarico*, a play founded on a Barbadian story, which our family must have gone with delight to see. Another favourite, which used to make my mother shed tears, on account of my sister Eliza, who died early, was Jackson of Exeter's song—

> Encompass'd in an angel's frame.

It is, indeed, a touching specimen of that master. The " Hardy Tar," also, and " The topsails shiver in the wind," used to charm yet sadden her, on account of my eldest brother then living, who was at sea. The latter, written by the good-natured and gallant Captain Thompson, was set to music, I think, by Arne's son, Michael, who had a fine musical sea-vein, simple and strong. He was the composer of " Fresh and strong the breeze is blowing."

The other day I found two songs of that period on Robinson's music-stall in Wardour Street, one by Mr. Hook, entitled " Alone, by the light of the moon;" the other, a song with a French burden, called " Dans votre lit;" an innocent production, notwithstanding its title. They were the only songs I recollect singing when a child, and I looked on them with the accumulated tenderness of sixty-three years of age. I do not remember to have set eyes on them in the interval. What a difference between the little smooth-faced boy at his mother's knee, encouraged to lift up his voice to the pianoforte, and the battered grey-headed senior, looking again, for the first time, on what he had sung at the distance of more than half a century! Life often seems a dream; but there are occasions when the sudden re-appearance of early objects, by the intensity of their presence, not only renders the interval less present to the consciousness than a very dream, but makes the portion of life which preceded it seem to have been the most real of all things, and our only undreaming time.

"Alone, by the light of the moon," and "Dans votre lit!" how had they not been thumbed and thrown aside by all the pianoforte young ladies—our mothers and grandmothers— fifty years ago, never to be brought forth again, except by an explorer of old stalls, and to meet, perhaps, with no sympathy but in his single imagination! Yet there I stood; and Wardour Street, every street, all London, as it now exists, became to me as if it had never been. The universe itself was nothing but a poor sitting-room in the year '89 or '90, with my mother in it bidding me sing, Miss C. at the pianoforte—harpsichord more likely, and my little sister, Mary, with her round cheeks and blue eyes, wishing me to begin. What a great singer is that little boy to those loving relations, and how Miss C., with all her good nature, must be smiling at the importance of little boys to their mothers! "Alone, by the light of the moon," was the "show song," but "Dans votre lit" was the favourite with my sister, because, in her ignorance of the French language, she had associated the name of her brother with the sound of the last word.

The song was a somewhat gallant, but very decorous song, apostrophizing a lady as a lily in the flower-bed. It was "silly, sooth," and "dallied with the innocence of love" in those days, after a fashion which might have excited livelier ideas in the more restricted imaginations of the present. The reader has seen that my mother, notwithstanding her charitableness to the poor maid-servant, was a woman of strict morals; the tone of the family conversation was scrupulously correct, though, perhaps, a little flowery and Thomson-like (Thomson was the favourite poet of most of us); yet the songs that were sung at that time by the most fastidious might be thought a shade freer than would suit the like kind of society at present. Whether we are more innocent in having become more ashamed, I shall not judge. Assuredly, the singer of those songs was as innocent as the mother that bade him sing them.

My little sister Mary died not long after. She was so young, that my only recollection of her, besides her blue eyes, is her love of her brother, and her custom of leading me by the hand to some stool or seat on the staircase, and making me sing the song with her favourite burden. We were the two youngest children, and about of an age.

I please myself with picturing to my imagination what was going forward during my childhood in the world of politics, literature, and public amusements; how far they interested my parents; and what amount of impression they may have left on my own mind. The American Revolution, which had driven my father from Philadelphia, was not long over, and the French Revolution was approaching. My father, for reasons which have already been mentioned, listened more and more to the new opinions, and my mother listened, not only from love to her husband, but because she was still more deeply impressed by speculations regarding the welfare of human kind. The public mind, after a long and comparatively insipid tranquillity, had begun to be stirred by the eloquence of Burke; by the rivalries of Pitt and Fox; by the thanks which the king gave to heaven for his recovery from his first illness; by the warlike and licentious energies of the Russian Empress, Catherine II., who partly shocked and partly amused them; and by the gentler gallantries and showy luxury of the handsome young Prince of Wales, afterwards George IV.

In the world of literature and art, Goldsmith and Johnson had gone; Cowper was not yet much known; the most prominent poets were Hayley and Darwin; the most distinguished prose-writer, Gibbon. Sir Joshua Reynolds was in his decline, so was Horace Walpole. The Kembles had come up in the place of Garrick. There were excellent comic actors in the persons of Edwin, Lewis, young Bannister, &c. They had O'Keeffe, an original humourist, to write for them. I have already noticed the vocal portion of the theatres. Miss Burney, afterwards Madame d'Arblay, surprised the reading world with her entertaining, but somewhat vulgar novels; and Mrs. Inchbald, Mrs. Charlotte Smith, and a then anonymous author, Robert Bage (who wrote *Hermsprong*, and *Man as He Is*), delighted liberal politicians with theirs. Mrs. Inchbald was also a successful dramatist; but her novels, which were written in a style to endure, were her chief merits.

My mother was one of their greatest admirers. I have heard her expatiate with delight on the characters in *Nature and Art*, which, though not so masterly a novel as the *Simple Story*, and a little wilful in the treatment, was full of matter for reflection, especially on conventional, and what are now called "class" points. Dr. Philpotts would have accused my mother of disaffection to the Church; and she would not have mended the matter by retreating on her admiration of Bishops Hoadley and Shipley. Her regard for the reverend author of *Meditations in a Flower Garden* would have made the doctor smile, though she would have recovered, perhaps, something of his good opinion by her admiration of Dr. Young and his *Night Thoughts*. But Young deluded her with his groans against the world, and his lamentations for his daughter. She did not know that he was a preferment-hunter, who was prosperous enough to indulge in the "luxury of woe," and to groan because his toast was not thrice buttered.

Ranelagh and Vauxhall, as painted in Miss Burney's novels, were among the fashionable amusements of those days. My mother was neither rich nor gay enough to see much of them; but she was no ascetic, and she went where others did, as occasion served. My father, whose manners were at once high-bred and lively, had some great acquaintances; but I recollect none of them personally, except an old lady of quality, who (if memory does not strangely deceive me, and give me a personal share in what I only heard talked of; for old autobiographers of childhood must own themselves liable to such confusions) astounded me one day, by letting her false teeth slip out, and clapping them in again.

I had no idea of the existence of such phenomena, and could almost as soon have expected her to take off her head and re-adjust it. She lived in Red Lion Square, a quarter in different estimation from what it is now. It was at her house, I believe, that my father one evening met Wilkes. He did not know him by sight, and happening to fall into conversation with him, while the latter sat looking down, he said something in Wilkes's disparagement; on which the jovial demagogue looked up in his face, and burst out a laughing.

I do not exactly know how people dressed at that time; but I believe that sacks, and negligées, and toupees were going out, and the pigtail and the simpler modern style of dress coming in. I recollect hearing my mother describe the misery of having her hair dressed two or three stories high, and of lying in it all night ready for some visit or spectacle next day. I think I also recollect seeing Wilkes himself in an old-fashioned flap-waistcoated suit of scarlet and gold; and I am sure I have seen Murphy, the dramatist, a good deal later, in a suit of a like fashion, though soberer, and a large cocked-hat. The cocked-hat in general survived till nearly the present century. It was superseded by the round one during the French Revolution. I remember our steward at school, a very solemn personage, making his appearance in one, to our astonishment, and not a little to the diminution of his dignity. Some years later, I saw Mr. Pitt in a blue coat, buckskin breeches and boots, and a round hat, with powder and pigtail. He was thin and gaunt, with his hat off his forehead, and his nose in the air,—that nose on which Hazlitt said he "suspended the House of Commons." Much about the same time I saw his friend, the first Lord Liverpool, a respectable looking old gentleman, in a brown wig. Later still, I saw Mr. Fox, fat and jovial, though he was then declining. He, who had been a "beau" in his youth, then looked something quaker-like as to dress, with plain coloured clothes, a broad round hat, white waistcoat, and, if I am not mistaken, white stockings. He was standing in Parliament-street, just where the street commences as you leave Whitehall; and was making two young gentlemen laugh heartily at something which he seemed to be relating.

My father once took me—but I cannot say at what period of my juvenility—into both houses of Parliament. In the Commons, I saw Mr. Pitt sawing the air, and occasionally turning to appeal to those about him, while he spoke in a loud, important, and hollow voice. When the persons he appealed to, said "Hear! hear!" I thought they said "Dear! dear!" in objection; and I wondered that he did not seem in the least degree disconcerted. The House of Lords, I must say (without meaning disrespect to an assembly which must always have contained some of the most accomplished men in the country), surprised me with the personally insignificant look of its members. I had, to be sure, conceived exaggerated notions of the magnates of all countries; and perhaps might have expected to behold a set of conscript fathers; but in no respect, real or ideal, did they appear to me in their corporate aspect, like anything which is understood by the word "noble." The Commons seemed to me to have the advantage; though they surprised me with lounging on the benches and retaining their hats. I was not then informed enough to know the difference between apparent and substantial importance; much less aware of the positive exaltation, which that very simplicity, and that absence of pretension, gave to the most potent assembly in Europe.

CHAPTER III.

SCHOOL-DAYS.

Books for children during the latter part of the eighteenth century had been in a bad way, with sordid and merely plodding morals—ethics that were necessary perhaps for a certain stage in the progress of commerce and for its greatest ultimate purposes (undreamt of by itself), but which thwarted healthy and large views of society for the time being. They were the consequences of an altogether unintellectual state of trade, aided and abetted by such helps to morality as Hogarth's pictures of the Good and Bad Apprentice, which identified virtue with prosperity.

Hogarth, in most of his pictures, was as healthy a moralist as he supposed himself, but not for the reasons which he supposed. The gods he worshipped were Truth and Prudence; but he saw more of the carnal than spiritual beauties of either. He was somewhat of a vulgarian in intention as well as mode. But wherever there is genius, there is a genial something greater than the accident of breeding, than the prevailing disposition, or even than the conscious design; and this portion of divinity within the painter, saw fair-play between his conventional and immortal part. It put the beauty of colour into his mirth, the counteraction of mirth into his melancholy, and a lesson beyond his intention into all: that is to say, it suggested redemptions and first causes for the objects of his satire; and thus vindicated the justice of nature, at the moment when he was thinking of little but the pragmaticalness of art.

The children's books in those days were Hogarth's pictures taken in their most literal acceptation. Every good boy was to ride in his coach, and be a lord mayor; and every bad boy was to be hung, or eaten by lions. The gingerbread was gilt, and the books were gilt like the gingerbread,—a "take in" the more gross, inasmuch as nothing could be plainer or less dazzling than the books of the same boys when they grew a little older.   There was a lingering old ballad or so in favour of the gallanter apprentices who tore out lions' hearts and astonished gazing sultans; and in antiquarian corners, Percy's "Reliques" were preparing a nobler age, both in poetry and prose. But the first counteraction came, as it ought, in the shape of a new book for children. The pool of mercenary and time-serving ethics was first blown over by the fresh country breeze of Mr. Day's *Sandford and Merton*—a production that I well remember, and shall ever be grateful to. It came in aid of my mother's perplexities between delicacy and hardihood, between courage and conscientiousness. It assisted the cheerfulness I inherited from my father; showed me that circumstances were not to crush a healthy gaiety, or the most masculine self-respect; and helped to supply me with the resolution of standing by a principle, not merely as a point of lowly or lofty sacrifice, but as a matter of common sense and duty, and a simple co-operation with the elements of natural welfare.

I went, nevertheless, to school at Christ Hospital, an ultra-sympathizing and timid boy.* The sight of boys fighting, from which I had been so anxiously withheld, frightened me as something devilish; and the least threat of corporal chastisement to a schoolfellow (for the lesson I had learned would have enabled me to bear it myself) affected me to tears. I remember to this day, merely on that account, the name of a boy who was to receive punishment for some offence about a task. It was Lemoine. (I hereby present him with my respects, if he is an existing old gentleman, and hope he has not lost a pleasing countenance.) He had a cold and hoarseness; and his voice, while pleading in mitigation, sounded to me so pathetic, that I wondered how the master could have the heart to strike him.

Readers who have been at a public school may guess the consequence. I was not of a disposition to give offence, but neither was I quick to take it; and this, to the rude, energy-cultivating spirit of boys in general (not the worst thing in the world, till the pain in preparation for them can be diminished), was in itself an offence. I therefore "went to the wall," till address, and the rousing of my own spirit, tended to right me;

* In 1792.

but I went through a great deal of fear in the process. I became convinced, that if I did not put moral courage in the place of personal, or, in other words, undergo any stubborn amount of pain and wretchedness, rather than submit to what I thought wrong, there was an end for ever, as far as I was concerned, of all those fine things that had been taught me, in vindication of right and justice.

Whether it was, however, that by the help of animal spirits I possessed some portion of the courage for which the rest of the family was remarkable—or whether I was a veritable coward, born or bred, destined to show, in my person, how far a spirit of love and freedom could supersede the necessity of gall, and procure me the respect of those about me—certain it is, that although, except in one instance, I did my best to avoid, and succeeded honourably in avoiding, those personal encounters with my school-fellows, which, in confronting me on my own account with the face of a fellow-creature, threw me upon a sense of something devilish, and overwhelmed me with a sort of terror for both parties, yet I gained at an early period of boyhood the reputation of a romantic enthusiast, whose daring in behalf of a friend or a good cause nothing could put down. I was obliged to call in the aid of a feeling apart from my own sense of personal antagonism, and so merge the diabolical, as it were, into the human. In other words, I had not self-respect or gall enough to be angry on my own account, unless there was something at stake which, by concerning others, gave me a sense of support, and so pieced out my want with their abundance. The moment, however, that I felt thus supported, not only did all misgiving vanish from my mind, but contempt of pain took possession of my body ; and my poor mother might have gloried through her tears in the loving courage of her son.

I state the case thus proudly, both in justice to the manner in which she trained me, and because I conceive it may do good. I never fought with a boy but once, and then it was on my own account ; but though I beat him I was frightened, and eagerly sought his good will. I dared everything, however, from the biggest and strongest boys on other accounts, and was sometimes afforded an opportunity of showing my spirit of martyrdom. The truth is, I could suffer better than act ; for the utmost activity of martyrdom is supported by a certain sense of passiveness. We are not bold from ourselves, but from something which compels us to be so, and which supports us by a sense of the necessity.

I had not been long in the school, when this spirit within me broke out in a manner that procured me great esteem. There was a monitor or "big boy" in office, who had a trick of entertaining himself by pelting lesser boys' heads with a hard ball. He used to throw it at this boy and that; make the *throwee* bring it back to him; and then send a rap with it on his cerebellum, as he was going off.

I had borne this spectacle one day for some time, when the family precepts rising within me, I said to myself, "I must go up to the monitor and speak to him about this." I issued forth accordingly, and to the astonishment of all present, who had never witnessed such an act of insubordination, I said, "You have no right to do this." The monitor, more astounded than any one, exclaimed, "What?." I repeated my remonstrance. He treated me with the greatest contempt, as if disdaining even to strike me; and finished by ordering me to "stand out." "Standing out" meant going to a particular spot in the hall where we dined. I did so; but just as the steward (the master in that place) was entering it, the monitor called to me to come away; and I neither heard any more of standing out, nor saw any more of the ball. I do not recollect that he even "spited" me afterwards, which must have been thought very remarkable. I seemed fairly to have taken away the breath of his calculations. The probability is, that he was a good lad who had got a bad habit. Boys often become tyrants from a notion of its being grand and manly.

Another monitor, a year or two afterwards, took it into his head to force me to be his fag. Fag was not the term at our school, though it was in our vocabulary. Fag, with us, meant eatables. The learned derived the word from the Greek *phago*, to eat. I had so little objection to serve out of love, that there is no office I could not have performed for good will; but it had been given out that I had determined not to be a menial on any other terms, and the monitor in question undertook to bring me to reason. He was a mild, good-looking boy about fourteen, remarkable for the neatness, and even elegance, of his appearance.

Receiving the refusal, for which he had been prepared, he showed me a knot in a long handkerchief, and told me I should receive a lesson from that handkerchief every day,

with the addition of a fresh knot every time, unless I chose
to alter my mind. I did not choose. I received the daily or
rather nightly lesson, for it was then most convenient to strip
me, and I came out of the ordeal in triumph. I never was
fag to anybody; never made anybody's bed, or cleaned his
shoes, or was the boy to get his tea, much less expected to
stand as a screen for him before the fire, which I have seen
done; though, upon the whole, the boys were very mild
governors.

Lamb has noticed the character of the school for good
manners, which he truly describes as being equally removed
from the pride of aristocratic foundations and the servility of
the charity schools. I believe it retains this character still;
though the changes which its system underwent not long ago,
fusing all the schools into one another, and introducing a
more generous diet, is thought by some not to have been
followed by an advance in other respects. I have heard the
school charged, more lately, with having been suffered, in the
intervals between the school hours, to fall out of the liberal
and gentlemanly supervision of its best teachers, into the
hands of an officious and ignorant sectarianism. But this
may only have been a passing abuse.

I love and honour the school on private accounts; and I
feel a public interest in its welfare, inasmuch as it is one of
those judicious links with all classes, the importance of which,
especially at a time like the present, cannot be too highly
estimated; otherwise, I should have said nothing to its possible, and I hope transient disadvantage. Queen Victoria
recognized its importance, by visits and other personal con-
descensions, long before the late changes in Europe could
have diminished the grace of their bestowal; and I will
venture to say that every one of those attentions will have
sown for her generous nature a crop of loyalty worth having.

But for the benefit of such as are unacquainted with the
city, or with a certain track of reading, I must give a more
particular account of a school which in truth is a curiosity.
Thousands of inhabitants of the metropolis have gone from
west-end to east-end, and till the new hall was laid open
to view by the alterations in Newgate Street, never suspected
that in the heart of it lies an old cloistered foundation, where
a boy may grow up as I did, among six hundred others, and
know as little of the very neighbourhood as the world does
of him.

4

Perhaps there is not a foundation in the country so truly English, taking that word to mean what Englishmen wish it to mean—something solid, unpretending, of good character, and free to all. More boys are to be found in it, who issue from a greater variety of ranks, than in any school in the kingdom; and as it is the most various, so it is the largest, of all the free schools. Nobility do not go there, except as boarders. Now and then a boy of a noble family may be met with, and he is reckoned an interloper, and against the charter; but the sons of poor gentry and London citizens abound; and with them an equal share is given to the sons of tradesmen of the very humblest description, not omitting servants. I would not take my oath—but I have a strong recollection, that in my time there were two boys, one of whom went up into the drawing-room to his father, the master of the house; and the other, down into the kitchen to *his* father, the coachman. One thing, however, I know to be certain, and it is the noblest of all, namely, that the boys themselves (at least it was so in my time) had no sort of feeling of the difference of one another's ranks out of doors. The cleverest boy was the noblest, let his father be who he might. Christ Hospital is a nursery of tradesmen, of merchants, of naval officers, of scholars; it has produced some of the greatest ornaments of their time; and the feeling among the boys themselves is, that it is a medium between the patrician pretension of such schools as Eton and Westminster, and the plebeian submission of the charity schools. In point of university honours it claims to be equal with the best; and though other schools can show a greater abundance of eminent names, I know not where many will be found who are a greater host in themselves. One original author is worth a hundred transmitters of elegance: and such a one is to be found in Richardson, who here received what education he possessed. Here Camden also received the rudiments of his. Bishop Stillingfleet, according to the *Memoirs of Pepys*, was brought up in the school. We have had many eminent scholars, two of them Greek professors, to wit, Barnes and Scholefield, the latter of whom attained an extraordinary succession of university honours. The rest are Markland; Middleton, late Bishop of Calcutta; and Mitchell, the translator of *Aristophanes*. Christ Hospital, I believe, towards the close of the last century, and the beginning of the present, sent out more living writers, in its proportion, than any other school.

There was Dr. Richards, author of the *Aboriginal Britons;* Dyer, whose life was one unbroken dream of learning and goodness, and who used to make us wonder with passing through the school-room (where no other person in "town clothes" ever appeared) to consult books in the library; Le Grice, the translator of *Longus;* Horne, author of some well-known productions in controversial divinity; Surr, the novelist (not in the Grammar School); James White, the friend of Charles Lamb, and not unworthy of him, author of *Falstaff's Letters* (this was he who used to give an anniversary dinner to the chimney-sweepers, merrier than, though not so magnificent as Mrs. Montague's); Pitman, a celebrated preacher, editor of some school-books and religious classics (also a veritable man of wit); Mitchell, before mentioned, myself, who stood next him; Barnes, who came next, the Editor of the *Times,* than whom no man (if he had cared for it) could have been more certain of attaining celebrity for wit and literature; Townsend, a prebendary of Durham, author of *Armageddon,* and several theological works (it was he who went to see the Pope, in the hope of persuading him to concede points towards the amalgamation of the Papal and Protestant Churches); Gilly, another of the Durham prebendaries, an amiable man, who wrote the *Narrative of the Waldenses;* Scargill, a Unitarian minister, author of some tracts on Peace and War, &c.; and lastly, whom I have kept by way of climax, Coleridge and Charles Lamb, two of the most original geniuses, not only of the day, but of the country.

In the time of Henry the Eighth Christ Hospital was a monastery of Franciscan friars. Being dissolved among the others, Edward the Sixth, moved by a sermon of Bishop Ridley's, assigned the revenues of it to the maintenance and education of a certain number of poor orphan children, born of citizens of London. I believe there has been no law passed to alter the letter of this intention; which is a pity, since the alteration has taken place. An extension of it was probably very good, and even demanded by circumstances. I have reason, for one, to be grateful for it. But tampering with matters-of-fact among children is dangerous. They soon learn to distinguish between allowed poetical fiction and that which they are told, under severe penalties, never to be guilty of; and this early sample of contradiction between the thing asserted and the obvious fact, can do no good even in an establishment so plain-dealing in other respects as Christ

Hospital. The place is not only designated as an Orphan-house in its Latin title, but the boys, in the prayers which they repeat every day, implore the pity of heaven upon "us poor orphans." I remember the perplexity this caused me at a very early period. It is true, the word orphan may be used in a sense implying destitution of any sort; but this was not its Christ Hospital intention; nor do the younger boys give it the benefit of that scholarly interpretation. There was another thing (now, I believe, done away) which existed in my time, and perplexed me still more. It seemed a glaring instance of the practice likely to result from the other assumption, and made me prepare for a hundred falsehoods and deceptions, which, mixed up with contradiction, as most things in society are, I sometimes did find, and oftener dreaded. I allude to a foolish custom they had in the ward which I first entered, and which was the only one that the company at the public suppers were in the habit of going into, of hanging up, by the side of each bed, a clean white napkin, which was sup-posed to be the one used by the occupiers. Now these nap-kins were only for show, the real towels being of the largest and coarsest kind. If the masters had been asked about them, they would doubtless have told the truth ; perhaps the nurses would have done so. But the boys were not aware of this. There they saw these "white lies" hanging before them, a conscious imposition; and I well remember how alarmed I used to feel, lest any of the company should direct their inquiries to me.

Christ Hospital (for this is its proper name, and not Christ's Hospital) occupies a considerable portion of ground between Newgate Street, Giltspur Street, St. Bartholomew's, and Little Britain. There is a quadrangle with cloisters; and the square inside the cloisters is called the Garden, and most likely was the monastery garden. Its only delicious crop, for many years, has been pavement. Another large area, pre-senting the Grammar and Navigation Schools, is also mis-nomered the Ditch; the town-ditch having formerly run that way. In Newgate Street is seen the Hall, or eating-room, one of the noblest in England, adorned with enormously long paintings by Verrio and others, and with an organ. A por-tion of the old quadrangle once contained the library of the monks, and was built or repaired by the famous Whittington, whose arms were to be seen outside; but alterations of late years have done it away.

In the cloisters a number of persons lie buried, besides the officers of the house. Among them is Isabella, wife of Edward the Second, the "She-wolf of France." I was not aware of this circumstance then; but many a time, with a recollection of some lines in "Blair's Grave" upon me, have I run as hard as I could at night-time from my ward to another, in order to borrow the next volume of some ghostly romance. In one of the cloisters was an impression resembling a gigantic foot, which was attributed by some to the angry stamping of the ghost of a beadle's wife! A beadle was a higher sound to us than to most, as it involved ideas of detected apples in churchtime, "skulking" (as it was called) out of bounds, and a power of reporting us to the masters. But fear does not stand upon rank and ceremony.

The wards, or sleeping-rooms, are twelve, and contained, in my time, rows of beds on each side, partitioned off, but connected with one another, and each having two boys to sleep in it. Down the middle ran the binns for holding bread and other things, and serving for a table when the meal was not taken in the hall; and over the binns hung a great homely chandelier.

To each of these wards a nurse was assigned, who was the widow of some decent liveryman of London, and who had the charge of looking after us at night-time, seeing to our washing, &c., and carving for us at dinner: all of which gave her a good deal of power, more than her name warranted. The nurses, however, were almost invariably very decent people, and performed their duty; which was not always the case with the young ladies, their daughters. There were five schools; a grammar-school, a mathematical or navigation-school (added by Charles the Second, through the zeal of Mr. Pepys), a writing, a drawing, and a reading school. Those who could not read when they came on the foundation, went into the last. There were few in the last-but-one, and I scarcely know what they did, or for what object. The writing-school was for those who were intended for trade and commerce; the mathematical, for boys who went as midshipmen into the naval and East India service; and the grammar-school for such as were designed for the Church, and to go to the University. The writing-school was by far the largest; and, what is very curious (it has been altered since), all the schools were kept quite distinct; so that a boy might arrive at the age of fifteen in the grammar school, and not know his multiplication-table; which was the case with myself. Nor do I know it to this day! Shades of Horace, Walpole, and Lord Lyttelton! come to my assistance, and enable me to bear the confession: but so it is. The fault was not my fault at the time; but I ought to have repaired it when I went out in the world; and great is the mischief which it has done me.

Most of these schools had several masters; besides whom there was a steward, who took care of our subsistence, and who had a general superintendence over all hours and circumstances not connected with teaching. The masters had almost all been in the school, and might expect pensions or livings in their old age. Among those in my time, the mathematical master was Mr. Wales, a man well known for his science, who had been round the world with Captain Cook; for which we highly venerated him. He was a good man, of plain, simple manners, with a heavy large person and a benign countenance. When he was at Otaheite, the natives played him a trick while bathing, and stole his small-clothes; which we used to think a liberty scarcely credible. The name of the steward, a thin stiff man of invincible formality of demeanour, admirably fitted to render encroachment impossible, was Hathaway. We of the grammar-school used to call him "the Yeoman," on account of Shakspeare having married the daughter of a man of that name, designated as "a substantial yeoman."

Our dress was of the coarsest and quaintest kind, but was respected out of doors, and is so. It consisted of a blue drugget gown, or body, with ample skirts to it; a yellow vest underneath in winter-time; small-clothes of Russia duck; worsted yellow stockings; a leathern girdle; and a little black worsted cap, usually carried in the hand. I believe it was the ordinary dress of children in humble life during the reign of the Tudors. We used to flatter ourselves that it was taken from the monks; and there went a monstrous tradition, that at one period it consisted of blue velvet with silver buttons. It was said, also, that during the blissful era of the blue velvet, we had roast mutton for supper; but that the small-clothes not being then in existence, and the mutton suppers too luxurious, the eatables were given up for the ineffables.

A malediction, at heart, always followed the memory of him who had taken upon himself to decide so preposterously.

To say the truth, we were not too well fed at that time, either in quantity or quality; and we could not enter with our hungry imaginations into these remote philosophies. Our breakfast was bread and water, for the beer was too bad to drink. The bread consisted of the half of a three-halfpenny loaf, according to the prices then current. This was not much for growing boys, who had had nothing to eat from six or seven o'clock the preceding evening. For dinner we had the same quantity of bread, with meat only every other day, and that consisting of a small slice, such as would be given to an infant three or four years old. Yet even that, with all our hunger, we very often left half-eaten—the meat was so tough. On the other days we had a milk-porridge, ludicrously thin; or rice-milk, which was better. There were no vegetables or puddings. Once a month we had roast beef; and twice a year (I blush to think of the eagerness with which it was looked for!) a dinner of pork. One was roast, and the other boiled; and on the latter occasion we had our only pudding, which was of peas. I blush to remember this, not on account of our poverty, but on account of the sordidness of the custom. There had much better have been none. For supper we had a like piece of bread, with butter or cheese; and then to bed, " with what appetite we might."

Our routine of life was this. We rose to the call of a bell, at six in summer, and seven in winter; and after combing ourselves, and washing our hands and faces, went, at the call of another bell, to breakfast. All this took up about an hour. From breakfast we proceeded to school, where we remained till eleven, winter and summer, and then had an hour's play. Dinner took place at twelve. Afterwards was a little play till one, when we again went to school, and remained till five in summer and four in winter. At six was the supper. We used to play after it in summer till eight. In winter, we proceeded from supper to bed. On Sundays, the school-time of the other days was occupied in church, both morning and evening ; and as the Bible was read to us every day before every meal, and on going to bed, besides prayers and graces, we rivalled the monks in the religious part of our duties.

The effect was certainly not what was intended. The Bible, perhaps, was read thus frequently, in the first instance, out of contradiction to the papal spirit that had so long kept it locked up; but, in the eighteenth century, the repetition was not so desirable among a parcel of hungry boys, anxious to get their modicum to eat. On Sunday, what with the long service in the morning, the service again after dinner, and the inaudible and indifferent tones of some of the preachers, it was unequivocally tiresome. I, for one, who had been piously brought up, and continued to have religion inculcated on me by father and mother, began secretly to become as indifferent as I thought the preachers; and, though the morals of the school were in the main excellent and exemplary, we all felt, without knowing it, that it was the orderliness and example of the general system that kept us so, and not the religious part of it, which seldom entered our heads at all, and only tired us when it did.

I am not begging any question here, or speaking for or against. I am only stating a fact. Others may argue that, however superfluous the readings and prayers might have been, a good general spirit of religion must have been inculcated, because a great deal of virtue and religious charity is known to have issued out of that school, and no fanaticism. I shall not dispute the point. The case is true; but not the less true is what I speak of. Latterly there came, as our parish clergyman, Mr. Crowther, a nephew of our famous Richardson, and worthy of the talents and virtues of his kinsman, though inclining to a mode of faith which is supposed to produce more faith than charity. But, till then, the persons who were in the habit of getting up in our church pulpit and reading-desk, might as well have hummed a tune to their diaphragms. They inspired us with nothing but mimicry. The name of the morning reader was Salt. He was a worthy man, I believe, and might, for aught we knew, have been a clever one; but he had it all to himself. He spoke in his throat, with a sound as if he were weak and corpulent; and was famous among us for saying "murracles" instead of "miracles." When we imitated him, this was the only word we drew upon: the rest was unintelligible suffocation. Our usual evening preacher was Mr. Sandiford, who had the reputation of learning and piety. It was of no use to us, except to make us associate the ideas of learning and piety in the pulpit with inaudible humdrum. Mr. Sandiford's voice was hollow and low; and he had a habit of dipping up and down over his book, like a chicken drinking. Mr. Salt was eminent for a single word. Mr. Sandiford surpassed him, for he had two audible phrases. There was, it is true, no great variety in them. One was "the dispensation of Moses;" the other (with a due interval of hum), "the Mosaic dispensation." These he used to repeat so often, that in our caricatures of him they sufficed for an entire portrait. The reader may conceive a large church (it was Christ Church, Newgate Street), with six hundred boys, seated like charity-children up in the air, on each side of the organ, Mr. Sandiford humming in the valley, and a few maid-servants who formed his afternoon congregation. We did not dare to go to sleep. We were not allowed to read. The great boys used to get those that sat behind them to play with their hair. Some whispered to their neighbours, and the others thought of their lessons and tops. I can safely say, that many of us would have been good listeners, and most of us attentive ones, if the clergyman could have been heard. As it was, I talked as well as the rest, or thought of my exercise. Sometimes we could not help joking and laughing over our weariness ; and then the fear was, lest the steward had seen us. It was part of the business of the steward to preside over the boys in church-time. He sat aloof, in a place where he could view the whole of his flock. There was a ludicrous kind of revenge we had of him, whenever a particular part of the Bible was read. This was the parable of the Unjust Steward. The boys waited anxiously till the passage commenced ; and then, as if by a general conspiracy, at the words "thou unjust steward," the whole school turned their eyes upon this unfortunate officer, who sat

"Like Teneriff or Atlas unremoved."

We persuaded ourselves, that the more unconscious he looked, the more he was acting.

By a singular chance, there were two clergymen, occasional preachers in our pulpit, who were as loud and startling as the others were somniferous. One of them, with a sort of flat, high voice, had a remarkable way of making a ladder of it, climbing higher and higher to the end of the sentence. It ought to be described by the gamut, or written up-hill. Perhaps it was an association of ideas, that has made me recollect one particular passage. It is where Ahab consults the prophets, asking them whether he shall go up to Ramoth Gilead to battle. "Shall I go against Ramoth Gilead to battle, or shall I forbear ? and they said, Go up ; for the Lord shall deliver it into the hand of the king." He used to give this out in such a manner, that you might have fancied him climb-

ing out of the pulpit, sword in hand. The other was a tall
thin man, with a noble voice. He would commence a prayer
in a most stately and imposing manner, full both of dignity
and feeling ; and then, as if tired of it, would hurry over all
the rest. Indeed, he began every prayer in this way, and was
as sure to hurry it ; for which reason, the boys hailed the
sight of him, as they knew they should get sooner out of
church. When he commenced, in his noble style, the band
seemed to tremble against his throat, as though it had been
a sounding-board.

Being able to read, and knowing a little Latin, I was put
at once into the Under Grammar School. How much time I
wasted there in learning the accidence and syntax, I cannot
say ; but it seems to me a long while. My grammar seemed
always to open at the same place. Things are managed differently now, I believe, in this as well as in many other respects. Great improvements have been made in the whole
establishment. The boys feed better, learn better, and have
longer holidays in the country. In my time, they never slept
out of the school, but on one occasion, during the whole of
their stay ; this was for three weeks in summer-time, which
they were bound to pass at a certain distance from London.
They now have these holidays with a reasonable frequency ;
and they all go to the different schools, instead of being confined, as they were then, some to nothing but writing and
cyphering, and some to the languages. It has been doubted
by some of us elders, whether this system will beget such
temperate, proper students, with pale faces, as the other did.
I dare say, our successors are not afraid of us. I had the
pleasure, some years since, of dining in company with a Deputy
Grecian, who, with a stout rosy-faced person, had not failed
to acquire the scholarly turn for joking which is common to
a classical education ; as well as those simple, becoming manners, made up of modesty and proper confidence, which have
been often remarked as distinguishing the boys on this foundation.

"But what is a Deputy Grecian?" Ah, reader! to ask
that question, and at the same time to know anything at all
worth knowing, would at one time, according to our notion of
things, have been impossible. When I entered the school,
I was shown three gigantic boys, young men rather (for the
eldest was between seventeen and eighteen), who, I was told,
were going to the University. These were the Grecians.

They were the three head boys of the Grammar School, and were understood to have their destiny fixed for the Church. The next class to these, like a College of Cardinals to those three Popes (for every Grecian was in our eyes infallible), were the Deputy Grecians. The former were supposed to have completed their Greek studies, and were deep in Sophocles and Euripides. The latter were thought equally competent to tell you anything respecting Homer and Demosthenes. These two classes, and the head boys of the Navigation School, held a certain rank over the whole place, both in school and out. Indeed, the whole of the Navigation School, upon the strength of cultivating their valour for the navy, and being called King's Boys, had succeeded in establishing an extraordinary pretension to respect. This they sustained in a manner as laughable to call to mind as it was grave in its reception. It was an etiquette among them never to move out of a right line as they walked, whoever stood in their way. I believe there was a secret understanding with Grecians and Deputy Grecians, the former of whom were unquestionably lords paramount in point of fact, and stood and walked aloof when all the rest of the school were marshalled in bodies. I do not remember any clashing between these civil and naval powers; but I remember well my astonishment when I first beheld some of my little comrades overthrown by the progress of one of these very straightforward marine personages, who walked on with as tranquil and unconscious a face as if nothing had happened. It was not a fierce-looking push ; there seemed to be no intention in it. The insolence lay in the boy not appearing to know that such inferior creatures existed. It was always thus, wherever he came. If aware, the boys got out of his way ; if not, down they went, one or more ; away rolled the top or the marbles, and on walked the future captain—

" In maiden navigation, frank and free."

These boys wore a badge on the shoulder, of which they were very proud; though in the streets it must have helped to confound them with charity boys. For charity boys, I must own, we all had a great contempt, or thought so. We did not dare to know that there might have been a little jealousy of our own position in it, placed as we were midway between the homeliness of the common charity-school and the dignity of the foundations. We called them " *chizzy-wags*," and had a particular scorn and hatred of their nasal tone in singing.

The under grammar-master, in my time, was the Rev. Mr. Field. He was a good-looking man, very gentlemanly, and always dressed at the neatest. I believe he once wrote a play. He had the reputation of being admired by the ladies. A man of a more handsome incompetence for his situation perhaps did not exist. He came late of a morning; went away soon in the afternoon; and used to walk up and down, languidly bearing his cane, as if it were a lily, and hearing our eternal *Dominuses* and *As in præsentis* with an air of ineffable endurance. Often he did not hear at all. It was a joke with us, when any of our friends came to the door, and we asked his permission to go to them, to address him with some preposterous question wide of the mark ; to which he used to assent. We would say, for instance, " Are you not a great fool, sir ?" or, " Isn't your daughter a pretty girl ?" to which he would reply, " Yes, child." When he condescended to hit us with the cane, he made a face as if he were taking physic. Miss Field, an agreeable-looking girl, was one of the goddesses of the school ; as far above us as if she had lived on Olympus. Another was Miss Patrick, daughter of the lamp-manufacturer in Newgate Street. I do not remember her face so well, not seeing it so often; but she abounded in admirers. I write the names of these ladies at full length, because there is nothing that should hinder their being pleased at having caused us so many agreeable visions. We used to identify them with the picture of Venus in Tooke's *Pantheon*.

The other master, the upper one, Boyer—famous for the mention of him by Coleridge and Lamb—was a short stout man, inclining to punchiness, with large face and hands, an aquiline nose, long upper lip, and a sharp mouth. His eye was close and cruel. The spectacles which he wore threw a balm over it. Being a clergyman, he dressed in black, with a powdered wig. His clothes were cut short; his hands hung out of the sleeves, with tight wristbands, as if ready for execution ; and as he generally wore gray worsted stockings, very tight, with a little balustrade leg, his whole appearance presented something formidably succinct, hard, and mechanical. In fact, his weak side, and undoubtedly his natural destination, lay in carpentry; and he accordingly carried, in a side-pocket made on purpose, a carpenter's rule.

The merits of Boyer consisted in his being a good verbal scholar, and conscientiously acting up to the letter of time and attention. I have seen him nod at the close of the long summer school-hours, wearied out; and I should have pitied him if he had taught us to do anything but fear. Though a clergyman, very orthodox, and of rigid morals, he indulged himself in an oath, which was "God's-my-life!" When you were out in your lesson, he turned upon you a round staring eye like a fish; and he had a trick of pinching you under the chin, and by the lobes of the ears, till he would make the blood come. He has many times lifted a boy off the ground in this way. He was, indeed, a proper tyrant, passionate and capricious; would take violent likes and dislikes to the same boys; fondle some without any apparent reason, though he had a leaning to the servile, and, perhaps, to the sons of rich people; and he would persecute others in a manner truly frightful. I have seen him beat a sickly-looking, melancholy boy (C——n) about the head and ears, till the poor fellow, hot, dry-eyed, and confused, seemed lost in bewilderment. C——n, not long after he took orders, died, out of his senses. I do not attribute that catastrophe to the master; and of course he could not wish to do him any lasting mischief. He had no imagination of any sort. But there is no saying how far his treatment of the boy might have contributed to prevent a cure. Tyrannical schoolmasters nowadays are to be found, perhaps, exclusively in such inferior schools as those described with such masterly and indignant edification by my friend Charles Dickens; but they formerly seemed to have abounded in all; and masters, as well as boys, have escaped the chance of many bitter reflections, since a wiser and more generous intercourse has come up between them.

I have some stories of Boyer that will completely show his character, and at the same time relieve the reader's indignation by something ludicrous in their excess. We had a few boarders at the school: boys whose parents were too rich to let them go on the foundation. Among them, in my time, was Carlton, a son of Lord Dorchester; Macdonald, one of the Lord Chief Baron's sons; and R——, the son of a rich merchant. Carlton, who was a fine fellow, manly and full of good sense, took his new master and his caresses very coolly, and did not want them. Little Macdonald also could dispense with them, and would put on his delicate gloves after lesson, with an air as if he resumed his patrician plumage. R—— was meeker, and willing to be encouraged; and there would the master sit, with his arm round his tall waist, helping him to his Greek verbs, as a nurse does bread and milk to an infant ; and repeating them, when he missed, with a fond patience, that astonished us criminals in drugget.

Very different was the treatment of a boy on the foundation, whose friends, by some means or other, had prevailed on the master to pay him an extra attention, and try to get him on. He had come into the school at an age later than usual, and could hardly read. There was a book used by the learners in reading, called *Dialogues between a Missionary and an Indian*. It was a poor performance, full of inconclusive arguments and other commonplaces. The boy in question used to appear with this book in his hand in the middle of the school, the master standing behind him. The lesson was to begin. Poor ——, whose great fault lay in a deep-toned drawl of his syllables and the omission of his stops, stood half looking at the book, and half casting his eye towards the right of him, whence the blows were to proceed. The master looked over him, and his hand was ready. I am not exact in my quotation at this distance of time ; but the *spirit* of one of the passages that I recollect was to the following purport, and thus did the teacher and his pupil proceed :—

Master.—" Now, young man, have a care ; or I'll set you a *swingeing* task." (A common phrase of his.)

Pupil.—(Making a sort of heavy bolt at his calamity, and never remembering his stop at the word Missionary.) " *Missionary* Can you see the wind ? "

(Master gives him a slap on the cheek.)

Pupil.—(Raising his voice to a cry, and still forgetting his stop.) " *Indian* No ! "

Master.—" God's-my-life, young man ! have a care how you provoke me ! "

Pupil.—(Always forgetting the stop.) " *Missionary* How then do you know that there is such a thing ? "

(Here a terrible thump.)

Pupil.—(With a shout of agony.) " *Indian* Because I feel it."

One anecdote of his injustice will suffice for all. It is of ludicrous enormity ; nor do I believe anything more flagrantly wilful was ever done by himself. I heard Mr. C——, the sufferer, now a most respectable person in a Government office, relate it with a due relish, long after quitting the school. The master was in the habit of " spiting " C—— ;

that is to say, of taking every opportunity to be severe with him; nobody knew why. One day he comes into the school, and finds him placed in the middle of it with three other boys. He was not in one of his worst humours, and did not seem inclined to punish them, till he saw his antagonist. "Oh, oh! sir," said he: "what! you are among them, are you?" and gave him an exclusive thump on the face. He then turned to one of the Grecians, and said, "I have not time to flog all these boys; make them draw lots, and I'll punish one." The lots were drawn, and C——'s was favourable. "Oh, oh!" returned the master, when he saw them, "you have escaped, have you, sir?" and pulling out his watch, and turning again to the Grecian, observed, that he found he *had* time to punish the whole three; "and, sir," added he to C——, with another slap, "I'll begin with *you*. He then took the boy into the library and flogged him; and, on issuing forth again, had the face to say, with an air of indifference, "I have not time, after all, to punish these two other boys; let them take care how they provoke me another time."

Often did I wish that I were a fairy, in order to play him tricks like a Caliban. We used to sit and fancy what we should do with his wig; how we would hamper and vex him; "put knives in his pillow, and halters in his pew." To venture on a joke in our own mortal persons, was like playing with Polyphemus. One afternoon, when he was nodding with sleep over a lesson, a boy of the name of Meader, who stood behind him, ventured to take a pin, and begin advancing with it up his wig. The hollow, exhibited between the wig and the nape of the neck, invited him. The boys encouraged this daring act of gallantry. Nods and becks, and then whispers of "Go it, M.!" gave more and more valour to his hand. On a sudden, the master's head falls back; he starts with eyes like a shark; and seizing the unfortunate culprit, who stood helpless in the act of holding the pin, caught hold of him, fiery with passion. A "swingeing task" ensued, which kept him at home all the holidays. One of these tasks would consist of an impossible quantity of Virgil, which the learner, unable to retain it at once, wasted his heart and soul out "to get up," till it was too late.

Sometimes, however, our despot got into a dilemma, and then he did not know how to get out of it. A boy, now and then, would be roused into open and fierce remonstrance. I recollect S., afterwards one of the mildest of preachers, start-ing up in his place, and pouring forth on his astonished hearer a torrent of invectives and threats, which the other could only answer by looking pale, and uttering a few threats in return. Nothing came of it. He did not like such matters to go before the governors. Another time, Favell, a Grecian, a youth of high spirit, whom he had struck, went to the school-door, opened it, and, turning round with the handle in his grasp, told him he would never set foot again in the place, unless he promised to treat him with more delicacy. "Come back, child; come back!" said the other, pale, and in a faint voice. There was a dead silence. Favell came back, and nothing more was done.

A sentiment, unaccompanied with something practical, would have been lost upon him. D——, who went after-wards to the Military College at Woolwich, played him a trick, apparently between jest and earnest, which amused us exceedingly. He was to be flogged; and the dreadful door of the library was approached. (They did not invest the books with flowers, as Montaigne recommends.) Down falls the criminal, and twisting himself about the master's legs, which he does the more when the other attempts to move, repeats without ceasing, "Oh, good God! consider my father, sir; my father, sir; you know my father!" The point was felt to be getting ludicrous, and was given up. P——, now a popular preacher, was in the habit of entertaining the boys that way. He was a regular wag; and would snatch his jokes out of the very flame and fury of the master, like snap-dragon. Whenever the other struck him, P. would get up; and, half to avoid the blows, and half render them ridiculous, begin moving about the school-room, making all sorts of antics. When he was struck in the face, he would clap his hand with affected vehemence to the place, and cry as rapidly, "*Oh*, Lord!" If the blow came on the arm, he would grasp his arm, with a similar exclamation. The master would then go, driving and kicking him; while the patient accompanied every blow with the same comments and illustrations, making faces to us by way of index.

What a bit of a golden age was it, when the Rev. Mr. Steevens, one of the under grammar-masters, took his place, on some occasion, for a short time! Steevens was short and fat, with a handsome, cordial face. You loved him as you looked at him; and seemed as if you should love him the more the fatter he became. I stammered when I was at that time of life : which was an infirmity that used to get me into terrible trouble with the master. Steevens used to say, on the other hand, "Here comes our little black-haired friend, who stammers so. Now, let us see what we can do for him." The consequence was, I did not hesitate half so much as with the other. When I did, it was out of impatience to please him.

Such of us were not liked the better by the master as were in favour with his wife. She was a sprightly, good-looking woman, with black eyes; and was beheld with trans-port by the boys, whenever she appeared at the school-door. Her husband's name, uttered in a mingled tone of good-nature and imperativeness, brought him down from his seat with smiling haste. Sometimes he did not return. On entering the school one day, he found a boy eating cherries. " Where did you get those cherries ? " exclaimed he, thinking the boy had nothing to say for himself. " Mrs. Boyer gave them me, sir." He turned away, scowling with disappointment.

Speaking of fruit, reminds me of a pleasant trait on the part of a Grecian of the name of Le Grice. He was the mad-dest of all the great boys in my time; clever, full of address, and not hampered with modesty. Remote humours, not lightly to be heard, fell on our ears, respecting pranks of his amongst the nurses' daughters. He had a fair handsome face, with delicate aquiline nose, and twinkling eyes. I remember his astonishing me when I was " a new boy," with sending me for a bottle of water, which he proceeded to pour down the back of G., a grave Deputy Grecian. On the master asking him one day why he, of all the boys, had given up no exer-cise (it was a particular exercise that they were bound to do in the course of a long set of holidays), he said he had had " a lethargy." The extreme impudence of this puzzled the master ; and, I believe, nothing came of it. But what I alluded to about the fruit was this. Le Grice was in the habit of eating apples in school-time, for which he had been often rebuked. One day, having particularly pleased the master, the latter, who was eating apples himself, and who would now and then with great ostentation present a boy with some halfpenny token of his mansuetude, called out to his favourite of the moment, " Le Grice, here is an apple for you." Le Grice, who felt his dignity hurt as a Grecian, but was more pleased at having this opportunity of mortifying his reprover, replied, with an exquisite tranquillity of assurance, " Sir, I never eat apples." For this, among other things, the boys adored him. Poor fellow! He and Favell (who, though very generous, was said to be a little too sensible of an humble origin) wrote to the Duke of York, when they were at College, for commissions in the army. The Duke good-naturedly sent them. Le Grice died in the West Indies. Favell was killed in one of the battles in Spain, but not before he had distinguished himself as an officer and a gentleman.

The Upper Grammar School was divided into four classes or forms. The two under ones were called Little and Great Erasmus; the two upper were occupied by the Grecians and Deputy Grecians. We used to think the title of Erasmus taken from the great scholar of that name; but the sudden appearance of a portrait among us, bearing to be the likeness of a certain Erasmus Smith, Esq., shook us terribly in this opinion, and was a hard trial of our gratitude. We scarcely relished this perpetual company of our benefactor, watching us, as he seemed to do, with his omnipresent eyes. I believe he was a rich merchant, and that the forms of Little and Great Erasmus were really named after him. It was but a poor consolation to think that he himself, or his great-uncle, might have been named after Erasmus. Little Erasmus learned Ovid; Great Erasmus, Virgil, Terence, and the Greek Testament. The Deputy Grecians were in Homer, Cicero, and Demosthenes; the Grecians, in the Greek plays and the mathematics.

When a boy entered the Upper School, he was understood to be in the road to the University, provided he had inclination and talents for it; but, as only one Grecian a year went to College, the drafts out of Great and Little Erasmus into the writing-school were numerous. A few also became Deputy Grecians without going farther, and entered the world from that form. Those who became Grecians always went to the University, though not always into the Church; which was reckoned a departure from the contract. When I first came to school, at seven years old, the names of the Grecians were Allen, Favell, Thomson, and Le Grice, brother of the Le Grice above mentioned, and now a clergyman in Cornwall. Charles Lamb had lately been Deputy Grecian; and Coleridge had left for the University.

The master, inspired by his subject with an eloquence beyond himself, once called him, "that sensible fool, Collĕrĭdge," pronouncing the word like a dactyl. Coleridge must have alternately delighted and bewildered him. The compliment, as to the bewildering was returned, if not the delight. The pupil, I am told, said he dreamt of the master all his life, and that his dreams were horrible. A *bon-mot* of his is recorded, very characteristic both of pupil and master. Coleridge, when he heard of his death, said, "It was lucky that the cherubim who took him to heaven were nothing but faces and wings, or he would infallibly have flogged them by the way." This was his esoterical opinion of him. His outward and subtler opinion, or opinion exoterical, he favoured the public with in his *Literary Life.* He praised him, among other things, for his good taste in poetry, and his not suffering the boys to get into the commonplaces of Castalian Streams, Invocations to the Muses, &c. Certainly, there were no such things in our days—at least, to the best of my remembrance. But I do not think the master saw through them, out of a perception of anything further. His objection to a commonplace must have been itself commonplace.

I do not remember seeing Coleridge when I was a child. Lamb's visits to the school, after he left it, I remember well, with his fine intelligent face. Little did I think I should have the pleasure of sitting with it in after-times as an old friend, and seeing it careworn and still finer. Allen, the Grecian, was so handsome, though in another and more obvious way, that running one day against a barrow-woman in the street, and turning round to appease her in the midst of her abuse, she said, "Where are you driving to, you great hulking, good-for-nothing—beautiful fellow, God bless you!" Le Grice the elder was a wag, like his brother, but more staid. He went into the Church, as he ought to do, and married a rich widow. He published a translation, abridged, of the celebrated pastoral of Longus; and report at school made him the author of a little anonymous tract on the *Art of Poking the Fire.*

Few of us cared for any of the books that were taught : and no pains were taken to make us do so. The boys had no helps to information, bad or good, except what the master afforded them respecting manufactures—a branch of knowledge to which, as I before observed, he had a great tendency, and which was the only point on which he was enthusiastic and gratuitous. I do not blame him for what he taught us of

5—2

this kind: there was a use in it, beyond what he was aware
of; but it was the only one on which he volunteered any
assistance. In this he took evident delight. I remember, in
explaining pigs of iron or lead to us, he made a point of
crossing one of his legs with the other, and, cherishing it up
and down with great satisfaction, saying, "A pig, children, is
about the thickness of my leg." Upon which, with a slavish
pretence of novelty, we all looked at it, as if he had not told
us so a hundred times. In everything else we had to hunt
out our own knowledge. He would not help us with a word
till he had ascertained that we had done all we could to learn
the meaning of it ourselves. This discipline was useful; and
in this and every other respect, we had all the advantages
which a mechanical sense of right, and a rigid exaction of
duty, could afford us; but no further. The only superfluous
grace that he was guilty of, was the keeping a manuscript
book, in which, by a rare luck, the best exercise in English
verse was occasionally copied out for immortality! To have
verses in "the Book" was the rarest and highest honour
conceivable to our imaginations. I never, alas! attained it.

How little did I care for any verses at that time, except
English ones; I had no regard even for Ovid. I read and
knew nothing of Horace; though I had got somehow a liking
for his character. Cicero I disliked, as I cannot help doing
still. Demosthenes I was inclined to admire, but did not know
why, and would very willingly have given up him and his
difficulties together. Homer I regarded with horror, as a
series of lessons which I had to learn by heart before I understood him. When I had to conquer, in this way, lines which
I had not construed, I had recourse to a sort of artificial
memory, by which I associated the Greek words with sounds
that had a meaning in English. Thus, a passage about Thetis
I made to bear on some circumstance that had taken place in
the school. An account of a battle was converted into a
series of jokes; and the master, while I was saying my lesson
to him in trepidation, little suspected what a figure he was
often cutting in the text. The only classic I remember having any love for was Virgil; and that was for the episode of
Nisus and Euryalus.

But there were three books which I read in whenever I
could, and which often got me into trouble. These were
Tooke's *Pantheon*, Lempriere's *Classical Dictionary*, and
Spence's *Polymetis*, the great folio edition with plates. Tooke

was a prodigious favourite with us. I see before me, as vividly now as ever, his Mars and Apollo, his Venus and Aurora, which I was continually trying to copy; the Mars, coming on furiously in his car; Apollo, with his radiant head, in the midst of shades and fountains; Aurora with hers, a golden dawn; and Venus, very handsome, we thought, and not looking too modest in " a slight cymar." It is curious how completely the graces of the Pagan theology overcame with us the wise cautions and reproofs that were set against it in the pages of Mr. Tooke. Some years after my departure from school, happening to look at the work in question, I was surprised to find so much of that matter in him. When I came to reflect, I had a sort of recollection that we used occasionally to notice it, as something inconsistent with the rest of the text—strange, and odd, and like the interference of some pedantic old gentleman. This, indeed, is pretty nearly the case. The author has also made a strange mistake about Bacchus, whom he represents, both in his text and his print, as a mere belly-god; a corpulent child, like the Bacchus bestriding a tun. This is anything but classical. The truth is, it was a sort of pious fraud, like many other things palmed upon antiquity. Tooke's *Pantheon* was written originally in Latin by the Jesuits.

Our Lempriere was a fund of entertainment. Spence's *Polymetis* was not so easily got at. There was also something in the text that did not invite us; but we admired the fine large prints. However, Tooke was the favourite. I cannot divest myself of a notion, to this day, that there is something really clever in the picture of Apollo. The Minerva we " could not abide;" Juno was no favourite, for all her throne and her peacock; and we thought Diana too pretty. The instinct against these three goddesses begins early. I used to wonder how Juno and Minerva could have the insolence to dispute the apple with Venus.

In those times, Cooke's edition of the British poets came up. I had got an odd volume of Spenser; and I fell passionately in love with Collins and Gray. How I loved those little sixpenny numbers containing whole poets! I doted on their size; I doted on their type, on their ornaments, on their wrappers containing lists of other poets, and on the engravings from Kirk. I bought them over and over again, and used to get up select sets, which disappeared like buttered crumpets; for I could resist neither giving them away, nor possessing

them. When the master tormented me—when I used to hate
and loathe the sight of Homer, and Demosthenes, and Cicero—
I would comfort myself with thinking of the sixpence in my
pocket, with which I should go out to Paternoster Row, when
school was over, and buy another number of an English poet.

I was already fond of writing verses. The first I remember were in honour of the Duke of York's " Victory at Dun-
kirk;" which victory, to my great mortification, turned out
to be a defeat. I compared him with Achilles and Alexander;
or should rather say, trampled upon those heroes in the comparison. I fancied him riding through the field, and shooting
right and left of him! Afterwards, when in Great Erasmus,
I wrote a poem called *Winter*, in consequence of reading
Thomson; and when Deputy Grecian, I completed some hundred stanzas of another, called the *Fairy King*, which was to
be in emulation of Spenser! I also wrote a long poem in
irregular Latin verses (such as they were) entitled *Thor;* the
consequence of reading Gray's Odes and Mallett's *Northern
Antiquities*. English verses were the only exercise I performed with satisfaction. Themes, or prose essays, I wrote so
badly, that the master was in the habit of contemptuously
crumpling them up in his hand, and calling out, " Here,
children, there is something to amuse you!" Upon which
the servile part of the boys would jump up, seize the paper,
and be amused accordingly.

The essays must have been very absurd, no doubt; but
those who would have tasted the ridicule best were the last
to move. There was an absurdity in giving us such essays
to write. They were upon a given subject, generally a moral
one, such as Ambition or the Love of Money: and the regular
process in the manufacture was this:—You wrote out the subject very fairly at top, *Quid non mortalia*, &c., or, *Crescit amor
nummi*. Then the ingenious thing was to repeat this
apophthegm in as many words and roundabout phrases as
possible, which took up a good bit of the paper. Then you
attempted to give a reason or two, why *amor nummi* was bad;
or on what accounts heroes ought to eschew ambition; after
which naturally came a few examples, got out of Plutarch or
the *Selectæ è Profanis;* and the happy moralist concluded
with signing his name. Somebody speaks of schoolboys going
about to one another on these occasions, and asking for " a
little sense." That was not the phrase with us; it was " a
thought." " P——, can you give me a thought?" " C——,

for God's sake, help me to a thought, for it only wants ten minutes to eleven." It was a joke with P——, who knew my hatred of themes, and how I used to hurry over them, to come to me at a quarter to eleven, and say, " Hunt, have you *begun* your theme ?"—" Yes, P——." He then, when the quarter of an hour had expired, and the bell tolled, came again, and, with a sort of rhyming formula to the other question, said, " Hunt, have you *done* your theme ? "— " Yes, P——."

How I dared to trespass in this way upon the patience of the master, I cannot conceive. I suspect that the themes appeared to him more absurd than careless. Perhaps another thing perplexed him. The master was rigidly orthodox ; the school establishment also was orthodox and high Tory ; and there was just then a little perplexity, arising from the free doctrines inculcated by the books we learned, and the new and alarming echo of them struck on the ears of power by the French Revolution. My father was in the habit of expressing his opinions. He did not conceal the new tendency which he felt to modify those which he entertained respecting both Church and State. His unconscious son at school, nothing doubting or suspecting, repeated his eulogies of Timoleon and the Gracchi, with all a schoolboy's enthusiasm ; and the master's mind was not of a pitch to be superior to this unwitting annoyance. It was on these occasions, I suspect, that he crumpled up my themes with a double contempt, and with an equal degree of perplexity.

There was a better school exercise, consisting of an abridgment of some paper in the *Spectator*. We made, however, little of it, and thought it very difficult and perplexing. In fact, it was a hard task for boys, utterly unacquainted with the world, to seize the best points out of the writings of masters in experience. It only gave the *Spectator* an unnatural gravity in our eyes. A common paper for selection, because reckoned one of the easiest, was the one beginning, "I have always preferred cheerfulness to mirth." I had heard this paper so often, and was so tired with it, that it gave me a great inclination to prefer mirth to cheerfulness.

My books were a never-ceasing consolation to me, and such they have ever continued. My favourites, out of school hours, were Spenser, Collins, Gray, and the *Arabian Nights*. Pope I admired more than loved; Milton was above me; and the only play of Shakspeare's with which I was conversant was *Hamlet*, of which I had a delighted awe. Neither then, however, nor at any time, have I been as fond of dramatic reading as of any other, though I have written many dramas myself, and have even a special propensity for so doing; a contradiction for which I have never been able to account. Chaucer, who has since been one of my best friends, I was not acquainted with at school, nor till long afterwards. *Hudibras* I remember reading through at one desperate plunge, while I lay incapable of moving, with two scalded legs. I did it as a sort of achievement, driving on through the verses without understanding a twentieth part of them, but now and then laughing immoderately at the rhymes and similes, and catching a bit of knowledge unawares. I had a schoolfellow of the name of Brooke, afterwards an officer in the East India Service—a grave, quiet boy, with a fund of manliness and good-humour. He would pick out the ludi-crous couplets, like plums; such as those on the astrologer,—

> "Who deals in destiny's dark counsels,
> And sage opinions of the moon sells;"

And on the apothecary's shop—

> "With stores of deleterious med'cines,
> Which whosoever took is dead since."

He had the little thick duodecimo edition, with Hogarth's plates—dirty, and well read, looking like Hudibras himself.

I read through, at the same time, and with little less sense of it as a task, Milton's *Paradise Lost*. The divinity of it was so much "Heathen Greek" to us. Unluckily, I could not taste the beautiful "Heathen Greek" of the style. Mil-ton's heaven made no impression; nor could I enter even into the earthly catastrophe of his man and woman. The only two things I thought of were their happiness in Paradise, where (to me) they eternally remained; and the strange malignity of the devil, who, instead of getting them out of it, as the poet represents, only served to bind them closer. He seemed an odd shade to the picture. The figure he cut in the engravings was more in my thoughts than anything said of him in the poem. He was a sort of human wild beast, lurk-ing about the garden in which they lived; though, in conse-quence of the dress given him in some of the plates, this man with a tail occasionally confused himself in my imagination with a Roman general. I could make little of it. I believe, the plates impressed me altogether much more than the poem. Perhaps they were the reason why I thought of Adam and Eve as I did; the pictures of them in their paradisaical state being more numerous than those in which they appear exiled. Besides, in their exile they were together ; and this constituting the best thing in their paradise, I suppose I could not so easily get miserable with them when out of it. I had the same impression from Dr. Johnson's *Rasselas.* I never thought of anything in it but the Happy Valley. I might have called to mind, with an effort, a shadowy something about disappointment, and a long remainder of talk which I would not read again, perhaps never thoroughly did read. The Happy Valley was new to me, and delightful, and everlasting; and there the princely inmates were everlastingly to be found.

The scald that I speak of as confining me to bed was a bad one. I will give an account of it, because it furthers the elucidation of our school manners. I had then become a monitor, or one of the chiefs of a ward ; and I was sitting before the fire one evening, after the boys had gone to bed, wrapped up in the perusal of the *Wonderful Magazine*, and having in my ear at the same time the bubbling of a great pot, or rather cauldron of water, containing what was by courtesy called a bread pudding ; being neither more nor less than a loaf or two of our bread, which, with a little sugar mashed up with it, was to serve for my supper. And there were eyes, not yet asleep, which would look at it out of their beds, and regard it as a lordly dish. From this dream of bliss I was roused up on the sudden by a great cry, and a horrible agony in my legs. A "boy," as a fag was called, wishing to get something from the other side of the fireplace, and not choosing either to go round behind the table, or to disturb the illustrious legs of the monitor, had endeavoured to get under them or between them, and so pulled the great handle of the pot after him. It was a frightful sensation. The whole of my being seemed collected in one fiery torment into my legs. Wood, the Grecian (afterwards Fellow of Pembroke, at Cambridge), who was in our ward, and who was always very kind to me (led, I believe, by my inclination for verses, in which he had a great name), came out of his study, and after helping me off with my stockings, which was a horrid operation, the stockings being very coarse, took me in his arms to the sick ward. I shall never forget the enchanting relief occasioned by the cold air, as it blew across the square of the sick ward. I lay there for several weeks, not allowed to move for some time; and caustics became necessary before I got well. The getting well was delicious. I had no tasks—no master; plenty of books to read; and the nurse's daughter (*absit calumnia*) brought me tea and buttered toast, and encouraged me to play the flute. My playing consisted of a few tunes by rote; my fellow-invalids (none of them in very desperate case) would have it rather than no playing at all; so we used to play and tell stories, and go to sleep, thinking of the blessed sick holiday we should have to-morrow, and of the bowl of milk and bread for breakfast, which was alone worth being sick for. The sight of Mr. Long's probe was not so pleasant. We preferred seeing it in the hands of Mr. Vincent, whose manners, quiet and mild, had double effect on a set of boys more or less jealous of the mixed humbleness and importance of their school. This was most likely the same gentleman of the name of Vincent, who afterwards became distinguished in his profession. He was dark, like a West Indian, and I used to think him handsome. Perhaps the nurse's daughter taught me to think so, for she was a considerable observer.

CHAPTER IV.

SCHOOL-DAYS (*continued*).

I AM grateful to Christ Hospital for having bred me up in old cloisters, for its making me acquainted with the languages of Homer and Ovid, and for its having secured to me, on the whole, a well-trained and cheerful boyhood. It pressed no superstition upon me. It did not hinder my growing mind from making what excursions it pleased into the wide and healthy regions of general literature. I might buy as much Collins and Gray as I pleased, and get novels to my heart's content from the circulating libraries. There was nothing prohibited but what would have been prohibited by all good fathers; and everything was encouraged which would have been encouraged by the Steeles, and Addisons, and Popes; by the Warburtons, and Atterburys, and Hoadleys. Boyer was a severe, nay, a cruel master; but age and reflection have made me sensible that I ought always to add my testimony to his being a laborious and a conscientious one. When his severity went beyond the mark, I believe he was always sorry for it : sometimes I am sure he was. He once (though the anecdote at first sight may look like a burlesque on the remark) knocked out one of my teeth with the back of a Homer, in a fit of impatience at my stammering. The tooth was a loose one, and I told him as much ; but the blood rushed out as I spoke : he turned pale, and, on my proposing to go out and wash the mouth, he said, " Go, child," in a tone of voice amounting to the paternal. Now " Go, child," from Boyer, was worth a dozen tender speeches from any one else; and it was felt that I had got an advantage over him, acknowledged by himself.

If I had reaped no other benefit from Christ Hospital, the school would be ever dear to me from the recollection of the friendships I formed in it, and of the first heavenly taste it gave me of that most spiritual of the affections. I use the word "heavenly" advisedly ; and I call friendship the most spiritual of the affections, because even one's kindred, in partaking of our flesh and blood, become, in a manner, mixed up with our entire being. Not that I would disparage any other form of affection, worshipping, as I do, all forms of it, love in particular, which, in its highest state, is friendship and something more. But if ever I tasted a disembodied transport on earth, it was in those friendships which I entertained at school, before I dreamt of any maturer feeling. I shall never forget the impression it first made on me. I loved my friend for his gentleness, his candour, his truth, his good repute, his freedom even from my own livelier manner, his calm and reasonable kindness. It was not any particular talent that attracted me to him, or anything striking whatsoever. I should say, in one word, it was his goodness. I doubt whether he ever had a conception of a tithe of the regard and respect I entertained for him ; and I smile to think of the perplexity (though he never showed it) which he probably felt sometimes at my enthusiastic expressions ; for I thought him a kind of angel. It is no exaggeration to say, that, take away the unspiritual part of it—the genius and the knowledge—and there is no height of conceit indulged in by the most romantic character in Shakspeare, which surpassed what I felt towards the merits I ascribed to him, and the delight which I took in his society. With the other boys I played antics, and rioted in fantastic jests; but in his society, or whenever I thought of him, I fell into a kind of Sabbath state of bliss; and I am sure I could have died for him.

I experienced this delightful affection towards three successive schoolfellows, till two of them had for some time gone out into the world and forgotten me; but it grew less with each, and in more than one instance became rivalled by a new set of emotions, especially in regard to the last, for I fell in love with his sister—at least, I thought so. But on the occurrence of her death, not long after, I was startled at finding myself assume an air of greater sorrow than I felt, and at being willing to be relieved by the sight of the first pretty face that turned towards me. I was in the situation of the page in *Figaro*:—

"Ogni donna cangiar di colore;
Ogni donna mi fa palpitar."

My friend, who died himself not long after his quitting the University, was of a German family in the service of the court, very refined and musical. I likened them to the people in the novels of Augustus La Fontaine; and with the younger of the two sisters I had a great desire to play the part of the hero in the *Family of Halden*.

The elder, who was my senior, and of manners too advanced for me to aspire to, became distinguished in private circles as an accomplished musician. How I used to rejoice when they struck their "harps in praise of Bragela!" and how ill-bred I must have appeared when I stopped beyond all reasonable time of visiting, unable to tear myself away! They lived in Spring Gardens, in a house which I have often gone out of my way to look at; and as I first heard of Mozart in their company, and first heard his marches in the Park, I used to associate with their idea whatsoever was charming and graceful.

Maternal notions of war came to nothing before love and music, and the steps of the officers on parade. The young ensign with his flag, and the ladies with their admiration of him, carried everything before them.

I had already borne to school the air of "*Non più andrai*;" and, with the help of instruments made of paper, into which we breathed what imitations we could of hautboys and clarionets, had inducted the boys into the "pride, pomp, and circumstance" of that glorious bit of war.

Thus is war clothed and recommended to all of us, and not without reason, as long as it is a necessity, or as long as it is something, at least, which we have not acquired knowledge or means enough to do away with. A bullet is of all pills the one that most requires gilding.

But I will not bring these night-thoughts into the morning of life. Besides, I am anticipating; for this was not my first love. I shall mention that presently.

I have not done with my school reminiscences; but in order to keep a straightforward course, and notice simultaneous events in their proper places, I shall here speak of the persons and things in which I took the greatest interest when I was not within school-bounds.

The two principal houses at which I visited, till the arrival of our relations from the West Indies, were Mr. West's (late President of the Royal Academy), in Newman-street, and Mr. Godfrey Thornton's (of the distinguished City family), in Austin Friars. How I loved the Graces in one, and everything in the other! Mr. West (who, as I have already mentioned, had married one of my relations) had bought his house, I believe, not long after he came to England; and he had added a gallery at the back of it, terminating in a couple of lofty rooms. The gallery was a continuation of the house-passage, and, together with one of those rooms and the parlour, formed three sides of a garden, very small but elegant, with a grass-plot in the middle, and busts upon stands under an arcade. The gallery, as you went up it, formed an angle at a little distance to the left, then another to the right, and then took a longer stretch into the two rooms; and it was hung with the artist's sketches all the way. In a corner between the two angles was a study-door, with casts of Venus and Apollo on each side of it. The two rooms contained the largest of his pictures; and in the farther one, after stepping softly down the gallery, as if reverencing the dumb life on the walls, you generally found the mild and quiet artist at his work; happy, for he thought himself immortal.

I need not enter into the merits of an artist who is so well known, and has been so often criticized. He was a man with regular, mild features; and, though of Quaker origin, had the look of what he was, a painter to a court. His appearance was so gentlemanly, that, the moment he changed his gown for a coat, he seemed to be full-dressed. The simplicity and self-possession of the young Quaker, not having time enough to grow stiff (for he went early to study at Rome), took up, I suppose, with more ease than most would have done, the urbanities of his new position. And what simplicity helped him to, favour would retain. Yet this man, so well bred, and so indisputably clever in his art (whatever

might be the amount of his genius), had received so careless,
or so homely an education when a boy, that he could hardly
read. He pronounced also some of his words, in reading,
with a puritanical barbarism, such as *haive* for *have*, as some
people pronounce when they sing psalms. But this was, perhaps, an American custom. My mother, who both read and
spoke remarkably well, would say *haive* and *shaul* (for *shall*),
when she sang her hymns. But it was not so well in reading
lectures to the Academy. Mr. West would talk of his art all
day long, painting all the while. On other subjects he was
not so fluent ; and on political and religious matters he tried
hard to maintain the reserve common with those about a court.
He succeeded ill in both. There were always strong suspicions of his leaning to his native side in politics ; and during
Bonaparte's triumph, he could not contain his enthusiasm for
the Republican chief, going even to Paris to pay him his
homage, when First Consul. The admiration of high colours
and powerful effects, natural to a painter, was too strong for
him. How he managed this matter with the higher powers
in England I cannot say. Probably he was the less heedful,
inasmuch as he was not very carefully paid. I believe he did
a great deal for George the Third with little profit. Mr. West
certainly kept his love for Bonaparte no secret ; and it was no
wonder, for the latter expressed admiration of his pictures.
The artist thought the conqueror's smile enchanting, and that
he had the handsomest leg he had ever seen. He was present
when the " Venus de' Medici " was talked of, the French
having just taken possession of her. Bonaparte, Mr. West
said, turned round to those about him, and said, with his eyes
lit up, " She's coming !" as if he had been talking of a living
person. I believe he retained for the Emperor the love that
he had had for the First Consul, a wedded love, " for better,
for worse." However, I believe also that he retained it after
the Emperor's downfall—which is not what every painter did.
   But I am getting out of my chronology. The quiet of
Mr. West's gallery, the tranquil, intent beauty of the statues,
and the subjects of some of the pictures, particularly Death
on the Pale Horse, the Deluge, the Scotch King hunting the
Stag, Moses on Mount Sinai, Christ Healing the Sick (a
sketch), Sir Philip Sidney giving up the Water to the Dying
Soldier, the Installation of the Knights of the Garter, and
Ophelia before the King and Queen (one of the best things
he ever did), made a great impression upon me. My mother

and I used to go down the gallery, as if we were treading on wool. She was in the habit of stopping to look at some of the pictures, particularly the Deluge and the Ophelia, with a countenance quite awe-stricken. She used also to point out to me the subjects relating to liberty and patriotism, and the domestic affections. Agrippina bringing home the ashes of Germanicus was a great favourite with her. I remember, too, the awful delight afforded us by the Angel slaying the Army of Sennacherib; a bright figure lording it in the air, with a chaos of human beings below.

As Mr. West was almost sure to be found at work, in the farthest room, habited in his white woollen gown, so you might have predicated, with equal certainty, that Mrs. West was sitting in the parlour, reading. I used to think, that if I had such a parlour to sit in, I should do just as she did. It was a good-sized room, with two windows looking out on the little garden I spoke of, and opening to it from one of them by a flight of steps. The garden, with its busts in it, and the pictures which you knew were on the other side of its wall, had an Italian look. The room was hung with engravings and coloured prints. Among them was the Lion Hunt, from Rubens; the Hierarchy with the Godhead, from Raphael, which I hardly thought it right to look at; and two screens by the fireside, containing prints (from Angelica Kauffman, I think, but I am not sure that Mr. West himself was not the designer) of the Loves of Angelica and Medoro, which I could have looked at from morning to night. Angelica's intent eyes, I thought, had the best of it; but I thought so without knowing why. This gave me a love for Ariosto before I knew him. I got Hoole's translation, but could make nothing of it. Angelica Kauffman seemed to me to have done much more for her namesake. She could see farther into a pair of eyes than Mr. Hoole with his spectacles. This reminds me that I could make as little of Pope's *Homer*, which a schoolfellow of mine was always reading, and which I was ashamed of not being able to like. It was not that I did not admire Pope; but the words in his translation always took precedence in my mind of the things, and the unvarying sweetness of his versification tired me before I knew the reason. This did not hinder me afterwards from trying to imitate it; nor from succeeding; that is to say, as far as everybody else succeeds, and writing smooth verses. It is Pope's wit and closeness that are the difficult things, and that make him what he is: a truism which the mistakes of critics on divers sides have rendered it but too warrantable to repeat.

Mrs. West and my mother used to talk of old times, and Philadelphia, and my father's prospects at court. I sat apart with a book, from which I stole glances at Angelica. I had a habit at that time of holding my breath, which forced me every now and then to take long sighs. My aunt would offer me a bribe not to sigh. I would earn it once or twice; but the sighs were sure to return. These wagers I did not care for; but I remember being greatly mortified when Mr. West offered me half-a-crown if I would solve the old question of "Who was the father of Zebedee's children?" and I could not tell him. He never made his appearance till dinner, and returned to his painting-room directly after it. And so at tea-time. The talk was very quiet; the neighbourhood quiet; the servants quiet; I thought the very squirrel in the cage would have made a greater noise anywhere else. James, the porter, a fine tall fellow, who figured in his master's pictures as an apostle, was as quiet as he was strong. Standing for his picture had become a sort of religion with him. Even the butler, with his little twinkling eyes, full of pleasant conceit, vented his notions of himself in half-tones and whispers. This was a strange fantastic person. He got my brother Robert to take a likeness of him, small enough to be contained in a shirt-pin. It was thought that his twinkling eyes, albeit not young, had some fair cynosure in the neighbourhood. What was my brother's amazement, when, the next time he saw him, the butler said, with a face of enchanted satisfaction, "Well, sir, you see!" making a movement at the same time with the frill at his waistcoat. The miniature that was to be given to the object of his affections, had been given accordingly. It was in his own bosom!

But, notwithstanding my delight with the house at the West End of the town, it was not to compare with my beloved one in the City. There was quiet in the one; there were beautiful statues and pictures; and there was my Angelica for me, with her intent eyes, at the fireside. But, besides quiet in the other, there was cordiality, and there was music, and a family brimful of hospitality and good-nature, and dear Almeria (now Mrs. P——e), who in vain pretends that she has become aged, which is what she never did, shall, would, might, should, or could do. Those were indeed holidays, on which I used to go to Austin Friars. The house (such, at least, are my boyish recollections) was of the description I have been ever fondest of,—large, rambling, old-fashioned, solidly built, resembling the mansions about Highgate and other old villages.

It was furnished as became the house of a rich merchant and a sensible man, the comfort predominating over the costliness. At the back was a garden with a lawn; and a private door opened into another garden, belonging to the Company of Drapers; so that, what with the secluded nature of the street itself, and these verdant places behind it, it was truly *rus in urbe*, and a retreat. When I turned down the archway, I held my mother's hand tighter with pleasure, and was full of expectation, and joy, and respect. My first delight was in mounting the staircase to the rooms of the young ladies, setting my eyes on the comely and bright countenance of my fair friend, with her romantic name, and turning over for the hundredth time the books in her library. What she did with the volumes of the *Turkish Spy*, what they meant, or what amusement she could extract from them, was an eternal mystification to me. Not long ago, meeting with a copy of the book accidentally, I pounced upon my old acquaintance, and found him to contain better and more amusing stuff than people would suspect from his dry look and his obsolete politics.*

The face of tenderness and respect with which Almeria used to welcome my mother, springing forward with her fine buxom figure to supply the strength which the other wanted, and showing what an equality of love there may be between youth and middle age, and rich and poor, I should never cease to love her for, had she not been, as she was, one of the best-natured persons in the world in everything. I have not seen her now for a great many years; but, with that same face, whatever change she may pretend to find in it, she will go to heaven; for it is the face of her spirit. A good heart never grows old.

Of George T——, her brother, who will pardon this omission of his worldly titles, whatever they may be, I have

---

* The *Turkish Spy* is a sort of philosophical newspaper, in volumes; and, under a mask of bigotry, speculates very freely on all subjects. It is said to have been written by an Italian Jesuit of the name of Marana. The first volume has been attributed, however, to Sir Roger Manley, father of the author of the *Atalantis;* and the rest to Dr. Midgeley, a friend of his.

a similar kind of recollection, in its proportion; for, though we knew him thoroughly, we saw him less. The sight of his face was an additional sunshine to my holiday. He was very generous and handsome-minded; a genuine human being.

Mrs. T——, the mother, a very lady-like woman, in a delicate state of health, we usually found reclining on a sofa, always ailing, but always with a smile for us. The father, a man of a large habit of body, panting with asthma, whom we seldom saw but at dinner, treated us with all the family delicacy, and would have me come and sit next him, which I did with a mixture of joy and dread; for it was painful to hear him breathe. I dwell the more upon these attentions, because the school that I was in held a sort of equivocal rank in point of what is called respectability; and it was no less an honour to another, than to ourselves, to know when to place us upon a liberal footing. Young as I was, I felt this point strongly; and was touched with as grateful a tenderness towards those who treated me handsomely, as I retreated inwardly upon a proud consciousness of my Greek and Latin, when the supercilious would have humbled me. Blessed house! May a blessing be upon your rooms, and your lawn, and your neighbouring garden, and the quiet old monastic name of your street! and may it never be a thoroughfare! and may all your inmates be happy! Would to God one could renew, at a moment's notice, the happy hours we have enjoyed in past times, with the same circles, and in the same houses! A planet with such a privilege would be a great lift nearer heaven. What prodigious evenings, reader, we would have of it! What fine pieces of childhood, of youth, of manhood—ay, and of age, as long as our friends lasted!

The old gentleman in *Gil Blas*, who complained that the peaches were not so fine as they used to be when he was young, had more reason than appears on the face of it. He missed not only his former palate, but the places he ate them in, and those who ate them with him. I have been told, that the cranberries I have met with since must have been as fine as those I got with the T——'s; as large and as juicy; and that they came from the same place. For all that, I never ate a cranberry-tart since I dined in Austin Friars.

I should have fallen in love with A. T——, had I been old enough. As it was, my first flame, or my first notion of a flame, which is the same thing in those days, was for my giddy cousin Fanny Dayrell, a charming West Indian. Her

mother, the aunt I spoke of, had just come from Barbados
with her two daughters and a sister. She was a woman of a
princely spirit ; and having a good property, and every wish
to make her relations more comfortable, she did so. It
became holiday with us all. My mother raised her head ;
my father grew young again ; my cousin Kate (Christiana
rather, for her name was not Catherine; Christiana Arabella
was her name) conceived a regard for one of my brothers,
and married him ; and for my part, besides my pictures and
Italian garden at Mr. West's, and my beloved old English
house in Austin Friars, I had now another paradise in Great
Ormond Street.

My aunt had something of the West Indian pride, but all
in a good spirit, and was a mighty cultivator of the gentilities,
inward as well as outward. I did not dare to appear before
her with dirty hands, she would have rebuked me so handsomely. For some reason or other, the marriage of my
brother and his cousin was kept secret a little while. I became acquainted with it by chance, coming in upon a holiday,
the day the ceremony took place. Instead of keeping me out
of the secret by a trick, they very wisely resolved upon trusting
me with it, and relying upon my honour. My honour happened
to be put to the test, and I came off with flying colours. It
is to this circumstance I trace the religious idea I have ever
since entertained of keeping a secret. I went with the bride
and bridegroom to church, and remember kneeling apart and
weeping bitterly. My tears were unaccountable to me then.
Doubtless they were owing to an instinctive sense of the great
change that was taking place in the lives of two human
beings, and of the unalterableness of the engagement. Death
and Life seem to come together on these occasions, like awful
guests at a feast, and look one another in the face.

It was not with such good effect that my aunt raised my
notions of a schoolboy's pocket-money to half-crowns, and
crowns, and half-guineas. My father and mother were both
as generous as daylight ; but they could not give what they
had not. I had been unused to spending, and accordingly I
spent with a vengeance. I remember a ludicrous instance.
The first half-guinea that I received brought about me a con-
sultation of companions to know how to get rid of it. One
shilling was devoted to pears, another to apples, another to
cakes, and so on, all to be bought immediately, as they were ;
till coming to the sixpence, and being struck with a recollec-

tion that I ought to do something useful with that, I bought sixpenn'rth of shoe-strings: these, no doubt, vanished like the rest. The next half-guinea came to the knowledge of the master : he interfered, which was one of his proper actions ; and my aunt practised more self-denial in future.

Our new family from abroad were true West Indians, or, as they would have phrased it, "true Barbadians born." They were generous, warm-tempered, had great good-nature ; were proud, but not unpleasantly so; lively, yet indolent; temperately epicurean in their diet; fond of company, and dancing, and music; and lovers of show, but far from with-holding the substance. I speak chiefly of the mother and daughters. My other aunt, an elderly maiden, who piqued herself on the delicacy of her hands and ankles, and made you understand how many suitors she had refused (for which she expressed anything but repentance, being extremely vexed), was not deficient in complexional good-nature ; but she was narrow-minded, and seemed to care for nothing in the world but two things : first, for her elder niece Kate, whom she had helped to nurse ; and second, for a becoming set-out of coffee and buttered toast, particularly of a morning, when it was taken up to her in bed, with a suitable equipage of silver and other necessaries of life. Yes ; there was one more in-dispensable thing—slavery. It was frightful to hear her small mouth and little mincing tones assert the necessity not only of slaves, but of robust corporal punishment to keep them to their duty. But she did this, because her want of ideas could do no otherwise. Having had slaves, she won-dered how anybody could object to so natural and lady-like an establishment. Late in life, she took to fancying that every polite old gentleman was in love with her ; and thus she lived on, till her dying moment, in a flutter of expectation.

The black servant must have puzzled this aunt of mine sometimes. All the wonder of which she was capable, he certainly must have roused, not without a "quaver of con-sternation." This man had come over with them from the West Indies. He was a slave on my aunt's estate, and as such he demeaned himself, till he learned that there was no such thing as a slave in England; that the moment a man set his foot on English ground he was free. I cannot help smiling to think of the bewildered astonishment into which his first overt act, in consequence of this knowledge, must have put my poor aunt Courthope (for that was her Christian name). Most likely it broke out in the shape of some remonstrance about his fellow-servants. He partook of the pride common to all the Barbadians, black as well as white; and the maid-servants tormented him. I remember his coming up in the parlour one day, and making a ludicrous representation of the affronts put upon his office and person, interspersing his chattering and gesticulations with explanatory dumb show. One of the maids was a pretty girl, who had manœuvred till she got him stuck in a corner; and he insisted upon telling us all that she said and did. His respect for himself had naturally increased since he became free; but he did not know what to do with it. Poor Samuel was not ungenerous, after his fashion. He also wished, with his freedom, to acquire a freeman's knowledge, but stuck fast at pothooks and hangers. To frame a written B he pronounced a thing impossible. Of his powers on the violin he made us more sensible, not without frequent remonstrances, which it must have taken all my aunt's good-nature to make her repeat. He had left two wives in Barbados, one of whom was brought to bed of a son a little after he came away. For this son he wanted a name, that was new, sounding, and long. They referred him to the reader of Homer and Virgil. With classical names he was well acquainted, Mars and Venus being among his most intimate friends, besides Jupiters and Adonises, and Dianas with large families. At length we succeeded with Neoptolemus. He said he had never heard it before; and he made me write it for him in a great text-hand, that there might be no mistake.

My aunt took a country-house at Merton, in Surrey, where I passed three of the happiest weeks of my life. It was the custom at our school, in those days, to allow us only one set of unbroken holidays during the whole time we were there—I mean, holidays in which we remained away from school by night as well as by day. The period was always in August. Imagine a schoolboy passionately fond of the green fields, who had never slept out of the heart of the City for years. It was a compensation even for the pang of leaving my friend; and then what letters I would write to him! And what letters I did write! What full measure of affection pressed down, and running over! I read, walked, had a garden and orchard to run in; and fields that I could have rolled in, to have my will of them.

My father accompanied me to Wimbledon to see Horne Tooke, who patted me on the head. I felt very differently under his hand, and under that of the bishop of London, when he confirmed a crowd of us in St. Paul's. Not that I thought of politics, though I had a sense of his being a patriot; but patriotism, as well as everything else, was connected in my mind with something classical, and Horne Tooke held his political reputation with me by the same tenure that he held his fame for learning and grammatical knowledge. " The learned Horne Tooke " was the designation by which I styled him in some verses I wrote; in which verses, by the way, with a poetical licence which would have been thought more classical by Queen Elizabeth than my master, I called my aunt a " nymph." In the ceremony of confirmation by the bishop, there was something too official and like a despatch of business, to excite my veneration. My head only anticipated the coming of his hand with a thrill in the scalp : and when it came, it tickled me.

My cousins had the celebrated Dr. Callcott for a music-master. The doctor, who was a scholar and a great reader, was so pleased with me one day for being able to translate the beginning of Xenophon's *Anabasis* (one of our schoolbooks), that he took me out with him to Nunn's the bookseller's in Great Queen Street, and made me a present of Schrevelius's *Lexicon*. When he came down to Merton, he let me ride his horse. What days were those ! Instead of being roused against my will by a bell, I jumped up with the lark, and strolled " out of bounds." Instead of bread and water for breakfast, I had coffee, and tea, and buttered toast: for dinner, not a hunk of bread and a modicum of hard meat, or a bowl of pretended broth; but fish, and fowl, and noble hot joints, and puddings, and sweets, and Guava jellies, and other West Indian mysteries of peppers and preserves, and wine; and then I had tea; and I sat up to supper like a man, and lived so well, that I might have been very ill, had I not run about all the rest of the day.

My strolls about the fields with a book were full of happiness: only my dress used to get me stared at by the villagers. Walking one day by the little river Wandle, I came upon one of the loveliest girls I ever beheld, standing in the water with bare legs, washing some linen. She turned as she was stooping, and showed a blooming oval face with blue eyes, on either side of which flowed a profusion of flaxen locks. With the exception of the colour of the hair, it was like Raphael's own head turned into a peasant girl's. The eyes were full of gentle astonishment at the sight of me; and mine must have wondered no less. However, I was prepared for such wonders. It was only one of my poetical visions realized, and I expected to find the world full of them. What she thought of my blue skirts and yellow stockings is not so clear. She did not, however, taunt me with my " petticoats," as the girls in the streets of London would do, making me blush, as I thought they ought to have done instead. My beauty in the brook was too gentle and diffident; at least I thought so, and my own heart did not contradict me. I then took every beauty for an Arcadian, and every brook for a fairy stream; and the reader would be surprised if he knew to what an extent I have a similar tendency still. I find the same possibilities by another path.

I do not remember whether an Abbé Paris, who taught my cousins French, used to see them in the country; but I never shall forget him in Ormond Street. He was an emigrant, very gentlemanly, with a face of remarkable benignity, and a voice that became it. He spoke English in a slow manner, that was very graceful. I shall never forget his saying one day, in answer to somebody who pressed him on the subject, and in the mildest of tones, that without doubt it was impossible to be saved out of the pale of the Catholic Church.

One contrast of this sort reminds me of another. My aunt Courthope had something growing out on one of her knuckles, which she was afraid to let a surgeon look at. There was a Dr. Chapman, a West Indian physician, who came to see us, a person of great suavity of manners, with all that air of languor and want of energy which the West Indians often exhibit. He was in the habit of inquiring, with the softest voice in the world, how my aunt's hand was; and coming one day upon us in the midst of dinner, and sighing forth his usual question, she gave it him over her shoulder to look at. In a moment she shrieked, and the swelling was gone. The meekest of doctors had done it away with his lancet.

I had no drawback on my felicity at Merton, with the exception of an occasional pang at my friend's absence, and a new vexation that surprised and mortified me. I had been accustomed at school to sleep with sixty boys in the room, and some old night-fears that used to haunt me were forgotten. No Mantichoras there!—no old men crawling on the floor! What was my chagrin, when on sleeping alone, after so long a period, I found my terrors come back again!—not, indeed, in all the same shapes. Beasts could frighten me no longer; but I was at the mercy of any other ghastly fiction that presented itself to my mind, crawling or ramping. I struggled hard to say nothing about it; but my days began to be discoloured with fears of my nights; and with unutterable humiliation I begged that the footman might be allowed to sleep in the same room. Luckily, my request was attended to in the kindest and most reconciling manner. I was pitied for my fears, but praised for my candour—a balance of qualities which, I have reason to believe, did me a service far beyond that of the moment. Samuel, who, fortunately for my shame, had a great respect for fear of this kind, had his bed removed accordingly into my room. He used to entertain me at night with stories of Barbados and the negroes; and in a few days I was reassured and happy.

It was then (oh, shame that I must speak of fair lady after confessing a heart so faint!)—it was then that I fell in love with my cousin Fan. However, I would have fought all her young acquaintances round for her, timid as I was, and little inclined to pugnacity.

Fanny was a lass of fifteen, with little laughing eyes, and a mouth like a plum. I was then (I feel as if I ought to be ashamed to say it) not more than thirteen, if so old; but I had read Tooke's *Pantheon*, and came of a precocious race. My cousin came of one too, and was about to be married to a handsome young fellow of three-and-twenty. I thought nothing of this, for nothing could be more innocent than my intentions. I was not old enough, or grudging enough, or whatever it was, even to be jealous. I thought everybody must love Fanny Dayrell; and if she did not leave me out in permitting it, I was satisfied. It was enough for me to be with her as long as I could; to gaze on her with delight as she floated hither and thither; and to sit on the stiles in the neighbouring fields, thinking of Tooke's *Pantheon*. My friendship was greater than my love. Had my favourite schoolfellow been ill, or otherwise demanded my return, I should certainly have chosen his society in preference. Three-fourths of my heart were devoted to friendship; the rest was in a vague dream of beauty, and female cousins, and nymphs, and green fields, and a feeling which, though of a warm nature, was full of fear and respect.

Had the jade put me on the least equality of footing as to age, I know not what change might have been wrought in me; but though too young herself for the serious duties she was about to bring on her, and full of sufficient levity and gaiety not to be uninterested with the little black-eyed schoolboy that lingered about her, my vanity was well paid off by hers, for she kept me at a distance by calling me *petit garçon*. This was no better than the assumption of an elder sister in her teens over a younger one ; but the latter feels it, nevertheless; and I persuaded myself that it was particularly cruel. I wished the Abbé Paris at Jamaica with his French. There would she come in her frock and tucker (for she had not yet left off either), her curls dancing, and her hands clasped together in the enthusiasm of something to tell me, and when I flew to meet her, forgetting the difference of ages, and alive only to my charming cousin, she would repress me with a little fillip on the cheek, and say, " Well, *petit garçon*, what do you think of that ?" The worst of it was, that this odious French phrase sat insufferably well upon her plump little mouth. She and I used to gather peaches before the house were up. I held the ladder for her ; she mounted like a fairy ; and when I stood doting on her as she looked down and threw the fruit in my lap, she would cry, " *Petit garçon*, you will let 'em all drop!" On my return to school, she gave me a locket for a keepsake, in the shape of a heart ; which was the worst thing she ever did to the *petit garçon*, for it touched me on my weak side, and looked like a sentiment. I believe I should have had serious thoughts of becoming melancholy, had I not, in returning to school, returned to my friend, and so found means to occupy my craving for sympathy. However, I wore the heart a long while. I have sometimes thought there was more in her French than I imagined; but I believe not. She naturally took herself for double my age, with a lover of three-and-twenty. Soon after her marriage, fortune separated us for many years. My passion had almost as soon died away; but I have loved the name of Fanny ever since; and when I met her again, which was under circumstances of trouble on her part, I could not see her without such an emotion as I was fain to confess to a person " near and dear," who forgave me for it; which made me love the forgiver the more. Yes! the " black ox " trod on the fairy foot of my light-hearted cousin Fan; of her, whom I could no more have thought of in conjunction with sorrow, than of a ball-room with a tragedy. To know that she was rich and admired, and abounding in mirth and music, was to me the same thing as to know that she existed. How often did I afterwards wish myself rich in turn, that I might have restored to her all the graces of life! She was generous, and would not have denied me the satisfaction.

This was my first love. That for a friend's sister was my second, and not so strong; for it was divided with the admiration of which I have spoken for the Park music and "the soldiers." Nor had the old tendency to mix up the clerical with the military service been forgotten. Indeed, I have never been without a clerical tendency; nor, after what I have written for the genial edification of my fellow-creatures, and the extension of charitable and happy thoughts in matters of religion, would I be thought to speak of it without even a certain gravity, not compromised or turned into levity, in my opinion, by any cheerfulness of tone with which it may happen to be associated; for Heaven has made smiles as well as tears: has made laughter itself, and mirth; and to appreciate its gifts thoroughly is to treat none of them with disrespect, or to affect to be above them. The wholly gay and the wholly grave spirit is equally but half the spirit of a right human creature.

I mooted points of faith with myself very early, in consequence of what I heard at home. The very inconsistencies which I observed round about me in matters of belief and practice, did but the more make me wish to discover in what the right spirit of religion consisted: while, at the same time, nobody felt more instinctively than myself, that forms were necessary to preserve essence. I had the greatest respect for them, wherever I thought them sincere. I got up imitations of religious processions in the school-room, and persuaded my coadjutors to learn even a psalm in the original Hebrew, in order to sing it as part of the ceremony. To make the lesson as easy as possible, it was the shortest of all the psalms, the hundred and seventeenth, which consists but of two verses. A Jew, I am afraid, would have been puzzled to recognize it; though, perhaps, I got the tone from his own synagogue; for I was well acquainted with that place of worship. I was led to dislike Catholic chapels, in spite of their music and their paintings, by what I had read of Inquisitions, and by the impiety which I found in the doctrine of eternal punishment,—a monstrosity which I never associated with

the Church of England, at least not habitually. But identi-
fying no such dogmas with the Jews, who are indeed free
from them (though I was not aware of that circumstance
at the time), and reverencing them for their ancient connection with the Bible, I used to go with some of my companions
to the synagogue in Duke's Place ; where I took pleasure
in witnessing the semi-Catholic pomp of their service, and
in hearing their fine singing ; not without something of a
constant astonishment at their wearing their hats. This custom, however, kindly mixed itself up with the recollection
of my cocked hat and band. I was not aware that it originated in the immovable Eastern turban.

These visits to the synagogue did me, I conceive, a great
deal of good. They served to universalize my notions of
religion, and to keep them unbigoted. It never became necessary to remind me that Jesus was himself a Jew. I have also
retained through life a respectful notion of the Jews as a body.

There were some school rhymes about "pork upon a fork,"
and the Jews going to prison. At Easter, a strip of bordered
paper was stuck on the breast of every boy, containing the
words " He is risen." It did not give us the slightest thought
of what it recorded. It only reminded us of an old rhyme,
which some of the boys used to go about the school repeating:—

> " He is risen, he is risen,
> All the Jews must go to prison."

A beautiful Christian deduction ! Thus has charity itself
been converted into a spirit of antagonism ; and thus it is that
the antagonism, in the progress of knowledge, becomes first
a pastime and then a jest.

I never forgot the Jews' synagogue, their music, their
tabernacle, and the courtesy with which strangers were
allowed to see it. I had the pleasure, before I left school,
of becoming acquainted with some members of their community, who were extremely liberal towards other opinions,
and who, nevertheless, entertained a sense of the Supreme
Being far more reverential than I had observed in any
Christian, my mother excepted. My feelings towards them
received additional encouragement from the respect shown to
their history in the paintings of Mr. West, who was anything
but a bigot himself, and who often had Jews to sit to him.
I contemplated Moses and Aaron, and the young Levites, by
the sweet light of his picture-rooms, where everybody trod

about in stillness, as though it were a kind of holy ground; and if I met a Rabbi in the street, he seemed to me a man coming, not from Bishopsgate or Saffron Hill, but out of the remoteness of time.

I have spoken of the distinguished individuals bred at Christ Hospital, including Coleridge and Lamb, who left the school not long before I entered it. Coleridge I never saw till he was old. Lamb I recollect coming to see the boys, with a pensive, brown, handsome, and kindly face, and a gait advancing with a motion from side to side, between involuntary consciousness and attempted ease. His brown complexion may have been owing to a visit in the country; his air of uneasiness to a great burden of sorrow. He dressed with a quaker-like plainness. I did not know him as Lamb: I took him for a Mr. "Guy," having heard somebody address him by that appellative, I suppose in jest.

The boy whom I have designated in these notices as C——n, and whose intellect in riper years became clouded, had a more than usual look of being the son of old parents. He had a reputation among us, which, in more superstitious times, might have rendered him an object of dread. We thought he knew a good deal out of the pale of ordinary inquiries. He studied the weather and the stars, things which boys rarely trouble their heads with; and as I had an awe of thunder, which always brought a reverential shade on my mother's face, as if God had been speaking, I used to send to him on close summer days, to know if thunder was to be expected.

In connection with this mysterious schoolfellow, though he was the last person, in some respects, to be associated with him, I must mention a strange epidemic fear which occasionally prevailed among the boys respecting a personage whom they called the Fazzer.

The Fazzer was known to be nothing more than one of the boys themselves. In fact, he consisted of one of the most impudent of the bigger ones; but as it was his custom to disguise his face, and as this aggravated the terror which made the little boys hide their own faces, his participation of our common human nature only increased the supernatural fearfulness of his pretensions. His office as Fazzer consisted in being audacious, unknown, and frightening the boys at night; sometimes by pulling them out of their beds; sometimes by simply *fazzing* their hair ("fazzing" meant pulling or vexing, like a goblin); sometimes (which was horriblest of all) by quietly giving us to understand, in some way or other, that the " Fazzer was out," that is to say, out of his own bed, and then being seen (by those who dared to look) sitting, or otherwise making his appearance, in his white shirt, motionless and dumb. It was a very good horror, of its kind. The Fazzer was our Dr. Faustus, our elf, our spectre, our Flibbertigibbet, who " put knives in our pillows and halters in our pews." He was Jones, it is true, or Smith; but he was also somebody else—an anomaly, a duality, Smith and sorcery united. My friend Charles Ollier should have written a book about him. He was our Old Man of the Mountain, and yet a common boy.

One night I thought I saw this phenomenon under circumstances more than usually unearthly. It was a fine moonlight night; I was then in a ward the casements of which looked (as they still look) on the churchyard. My bed was under the second window from the east, not far from the statue of Edward the Sixth. Happening to wake in the middle of the night, and cast up my eyes, I saw, on a bed's head near me, and in one of these casements, a figure in its shirt, which I took for the Fazzer. The room was silent; the figure motionless; I fancied that half the boys in the ward were glancing at it, without daring to speak. It was poor C——n, gazing at that lunar orb, which might afterwards be supposed to have malignantly fascinated him.

Contemporary with C——n was Wood, before mentioned, whom I admired for his verses, and who was afterwards Fellow of Pembroke College, Cambridge, where I visited him, and found him, to my astonishment, a head shorter than myself. Every upper boy at school appears a giant to a little one. " Big boy" and senior are synonymous. Now and then, however, extreme smallness in a senior scholar gives a new kind of dignity, by reason of the testimony it bears to the ascendancy of the intellect. It was the custom for the monitors at Christ Hospital, during prayers before meat, to stand fronting the tenants of their respective wards, while the objects of their attention were kneeling. Looking up, on one of these occasions, towards a new monitor who was thus standing, and whose face was unknown to me (for there were six hundred of us, and his ward was not mine), I thought him the smallest boy that could ever have attained to so distinguished an eminence. He was little in person, little in face, and he had a singularly juvenile cast of features, even for one so *petit*.

It was Mitchell, the translator of *Aristophanes*. He had really attained his position prematurely. I rose afterwards to be next to him in the school; and from a grudge that existed between us, owing probably to a reserve, which I thought pride, on his part, and to an ardency which he may have considered frivolous on mine, we became friends. Circumstances parted us in after-life: I became a Reformist, and he a Quarterly Reviewer; but he sent me kindly remembrances not long before he died. I did not know he was declining; and it will ever be a pain to me to reflect that delay conspired with accident to hinder my sense of it from being known to him; especially as I learned that he had not been so prosperous as I supposed. He had his weaknesses as well as myself, but they were mixed with conscientious and noble qualities. Zealous as he was for aristocratical government, he was no indiscriminate admirer of persons in high places; and, though it would have bettered his views in life, he had declined taking orders, from nicety of religious scruple. Of his admirable scholarship I need say nothing.

Equally good scholar, but of a less zealous temperament, was Barnes, who stood next me on the Deputy Grecian form, and who was afterwards identified with the sudden and striking increase of the *Times* newspaper in fame and influence. He was very handsome when young, with a profile of Grecian regularity; and was famous among us for a certain dispassionate humour, for his admiration of the works or Fielding, and for his delight, nevertheless, in pushing a narrative to its utmost, and drawing upon his stores of fancy for intensifying it; an amusement for which he possessed an understood privilege. It was painful in after-life to see his good looks swallowed up in corpulency, and his once handsome mouth thrusting its under lip out, and panting with asthma. I believe he was originally so well constituted in point of health and bodily feeling, that he fancied he could go on, all his life, without taking any of the usual methods to preserve his comfort. The editorship of the *Times*, which turned his night into day, and would have been a trying burden to any man, completed the bad consequences of his negligence; and he died painfully before he was old. Barnes wrote elegant Latin verse, a classical English style, and might assuredly have made himself a name in wit and literature, had he cared much for anything beyond his glass of wine and his Fielding. He left money to found a Barnes scholarship at Cambridge.

What pleasant days have I not passed with him, and other schoolfellows, bathing in the New River, and boating on the Thames! He and I began to learn Italian together; and anybody not within the pale of the enthusiastic, might have thought us mad, as we went shouting the beginning of Metastasio's Ode to Venus, as loud as we could bawl, over the Hornsey fields. I can repeat it to this day, from those first lessons.

"Scendi propizia
Col tuo splendore,
O bella Venere,
Madre d'Amore;
Madre d'Amore,
Che sola sei
Piacer degli uomini,
E degli dei." *

On the same principle of making invocations as loud as possible, and at the same time of fulfilling the prophecy of a poet, and also for the purpose of indulging ourselves with an echo, we used to lie upon our oars at Richmond, and call, in the most vociferous manner, upon the spirit of Thomson to "rest."

"Remembrance oft shall haunt the shore,
When Thames in summer wreaths is drest,
And oft suspend the dashing oar
To bid his gentle spirit rest."
Collins's Ode on the Death of Thomson.

It was more like "perturbing" his spirit than laying it.

One day Barnes fell overboard, and, on getting into the boat again, he drew a little edition of Seneca out of his pocket, which seemed to have become fat with the water. It was like an extempore dropsy.

Another time, several of us being tempted to bathe on a very hot day, near Hammersmith, and not exercising sufficient patience in selecting our spot, we were astonished at receiving a sudden lecture from a lady. She was in a hat and feathers, and riding-habit; and as the grounds turned out to belong to the Margravine of Anspach (Lady Craven), we persuaded ourselves that our admonitrix, who spoke in no

* "Descend propitious with thy brightness, O beautiful Venus, Mother of Love;—Mother of Love, who alone art the pleasure of men and of gods."

measured terms, was her Serene Highness herself. The obvious reply to her was, that if it was indiscreet in us not to have chosen a more sequestered spot, it was not excessively the reverse in a lady to come and rebuke us. I related this story to my acquaintance, Sir Robert Ker Porter, who knew her. His observation was, that nothing wonderful was to be wondered at in the Margravine.

I was fifteen when I put off my band and blue skirts for a coat and neckcloth. I was then first Deputy Grecian, and I had the honour of going out of the school in the same rank, at the same age, and for the same reason, as my friend Charles Lamb. The reason was, that I hesitated in my speech. I did not stammer half so badly as I used ; and it is very seldom that I halt at a syllable now ; but it was understood that a Grecian was bound to deliver a public speech before he left school, and to go into the Church afterwards; and as I could do neither of these things, a Grecian I could not be. So I put on my coat and waistcoat, and, what was stranger, my hat ; a very uncomfortable addition to my sensations. For eight years I had gone bareheaded, save now and then a few inches of pericranium, when the little cap, no larger than a crumpet, was stuck on one side, to the mystification of the old ladies in the streets.

I then cared as little for the rains as I did for anything else. I had now a vague sense of worldly trouble, and of a great and serious change in my condition ; besides which, I had to quit my old cloisters, and my playmates, and long habits of all sorts ; so that what was a very happy moment to schoolboys in general, was to me one of the most painful of my life. I surprised my schoolfellows and the master with the melancholy of my tears. I took leave of my books, of my friends, of my seat in the grammar-school, of my good-hearted nurse and her daughter, of my bed, of the cloisters, and of the very pump out of which I had taken so many delicious draughts, as if I should never see them again, though I meant to come every day. The fatal hat was put on ; my father was come to fetch me.

> "We, hand in hand, with strange new steps and slow,
> Through Holborn took our meditative way."

CHAPTER V.

YOUTH.

FOR some time after I left school, I did nothing but visit my schoolfellows, haunt the book-stalls, and write verses. My father collected the verses, and published them [in 1802, under the title of *Juvenilia*], with a large list of subscribers, numbers of whom belonged to his old congregations. [The volume had a portrait by Jackson in the manner of that artist, imparti g to it an air of heavy laziness, said to have characterized the artist, but certainly foreign to the sitter.] I was as proud, perhaps, of the book at that time as I am ashamed of it now. The French Revolution, though the worst portion of it was over, had not yet shaken up and reinvigorated the sources of thought all over Europe. At least I was not old enough, perhaps was not able, to get out of the trammels of the regular imitative poetry, or versification rather, which was taught in the schools. My book was a heap of imitations, all but absolutely worthless. But absurd as it was, it did me a serious mischief; for it made me suppose that I had attained an end, instead of not having reached even a commencement; and thus caused me to waste in imitation a good many years which I ought to have devoted to the study of the poetical art and of nature. Coleridge has praised Boyer for teaching us to laugh at "muses" and "Castalian streams;" but he ought rather to have lamented that he did not teach us how to love them wisely, as he might have done had he really known anything about poetry, or loved Spenser and the old poets, as he thought, and admired the new. Even Coleridge's juvenile poems were none the better for Boyer's training. As to mine, they were for the most part as mere trash as anti-Castalian heart could have desired. I wrote "odes" because Collins and Gray had written them, "pastorals" because Pope had written them, "blank verse" because Akenside and Thomson had written blank verse, and a "Palace of Pleasure" because Spenser had written a "Bower of Bliss." But in all these authors I saw little but their words, and imitated even those badly. I had nobody to bid me to go to the nature which had originated the books. Coleridge's lauded teacher put into my hands, at one time, the life of Pope by Ruffhead (the worst he could have chosen), and at another (for the express purpose of cultivating my love of poetry) the *Irene* and other poems of Dr. Johnson! Pope's smooth but unartistical versification spell-bound me for a long time. Of Johnson's poems I retained nothing but the epigram beginning "Hermit hoar—"

> "'Hermit hoar, in solemn cell,
>   Wearing out life's evening gray,
> Strike thy bosom, sage, and tell,
>   What is bliss, and which the way?'
> Thus I spoke, and speaking, sighed,
>   Scarce repressed the starting tear,
> When the hoary sage replied,
>   'Come, my lad, and drink some beer.'"

This was the first epigram of the kind which I had seen; and it had a cautionary effect upon me to an extent which its author might hardly have desired. The grave Dr. Johnson and the rogue Ambrose de Lamela, in *Gil Blas*, stood side by side in my imagination as unmaskers of venerable appearances; that is to say, as persons who had no objection to the jolly hypocrisy which they unmasked.

Not long after the publication of my book, I visited two of my schoolfellows, who had gone to Cambridge and Oxford. The repute of it, unfortunately, accompanied me, and gave a foolish increase to my self-complacency. At Oxford, I was introduced to Kett, the poetry professor,—a good-natured man with a face like a Houyhnhnm (had Swift seen it, he would have thought it a pattern for humanity). It was in the garden of the professor's college (Trinity); and he expressed a hope that I should feel inspired then "by the muse of Warton." I was not acquainted with the writings of Warton at that time; and perhaps my ignorance was fortunate; for it was not till long after my acquaintance with them that I saw farther into their merits than the very first anti-commonplaces would have discerned, and as I had not acquired even those at that period, and my critical presumption was on a par with my poetical, I should probably have given the professor to understand that I had no esteem for that kind of secondhand inspiration. I was not aware that my own was precisely of the same kind, and as different from Warton's as poverty from acquirement.

At Oxford, my love of boating had nearly cost me my life. I had already had a bit of a taste of drowning in the river Thames, in consequence of running a boat too hastily on shore; but it was nothing to what I experienced on this occasion. The schoolfellow whom I was visiting was the friend whose family lived in Spring Gardens. We had gone out in a little decked skiff, and not expecting disasters in the "gentle Isis," I had fastened the sail-line, of which I had the direction, in order that I might read a volume which I had with me, of Mr. Cumberland's novel called *Henry*. My friend was at the helm. The wind grew a little strong; and we had just got into Iffley Reach, when I heard him exclaim, "Hunt, we are over!" The next moment I was under the water, gulping it, and giving myself up for lost. The boat had a small opening in the middle of the deck, under which I had thrust my feet; this circumstance had carried me over with the boat, and the worst of it was, I found I had got the sail-line round my neck. My friend, who sat on the deck itself, had been swept off, and got comfortably to shore, which was at a little distance.

My bodily sensations were not so painful as I should have fancied they would have been. My mental reflections were very different, though one of them, by a singular meeting of extremes, was of a comic nature. I thought that I should never see the sky again, that I had parted with all my friends, and that I was about to contradict the proverb which said that a man who was born to be hanged, would never be drowned; for the sail-line, in which I felt entangled, seemed destined to perform for me both the offices. On a sudden, I found an oar in my hand, and the next minute I was climbing, with assistance, into a wherry, in which there sat two Oxonians, one of them helping me, and loudly and laughingly differing with the other, who did not at all like the rocking of the boat, and who assured me, to the manifest contradiction of such senses as I had left, that there was no room. This gentleman is now no more; and I shall not mention his name, because I might do injustice to the memory of a brave man struck with a panic. The name of his companion, if I mistake not, was Russell. I hope he was related to an illustrious person of the same name, to whom I have lately been indebted for what may have been another prolongation of my life.

On returning to town, which I did on the top of an Oxford coach, I was relating this story to the singular person who then drove it (Bobart, who had been a collegian), when a man who was sitting behind surprised us with the excess of his laughter. On asking him the reason, he touched his hat, and said, "Sir, I'm his footman." Such are the delicacies of the livery, and the glorifications of their masters with which they entertain the kitchen.

This Bobart was a very curious person. I have noticed him in the *Indicator*, in the article on "Coaches." He was a descendant of a horticultural family, who had been keepers of the Physic Garden at Oxford, and one of whom palmed a rat upon the learned world for a dragon, by stretching out its skin into wings. Tillimant Bobart (for such was the name of our charioteer) had been at college himself, probably as a sizer; but having become proprietor of a stage-coach, he thought fit to be his own coachman; and he received your money and touched his hat like the rest of the fraternity. He had a round, red face, with eyes that stared, and showed the white; and having become, by long practice, an excellent capper of verses, he was accustomed to have bouts at that pastime with the collegians whom he drove. It was curious to hear him whistle and grunt, and urge on his horses with the other customary euphonics of his tribe, and then see him flash his eye round upon the capping gentleman who sat behind him, and quote his never-failing line out of Virgil or Horace. In the evening (for he only drove his coach half way to London) he divided his solace after his labours between his book and his brandy-and-water; but I am afraid with a little too much of the brandy, for his end was not happy.* There was eccentricity in the family, without anything much to show for it. The Bobart who invented the dragon chuckled over the secret for a long time with a satisfaction that must have cost him many falsehoods; and the first Bobart that is known used to tag his beard with silver on holidays.

If female society had not been wanting, I should have longed to reside at an university; for I have never seen trees, books, and a garden to walk in, but I saw my natural home, provided there was no "monkery" in it. I have always thought it a brave and great saying of Mohammed,— "There is no monkery in Islam."

> "From women's eyes this doctrine I derive:
> They are the books, the arts, the academes,
> Which shew, contain, and nourish all the world."

* On the information of Mr. George Hooper, who kindly volunteered the communication as a reader of the *Indicator*, and sent me a very curious letter on the subject; with details, however, that were rather of private than of public interest.

Were I to visit the universities now, I should explore every corner, and reverently fancy myself in the presence of every great and good man that has adorned them; but the most important people to young men are one another; and I was content with glancing at the haunts of Addison and Warton in Oxford, and at those of Gray, Spenser, and Milton, in Cambridge. Oxford, I found, had greatly the advantage of Cambridge in point of country. You could understand well enough how poets could wander about Iffley and Woodstock; but when I visited Cambridge, the nakedness of the land was too plainly visible under a sheet of snow, through which gutters of ditches ran, like ink, by the side of leafless sallows, which resembled huge pincushions stuck on posts. The town, however, made amends; and Cambridge has the advantage of Oxford in a remarkable degree, as far as regards eminent names. England's two greatest philosophers, Bacon and Newton, and (according to Tyrwhitt) three out of its four great poets, were bred there, besides double the number of minor celebrities. Oxford even did not always know "the good the gods provided." It repudiated Locke; alienated Gibbon; and had nothing but angry sullenness and hard expulsion to answer to the inquiries which its very ordinances encouraged in the sincere and loving spirit of Shelley.

Yet they are divine places, both; full of grace, and beauty, and scholarship; of reverend antiquity, and ever-young nature and hope. Their faults, if of worldliness in some, are those of time and of conscience in more, and if the more pertinacious on those accounts, will merge into a like conservative firmness, when still nobler developments are in their keeping. So at least I hope; and so may the Fates have ordained; keeping their gowns among them as a symbol that learning is, indeed, something which ever learns; and instructing them to teach love, and charity, and inquiry, with the same accomplished authority as that with which they have taught assent.

My book was unfortunately successful everywhere, particularly in the metropolis. The critics were extremely kind; and, as it was unusual at that time to publish at so early a period of life, my age made me a kind of "Young Roscius" in authorship. I was introduced to literati, and shown about among parties. My father took me to see Dr. Raine, Master of the Charter-House. The doctor, who was very kind and pleasant, but who probably drew none of our deductions in favour of the young writer's abilities, warned me against the perils of authorship; adding, as a final dehortative, that " the shelves were full." It was not till we came away that I thought of an answer, which I conceived would have " annihilated " him. " Then, sir " (I should have said), " we will make another." Not having been in time with this repartee, I felt all that anguish of undeserved and unnecessary defeat, which has been so pleasantly described in the *Miseries of Human Life*. This, thought I, would have been an answer befitting a poet, and calculated to make a figure in biography.

A mortification that I encountered at a house in Cavendish Square affected me less, though it surprised me a good deal more. I had been held up, as usual, to the example of the young gentlemen and the astonishment of the young ladies, when, in the course of the dessert, one of mine host's daughters, a girl of exuberant spirits, and not of the austerest breeding, came up to me, and, as if she had discovered that I was not so young as I pretended to be, exclaimed, " What a beard you have got ! " at the same time convincing herself of the truth of her discovery by taking hold of it ! Had I been a year or two older, I should have taken my revenge. As it was, I know not how I behaved, but the next morning I hastened to have a beard no longer.

I was now a man, and resolved not to be out of countenance next time. Not long afterwards, my grandfather, sensible of the new fame in his family, but probably alarmed at the fruitless consequences to which it might lead, sent me word, that if I would come to Philadelphia, " he would make a man of me." I sent word, in return, that " men grew in England as well as America: " an answer which repaid me for the loss of my repartee at Dr. Raine's.

I had got a dislike of my grandfather for reasons in which his only surviving daughter tells me I was mistaken ; and partly on a similar account, I equally disliked his friend Dr. Franklin, author of *Poor Richard's Almanack:* a heap, as it appeared to me, of " scoundrel maxims." * I think I now

---

* Thomson's phrase, in the *Castle of Indolence,* speaking of a miserly money-getter :—

   " 'A penny saved is a penny got ;'
     Firm to this scoundrel maxim keepeth he,
     Ne of its rigour will he bate a jot,
     Till it hath quench'd his fire and banishèd his pot."

The reader will not imagine that I suppose all money-makers to be appreciate Dr. Franklin as I ought; but although I can see the utility of such publications as his *Almanack* for a rising commercial state, and hold it useful as a memorandum to uncalculating persons like myself, who happen to live in an old one, I think there is no necessity for it in commercial nations long established, and that it has no business in others, who do not found their happiness in that sort of power. Franklin, with all his abilities, is but at the head of those who think that man lives " by bread alone."

The respect which, in matters of religion, I felt for the " spirit which giveth life," in preference to the " letter which killeth," received a curious corroboration from a circumstance which I witnessed on board a Margate hoy. Having nothing to do, after the publication of my poor volume, but to read and to look about me, a friend proposed an excursion to Brighton. We were to go first to Margate, and then walk the rest of the way by the sea-side, for the benefit of the air.

We took places accordingly in the first hoy that was about to sail, and speedily found ourselves seated and moving. We thought the passengers a singularly staid set of people for holiday-makers, and could not account for it. The impression by degrees grew so strong, that we resolved to inquire into the reason; and it was with no very agreeable feelings, that we found ourselves fixed for the day on board what was called the " Methodist hoy." The vessel, it seems, was under the particular patronage of the sect of that denomination; and it professed to sail " by Divine Providence."

Dinner brought a little more hilarity into the faces of these children of heaven. One innocently proposed a game at riddles; another entertained a circle of hearers by a question in arithmetic; a third (or the same person, if I remember— a very dreary gentleman) raised his voice into some remarks on " atheists and deists," glancing, while he did it, at the

of this description. Very gallant spirits are to be found among them, who only take to this mode of activity for want of a better, and are as generous in disbursing as they are vigorous in acquiring. You may always know the common run, as in other instances, by the soreness with which they feel attacks on the body corporate.

For the assertion that Dr. Franklin cut off his son with a shilling, my only authority is family tradition. It is observable, however, that the friendliest of his biographers are not only forced to admit that he seemed a little too fond of money, but notice the mysterious secrecy in which his family history is involved.

small knot of the uninitiated who had got together in self-defence; on which a fourth gave out a hymn of Dr. Watts's, which says that—

> "Religion never was designed
> To make our pleasures less."

It was sung, I must say, in a tone of the most impartial misery, as if on purpose to contradict the opinion.

Thus passed the hours, between formality, and eating and drinking, and psalm-singing, and melancholy attempts at a little mirth, till night came on; when our godly friends vanished below into their berths. The wind was against us: we beat out to sea, and had a taste of some cold autumnal weather. Such of us as were not prepared for this, adjusted ourselves as well as we could to the occasion, or paced about the deck to warm ourselves, not a little amused with the small crew of sailors belonging to the vessel, who sat together singing songs in a low tone of voice, in order that the psalm-singers below might not hear them.

During one of these pacings about the deck, my foot came in contact with a large bundle which lay as much out of the way as possible, but which I had approached unawares. On stooping to see what it was, I found it was a woman. She was sleeping, and her clothes were cold and damp. As the captain could do nothing for her, except refer me to the "gentlefolks" below, in case any room could be made for her in their dormitory, I repaired below accordingly; and with something of a malicious benevolence, persisted in waking every sleeper in succession, and stating the woman's case. Not a soul would stir. They had paid for their places: the woman should have done the same; and so they left her to the care of the "Providence" under which they sailed. I do not wish to insinuate by this story that many excellent people have not been Methodists. All I mean to say is, that here was a whole Margate hoy full of them; that they had feathered their nests well below; that the night was trying; that to a female it might be dangerous; and that not one of them, nevertheless, would stir to make room for her.

As Methodism is a fact of the past and of the present, I trust it may have had its uses. The degrees of it are various, from the blackest hue of what is called Calvinistic Methodism to colours little distinguishable from the mildest and pleasantest of conventional orthodoxy. Accidents of birth, breeding, brain, heart, and temperament make worlds of difference in this respect, as in all others. But where the paramount doctrine of a sect, whatever it may profess to include, is Self-preservation, and where this paramount doctrine, as it needs must when actually paramount, blunts in very self-defence the greatest final sympathies with one's fellow-creatures, the transition of ideas is easy from unfeelingness in a future state to unfeelingness in the present; and it becomes a very little thing indeed to let a woman lie out in the cold all night, while saints are snoozing away in comfort.

My companion and I, much amused, and not a little indignant, took our way from Ramsgate along the coast, turning cottages into inns as our hunger compelled us, and sleeping at night the moment we laid our heads on our pillows.

The length of this journey, which did us good, we reckoned to be a hundred and twelve miles; and we did it in four days, which was not bad walking. But my brother Robert once went a hundred miles in two. He also, when a lad, kept up at a kind of trotting pace with a friend's horse all the way from Finchley to Pimlico. His limbs were admirably well set.

The friend who was my companion in this journey had not been long known to me; but he was full of good qualities. He died a few years afterwards in France, where he unhappily found himself among his countrymen, whom Bonaparte so iniquitously detained at the commencement of the second war. He was brother of my old friend Henry Robertson, treasurer of Covent Garden theatre, in whose company and that of Vincent Novello, Charles Cowden Clarke, and other gifted and estimable men, I have enjoyed some of the most harmonious evenings of my life, in every sense of the word.

Let me revert to a pleasanter recollection. The companion of my journey to Brighton, and another brother of his, who was afterwards in the Commissariat (all the brothers, alas! are now dead), set up a little club to which I belonged, called the "Elders," from our regard for the wine of that name, with hot goblets of which we finished the evening. It was not the wine so called which you buy in the shops, and which is a mixture of brandy and verjuice, but the vintage of the genuine berry, which is admired wherever it is known, and which the ancients unquestionably symbolized under the mystery of the Bearded Bacchus, the senior god of that name—

"Brother of Bacchus, *elder* born."

The great Boerhaave held the tree in such pleasant reverence for the multitude of its virtues, that he is said to have taken off his hat whenever he passed it.

Be this as it may, so happily it sent us to our beds, with such an extraordinary twofold inspiration of Bacchus and Somnus, that, falling to sleep, we would dream half an hour after of the last jest, and wake up again in laughter.

<hr>

CHAPTER VI.

PLAYGOING AND VOLUNTEERS.

A KNOCK at the doors of all England awoke us up from our dreams. It was Bonaparte, threatening to come among us, and bidding us put down "that glass." The "Elders," in common with the rest of the world, were moved to say him nay, and to drink, and drill themselves, to his confusion.

I must own that I never had the slightest belief in this coming of Bonaparte. It did, I allow, sometimes appear to me not absolutely impossible; and very strange it was to think that some fine morning I might actually find myself face to face with a parcel of Frenchmen in Kent or Sussex, instead of playing at soldiers in Piccadilly. But I did not believe in his coming: first, because I thought he had far wiser things to attend to; secondly, because he made such an ostentatious show of it; and thirdly, because I felt that whatever might be our party politics, it was not in the nature of things English to allow it. Nobody, I thought, could believe it possible, who did but see and hear the fine, unaffected, manly young fellows that composed our own regiment of volunteers, the St. James's, and whose counterparts had arisen in swarms all over the country. It was too great a jest. And with all due respect for French valour, I think so to this day.

The case was not the same as in the time of the Normans. The Normans were a more advanced people than the Saxons; they possessed a familiar and family interest among us; and they had even a right to the throne. But in the year 1802, the French and English had for centuries been utterly distinct as well as rival nations; the latter had twice beaten the French on French ground, and under the greatest disadvantages: how much less likely were they to be beaten on their own, under every circumstance of exasperation? They were an abler-bodied nation than the French; they had been bred up, however erroneously, in a contempt for them, which (in a military point of view) was salutary when it was not careless; and, in fine, here were all these volunteers, as well as troops of the line, taking the threat with an ease too great even to laugh at it, but at the same time sedulously attending to their drills, and manifestly resolved, if the struggle came, to make a personal business of it, and see which of the two nations had the greatest pluck.

The volunteers would not even take the trouble of patronizing a journal that was set up to record their movements and to flatter their self-respect. A word of praise from the king, from the commander-in-chief, or the colonel of the regiment, was well enough; it was all in the way of business; but why be told what they knew, or be encouraged when they did not require it? Wags used to say of the journal in question, which was called the *Volunteer*, that it printed only one number, sold only one copy, and that this copy had been purchased by a volunteer drummer-boy. The boy, seeing the paper set out for sale, exclaimed, "The *Volunteer!* why, I'm a volunteer;" and so he bought that solitary image of himself. The boy was willing to be told that he was doing something more than playing at soldiers; but what was this to the men?

This indifferent kind of self-respect and contentment did not hinder the volunteers, however, from having a good deal of pleasant banter of one another among themselves, or from feeling that there was something now and then among them ridiculous in respect to appearances. A gallant officer in our regiment, who was much respected, went among us by the name of Lieutenant Molly, on account of the delicacy of his complexion. Another, who was a strict disciplinarian, and had otherwise a spirit of love for the profession, as though he had been a born soldier, was not spared allusions to his balls of perfumery. Our major (now no more) was an undertaker in Piccadilly, of the name of Downs, very fat and jovial, yet active withal, and a good soldier. He had one of those lively, juvenile faces that are sometimes observed in people of a certain sleek kind of corpulency. This ample field-officer was "cut and come again" for jokes of all sorts. Nor was the colonel himself spared, though he was a highly respectable nobleman, and nephew to an actual troop-of-the-line conqueror, the victor of Montreal. But this requires a paragraph or two to itself.

We had been a regiment for some time without a colonel. The colonel was always about to be declared, but declared he was not; and meantime we mustered about a thousand strong, and were much amazed, and, perhaps, a little indignant. At length the moment arrived—the colonel was named; he was to be introduced to us; and that nothing might be wanting to our dignity, he was a lord, and a friend of the minister, and nephew to the victor aforesaid.

Our parade was the court-yard of Burlington House. The whole regiment attended. We occupied three sides of the ground. In front of us were the great gates, longing to be opened. Suddenly the word is given, "My lord is at hand!" Open burst the gates—up strikes the music. "Present arms!" vociferates the major.

In dashes his lordship, and is pitched right over his horse's head to the ground.

It was the most unfortunate anticlimax that could have happened. Skill, grace, vigour, address, example, ascendancy, mastery, victory, all were in a manner to have been presented to us in the heroical person of the noble colonel; and here they were, prostrated at our feet—ejected—cast out—humiliated—ground to the earth—subjected (for his merciful construction) to the least fellow-soldier that stood among us upright on his feet.

The construction, however, was accorded. Everybody felt indeed, that the greatest of men might have been subjected to the accident. It was the horse, not he, that was in fault—it was the music—the ringing of the arms, &c. His spirit had led him to bring with him too fiery a charger. Bucephalus might have thrown Alexander at such a moment. A mole-hill threw William the Third. A man might conquer Bonaparte, and yet be thrown from his horse. And the conclusion was singularly borne out in another quarter; for no conqueror, I believe, whose equitation is ascertained, ever combined more numerous victories with a greater number of falls from his saddle than his lordship's illustrious friend, the Duke of Wellington.

During our field-days, which sometimes took place in the neighbourhood celebrated by Foote in his *Mayor of Garrat*, it was impossible for those who were acquainted with his writings not to think of his city-trained bands and their

dreadful "marchings and counter-marchings from Acton to
Ealing, and from Ealing back again to Acton." We were
not "all robbed and murdered," however, as we returned
home, "by a single footpad." We returned, not by the
Ealing stage, but in right warlike style, marching and dusty.
We had even, one day, a small taste of the will and appetite
of campaigning. Some of us, after a sham-fight, were hastening towards Acton, in a very rage of hunger and thirst, when
we discerned coming towards us a baker with a basket full of
loaves. To observe the man, to see his loaves scattered on
the ground, to find ourselves each with one of them under
his arm, tearing the crumb out, and pushing on for the
village, heedless of the cries of the pursuing baker, was (in
the language of the novelists) the work of a moment. Next
moment we found ourselves standing in the cellar of an Acton
alehouse, with the spigots torn out of the barrels, and everybody helping himself as he could. The baker and the beer-
man were paid, but not till we chose to attend to them ; and
I fully comprehended, even from this small specimen of the
will and pleasure of soldiers, what savages they could become
on graver occasions.

In this St. James's regiment of volunteers were three
persons whom I looked on with great interest, for they were
actors. They were Farley, Emery, and De Camp, all well-
known performers at the time. The first was a celebrated
melodramatic actor, remarkable for combining a short
sturdy person with energetic activity; for which reason, if I
am not mistaken, in spite of his shortness and his sturdiness,
he had got into the light infantry company, where I think I
have had the pleasure of standing both with him and Mr. De
Camp. With De Camp certainly. The latter was brother
of Miss De Camp, afterwards Mrs. Charles Kemble, an
admirable actress in the same line as Farley, and in such
characters as *Beatrice* and *Lucy Lockitt*. She had a beautiful figure, fine large dark eyes, and elevated features, fuller
of spirit than softness, but still capable of expressing great
tenderness. Her brother was nobody in comparison with
her, though he was clever in his way, and more handsome.
But it was a sort of effeminate beauty, which made him look
as if he ought to have been the sister, and she the brother.
It was said of him, in a comprehensive bit of alliteration, that
he "failed in fops, but there was fire in his footmen."

The third of these histrionic patriots, Mr. Emery, was one

of the best actors of his kind the stage ever saw. He excelled, not only in Yorkshiremen, and other rustical comic characters, but in parts of homely tragedy, such as criminals of the lower order; whose conscious guilt he exhibited with such a lively, truthful mixture of clownishness in the mode and intensity in the feeling, as made a startling and terrible picture of the secret passions to which all classes of men are liable.

Emery was also an amateur painter—of landscape, I believe, and of no mean repute. He was a man of a middle height, rather tall perhaps than otherwise, and with quiet, respectable manners; but with something of what is called a pudding face, and an appearance on the whole not unlike a gentleman farmer. You would not have supposed there was so much emotion in him, though he had purpose, too, in his look, and he died early.

I have been tempted to dilate somewhat on these gentlemen; for though I made no acquaintance with them privately, I was now beginning to look with peculiar interest on the stage, to which I had already wished to be a contributor, and of which I was then becoming a critic. I had written a tragedy, a comedy, and a farce; and my Spring Garden friends had given me an introduction to their acquaintance, Mr. Kelly, of the Opera House, with a view to having the farce brought out by some manager with whom he was intimate. I remember lighting upon him at the door of his music-shop or saloon, at the corner of the lane in Pall Mall, where the Arcade now begins, and giving him my letter of introduction and my farce at once. He had a quick, snappish, but not ill-natured voice, and a flushed, handsome, and good-humoured face, with the hair about his ears. The look was a little rakish or so, but very agreeable.

Mr. Kelly was extremely courteous to me; but what he said of the farce, or did with it, I utterly forget. Himself I shall never forget; for as he was the first actor I ever beheld anywhere, so he was one of the first whom I saw on the stage. Actor, indeed, he was none, except inasmuch as he was an acting singer, and not destitute of a certain spirit in everything he did. Neither had he any particular power as a singer, or even a voice. He said it broke down while he was studying in Italy; where, indeed, he had sung with applause. The little snappish tones I spoke of were very manifest on the stage: he had short arms, as if to match them, and a hasty step: and yet, notwithstanding these drawbacks, he was heard with pleasure, for he had taste and feeling. He was a delicate composer, as the music in *Blue Beard* evinces; and he selected so happily from other composers, as to give rise to his friend Sheridan's banter, that he was an "importer of music and composer of wines" (for he once took to being a wine-merchant). While in Ireland, during the early part of his career, he adapted a charming air of Martini's to English words, which, under the title of "Oh, thou wert born to please me," he sang with Mrs. Crouch to so much effect, that not only was it always called for three times, but no play was suffered to be performed without it. It should be added, that Mrs. Crouch was a lovely woman, as well as a beautiful singer, and that the two performers were in love. I have heard them sing it myself, and do not wonder at the impression it made on the susceptible hearts of the Irish. Twenty years afterwards, when Mrs. Crouch was no more, and while Kelly was singing a duet in the same country with Madame Catalani, a man in the gallery cried out, "Mr. Kelly, will you be good enough to favour us with 'Oh, thou wert born to please me?'" The audience laughed; but the call went to the heart of the singer, and probably came from that of the honest fellow who made it. The man may have gone to the play in his youth, with somebody whom he loved by his side, and heard two lovers, as happy as himself, sing what he now wished to hear again.

Madame Catalani was also one of the singers I first remember. I first heard her at an oratorio, where, happening to sit in a box right opposite to where she stood, the leaping forth of her amazingly powerful voice absolutely startled me. Women's voices on the stage are apt to rise above all others, but Catalani's seemed to delight in trying its strength with choruses and orchestras; and the louder they became, the higher and more victorious she ascended. In fact, I believe she is known to have provoked and enjoyed this sort of contest. I suspect, however, that I did not hear her when she was at her best or sweetest. My recollection is, that with a great deal of taste and brilliancy, there was more force than feeling. She was a Roman, with the regular Italian antelope face (if I may so call it); large eyes, with a sensitive elegant nose, and lively expression.

Mrs. Billington also appeared to me to have more brilliancy of execution than depth of feeling. She was a fat beauty, with regular features, and may be seen drawn to the life, in a portrait in Mr. Hogarth's *Memoirs of the Musical Drama*, where she is frightfully dressed in a cropped head of hair, and a waist tucked under her arms—the fashion of the day.

Not so Grassini, a large but perfectly well-made as well as lovely woman, with black hair and eyes, and her countenance as full of feeling as her divine contralto voice. Largeness, or what is called fineness of person, was natural to her, and did not hinder her from having a truly feminine appearance. She was an actress as well as singer. She acted Proserpina in Winter's beautiful opera, and might have remained in the recollection of any one who heard and beheld her, as an image of the goddess she represented. My friend, Vincent Novello, saw the composer when the first performance of the piece was over, stoop down (he was a very tall man) and kiss Mrs. Billington's hand for her singing in the character of Ceres. I wonder he did not take Grassini in his arms. She must have had a fine soul, and would have known how to pardon him. But, perhaps he did.

With Billington used to perform Braham, from whose wonderful remains of power in his old age we may judge what he must have been in his prime. I mean, with regard to voice; for as to general manner and spirit, it is a curious fact that, except when he was in the act of singing, he used to be a remarkably insipid performer; and that it was not till he was growing elderly that he became the animated person we now see him. This, too, he did all on a sudden, to the amusement as well as astonishment of the beholders. When he sang, he was always animated. The probability is, that he had been bred up under masters who were wholly untheatrical, and that something had occurred to set his natural spirit reflecting on the injustice they had done him; though, for a reason which I shall give presently, the theatre, after all, was not the best field for his abilities. He had wonderful execution as well as force, and his voice could also be very sweet, though it was too apt to betray something of that nasal tone which has been observed in Jews, and which is, perhaps, quite as much, or more, a habit in which they have been brought up than a consequence of organization. The same thing has been noticed in Americans; and it might not be difficult to trace it to moral, and even to monied causes; those, to wit, that induce people to retreat inwardly upon themselves; into a sense of their shrewdness and resources; and to clap their finger in self-congratulation upon the organ through which it pleases them occasionally to intimate as much to a bystander, not choosing to trust it wholly to the mouth.

Perhaps it was in some measure the same kind of breeding (I do not say it in disrespect, but in reference to matters of caste, far more discreditable to Christians than Jews) which induced Mr. Braham to quit the Italian stage, and devote himself to his popular and not very refined style of bravura-singing on the English. It was what may be called the loud-and-soft style. There was admirable execution; but the expression consisted in being very soft on the words *love*, *peace*, &c., and then bursting into roars of triumph on the words *hate*, *war*, and *glory*. To this pattern Mr. Braham composed many of the songs written for him; and the public were enchanted with a style which enabled them to fancy that they enjoyed the highest style of the art, while it required only the vulgarest of their perceptions. This renowned vocalist never did himself justice except in the compositions of Handel. When he stood in the concert-room or the oratorio, and opened his mouth with plain, heroic utterance in the mighty strains of "Deeper and deeper still," or "Sound an alarm," or, "Comfort ye my people," you felt indeed that you had a great singer before you. His voice which too often sounded like a horn vulgar, in the catchpenny lyrics of Tom Dibdin, now became a veritable trumpet of grandeur and exaltation; the tabernacle of his creed seemed to open before him in its most victorious days; and you might have fancied yourself in the presence of one of the sons of Aaron, calling out to the host of the people from some platform occupied by their prophets.

About the same time Pasta made her first appearance in England, and produced no sensation. She did not even seem to attempt any. Her nature was so truthful, that, having as yet no acquirements to display, it would appear that she did not pretend she had. She must either have been prematurely put forward by others, or, with an instinct of her future greatness, supposed that the instinct itself would be recognized. When she came the second time, after completing her studies, she took rank at once as the greatest genius in her line which the Italian theatre in England had witnessed. She was a great tragic actress; and her singing, in point of force, tenderness, and expression, was equal to her acting. All noble passions belonged to her; and her very scorn seemed equally noble, for it trampled only on what was mean. When she measured her enemy from head to foot, in *Tancredi*, you really felt for the man, at seeing him so reduced into nothingness. When she made her entrance on the stage, in the same character—which she did right in front of the audience, midway between the side scenes, she waved forth her arms, and drew them quietly together again over her bosom, as if she sweetly, yet modestly, embraced the whole house. And when, in the part of Medea, she looked on the children she was about to kill, and tenderly parted their hair, and seemed to mingle her very eyes in lovingness with theirs, uttering, at the same time, notes of the most wandering and despairing sweetness, every gentle eye melted into tears. She wanted height, and had somewhat too much flesh; but it seemed the substance of the very health of her body, which was otherwise shapely. Her head and bust were of the finest classical mould. An occasional roughness in her lower tones did but enrich them with passion, as people grow hoarse with excess of feeling; and while her voice was in its prime, even a little incorrectness now and then in the notes would seem the consequence of a like boundless emotion; but, latterly, it argued a failure of ear, and consoled the mechanical artists who had been mystified by her success. In every other respect, perfect truth, graced by idealism, was the secret of Pasta's greatness. She put truth first always; and, in so noble and sweet a mind, grace followed it as a natural consequence.

With the exception of Lablache, that wonderful barytone singer, full of might as well as mirth, in whom the same truth, accompanied in some respects by the same grace of feeling, suffered itself to be overlaid with comic fat (except when he turned it into an heroic amplitude with drapery), I remember no men on our Italian stage equal to the women. Women have carried the palm out and out, in acting, singing, and dancing. The pleasurable seems more the forte of the sex; and the opera house is essentially a palace of pleasure, even in its tragedy. Bitterness there cannot but speak sweetly; there is no darkness, and no poverty; and every death is the death of the swan. When the men are sweet, they either seem feeble, or, as in the case of Rubini, have execution without passion. Naldi was amusing; Tramezzani was elegant; Ambrogetti (whose great big calves seemed as if they ought to have saved him from going into La Trappe) was a fine dashing representative of Don Juan, without a voice. But what were these in point of impression on the public, compared with the woman I have mentioned, or even with voluptuous Fodor, with amiable Sontag, with charming Malibran (whom I never saw), or with adorable Jenny Lind (whom, as an Irishman would say, I have seen still less ; for not to see her appears to be a deprivation beyond all ordinary conceptions of musical loss and misfortune)?

As to dancers, male dancers are almost always *gawkies*, compared with female. One forgets the names of the best of them ; but who, that ever saw, has forgotten Heberle, or Cerito, or Taglioni? There was a great noise once in France about the Vestrises ; particularly old Vestris ; but (with all due respect to our gallant neighbours) I have a suspicion that he took the French in with the gravity and *imposingness* of his twirls. There was an imperial demand about Vestris, likely to create for him a corresponding supply of admiration. The most popular dancers of whom I have a recollection, when I was young, were Deshayes, who was rather an elegant posture-master than dancer, and Madame Parisot, who was very thin, and always smiling. I could have seen little dancing in those times, or I should have something to say of the Presles, Didelots, and others, who turned the heads of the Yarmouths and Barrymores of the day. Art, in all its branches, has since grown more esteemed ; and I suspect that neither dancing nor singing ever attained so much grace and beauty as they have done within the last twenty years. The Farinellis and Pacchierottis were a kind of monsters of execution. There were tones, also, in their voices which, in all probability, were very touching. But, to judge from their printed songs, their chief excellence lay in difficult and everlasting roulades. And we may guess, even now, from the prevailing character of French dancing, that difficulty was the great point of conquest with Vestris. There was no such graceful understanding between the playgoers and the performers, no such implied recognition of the highest principles of emotion, as appears to be the case in the present day with the Taglionis and Jenny Linds.

To return to the English boards,—the first actor whom I remember seeing upon them was excellent Jack Bannister. He was a handsome specimen of the best kind of Englishman, —jovial, manly, good-humoured, unaffected, with a great deal of whim and drollery, but never passing the bounds of the decorous ; and when he had made you laugh heartily as some yeoman or seaman in a comedy, he could bring the tears into your eyes for some honest sufferer in an afterpiece. He gave you the idea of a good fellow,—a worthy household humourist, —whom it would be both pleasant and profitable to live with; and this was his real character. He had a taste for pictures, and settled down into a good English gout and the love of his family. I saw him one day hobbling with a stick in Gower Street, where he lived, and the same evening performing the part either of the young squire, Tony Lumpkin, in *She Stoops to Conquer*, or of Acres, in the Comedy of the *Rivals*, I forget which; but in either character he would be young to the last. Next day he would perform the old father, the Brazier, in Colman's sentimental comedy, *John Bull;* and everybody would see that it was a father indeed who was suffering.

This could not be said of Fawcett in the same character, who roared like *Bull,* but did not feel like *John.* He was affecting, too, in his way; but it was after the fashion of a great noisy boy, whom you cannot help pitying for his tears, though you despise him for his vulgarity. Fawcett had a harsh, brazen face, and a voice like a knife-grinder's wheel. He was all pertness, coarseness, and effrontery, but with a great deal of comic force; and whenever he came trotting on to the stage (for such was his walk) and pouring forth his harsh, rapid words, with his nose in the air, and a facetious grind in his throat, the audience were prepared for a merry evening.

Munden was a comedian famous for the variety and significance of his grimaces, and for making something out of nothing by a certain intensity of contemplation. Lamb, with exquisite wit, described him in one sentence, by saying, that Munden " beheld a leg of mutton in its quiddity." If he laid an emphasis on the word " Holborn," or " button," he did it in such a manner that you thought there was more in " Holborn," or " button," than it ever before entered into your head to conceive. I have seen him, while playing the part of a vagabond loiterer about inn-doors, look at, and gradually approach, a pot of ale on a table from a distance, for ten minutes together, while he kept the house in roars of laughter by the intense idea which he dumbly conveyed of its contents, and the no less intense manifestation of his cautious but inflexible resolution to drink it. So, in acting the part of a credulous old antiquary, on whom an old beaver is palmed for the " hat of William Tell," he reverently put the hat on his head, and then solemnly walked to and fro with such an excessive sense of the glory with which he was crowned, such a weight of reflected heroism, and accumulation of Tell's whole history on that single representative culminating point, elegantly halting every now and then to put himself in the attitude of one drawing a bow, that the spectators could hardly have been astonished had they seen his hair stand on end, and carry the hat aloft with it. But I must not suffer myself to be led into these details.

Lewis was a comedian of the rarest order, for he combined whimsicality with elegance, and levity with heart. He was the fop, the lounger, the flatterer, the rattlebrain, the sower of wild oats; and in all he was the gentleman. He looked on the stage what he was off it, the companion of wits and men of quality. It is pleasant to know that he was a descendant of Erasmus Lewis, the secretary of Lord Oxford, and friend of Pope and Swift. He was airiness personified. He had a light person, light features, a light voice, a smile that showed the teeth, with good-humoured eyes; and a genial levity pervaded his action, to the very tips of his delicately-gloved fingers. He drew on his glove like a gentleman, and then darted his fingers at the ribs of the character he was talking with, in a way that carried with it whatever was suggestive, and sparkling, and amusing. When he died, they put up a classical Latin inscription to his memory, about *elegantiæ* and *lepores* (whims and graces); and you felt that no man better deserved it. He had a right to be recorded as the type of airy genteel comedy.

Elliston was weightier both in manner and person; and he was a tragedian as well as comedian. Not a great tragedian, though able to make a serious and affecting impression; and when I say weightier in comedy than Lewis, I do not mean heavy; but that he had greater bodily substance and force. In Sir Harry Wildair, for instance, he looked more like the man who could bear rakery and debauch. The engraved portrait of him in a coat bordered with fur is very like. He had dry as well as genial humour, was an admirable representative of the triple hero in *Three and the Deuce*, of Charles Surface, Don Felix, the Duke in the *Honeymoon*, and of all gallant and gay lovers of a robust order, not omitting the most cordial. Indeed, he was the most genuine lover that I ever saw on the stage. No man approached a woman as he did,— with so flattering a mixture of reverence and passion—such closeness without insolence, and such a trembling energy in his words. His utterance of the single word "charming" was a volume of rapturous fervour. I speak, of course, only of his better days. Latterly, he grew flustered with imprudence and misfortune ; and from the accounts I have heard of his acting, nobody who had not seen him before could have guessed what sort of man he had been. Elliston, like Lewis, went upon the stage with advantages of training and connections. He was nephew of Dr. Elliston, master of one of the colleges at Cambridge ; and he was educated at Saint Paul's school.

These are the actors of those days whom I recollect with the greatest pleasure. I include Fawcett, because he was identified with some of the most laughable characters in farce.

To touch on some others. Liston was renowned for an exquisitely ridiculous face and manner, rich with half-conscious, half-unconscious absurdity. The whole piece became *Listonized* the moment he appeared. People longed for his coming back, in order that they might dote on his oily, mantling face, and laugh with him and at him.

Mathews was a genius in mimicry, a facsimile in mind as well as manner; and he was a capital Sir Fretful Plagiary. It was a sight to see him looking wretchedly happy at his victimizers, and digging deeper and deeper into his mortification at every fresh button of his coat that he buttoned up.

Dowton was perfect in such characters as Colonel Oldboy and Sir Anthony Absolute. His anger was no petty irritability, but the boiling of a rich blood, and of a will otherwise genial. He was also by far the best Falstaff.

Cooke, a square-faced, hook-nosed, wide-mouthed, malignantly smiling man, was intelligent and peremptory, and a hard hitter : he seized and strongly kept your attention; but he was never pleasant. He was too entirely the satirist, the hypocrite, and the villain. He loved too fondly his own caustic and rascally words; so that his voice, which was otherwise harsh, was in the *habit* of melting and dying away inwardly in the secret satisfaction of its smiling malignity. As to his vaunted tragedy, it was a mere reduction of Shakspeare's poetry into indignant prose. He limited every character to its worst qualities; and had no idealism, no affections, no verse.

Kemble was a god compared with Cooke, as far as the ideal was concerned; though, on the other hand, I never could admire Kemble as it was the fashion to do. He was too artificial, too formal, too critically and deliberately conscious. Nor do I think that he had any genius whatsoever. His power was all studied acquirement. It was this, indeed, by the help of his stern Roman aspect, that made the critics like him. It presented, in a noble shape, the likeness of their own capabilities.

Want of genius could not be imputed to his sister, Mrs. Siddons. I did not see her, I believe, in her best days; but she must always have been a somewhat masculine beauty; and she had no love in her, apart from other passions. She was a mistress, however, of lofty, of queenly, and of appalling tragic effect. Nevertheless, I could not but think that something of too much art was apparent even in Mrs. Siddons; and she failed, I think, in the highest points of refinement. When she smelt the blood on her hand, for instance, in *Macbeth*, in the scene where she walked in her sleep, she made a face of ordinary disgust, as though the odour were offensive to the senses, not appalling to the mind.

Charles Kemble, who had an ideal face and figure, was the nearest approach I ever saw to Shakspeare's gentlemen, and to heroes of romance. He also made an excellent Cassio. But with the exception of Mrs. Siddons, who was declining, all the reigning school of tragedy had retrograded rather than otherwise, towards the time that preceded Garrick; and the consequence was, that when Kean brought back nature and impulse, he put an end to it at once, as Garrick had put an end to Quin.

In comedy nature had never been wanting; and there was one comic actress, who was nature herself in one of her most genial forms. This was Mrs. Jordan; who, though she was neither beautiful, nor handsome, nor even pretty, nor accomplished, nor "a lady," nor anything conventional or *comme il faut* whatsoever, yet was so pleasant, so cordial, so natural, so full of spirits, so healthily constituted in mind and body, had such a shapely leg withal, so charming a voice, and such a happy and happy-making expression of countenance, that she appeared something superior to all those requirements of acceptability, and to hold a patent from nature herself for our delight and good opinion. It is creditable to the feelings of society in general, that allowances are made for the temptations to which the stage exposes the sex; and in Mrs. Jordan's case these were not diminished by a sense of the like consideration due to princely restrictions, and to the manifest domestic dispositions of more parties than one. But she made even Methodists love her. A touching story is told of her apologizing to a poor man of that persuasion for having relieved him. He had asked her name; and she expressed a hope that he would not feel offended when the name was told him. On hearing it, the honest Methodist (he could not have been one on board the hoy) shed tears of pity and admiration, and trusted that he could not do wrong in begging a blessing on her head.

(*Serious Reviewer, interrupting.* But, my good sir, suppose some of your female readers should take it into their heads to be Mrs. Jordan?

Author. Oh, my good sir, don't be alarmed. My female readers are not persons to be so much afraid for, as you seem to think yours are. The stage itself has taught them large measures both of charity and discernment. They have not been so locked up in restraint, as to burst out of bounds the moment they see a door open for consideration.)

Mrs. Jordan was inimitable in exemplifying the consequences of too much restraint in ill-educated Country Girls, in Romps, in Hoydens, and in Wards on whom the mercenary have designs. She wore a bib and tucker, and pinafore, with a bouncing propriety, fit to make the boldest spectator alarmed at the idea of bringing such a household responsibility on his shoulders. To see her when thus attired shed blubbering tears for some disappointment, and eat all the while a great thick slice of bread and butter, weeping, and moaning, and munching, and eyeing at every bite the part she meant to bite next, was a lesson against will and appetite worth a hundred sermons of our friends on board the hoy; and, on the other hand, they could assuredly have done and said nothing at all calculated to make such an impression in favour of amiableness as she did, when she acted in gentle, generous, and confiding characters. The way in which she would take a friend by the cheek and kiss her, or make up a quarrel with a lover, or coax a guardian into good-humour, or sing (without accompaniment) the song of "Since then I'm doom'd," or "In the dead of the night," trusting, as she had a right to do, and as the house wished her to do, to the sole effect of her sweet, mellow, and loving voice—the reader will pardon me, but tears of pleasure and regret come into my eyes at the recollection, as if she personified whatsoever was happy at that period of life, and which has gone like herself. The very sound of the little familiar word *bud* from her lips (the abbreviation of husband), as she packed it closer, as it were, in the utterance, and pouted it up with fondness in the man's face, taking him at the same time by the chin, was a whole concentrated world of the power of loving.

That is a pleasant time of life, the playgoing time in youth, when the coach is packed full to go to the theatre, and brothers and sisters, parents and lovers (none of whom, perhaps, go very often) are all wafted together in a flurry of expectation; when the only wish as they go (except with the lovers) is to go as fast as possible, and no sound is so delightful as the cry of " Bill of the Play;" when the smell of links in the darkest and muddiest winter's night is charming; and the steps of the coach are let down; and a roar of hoarse voices round the door, and *mud-shine* on the pavement, are accompanied with the sight of the warm-looking lobby which is about to be entered; and they enter, and pay, and ascend the pleasant stairs, and begin to hear the *silence* of the house, perhaps the first jingle of the music; and the box is entered amidst some little awkwardness in descending to their places, and being looked at; and at length they sit, and are become used to by their neighbours, and shawls and smiles are adjusted, and the play-bill is handed round or pinned to the cushion, and the gods are a little noisy, and the music veritably commences, and at length the curtain is drawn up, and the first delightful syllables are heard:—

" Ah! my dear Charles, when did you see the lovely Olivia?"

" Oh! my dear Sir George, talk not to me of Olivia. The cruel guardian," &c.

Anon the favourite of the party makes his appearance, and then they are quite happy; and next day, besides his own merits, the points of the dialogue are attributed to him as if he were their inventor. It is not Sir Harry, or old Dornton, or Dubster, who said this or that; but " Lewis," " Munden," or " Keeley." They seem to think the wit really originated with the man who uttered it so delightfully.

Critical playgoing is very inferior in its enjoyments to this. It must of necessity blame as well as praise; it becomes difficult to please; it is tempted to prove its own merits, instead of those of its entertainers; and the enjoyments of self-love, besides, perhaps, being ill-founded, and subjecting it to the blame which it bestows, are sorry substitutes, at the best, for hearty delight in others. Never, after I had taken critical pen in hand, did I pass the thoroughly delightful evenings at the playhouse which I had done when I went only to laugh or be moved. I had the pleasure, it is true, of praising those whom I admired; but the retributive uneasiness of the very pleasure of blaming attended it; the consciousness of self, which on all occasions except loving ones contains a bitter in its sweet, put its sorry obstacle in the way of an unembarrassed delight; and I found the days flown when I retained none but the good passages of plays and performers, and when I used to carry to my old school-fellows rapturous accounts of the farces of Colman, and the good-natured comedies of O'Keefe.

I speak of my own feelings, and at a particular time of life: but forty or fifty years ago people of all times of life were much greater playgoers than they are now. They dined earlier, they had not so many newspapers, clubs, and pianofortes; the French Revolution only tended at first to endear the nation to its own habits; it had not yet opened a thousand new channels of thought and interest; nor had railroads conspired to carry people, bodily as well as mentally, into as many analogous directions. Everything was more concentrated, and the various classes of society felt a greater concern in the same amusements. Nobility, gentry, citizens, princes, —all were frequenters of theatres, and even more or less acquainted personally with the performers. Nobility intermarried with them; gentry, and citizens too, wrote for them; princes conversed and lived with them. Sheridan, and other members of Parliament, were managers as well as dramatists. It was Lords Derby, Craven, and Thurlow that sought wives on the stage. Two of the most popular minor dramatists were Cobb, a clerk in the India House, and Birch, the pastrycook. If Mrs. Jordan lived with the Duke of Clarence (William IV.) as his mistress, nobody doubts that she was as faithful to him as a wife. His brother, the Prince of Wales (George the Fourth), besides his intimacy with Sheridan and the younger Colman, and to say nothing of Mrs. Robinson, took a pleasure in conversing with Kemble, and was the personal patron of O'Keefe and of Kelly. The Kembles, indeed, as Garrick had been, were received everywhere among the truly best circles; that is to say, where intelligence was combined with high breeding; and they deserved it : for whatever difference of opinion may be entertained as to the amount of genius in the family, nobody who recollects them will dispute that they were a remarkable race, dignified and elegant in manners, with intellectual tendencies, and in point of aspect very like what has been called " God Almighty's nobility."

I remember once standing behind John Kemble and a noble lord at a sale. It was the celebrated book sale of the Duke of Roxburgh; and by the same token I recollect another person that was present, of whom more by-and-by. The player and the nobleman were conversing, the former in his high, dignified tones, the latter in a voice which I heard but indistinctly. Presently, the actor turned his noble profile to his interlocutor, and on his moving it back again, the man of quality turned his. What a difference ! and what a voice ! Kemble's voice was none of the best; but, like his profile, it was nobleness itself compared with that of the noble lord. I had taken his lordship for a young man, by the trim cut of his body and of his clothes, the " fall in " of his back, and the smart way in which he had stuck his hat on the top of his head ; but when I saw his profile and heard his voice, I seemed to have before me a premature old one. His mouth seemed toothless; his voice was a hasty mumble. Without being aquiline, the face had the appearance of being what may be called an old " nose-and-mouth face." The suddenness with which it spoke added to the surprise. It was like a flash of decrepitude on the top of a young body.

This was the sale at which the unique copy of Boccaccio fetched a thousand and four hundred pounds. It was bought by the Marquis of Blandford (the late Duke of Marlborough) in competition with Earl Spencer, who conferred with his son, Lord Althorp, and gave it up. So at least I understand, for I was not aware of the conference, or of the presence of Lord Althorp (afterwards minister, and late Earl Spencer). I remember his father well at the sale, and how he sat at the farther end of the auctioneer's table, with an air of intelligent indifference, leaning his head on his hand so as to push up the hat a little from off it. I beheld with pleasure in his person the pupil of Sir William Jones and brother of Coleridge's Duchess of Devonshire. It was curious, and scarcely pleasant, to see two Spencers thus bidding against one another, even though the bone of contention was a book; and the ghost of their illustrious kinsman, the author of the *Faerie Queene*, might have been gratified to see what book it was, and how high the prices of old folios had risen. What satisfaction the Marquis got out of his victory I cannot say. The Earl, who, I believe, was a genuine lover of books, could go home and reconcile himself to his defeat by reading the work in a cheaper edition.

I shall have occasion to speak of Mr. Kemble again presently, and of subsequent actors by-and-by.

CHAPTER VII.

ESSAYS IN CRITICISM.

I HAD not been as misdirected in the study of prose as in that of poetry. It was many years before I discovered what was requisite in the latter. In the former, the very commonplaces of the schoolmaster tended to put me in the right path, for (as I have already intimated) he found the *Spectator* in vogue, and this became our standard of prose writing.

It is true (as I have also mentioned) that in consequence of the way in which we were taught to use them by the schoolmaster, I had become far more disgusted than delighted with the charming papers of Addison, and with the exaction of moral observations on a given subject. But the seed was sown, to ripen under pleasanter circumstances; and my father, with his usual good-natured impulse, making me a present one day of a set of the British classics, which attracted my eyes on the shelves of Harley, the bookseller in Cavendish Street, the tenderness with which I had come to regard all my school recollections, and the acquaintance which I now made for the first time with the lively papers of the *Connoisseur*, gave me an entirely fresh and delightful sense of the merits of essay-writing. I began to think that when Boyer crumpled up and chucked away my "themes" in a passion, he had not done justice to the honest weariness of my antiformalities, and to their occasional evidences of something better.

The consequence was a delighted perusal of the whole set of classics (for I have ever been a "glutton of books"); and this was followed by my first prose endeavours in a series of papers called the *Traveller*, which appeared in the evening paper of that name [long since incorporated with the *Globe*], under the signature of " Mr. Town, *junior*, Critic and Censor-general"—the senior Mr. Town, with the same titles, being no less a person than my friend of the *Connoisseur*, with whom I thus had the boldness to fraternize. I offered them with fear and trembling to the editor of the *Traveller*, Mr. Quin, and was astonished at the gaiety with which he accepted them. What astonished me more was a perquisite of five or six copies of the paper, which I enjoyed every Saturday when my essays appeared, and with which I used to reissue from Bolt Court in a state of transport. I had been told, but could not easily conceive, that the editor of a new evening paper would be happy to fill up his pages with any decent writing; but Mr. Quin praised me besides; and I could not behold the long columns of type, written by myself, in a public paper, without thinking there must be some merit in them, besides that of being a stop-gap.

Luckily, the essays were little read; they were not at all noticed in public; and I thus escaped the perils of another premature laudation for my juvenility. I was not led to repose on the final merits either of my prototype or his imitator. The *Connoisseur*, nevertheless, gave me all the transports of a first love. His citizen at Vauxhall, who says, at every mouthful of beef, " There goes twopence;" and the creed of his unbeliever, who " believes in all unbelief," competed for a long time in my mind with the humour of Goldsmith. I was also greatly delighted with the singular account of himself, in the dual number, with which he concludes his work, shadowing forth the two authors of it in one person:—

" Mr. Town" (says he) "is a fair, black, middle-sized, very short person. He wears his own hair, and a periwig. He is about thirty years of age, and not more than four-and-twenty. He is a student of the law and a bachelor of physic. He was bred at the University of Oxford; where, having taken no less than three degrees, he looks down on many learned professors as his inferiors; yet, having been there but little longer than to take the first degree of bachelor of arts, it has more than once happened that the censor-general of all England has been reprimanded by the censor of his college for neglecting to furnish the usual essay, or (in the collegiate phrase) the theme of the week."

Probably these associations with school-terms, and with a juvenile time of life, gave me an additional liking for the

Connoisseur. The twofold author, which he thus describes himself, consisted of Bonnell Thornton, afterwards the translator of *Plautus*, and Colman, the dramatist, author of the *Jealous Wife*, and translator of *Terence*. Colman was the "very short person" of four-and-twenty, and Thornton was the bachelor of physic, though he never practised. The humour of these writers, compared with Goldsmith's, was caricature, and not deep; they had no pretensions to the genius of the *Vicar of Wakefield :* but they possessed great animal spirits, which are a sort of merit in this climate; and this was another claim on my regard. The name of Bonnell Thornton (whom I had taken to be the sole author of the *Connoisseur*) was for a long time, with me, another term for animal spirits, humour, and wit. I then discovered that there was more smartness in him than depth; and had I known that he and Colman had ridiculed the odes of Gray, I should, perhaps, have made the discovery sooner; though I was by no means inclined to confound parody with disrespect. But the poetry of Gray had been one of my first loves; and I could as soon have thought of friendship or of the grave with levity, as of the friend of West, and the author of the *Elegy* and the *Bard*.

An amusing story is told of Thornton, which may show the quick and ingenious, but, perhaps, not very feeling turn of his mind. It is said that he was once discovered by his father sitting in a box at the theatre, when he ought to have been in his rooms at college. The old gentleman addressing him accordingly, that youngster turned in pretended amazement to the people about him, and said, "Smoke old wigsby, who takes me for his son." Thornton, senior, upon this, indignantly hastens out of the box, with the manifest intention of setting off for Oxford, and finding the rooms vacant. Thornton, junior, takes double post-horses, and is there before him, quietly sitting in his chair. He rises from it on his father's appearance, and cries, "Ah! dear sir, is it you? To what am I indebted for this unexpected pleasure?"

Goldsmith enchanted me. I knew no end of repeating passages out of the *Essays* and the *Citizen of the World*—such as the account of the Club, with its Babel of talk; of Beau Tibbs, with his dinner of ox-cheek which "his grace was so fond of;" and of the wooden-legged sailor, who regarded those that were lucky enough to have their "legs shot off" on board king's ships (which entitled them to a penny a day), as being "born with golden spoons in their mouths." Then there was his correct, sweet style; the village-painting in his poems; the *Retaliation*, which, though on an artificial subject, seemed to me (as it yet seems) a still more genuine effusion; and, above all, the *Vicar of Wakefield* —with Burchell, whom I adored; and Moses, whom I would rather have been cheated with, than prosper; and the Vicar himself in his cassock, now presenting his "Treatise against Polygamy" (in the family picture) to his wife, habited as Venus; and now distracted for the loss of his daughter Olivia, who is seduced by the villanous squire. I knew not whether to laugh at him, or cry with him most.

These, with Fielding and Smollett, Voltaire, Charlotte Smith, Bage, Mrs. Radcliffe, and Augustus La Fontaine, were my favourite prose authors. I had subscribed, while at school, to the famous circulating library in Leadenhall Street, and I have continued to be such a glutton of novels ever since, that, except where they repel me in the outset with excessive wordiness, I can read their three-volume enormities to this day without skipping a syllable; though I guess pretty nearly all that is going to happen, from the mysterious gentleman who opens the work in the dress of a particular century, down to the distribution of punishments and the drying up of tears in the last chapter. I think the authors wonderfully clever people, particularly those who write most; and I should like the most contemptuous of their critics to try their hands at doing something half as engaging.

Should any chance observer of these pages (for I look upon my customary perusers as people of deeper insight) pronounce such a course of reading frivolous, he will be exasperated to hear that, had it not been for reverence to opinion, I should have been much inclined at that age (as, indeed, I am still) to pronounce the reading of far graver works frivolous; history, for one. I read every history that came in my way, and could not help liking good old Herodotus, ditto Villani, picturesque, festive Froissart, and accurate and most entertaining, though artificial, Gibbon. But the contradictions of historians in general, their assumption of a dignity for which I saw no particular grounds, their unphilosophic and ridiculous avoidance (on that score) of personal anecdote, and, above all, the narrow-minded and time-serving confinement of their subjects to wars and party-government (for there are time-servings, as there are fashions, that last for centuries), instinctively repelled me. I felt, though I did not know, till Fielding told me, that there was more truth in the verisimilitudes of fiction than in the assumptions of history; and I rejoiced over the story told of Sir Walter Raleigh, who, on receiving I forget how many different accounts of an incident that occurred under his own windows, laughed at the idea of his writing a *History of the World*.

But the writer who made the greatest impression on me was Voltaire. I did not read French at that time, but I fell in with the best translation of some of his miscellaneous works; and I found in him not only the original of much which I had admired in the style and pleasantry of my favourite native authors, Goldsmith in particular (who adored him), but the most formidable antagonist of absurdities which the world had seen; a discloser of lights the most overwhelming, in flashes of wit; a destroyer of the strongholds of superstition, that were never to be built up again, let the hour of renovation seem to look forth again as it might. I was transported with the gay courage and unquestionable humanity of this extraordinary person, and I soon caught the tone of his cunning implications and provoking turns. He did not frighten me. I never felt for a moment, young as I was, and Christianly brought up, that true religion would suffer at his hands. On the contrary, I had been bred up (in my home circle) to look for reforms in religion : I had been led to desire the best and gentlest form of it, unattended with threats and horrors : and if the school orthodoxy did not countenance such expectations, it took no pains to discountenance them. I had privately accustomed myself, of my own further motion, to doubt and to reject every doctrine, and every statement of facts, that went counter to the plainest precepts of love, and to the final happiness of all the creatures of God. I could never see, otherwise, what Christianity could mean, that was not meant by a hundred inferior religions; nor could I think it right and holy to accept of the greatest hopes, apart from that universality—*Fiat justitia, ruat cœlum*. I was prepared to give up heaven itself (as far as it is possible for human hope to do so) rather than that anything so unheavenly as a single exclusion from it should exist. Therefore, to me, Voltaire was a putter down of a great deal that was wrong, but of nothing that was right. I did not take him for a builder; neither did I feel that he knew much of the sanctuary which was inclosed in what he pulled down. He found a heap of rubbish pretending to be the shrine itself, and he set about denying its pretensions and abating it as a nuisance, without knowing, or considering (at least I thought so) what there remained of beauty and durability, to be disclosed on its demolition. I fought for him, then and afterwards, with those who challenged me to the combat; and I was for some time driven to take myself for a Deist in the most ordinary sense of the word, till I had learned to know what a Christian truly was, and so arrived at opinions on religious matters in general which I shall notice at the conclusion of these volumes.

It is a curious circumstance respecting the books of Voltaire—the greatest writer upon the whole that France has produced, and undoubtedly the greatest name in the eighteenth century—that to this moment they are far less known in England than talked of; so much so, that, with the exception of a few educated circles, chiefly of the upper class, and exclusively among the men even in those, he has not only been hardly read at all, even by such as have talked of him with admiration, or loaded him with reproach, but the portions of his writings that have had the greatest effect on the world are the least known among readers the most popularly acquainted with him. The reasons of this remarkable ignorance respecting so great a neighbour—one of the movers of the world, and an especial admirer of England—are to be found, first, in the exclusive and timid spirit, under the guise of strength, which came up with the accession of George the Third; second, as a consequence of this spirit, a studious ignoring of the Frenchman in almost all places of education, the colleges and foundations in particular; third, the anti-Gallican spirit which followed and exasperated the prejudice against the French Revolution; and fourth, the very translation and popularity of two of his novels, the *Candide* and *Zadig*, which, though by no means among his finest productions, had yet enough wit and peculiarity to be accepted as sufficing specimens of him, even by his admirers. Unfortunately one of these, the *Candide*, contained some of his most licentious and even revolting writing. This enabled his enemies to adduce it as a sufficing specimen on their own side of the question; and the idea of him which they succeeded in imposing upon the English community in general was that of a mere irreligious scoffer, who was opposed to everything good and serious, and who did but mingle a little frivolous wit with an abundance of vexatious, hard-hearted, and disgusting effrontery.

There is, it is true, a version, purporting to be that of his whole works, by Smollett, Thomas Franklin, and others, which is understood to have been what is called a bookseller's job; but I never met with it except in an old catalogue; and I believe it was so dull and bad, that readers instinctively recoiled from it as an incredible representation of anything lively. The probability is, that Smollett only lent his name; and Franklin himself may have done as little, though the "translator of Sophocles" (as he styled himself) was well enough qualified to misrepresent any kind of genius.

Be this as it may, I have hardly ever met, even in literary circles, with persons who knew anything of Voltaire, except through the medium of these two novels, and of later school editions of his two histories of *Charles the Twelfth* and *Peter the Great:* books which teachers of all sorts in his own country have been gradually compelled to admit into their courses of reading by national pride and the imperative growth of opinion. Voltaire is one of the three great tragic writers of France, and excels in pathos; yet not one Englishman in a thousand knows a syllable of his tragedies, or would do anything but stare to hear of his pathos. Voltaire inducted his countrymen into a knowledge of English science and metaphysics, nay, even of English poetry; yet Englishmen have been told little about him in connection with them, except of his disagreements with Shakspeare. Voltaire created a fashion for English thinking, manner, and policy, and fell in love with the simplicity and truthfulness of their very Quakers; and yet, I will venture to say, the English knew far less of all this than they do of a licentious poem with which he degraded his better nature in burlesquing the history of Joan of Arc.

There are, it is admitted, two sides to the character of Voltaire; one licentious, merely scoffing, saddening, defective in sentiment, and therefore wanting the inner clue of the beautiful to guide him out of the labyrinth of scorn and perplexity; all owing, be it observed, to the errors which he found prevailing in his youth, and to the impossible demands which they made on his acquiescence; but the other side of his character is moral, cheerful, beneficent, prepared to encounter peril, nay, actually encountering it, in the only true Christian causes, those of toleration and charity, and raising that voice of demand for the advancement of reason and justice which is now growing into the whole voice of Europe. He was the only man perhaps that ever existed who represented in his single person the entire character, with one honourable exception (for he was never sanguinary), of the nation in which he was born; nay, of its whole history, past, present, and to come. He had the licentiousness of the old monarchy under which he was bred, the cosmopolite ardour of the Revolution, the science of the Consulate and the "savans," the unphilosophic love of glory of the Empire, the worldly wisdom (without pushing it into folly) of Louis Philippe, and the changeful humours, the firmness, the weakness, the flourishing declamation, the sympathy with the poor, the *bonhomie*, the unbounded hopes of the best actors in the extraordinary scenes acted before the eyes of Europe in these last ten years. As he himself could not construct as well as he could pull down, so neither do his countrymen, with all the goodness and greatness among them, appear to be less truly represented by him in that particular than in others; but in pulling down he had the same vague desire of the best that could set up; and when he was most thought to oppose Christianity itself, he only did it out of an impatient desire to see the law of love triumphant, and was only thought to be the adversary of its spirit, because his revilers knew nothing of it themselves.

Voltaire, in an essay written by himself in the English language, has said of Milton, in a passage which would do honour to our best writers, that when the poet saw the Adamo of Andreini at Florence, he "pierced through the absurdity of the plot to the hidden majesty of the subject." It may be said of himself, that he pierced through the conventional majesty of a great many subjects, to the hidden absurdity of the plot. He laid the axe to a heap of savage abuses; pulled the corner-stones out of dungeons and inquisitions; bowed and mocked the most tyrannical absurdities out of countenance; and raised one prodigious peal of laughter at superstition, from Naples to the Baltic. He was the first man who got the power of opinion and common sense openly recognized as a reigning authority; and who made the acknowledgment of it a point of wit and cunning, even with those who had hitherto thought they had the world to themselves.

An abridgment that I picked up of the *Philosophical Dictionary* (a translation) was for a long while my text-book, both for opinion and style. I was also a great admirer of

L'Ingénu, or the Sincere Huron, and of the *Essay on the Philosophy of History.* In the character of the *Sincere Huron* I thought I found a resemblance to my own, as most readers do in those of their favourites: and this piece of self-love helped me to discover as much good-heartedness in Voltaire as I discerned wit. *Candide,* I confess, I could not like. I enjoyed passages; but the laughter was not as good-humoured as usual ; there was a view of things in it which I never entertained then or afterwards, and into which the author had been led, rather in order to provoke Leibnitz, than because it was natural to him ; and, to crown my unwilling dislike, the book had a coarseness, apart from graceful and pleasurable ideas, which I have never been able to endure. There were passages in the abridgment of the *Philosophical Dictionary* which I always passed over; but the rest delighted me beyond measure. I can repeat things out of it now.

It must have been about the time of my first acquaintance with Voltaire, that I became member, for a short time, of a club of young men, who associated for the purpose of cultivating public speaking. With the exception of myself, I believe the whole of them were students at law ; but, to the best of my recollection, the subjects they discussed were as miscellaneous as if they were of no profession; though the case probably became otherwise, as their powers advanced. At all events I did not continue long with them, my entrance into the club having mainly originated in a wish to please my friend Barron Field, and public speaking not being one of my objects in life. It might have been much to my benefit if it had ; for it would in all probability have sooner rid me of my stammering, and delivered me from my fear of it among strangers and in the presence of assembled audiences ;—an anxiety, of which I have never been able to get rid, and which has deprived me of serious advantages. Far different was the case with another member of the club, Thomas Wilde, then an attorney in Castle Street, Falcon Square, afterwards Lord Chancellor, and a peer of the realm. Wilde had an impediment in his speech, which he inflexibly determined to mend : an underhung jaw and a grave and fixed expression of countenance seemed constantly to picture this resolution to me, as I beheld him. The world has seen how well he succeeded. Another member of the club, who had no such obstacle to surmount, but who might have been diverted from success by wider intellectual sympathies and the very pleasurableness of his nature, conquered those perils by an energy still more admirable, and is the present Lord Chief Baron Pollock. My friend Field himself, though suffering under a state of health which prevented his growing old, became a judge in the colonies ; and very likely I should have more honours of the club to refer to, had I known it longer. I can with truth aver, that however much I admired the energy of Wilde, and have more than admired that of the Chief Baron (of whose legal as well as general knowledge, the former, if I am not mistaken, was in the habit of taking friendly counsel to the last), my feelings toward them, as far as ambition was concerned, never degenerated into envy. My path was chosen before I knew them ; my entire inclinations were in it ; and I never in my life had any personal ambition whatsoever, but that of adding to the list of authors, and doing some good as a cosmopolite. Often, it is true, when I considered my family, have I wished that the case could have been otherwise, and the cosmopolitism still not ineffectual ; nor do I mean to cast the slightest reflection on the views, personal or otherwise, of the many admirable and estimable men who have adorned the bench in our courts of law. My reverence, indeed, for the character of the British judge, notwithstanding a few monstrous exceptions in former times, and one or two subsequently of a very minor kind, is of so deep a nature, that I can never disassociate the feeling from their persons, however social and familiar it may please the most amiable of them to be in private. I respected as well as loved my dear friend Talfourd more and more to the last ; entertain the like sentiments for others, of whose acquaintance, while living, it would not become me openly to boast ; and believe it would have been impossible for them to have done better or more nobly for the world as well as for themselves, than by obeying the inclination which took them where they ascended. Under these circumstances, it will be considered, I trust, neither indecorous nor invidious in me, if I close these legal reminiscences with relating, that having, when I was young, been solemnly rebuked one evening in company by a subsequently eminent person of my own age, now dead, and of no remarkable orthodoxy, for making what he pronounced to be an irreverent remark on a disputed point of Mosaic history, I said to a friend of mine on coming away, " Now mark me, B——, so and so (naming him) will go straight up the high road to preferment, while I shall as surely be found in the opposite direction."

Besides Voltaire and the *Connoisseur*, I was very fond at that time of Johnson's *Lives of the Poets*, and a great reader of Pope. My admiration of the *Rape of the Lock* led me to write a long mock-heroic poem, entitled the *Battle of the Bridal Ring*, the subject of which was a contest between two rival orders of spirits, on whom to bestow a lady in marriage. I venture to say, that it would have been well spoken of by the critics, and was not worth a penny. I recollect one couplet, which will serve to show how I mimicked the tone of my author. It was an apostrophe to Mantua,—

"Mantua, of great and small the long renown,
That now a Virgil giv'st, and now a gown."

Dryden, I read, too, but not with that relish for his nobler versification which I afterwards acquired. To dramatic reading, with all my love of the theatre, I have already mentioned my disinclination; yet, in the interval of my departure from school, and my getting out of my teens, I wrote two farces, a comedy, and a tragedy; and the plots of all (such as they were) were inventions. The hero of my tragedy was the *Earl of Surrey* (Howard, the poet), who was put to death by Henry the Eighth. I forget what the comedy was upon. The title of one of the farces was the *Beau Miser*, which may explain the nature of it. The other was called *A Hundred a Year*, and turned upon a hater of the country, who, upon having an annuity to that amount given him, on condition of his never going out of London, becomes a hater of the town. In the last scene, his annuity died a jovial death in a country tavern; the bestower entering the room just as my hero had got on a table, with a glass in his hand, to drink confusion to the metropolis. All these pieces were, I doubt not, as bad as need be. About thirty years ago, being sleepless one night with a fit of enthusiasm, in consequence of reading about the Spanish play of the *Cid*, in Lord Holland's *Life of Guillen de Castro*, I determined to write a tragedy on the same subject, which was accepted at Drury Lane. Perhaps the conduct of this piece was not without merit, the conclusion of each act throwing the interest into the succeeding one: but I had great doubts of all the rest of it; and on receiving it from Mr. Elliston to make an alteration in the third act, very judiciously proposed by him, I looked the whole of the play over again, and convinced myself it was unfit for the stage. I therefore withheld it. I had painted my hero too after the beau-ideal of a modern reformer, instead of the half-godlike, half-bigoted soldier that he was. I began afterwards to re-cast the play, but grew tired and gave it up. The *Cid* would make a delicious character for the stage, or in any work; not, indeed, as Corneille declaimed him, nor as inferior writers might adapt him to the reigning taste; but taken, I mean, as he was, with the noble impulses he received from nature, the drawbacks with which a bigoted age qualified them, and the social and open-hearted pleasantry (not the least evidence of his nobleness) which brings forth his heart, as it were, in flashes through the stern armour. But this would require a strong hand, and readers capable of grappling with it. In the mean-time, they should read of him in Mr. Southey's *Chronicle of the Cid* (an admirable summary from the old Spanish writers), and in the delightful verses at the end of it, translated from an old Spanish poem by Mr. Hookham Frere, with a trium-phant force and fidelity, that you feel to be true to the original at once.

About the period of my writing the above essays, circum-stances introduced me to the acquaintance of Mr. Bell, the proprietor of the *Weekly Messenger*. In his house in the Strand I used to hear of politics and dramatic criticism, and of the persons who wrote them. Mr. Bell had been well known as a bookseller, and a speculator in elegant typo-graphy. It is to him the public are indebted for the small edition of the Poets that preceded Cooke's, and which, with all my predilections for that work, was unquestionably supe-rior to it. Besides, it included Chaucer and Spenser. The omission of these in Cooke's edition was as unpoetical a sign of the times, as the present familiarity with their names is the reverse. It was thought a mark of good sense :—as if good sense, in matters of literature, did not consist as much in knowing what was poetical poetry, as brilliant in wit. Bell was upon the whole a remarkable person. He was a plain man, with a red face, and a nose exaggerated by intem-perance; and yet there was something not unpleasing in his countenance, especially when he spoke. He had sparkling black eyes, a good-natured smile, gentlemanly manners, and one of the most agreeable voices I ever heard. He had no acquirements, perhaps not even grammar; but his taste in putting forth a publication, and getting the best artists to adorn it, was new in those times, and may be admired in any; and the same taste was observable in his house. He knew nothing of poetry. He thought the *Della Cruscans* fine people, because they were known in the circles; and for Milton's *Paradise Lost* he had the same epithet as for Mrs. Crouch's face, or the phaeton of Major Topham: he thought it "pretty." Yet a certain liberal instinct, and turn for large dealing, made him include Chaucer and Spenser in his edition; he got Stothard to adorn the one, and Mortimer the other; and in the midst, I suspect, of very equivocal returns, issued a *British Theatre* with embellishments, and a similar edition of the plays of Shakspeare—the incorrectest publication, according to Mr. Chalmers, that ever issued from the press.

Unfortunately for Mr. Bell, he had as great a taste for neat wines and ankles as for pretty books; and, to crown his misfortunes, the Prince of Wales, to whom he was bookseller, once did him the honour to partake of an entertainment, or refreshment (I forget which, most probably the latter), at his house. He afterwards became a bankrupt. He was one of those men whose temperament and turn for enjoyment throw a sort of grace over whatsoever they do, standing them in stead of everything but prudence, and sometimes even supplying them with the consolations which imprudence has forfeited. After his bankruptcy he set up a newspaper, which became profitable to everybody but himself. He had become so used to lawyers and bailiffs, that the more his concerns flourished, the more his debts flourished with him. It seemed as if he would have been too happy without them; too exempt from the cares that beset the prudent. The first time I saw him he was standing in a chemist's shop, waiting till the road was clear for him to issue forth. He had a toothache, for which he held a handkerchief over his mouth; and, while he kept a sharp look-out with his bright eye, was alternately groaning in a most gentlemanly manner over his gums, and addressing some polite words to the shopman. I had not then been introduced to him, and did not know his person; so that the effect of his voice upon me was unequivocal. I liked him for it, and wished the bailiff at the devil.*

* An intelligent compositor (Mr. J. P. S. Bicknell), who has been a noter of curious passages in his time, informs me, that Bell was the first printer who confined the small letter *s* to its present shape, and rejected altogether the older form, ∫. He tells me, that this innovation, besides the handsomer form of the new letter, was "a boon to both master-printers and the compositor, inasmuch as it lessened the amount of capital necessary to be laid out under the old system, and saved to the workman no small portion of his valuable time and labour." My informant adds, as a curious instance of conservative tendency

In the office of the *Weekly Messenger*, I saw one day a person who looked the epitome of squalid authorship. He was wretchedly dressed and dirty; and the rain, as he took his hat off, came away from it as from a spout. This was a man of the name of Badini, who had been poet at the Opera, and was then editor of the *Messenger*. He was afterwards sent out of the country under the Alien Act, and became reader of the English papers to Bonaparte. His intimacy with some of the first families in the country, among whom he had been a teacher, is supposed to have been of use to the French Government. He wrote a good idiomatic English style, and was a man of abilities. I had never before seen a *poor author*, such as are described in books; and the spectacle of the reality startled me. Like most authors, however, who are at once very poor and very clever, his poverty was his own fault. When he received any money he disappeared, and was understood to spend it in alehouses. We heard that in Paris he kept his carriage. I have since met with authors of the same squalid description; but they were destitute of ability, and had no more right to profess literature as a trade than alchemy. It is from these that the common notions about the poverty of the tribe are taken. One of them, poor fellow! might have cut a figure in Smollett. He was a proper ideal author, in rusty black, out at elbows, thin and pale. He brought me an ode about an eagle; for which the publisher of a magazine, he said, had had "the inhumanity" to offer him half-a-crown. His necessity for money he did not deny; but his great anxiety was to know whether, as a poetical composition, his ode was not worth more. "Is that *poetry*, sir?" cried he: "that's what I want to know—is that *poetry?*" rising from his chair, and staring and trembling in all the agony of contested excellence.

My brother John, at the beginning of the year 1805, set

on small points, that Messrs. Rivington having got as far as three sheets, on a work of a late Bishop of Durham, in which the new plan was adopted, the Bishop sent back the sheets, in order to have the old letter restored, which compelled the booksellers to get a new supply from the type-foundry, the fount containing the venerable ∫ having been thrown away.

Mr. Bicknell also informs me, that when Bell set up his newspaper, the *Weekly Messenger* (which had a wood-cut at the top of it, of a newsman blowing his horn), he is said to have gone to a masquerade in the newsman's character, and distributed prospectuses to the company.

up a paper, called the *News*, and I went to live with him in Brydges Street, and write the theatricals in it.

[Between quitting the Bluecoat School, and the establishment of the *News*, Leigh Hunt had been for some time in the law office of his brother Stephen.]

It was the custom at that time for editors of papers to be intimate with actors and dramatists. They were often proprietors, as well as editors; and, in that case, it was not expected that they should escape the usual intercourse, or wish to do so. It was thought a feather in the cap of all parties; and with their feathers they tickled one another. The newspaper man had consequence in the green-room, and plenty of tickets for his friends; and he dined at amusing tables. The dramatist secured a good-natured critique in his journal, sometimes got it written himself, or, according to Mr. Reynolds, was even himself the author of it. The actor, if he was of any evidence, stood upon the same ground of reciprocity; and not to know a pretty actress would have been a want of the knowing in general. Upon new performers, and upon writers not yet introduced, a journalist was more impartial; and sometimes, where the proprietor was in one interest more than another, or for some personal reason grew offended with an actor, or set of actors, a criticism would occasionally be hostile, and even severe. An editor, too, would now and then suggest to his employer the policy of exercising a freer authority, and obtain influence enough with him to show symptoms of it. I believe Bell's editor, who was more clever, was also more impartial than most critics; though the publisher of the *British Theatre*, and patron of the *Della Cruscans*, must have been hampered with literary intimacies. The best chance for an editor, who wished to have anything like an opinion of his own, was the appearance of a rival newspaper with a strong theatrical connection. Influence was here threatened with diminution. It was to be held up on other grounds; and the critic was permitted to find out that a bad play was not good, or an actress's petticoat of the lawful dimensions.

Puffing and plenty of tickets were, however, the system of the day. It was an interchange of amenities over the dinner-table; a flattery of power on the one side, and puns on the other; and what the public took for a criticism on a play was a draft upon the box-office, or reminiscences of last Thursday's salmon and lobster-sauce. The custom was, to write as short and as favourable a paragraph on the new piece as could be; to say that Bannister was "excellent" and Mrs. Jordan "charming;" to notice the "crowded house" or invent it, if necessary; and to conclude by observing that "the whole went off with *éclat*." For the rest, it was a critical religion in those times to admire Mr. Kemble: and at the period in question Master Betty had appeared, and been hugged to the hearts of the town as the young Roscius.

We saw that independence in theatrical criticism would be a great novelty. We announced it, and nobody believed us; we stuck to it, and the town believed everything we said. The proprietors of the *News*, of whom I knew so little that I cannot recollect with certainty any one of them, very handsomely left me to myself. My retired and scholastic habits kept me so; and the pride of success confirmed my independence with regard to others. I was then in my twentieth year, an early age at that time for a writer. The usual exaggeration of report made me younger than I was: and after being a "young Roscius" political, I was now looked upon as one critical. To know an actor personally appeared to me a vice not to be thought of; and I would as lief have taken poison as accepted a ticket from the theatres.

Good God! To think of the grand opinion I had of myself in those days, and what little reason I had for it! Not to accept the tickets was very proper, considering that I bestowed more blame than praise. There was also more good-nature than I supposed in not allowing myself to know any actors; but the vanity of my position had greater weight with me than anything else, and I must have proved it to discerning eyes by the small quantity of information I brought to my task, and the ostentation with which I produced it. I knew almost as little of the drama as the young Roscius himself. Luckily, I had the advantage of him in knowing how unfit *he* was for his office; and, probably, he thought me as much so, though he could not have argued upon it; for I was in the minority respecting his merits, and the balance was then trembling on the beam; the *News*, I believe, hastened the settlement of the question. I wish with all my heart we had let him alone, and he had got a little more money. However, he obtained enough to create him a provision for life. His position, which appeared so brilliant at first, had a remarkable cruelty in it. Most men begin life with struggles, and have their vanity sufficiently knocked

about the head and shoulders to make their kinder fortunes
the more welcome. Mr. Betty had his sugar first, and his
physic afterwards. He began life with a double childhood,
with a new and extraordinary felicity added to the natural
enjoyments of his age; and he lived to see it speedily come
to nothing, and to be taken for an ordinary person. I am
told that he acquiesces in his fate, and agrees that the town
were mistaken. If so, he is no ordinary person still, and has
as much right to our respect for his good sense, as he is declared on all hands to deserve it for his amiableness. I have
an anecdote of him to both purposes, which exhibits him in
a very agreeable light. Hazlitt happened to be at a party
where Mr. Betty was present; and in coming away, when
they were all putting on their great-coats, the critic thought
fit to compliment the dethroned favourite of the town, by
telling him that he recollected him in old times, and had
been "much pleased with him." Betty looked at his me-
morialist, as much as to say, "You don't tell me so!" and
then starting into a tragical attitude, exclaimed, "Oh, memory!
memory!"

I was right about Master Betty, and I am sorry for it; though
the town was in fault, not he. I think I was right also about
Kemble; but I have no regret upon that score. He flourished
long enough after my attack on his majestic dryness and
deliberate nothings; and Kean would have taken the public
by storm, whether they had been prepared for him or not:

"One touch of nature makes the whole world kin."

Kemble faded before him, like a tragedy ghost. I never
denied the merits which that actor possessed. He had the
look of a Roman; made a very good ideal, though not a very
real Coriolanus, for his pride was not sufficiently blunt and
unaffected: and in parts that suited his natural deficiency,
such as Penruddock and the Abbé de l'Epée, would have
been altogether admirable and interesting, if you could have
forgotten that their sensibility, in his hands, was not so much
repressed, as wanting. He was no more to be compared to
his sister, than stone is to flesh and blood. There was much
of the pedagogue in him. He made a fuss about trifles; was
inflexible on a pedantic reading: in short, was rather a
teacher of elocution than an actor; and not a good teacher,
on that account. There was a merit in his idealism, as far as
it went. He had, at least, faith in something classical and

scholastic, and he made the town partake of it; but it was all
on the surface—a hollow trophy : and I am persuaded, that
he had no idea in his head but of a stage Roman, and the dignity he added to his profession.

But if I was right about Kemble, whose admirers I plagued
enough, I was not equally so about the living dramatists,
whom I plagued more. I laid all the deficiencies of the
modern drama to their account, and treated them like a
parcel of mischievous boys, of whom I was the schoolmaster
and whipper-in. I forgot that it was I who was the boy,
and that they knew twenty times more of the world than I
did. Not that I mean to say their comedies were excellent,
or that my commonplaces about the superior merits of Con-
greve and Sheridan were not well founded; but there was
more talent in their "five-act farce" than I supposed; and I
mistook, in a great measure, the defect of the age—its dearth
of dramatic character—for that of the writers who were to
draw upon it. It is true, a great wit, by a laborious process,
and the help of his acquirements, might extract a play or
two from it, as was Sheridan's own case; but there was a
great deal of imitation even in Sheridan, and he was fain to
help himself to a little originality out of the characters of his
less formalized countrymen, his own included.

It is remarkable, that the three most amusing dramatists
of the last age, Sheridan, Goldsmith, and O'Keefe, were all
Irishmen, and all had characters of their own. Sheridan,
after all, was Swift's Sheridan come to life again in the person
of his grandson, with the oratory of Thomas Sheridan, the
father, superadded and brought to bear. Goldsmith, at a
disadvantage in his breeding, but full of address with his pen,
drew upon his own absurdities and mistakes, and filled his
dramas with ludicrous perplexity. O'Keefe was all for whim
and impulse, but not without a good deal of conscience; and,
accordingly, in his plays we have a sort of young and pastoral
taste of life in the very midst of its sophistications. Animal
spirits, quips and cranks, credulity, and good intention, are
triumphant throughout and make a delicious mixture. It is
a great credit to O'Keefe, that he ran sometimes close upon the
borders of the sentimental drama, and did it not only with im-
punity but advantage; but sprightliness and sincerity enable
a man to do everything with advantage.

It was a pity that as much could not be said of Mr. Colman, who, after taking more licence in his writings than

anybody, became a licenser *ex officio*, and seemed inclined to license nothing but cant. When this writer got into the sentimental, he made a sad business of it, for he had no faith in sentiment. He mouthed and overdid it, as a man does when he is telling a lie. At a farce he was admirable : and he remained so to the last, whether writing or licensing.

Morton seemed to take a colour from the writers all round him, especially from O'Keefe and the sentimentalists. His sentiment was more in earnest than Colman's, yet, somehow, not happy either. There was a gloom in it, and a smack of the Old Bailey. It was best when he put it in a shape of humour, as in the paternal and inextinguishable *tailorism* of Old Rapid, in a *Cure for the Heart-Ache*. Young Rapid, who complains that his father " sleeps so slow," is also a pleasant fellow, and worthy of O'Keefe. He is one of the numerous crop that sprang up from *Wild Oats*, but not in so natural a soil.

The character of the modern drama at that time was singularly commercial : nothing but gentlemen in distress, and hard landlords, and generous interferers, and fathers who got a great deal of money, and sons who spent it. I remember one play in particular, in which the whole wit ran upon prices, bonds, and post-obits. You might know what the pit thought of their pound-notes by the ostentatious indifference with which the heroes of the pieces gave them away, and the admiration and pretended approval with which the spectators observed it. To make a present of a hundred pounds was as if a man had uprooted and given away an Egyptian pyramid.

Mr. Reynolds was not behindhand with his brother dramatists in drawing upon the taste of the day for gains and distresses. It appears by his Memoirs that he had too much reason for so doing. He was, perhaps, the least ambitious, and the least vain (whatever charges to the contrary his animal spirits might have brought on him) of all the writers of that period. In complexional vivacity he certainly did not yield to any of them ; his comedies, if they were fugitive, were genuine representations of fugitive manners, and went merrily to their death ; and there is one of them, the *Dramatist*, founded upon something more lasting, which promises to remain in the collections, and deserves it : which is not a little to say of any writer. I never wish for a heartier laugh than I have enjoyed, since I grew wiser, not only in seeing, but in reading the vagaries of his dramatic hero, and his mystifications of "Old Scratch." When I read the good-humoured Memoirs of this writer the other day, I felt quite ashamed of the ignorant and boyish way in which I used to sit in judgment upon his faults, without being aware of what was good in him; and my repentance was increased by the very proper manner in which he speaks of his critics, neither denying the truth of their charges in letter, nor admitting them altogether in spirit; in fact, showing that he knew very well what he was about, and that they, whatsoever they fancied to the contrary, did not.

Mr. Reynolds, agreeably to his sense and good-humour, never said a word to his critics at the time. Mr. Thomas Dibdin, not quite so wise, wrote me a letter, which Incledon, I am told, remonstrated with him for sending, saying, it would do him no good with the "d——d boy." And he was right. I published it, with an answer, and only thought that I made dramatists "come bow to me." Mr. Colman attacked me in a prologue, which, by a curious chance, Fawcett spoke right in my teeth, the box I sat in happening to be directly opposite him. I laughed at the prologue; and only looked upon Mr. Colman as a great monkey pelting me with nuts, which I ate. Attacks of this kind were little calculated to obtain their end with a youth who persuaded himself that he wrote for nothing but the public good; who mistook the impression which anybody of moderate talents can make with a newspaper, for the result of something peculiarly his own; and who had just enough scholarship to despise the want of it in others. I do not pretend to think that the criticisms in the *News* had no merit at all. They showed an acquaintance with the style of Voltaire, Johnson, and others; were not unagreeably sprinkled with quotation; and, above all, were written with more care and attention than was customary with newspapers at that time. The pains I took to round a period with nothing in it, or to invent a simile that should appear offhand, would have done honour to better stuff.

A portion of these criticisms subsequently formed the appendix of an original volume on the same subject, entitled *Critical Essays on the Performers of the London Theatres* [1807]. I have the book now before me: and if I thought it had a chance of survival I should regret and qualify a good deal of uninformed judgment in it respecting the art of acting, which, with much inconsistent recommendation to the contrary, it too often confounded with a literal, instead of a liberal imitation of nature. I particularly erred with respect to comedians like Munden, whose superabundance of humour and expression I confounded with farce and buffoonery. Charles Lamb taught me better.

There was a good deal of truth, however, mixed up with these mistakes. One of the things on which I was always harping was Kemble's vicious pronunciation. Kemble had a smattering of learning, and a great deal of obstinacy. He was a reader of old books; and having discovered that pronunciation had not always been what it was, and that in one or two instances the older was metrically better than the new (as in the case of the word *aches*, which was originally a dissyllable—*aitches*), he took upon him to reform it in a variety of cases, where propriety was as much against him as custom. Thus the vowel *e* in the word " merchant," in defiance of its Latin etymology, he insisted upon pronouncing according to its French derivative, *marchant*. " Innocent " he called *innocint ;* " conscience " (in defiance even of his friend Chaucer), *conshince ;* " virtue," in proper slip-slop, *varchue ;* " fierce," *furse ;* " beard," *bird ;* " thy," *thĕ* (because we generally call " my," *mĕ*); and " odious," " hideous," and " perfidious," became *ojus, hijjus,* and *perfijjus.*

Nor were these all. The following banter, in the shape of an imaginary bit of conversation between an officer and his friend, was, literally, no caricature :—

A. Ha! captain! how dost ? (¹) *The* appearance would be much improved by a little more attention to *the* (²) *bird.*
B. Why, so I think : there's no (³) *sentimint* in a *bird.* But then it serves to distinguish a soldier, and there is no doubt much military (⁴) *varchue* in looking (⁵) *furful.*
A. But the girls, Jack, the girls ! Why, *the* mouth is enough to banish kissing from the (⁶) *airth* (⁷) *etairnally.*
B. In (⁸) *maircy,* no more of that ! Zounds, but the shopkeepers and the (⁹) *marchants* will get the better of us with the dear souls ! However, as it is now against military law to have a tender countenance, and as some *birds,* I thank heaven, are of a tolerable (¹⁰) *qual-ity,* I must make a *varchue* of necessity ; and as I can't look soft for the love of my girl, I must e'en look (¹¹) *hijjus* for the love of my country.

(¹) thy; (²) beard; (³) sentiment; (⁴) virtue; (⁵) fearful; (⁶) earth; (⁷) eternally; (⁸) mercy; (⁹) merchants; (¹⁰) quality (with the *a* as in *universality*); (¹¹) hideous.

CHAPTER VIII.

SUFFERING AND REFLECTION.

But the gay and confident spirit in which I began this critical career received a check, of which none of my friends suspected the anguish, and very few were told. I fell into a melancholy state of mind, produced by ill-health.

I thought it was owing to living too well; and as I had great faith in temperance, I went to the reverse extreme; not considering that temperance implies moderation in self-denial as well as in self-indulgence. The consequence was a nervous condition, amounting to hypochondria, which lasted me several months. I experienced it twice afterwards, each time more painfully than before, and for a much longer period; but I have never had it since; and I am of opinion that I need not have had it at all had I gone at once to a physician, and not repeated the mistake of being over abstinent.

I mention the whole circumstance for the benefit of others. The first attack came on me with palpitations of the heart. These I got rid of by horseback. I forget what symptoms attended the approach of the second. The third was produced by sitting out of doors too early in the spring. I attempted to outstarve them all, but egregiously failed. In one instance, I took wholly to a vegetable diet, which made me so weak and giddy, that I was forced to catch hold of rails in the streets to hinder myself from falling. In another, I confined myself for some weeks to a milk diet, which did nothing but jaundice my complexion. In the third, I took a modicum of meat, one glass of wine, no milk except in tea, and no vegetables at all; but though I did not suffer quite so much mental distress from this regimen as from the milk, I suffered more than from the vegetables, and for a much longer period than with either. To be sure, I continued it longer; and, perhaps, it gave me greater powers of endurance; but for upwards of four years, without intermission, and above six years in all, I underwent a burden of wretchedness, which I afterwards felt convinced I need not have endured for as many weeks, perhaps not as many days, had I not absurdly taken to the extreme I spoke of in the first instance, and then as absurdly persisted in seeking no advice, partly from fear of hearing worse things foretold me, and partly from a hope of wearing out the calamity by patience. At no time did my friends guess to what amount I suffered. They saw that my health was bad enough, and they condoled with me accordingly; but cheerful habits enabled me to retain an air of cheerfulness, except when I was alone; and I never spoke of it but once, which was to my friend Mitchell, whom I guessed to have undergone something of the kind.

And what was it that I suffered? and on what account? On no account. On none whatsoever, except my ridiculous super-abstinence, and my equally ridiculous avoidance of speaking about it. The very fact of having no cause whatsoever, was the thing that most frightened me. I thought that if I had but a cause, the cause might have been removed or palliated; but to be haunted by a ghost which was not even ghostly, which was something I never saw, or could even imagine, this, I thought, was the most terrible thing that could befall me. I could see no end to the persecutions of an enemy, who was neither visible nor even existing!

Causes for suffering, however, came. Not, indeed, the worst, for I was neither culpable nor superstitious. I had wronged nobody; and I now felt the inestimable benefit of having had cheerful opinions given me in religion. But I plagued myself with things which are the pastimes of better states of health, and the pursuits of philosophers. I mooted with myself every point of metaphysics that could get into a head into which they had never been put. I made a cause of causes for anxiety, by inquiring into causation, and outdid the Vicar of Wakefield's Moses, in being my own Sanchoniathan and Berosus on the subject of the cosmogony! I jest about it now; but oh! what pain was it to me then! and what pangs of biliary will and impossibility I underwent in the endeavour to solve these riddles of the universe! I felt, long before I knew Mr. Wordsworth's poetry,—

> "the burthen and the mystery
> Of all this unintelligible world."

I reverence the mystery still, but I no longer feel the burden, because for these five-and-thirty years I have known how to adjust my shoulders to it by taking care of my health. I should rather say because healthy shoulders have no such burden to carry. The elements of existence, like the air which we breathe, and which would otherwise crush us, are so nicely proportioned to one another within and around them, that we are unconsciously sustained by them, not thoughtfully oppressed.

One great benefit, however, resulted to me from this suffering. It gave me an amount of reflection, such as in all probability I never should have had without it; and if readers have derived any good from the graver portion of my writings, I attribute it to this experience of evil. It taught me patience; it taught me charity (however imperfectly I may have exercised either); it taught me charity even towards myself; it taught me the worth of little pleasures, as well as the dignity and utility of great pains ; it taught me that evil itself contained good ; nay, it taught me to doubt whether any such thing as evil, considered in itself, existed ; whether things altogether, as far as our planet knows them, could have been so good without it ; whether the desire, nevertheless, which nature has implanted in us for its destruction, be not the signal and the means to that end; and whether its destruction, finally, will not prove its existence, in the meantime, to have been necessary to the very bliss that supersedes it.

I have been thus circumstantial respecting this illness, or series of illnesses, in the hope that such readers as have not had experience or reflection enough of their own to dispense with the lesson, may draw the following conclusions from sufferings of all kinds, if they happen to need it :—

First,—That however any suffering may seem to be purely mental, body alone may occasion it; which was undoubtedly the case in my instance.

Second,—That as human beings do not originate their own bodies or minds, and as yet very imperfectly know how to manage them, they have a right to all the aid or comfort they can procure, under any sufferings whatsoever.

Third,—That whether it be the mind or body that is ailing, or both, they may save themselves a world of perplexity and of illness by going at once to a physician.

Fourth,—That till they do so, or in case they are unable to do it, a recourse to the first principles of health is their only wise proceeding; by which principles I understand air and exercise, bathing, amusements, and whatsoever else tends to enliven and purify the blood.

Fifth,—That the blackest day may have a bright morrow; for my last and worst illness suddenly left me, probably in consequence of the removal, though unconsciously, of some internal obstruction; and it is now for the long period above mentioned that I have not had the slightest return of it, though I have had many anxieties to endure, and a great deal of sickness.

Sixth,—That the far greater portion of a life thus tried may nevertheless be remarkable for cheerfulness ; which has been the case with my own.

Seventh,—That the value of cheerful opinions is inestimable; that they will retain a sort of heaven round a man, when everything else might fail him; and that, consequently, they ought to be religiously inculcated in children.

Eighth and last,—That evil itself has its bright, or at any rate its redeeming, side; probably is but the fugitive requisite of some everlasting good; and assuredly, in the meantime, and in a thousand obvious instances, is the admonisher, the producer, the increaser, nay, the very adorner and splendid investitor of good ; it is the pain that prevents a worse, the storm that diffuses health, the plague that enlarges cities, the fatigue that sweetens sleep, the discord that enriches harmonies, the calamity that tests affections, the victory and the crown of patience, the enrapturer of the embraces of joy.

I was reminded of the circumstance which gave rise to these reflections, by the mention of the friend of whom I spoke last, and another brother of whom I went to see during my first illness.   He was a young and amiable artist, residing at Gainsborough in Lincolnshire. He had no conception of what I suffered ; and one of his modes of entertaining me was his taking me to a friend of his, a surgeon, to see his anatomical preparations, and delight my hypochondriacal eyes with grinnings of skulls and delicacies of injected hearts. I have no more horror now, on reflection, of those frameworks and machineries of the beautiful body in which we live, than I have of the jacks and wires of a harpsichord. The first sight revolts us simply because life dislikes death, and the human being is jarred out of a sense of its integrity by these bits and scraps of the material portion of it. But I know it is no more *me*, than it is the feeling which revolts from it, or than the harpsichord itself is the music that Haydn or Beethoven put into it.   Indeed, I did not think otherwise at the time, with the healthier part of me ; nor did this healthier part ever forsake me. I always attributed what I felt to bodily ailment, and talked as reasonably, and for the most part as cheerfully, with my friends as usual, nor did I ever once gainsay the cheerfulness and hopefulness of my opinions. But I could not look comfortably on the bones and the skulls nevertheless, though I made a point of sustaining the exhibition. I bore anything that came, in order that I might be overborne by nothing; and I found this practice of patience very useful. I also took part in every diversion, and went into as many different places and new scenes as possible; which reminds me that I once rode with my Lincolnshire friend from Gainsborough to Doncaster, and that he and I, sick and serious as I was, or rather because I was sick and serious (for such extremes meet, and melancholy has a good-natured sister in mirth), made, in the course of our journey, a hundred and fifty rhymes on the word "philosopher." We stopped at that number, only because we had come to our journey's end. I shall not apologize to the reader for mentioning this boy's play, because I take every reader who feels an interest in this book to be a bit of a philosopher himself, and therefore prepared to know that boy's play and man's play are much oftener identical than people suppose, especially when the heart has need of the pastime. I need not remind him of the sage, who while playing with a parcel of schoolboys suddenly stopped at the approach of a solemn personage, and said, "We must leave off, boys, at present, for here's a fool coming."

The number of rhymes might be a little more surprising; but the wonder will cease when the reader considers that they must have been doggerel, and that there is no end to the forms in which rhymes can set off from new given points; as, *go* so far, *throw* so far; *nose* of her, *beaux* of her; *toss* of her, *cross* of her, &c.

Spirits of Swift and Butler! come to my aid, if any chance reader, not of our right reading fashion, happen to light upon this passage, and be inclined to throw down the book. Come to *his* aid; for he does not know what he is going to do;—how many illustrious jingles he is about to vituperate!

The surgeon I speak of was good enough one day to take me with him round the country, to visit his patients. I was startled in a respectable farmhouse to hear language openly talked in a mixed party of males and females, of a kind that seldom courts publicity, and that would have struck with astonishment an eulogizer of pastoral innocence. Yet nobody seemed surprised at it; nor did it bring a blush on the cheek of a very nice, modest-looking girl. She only smiled, and seemed to think it was the man's way. Probably it was nothing more than the language which was spoken in the first circles in times of old, and which thus survived among the peasantry, just as we find them retaining words that have grown obsolete in cities. The guilt and innocence of manners very much depend on conventional agreement; that is to say, on what is thought of them with respect to practice, and to the harm or otherwise which they are actually found to produce. The very dress which would be shameless in one age or country, is respectable in another; but in neither case is it a moral test. When the shame goes in one respect, it by no means comes in another; otherwise all Turks would be saints, and all Europeans sinners. The minds of the people in the Lincolnshire farmhouse were "naked and not ashamed." It must be owned, however, that there was an amount of consciousness about them, which savoured more of a pagan than a paradisaical state of innocence.

One of this gentleman's patients was very amusing. He was a pompous old gentleman-farmer, cultivating his gout on two chairs, and laying down the law on the state of the nation. Lord Eldon he called "my Lord *Eljin*" (Elgin); and he showed us what an ignorant man this chancellor was, and what a dreadful thing such want of knowledge was for the country. The proof of his own fitness for setting things right was thus given by his making three mistakes in one word. He took Lord Eldon for Lord Elgin; he took Lord Elgin for the chancellor; and he pronounced his lordship's name with a soft *g* instead of a hard one. His medical friend was of course not bound to cure his spelling as well as his gout; so we left him in the full-blown satisfaction of having struck awe on the Londoner.

Dr. Young talks of—

"That hideous sight—a naked human heart:"

a line not fit to have been written by a human being. The sight of the physical heart, it must be owned, was trying enough to sick eyes; that of the Doctor's moral heart, according to himself, would have been far worse. I don't believe it. I don't believe he had a right thus to calumniate it, much less that of his neighbour, and of the whole human race.

I saw a worse sight than the heart, in a journey which I took into a neighbouring country. It was an infant, all over sores, and cased in steel—the result of the irregularities of its father; and I confess that I would rather have seen the heart of the very father of that child, than I would the child himself. I am sure it must have bled at the sight. I am sure there would have been a feeling of some sort to vindicate nature, granting that up to that moment the man had been a fool or even a scoundrel. Sullenness itself would have been some amends; some sort of confession and regret. As to the poor child, let us trust that the horrible spectacle prevented more such; that he was a martyr, dying soon, and going to some heaven where little souls are gathered into comfort. I never beheld such a sight, before or since, except in one of the pictures of Hogarth, in his *Rake's Progress;* and I sadden this page with the recollection, for the same reason that induced him to paint it.

I have mentioned that I got rid of a palpitation of the heart, which accompanied my first visitation of hypochondria, by riding on horseback. The palpitation was so strong and incessant, that I was forced, for some nights, to sleep in a reclining posture, and I expected sudden death; but when I began the horseback, I soon found that the more I rode, and (I used to think) the harder I rode, the less the palpitation became. Galloping one day up a sloping piece of ground, the horse suddenly came to a stand, by a chalk-pit, and I was agreeably surprised to find myself not only unprecipitated over his head (for though a decent, I was not a skilful rider), but in a state of singular calmness and self-possession—a right proper masculine state of nerves. I might have discovered, as I did afterwards, what it was that so calmed and strengthened me. I was of a temperament of body in which the pores were not easily opened; and the freer they were kept, the better I was; but it took me a long time to discover that in order to be put into a state of vigour as well as composure, I required either vigorous exercise or some strong moral excitement connected with the sense of action. Unfortunately, I had a tendency to extremes in self-treatment. At one time I thought to cure myself by cold-water baths, in which I persevered through a winter season; and, subsequently, I hurt myself by hot baths. Late hours at night were not mended by lying in bed of a morning; nor incessant reading and writing, by weeks in which I did little but stroll and visit. It is true, I can hardly be said to have ever been without a book; for if not in my hand, it was at my side, or in my pocket; but what I needed was ordinary, regular habits, accompanied with a more than ordinary amount of exercise. I was never either so happy or so tranquil, as

when I was in a state the most active. I could very well
understand the character of an unknown individual, described
in the prose works of Ben Jonson, who would sit writing day
and night till he fainted, and then so entirely give himself up
to diversion, that people despaired of getting him to work
again. But I sympathized still more with one of the Rucellai
family, who was so devoted to a sedentary life, that he could
not endure the thought of being taken from it; till being
forced, in a manner, to accept a diplomatic mission, he became
as vehement for a life of action as he had before been absorbed
in indolence, and was never satisfied till he was driving everything before him, and spinning, with his chariot-wheels, from
one court to another. If I had not a reverence, indeed, for
whatever has taken place in the ordinance of things, great
and small, I should often have fancied that some such business
of diplomacy would have been my proper vocation; for I
delight in imagining conferences upon points that are to be
carried, or scenes in which thrones are looked upon, and
national compliments are to be conveyed; and I am sure
that a great deal of action would have kept me in the finest
health. Whatever dries up the surface of my body, inti-
midates me; but when the reverse has been effected by anything except the warm bath, fear has forsaken me, and my
spirit has felt as broad and healthy as my shoulders.

I did not discover this particular cause of healthy sensation
till long after my recovery. I attributed it entirely to exercise in general; but by exercise, at all events (and I mention
the whole circumstance for the benefit of the nervous), health
was restored to me; and I maintained it as long as I persevered in the means.

Not long after convalescence, the good that had been done
me was put further to the test. Some friends, among whom
were two of my brothers and myself, had a day's boating
up the Thames. We were very merry and jovial, and not
prepared to think any obstacle, in the way of our satisfaction,
possible. On a sudden we perceive a line stretched across
the river by some fishermen. We call out to them to lower,
or take it away. They say they will not. One of us holds
up a knife, and proclaims his intention to cut it. The fishermen defy the knife. Forward goes the knife with the boat,
and cuts the line in the most beautiful manner conceivable.
The two halves of the line rushed asunder.

"Off," cry the fishermen to one another, "and duck 'em."

They push out their boat. Their wives (I forget whence they issued) appear on the bank, echoing the cry of " Duck 'em!" We halt on our oars, and are come up with, the fishermen looking as savage as wild islanders, and swearing might and main. My brother and myself, not to let us all be run down (for the fishermen's boat was much larger than ours, and we had ladies with us, who were terrified) told the enemy we would come among them. We did so, going from our boat into theirs.

The determination to duck us now became manifest enough, and the fishermen's wives (cruel with their husbands' lost fishing) seemed equally determined not to let the intention remit. They screamed and yelled like so many furies. The fishermen seized my brother John, whom they took for the cutter of the line, and would have instantly effected their purpose, had he not been clasped round the waist by my brother Robert, who kept him tight down in a corner of the hold. A violent struggle ensued, during which a ruffianly fellow aiming a blow at my brother John's face, whose arms were pinioned, I had the good luck to intercept it. Meanwhile the wives of the boaters were screaming as well as the wives of the fishermen; and it was asked our antagonists, whether it was befitting brave men to frighten women out of their senses.

The fury seemed to relax a little at this. The word " payment" was mentioned, which seemed to relax it more; but it was still divided between threat and demand, when, in the midst of a fresh outbreak of the first resolution, beautiful evidence was furnished of the magical effects of the word "law."

Luckily for our friends and ourselves (for the enemy had the advantage of us, both in strength and numbers), the owner of the boat, it seems, had lately been worsted in some action of trespass, probably of the very nature of what they had been doing with their line. I was then living with my brother Stephen, who was in the law. I happened to be dressed in black; and I had gathered from some words which fell from them during their rage, that what they had been about with their fishing-net was in all probability illegal. I assumed it to be so. I mentioned the dreaded word "law;" my black coat corroborated its impression; and, to our equal relief and surprise, we found them on the sudden converting their rage and extortion into an assumption that we meant to settle with their master, and quietly permitting us to get back to our friends.

Throughout this little rough adventure, which at one time threatened very distressing, if not serious consequences, I was glad to find that I underwent no apprehensions but such as became me. The pain and horror that used to be given me at sight of human antagonism never entered my head. I felt nothing but a flow of brotherhood and determination, and returned in fine breathing condition to the oar. I subsequently found that all corporate occasions of excitement affected me in the same healthy manner. The mere fact of being in a crowd when their feelings were strongly moved, to whatever purpose, roused all that was strong in me; and from the alacrity, and even comfort and joy, into which I was warmed by the thought of resistance to whatever wrong might demand it, I learned plainly enough what a formidable thing a human being might become if he took wrong for right, and what reverence was due to the training and just treatment of the myriads that compose a nation.

I was now again in a state of perfect comfort and enjoyment, the gayer for the cloud which had gone, though occasionally looking back on it with gravity, and prepared, alas! or rather preparing myself by degrees, to undergo it again in the course of a few years by relapsing into a sedentary life. Suffer as I might have done, I had not, it seems, suffered enough. However, the time was very delightful while it lasted. I thoroughly enjoyed my books, my walks, my companions, my verses; and I had never ceased to be ready to fall in love with the first tender-hearted damsel that should encourage me. Now it was a fair charmer, and now a brunette; now a girl who sang, or a girl who danced; now one that was merry, or was melancholy, or seemed to care for nothing, or for everything, or was a good friend, or good sister, or good daughter. With this last, who completed her conquest by reading verses better than I had ever yet heard, I ultimately became wedded for life; and she reads verses better than ever to this day, especially some that shall be nameless.*

[* Written nearly ten years before the present edition was published: the reader had gone before the author revised his own writing, which he left unaltered.]

CHAPTER IX.

THE "EXAMINER."

At the beginning of the year 1808, my brother John and myself set up the weekly paper of the *Examiner* in joint partnership. It was named after the *Examiner* of Swift and his brother Tories. I did not think of their politics. I thought only of their wit and fine writing, which, in my youthful confidence, I proposed to myself to emulate; and I could find no previous political journal equally qualified to be its godfather. Even Addison had called his opposition paper the *Whig Examiner*.

Some years afterwards I had an editorial successor, Mr. Fonblanque, who had all the wit for which I toiled, without making any pretensions to it. He was, indeed, the genuine successor, not of me, but of the Swifts and Addisons themselves; profuse of wit even beyond them, and superior in political knowledge. Yet, if I laboured hard for what was so easy to Mr. Fonblanque, I will not pretend to think that I did not sometimes find it; and the study of Addison and Steele, of Goldsmith and Voltaire, enabled me, when I was pleased with my subject, to give it the appearance of ease. At other times, especially on serious occasions, I too often got into a declamatory vein, full of what I thought fine turns and Johnsonian antitheses. The new office of editor conspired with my success as a critic to turn my head. I wrote, though anonymously, in the first person, as if, in addition to my theatrical pretensions, I had suddenly become an oracle in politics; the words philosophy, poetry, criticism, statesmanship, nay, even ethics and theology, all took a final tone in my lips. When I remember the virtue as well as knowledge which I demanded from everybody whom I had occasion to notice, and how much charity my own juvenile errors ought to have considered themselves in need of (however they might have been warranted by conventional allowance), I will not say I was a hypocrite in the odious sense of the word, for it was all done out of a spirit of foppery and "fine writing," and I never affected any formal virtues in private; —but when I consider all the nonsense and extravagance of those assumptions, all the harm they must have done me in discerning eyes, and all the reasonable amount of resentment which it was preparing for me with adversaries, I blush to think what a simpleton I was, and how much of the consequences I deserved. It is out of no "ostentation of candour" that I make this confession. It is extremely painful to me.

Suffering gradually worked me out of a good deal of this kind of egotism. I hope that even the present most involuntarily egotistical book affords evidence that I am pretty well rid of it; and I must add, in my behalf, that, in every other respect, never, at that time or at any after time, was I otherwise than an honest man. I overrated my claims to public attention; but I set out perhaps with as good an editorial amount of qualification as most writers no older. I was fairly grounded in English history; I had carefully read De Lolme and Blackstone; I had no mercenary views whatsoever, though I was a proprietor of the journal; and all the levity of my animal spirits, and the foppery of the graver part of my pretensions, had not destroyed that spirit of martyrdom which had been inculcated in me from the cradle. I denied myself political as well as theatrical acquaintances; I was the reverse of a speculator upon patronage or employment; and I was prepared, with my excellent brother, to suffer manfully, should the time for suffering arrive.

The spirit of the criticism on the theatres continued the same as it had been in the *News*. In politics, from old family associations, I soon got interested as a man, though I never could love them as a writer. It was against the grain that I was encouraged to begin them; and against the grain I ever afterwards sat down to write, except when the subject was of a very general description, and I could introduce philosophy and the belles lettres.

The main objects of the *Examiner* newspaper were to assist in producing Reform in Parliament, liberality of opinion in general (especially freedom from superstition), and a fusion of literary taste into all subjects whatsoever. It began with being of no party; but Reform soon gave it one. It disclaimed all knowledge of statistics; and the rest of its politics were rather a sentiment, and a matter of general training, than founded on any particular political reflection. It possessed the benefit, however, of a good deal of reading. It never wanted examples out of history and biography, or a kind of adornment from the spirit of literature; and it gradually drew to its perusal many intelligent persons of both sexes, who would, perhaps, never have attended to politics under other circumstances.

In the course of its warfare with the Tories, the *Examiner* was charged with Bonapartism, with republicanism, with disaffection to Church and State, with conspiracy at the tables of Burdett, and Cobbett, and Henry Hunt. Now, Sir Francis, though he was for a long time our hero, we never exchanged a word with; and Cobbett and Henry Hunt (no relation of ours) we never beheld;—never so much as saw their faces. I was never even at a public dinner; nor do I believe my brother was. We had absolutely no views whatsoever but those of a decent competence and of the public good; and we thought, I dare affirm, a great deal more of the latter than of the former. Our competence we allowed too much to shift for itself. Zeal for the public good was a family inheritance; and this we thought ourselves bound to increase. As to myself, what I thought of, more than either, was the making of verses. I did nothing for the greater part of the week but write verses and read books. I then made a rush at my editorial duties; took a world of superfluous pains in the writing; sat up late at night, and was a very trying person to compositors and newsmen. I sometimes have before me the ghost of a pale and gouty printer whom I specially caused to suffer, and who never complained. I think of him and of some needy dramatist, and wish they had been worse men.

The *Examiner* commenced at the time when Bonaparte was at the height of his power. He had the continent at his feet; and three of his brothers were on thrones.

I thought of Bonaparte at that time as I have thought ever since; to wit, that he was a great soldier, and little else; that he was not a man of the highest order of intellect, much less a cosmopolite; that he was a retrospective rather than a prospective man, ambitious of old renown instead of new; and would advance the age as far, and no farther, as suited his views of personal aggrandizement. The *Examiner*, however much it differed with the military policy of Bonaparte's antagonists, or however meanly it thought of their understandings, never overrated his own, or was one of his partisans.

I now look upon war as one of the fleeting necessities of things in the course of human progress; as an evil (like most other evils) to be regarded in relation to some other evil that would have been worse without it, but always to be considered as an indication of comparative barbarism—as a necessity, the perpetuity of which is not to be assumed—or as a half-reasoning mode of adjustment, whether of disputes or of populations, which mankind, on arriving at years of discretion, and coming to a better understanding with one another, may, and must of necessity, do away. It would be as ridiculous to associate the idea of war with an earth covered with railroads and commerce, as a fight between Holborn and the Strand, or between people met in a drawing-room. Wars, like all other evils, have not been without their good. They have pioneered human intercourse; have thus prepared even for their own eventual abolition; and their follies, losses, and horrors have been made the best of by adornments and music, and consoled by the exhibition of many noble qualities. There is no evil unmixed with, or unproductive of, good. It could not, in the nature of things, exist. Antagonism itself prevents it. But nature incites us to the diminution of evil; and while it is pious to make the best of what is inevitable, it is no less so to obey the impulse which she has given us towards thinking and making it otherwise.

With respect to the charge of republicanism against the *Examiner*, it was as ridiculous as the rest. Both Napoleon and the Allies did, indeed, so conduct themselves on the high roads of empire and royalty, and the British sceptre was at the same time so unfortunately wielded, that kings and princes were often treated with less respect in our pages than we desired. But we generally felt, and often expressed, a wish to treat them otherwise. The *Examiner* was always quoting against them the Alfreds and Antoninuses of old. The " Constitution," with its King, Lords, and Commons, was its incessant watchword. The greatest political change which it desired was Reform in Parliament; and it helped to obtain it, because it was in earnest. As to republics, the United States, notwithstanding our family relationship, were no favourites with us, owing to what appeared to us to be an absorption in the love of money, and to their *then* want of the imaginative and ornamental; and the excesses of the French Revolution we held in abhorrence.

With regard to Church and State, the connection was of course duly recognized by admirers of the English constitution. We desired, it is true, reform in both, being far greater admirers of Christianity in its primitive than in any of its subsequent shapes, and hearty accorders with the dictum of the apostle, who said that the "letter killeth, but the spirit giveth life." Our version of religious faith was ever nearer to what M. Lamartine has called the "New Christianity," than to that of Doctors Horsley and Philpotts. But we heartily advocated the mild spirit of religious government, as exercised by the Church of England, in opposition to the bigoted part of dissent; and in furtherance of this advocacy, the first volume of the *Examiner* contained a series of *Essays on the Folly and Danger of Methodism*, which were afterwards collected into a pamphlet. So "orthodox" were these essays, short of points from which common sense and humanity always appeared to us to revolt, and from which the deliverance of the Church itself is now, I believe, not far off, that in duty to our hope of that deliverance, I afterwards thought it necessary to guard against the conclusions which might have been drawn from them, as to the amount of our assent. A church appeared to me then, as it still does, an instinctive want in the human family. I never to this day pass one, even of a kind the most unreformed, without a wish to go into it and join my fellow-creatures in their affecting evidence of the necessity of an additional tie with Deity and Infinity, with this world and the next. But the wish is accompanied with an afflicting regret that I cannot recognize it, free from barbarisms derogatory to both; and I sigh for some good old country church, finally delivered from the corruptions of the Councils, and breathing nothing but the peace and love befitting the Sermon on the Mount. I believe that a time is coming, when such doctrine, and such only, will be preached; and my future grave, in a certain beloved and flowery cemetery, seems quieter for the consummation. But I anticipate.

For a short period before and after the setting up of the *Examiner*, I was a clerk in the War Office. The situation was given me by Mr. Addington, then prime minister, afterwards Lord Sidmouth, who knew my father. My sorry stock of arithmetic, which I taught myself on purpose, was sufficient for the work which I had to do; but otherwise I made a bad clerk; wasting my time and that of others in perpetual jesting; going too late to office; and feeling conscious that if I did not quit the situation myself, nothing was more likely, or would have been more just, than a suggestion to that effect from others. The establishment of the *Examiner*, and the tone respecting the court and the ministry which I soon thought myself bound to adopt, increased the sense of the propriety of this measure; and, accordingly, I sent in my resignation. Mr. Addington had fortunately ceased to be minister before the *Examiner* was set up; and though I had occasion afterwards to differ extremely with the measures approved of by him as Lord Sidmouth, I never forgot the personal respect which I owed him for his kindness to myself, to his own amiable manners, and to his undoubted, though not wise, conscientiousness. He had been Speaker of the House of Commons, a situation for which his figure and deportment at that time of life admirably fitted him. I think I hear his fine voice, in his house at Richmond Park, good-naturedly expressing to me his hope, in the words of the poet, that it might be one day said of me,—

> " — Not in fancy's maze he wander'd long,
>   But stoop'd to truth, and moralized his song."

The sounding words, " moralized his song," came *toning* out of his dignified utterance like " sonorous metal." This was when I went to thank him for the clerkship. I afterwards sat on the grass in the park, feeling as if I were in a dream, and wondering how I should reconcile my propensity to verse-making with sums in addition. The minister, it was clear, thought them not incompatible: nor are they. Let nobody think otherwise, unless he is prepared to suffer for the mistake, and, what is worse, to make others suffer. The body of the British Poets themselves shall confute him, with Chaucer at their head, who was a " comptroller of wool" and " clerk of works."

> " Thou hearest neither that nor this"

(says the eagle to him in the House of Fame

> " For when thy labour all done is,
>   And hast made *all thy reckonings*,
>   Instead of rest and of new things,
>   Thou goest home to thine house anon,
>   And all so dumb as any stone
>   Thou sittest at another book,
>   Till fully dazèd is thy look."

Lamb, it is true, though he stuck to it, has complained of

> " The dry drudgery of the desk's dead wood:"

and Chaucer was unable to attend to his accounts in the month of May, when, as he tells us, he could not help passing whole days in the fields, looking at the daisies. The case, as in all other matters, can only be vindicated, or otherwise, by the consequences. But that is a perilous responsibility; and it involves assumptions which ought to be startling to the modesty of young rhyming gentlemen not in the receipt of an income.

I did not give up, however, a certainty for an uncertainty. The *Examiner* was fully established when I quitted the office [in 1808]. My friends thought that I should be better able to attend to its editorship; and it was felt, at any rate, that I could not with propriety remain. So I left my fellow-clerks to their better behaviour and quieter rooms; and set my face in the direction of stormy politics.

CHAPTER X.

LITERARY ACQUAINTANCE.

JUST after this period I fell in with a new set of acquaintances, accounts of whom may not be uninteresting. I forget what it was that introduced me to Mr. Hill, proprietor of the *Monthly Mirror*; but at his house at Sydenham I used to meet his editor, Du Bois; Thomas Campbell, who was his neighbour; and the two Smiths, authors of *The Rejected Addresses*. I saw also Theodore Hook, and Mathews the comedian. Our host was a jovial bachelor, plump and rosy as an abbot; and no abbot could have presided over a more festive Sunday. The wine flowed merrily and long; the discourse kept pace with it; and next morning, in returning to town, we felt ourselves very thirsty. A pump by the roadside, with a plash round it, was a bewitching sight.

Du Bois was one of those wits who, like the celebrated Eachard, have no faculty of gravity. His handsome hawk's eyes looked blank at a speculation; but set a joke or a piece of raillery in motion, and they sparkled with wit and malice. Nothing could be more trite or commonplace than his serious observations. Acquiescences they should rather have been called; for he seldom ventured upon a gravity, but in echo of another's remark. If he did, it was in defence of ortho-doxy, of which he was a great advocate; but his quips and cranks were infinite. He was also an excellent scholar. He, Dr. King, and Eachard would have made a capital trio over

11

a table, for scholarship, mirth, drinking, and religion. He was intimate with Sir Philip Francis, and gave the public a new edition of the *Horace* of Sir Philip's father. The literary world knew him well also as the writer of a popular novel in the genuine Fielding manner, entitled *Old Nick*.

Mr. Du Bois held his editorship of the *Monthly Mirror* very cheap. He amused himself with writing notes on Athenæus, and was a lively critic on the theatres; but half the jokes in his magazine were written for his friends, and must have mystified the uninitiated. His notices to correspondents were often made up of this by-play; and made his friends laugh, in proportion to their obscurity to every one else. Mr. Du Bois subsequently became a magistrate in the Court of Requests; and died the other day at an advanced age, in spite of his love of port. But then he was festive in good taste; no gourmand; and had a strong head withal. I do not know whether such men ever last as long as teetotallers; but they certainly last as long, and look a great deal younger, than the carking and severe.

They who knew Mr. Campbell only as the author of *Gertrude of Wyoming*, and the *Pleasures of Hope*, would not have suspected him to be a merry companion, overflowing with humour and anecdote, and anything but fastidious. These Scotch poets have always something in reserve. It is the only point in which the major part of them resemble their countrymen. The mistaken character which the lady formed of Thomson from his *Seasons* is well known. He let part of the secret out in his *Castle of Indolence;* and the more he let out, the more honour it did to the simplicity and cordiality of the poet's nature, though not always to the elegance of it. Allan Ramsay knew his friends Gay and Somerville as well in their writings as he did when he came to be personally acquainted with them; but Allan, who had bustled up from a barber's shop into a bookseller's, was "a cunning shaver;" and nobody would have guessed the author of the *Gentle Shepherd* to be penurious. Let none suppose that any insinuation to that effect is intended against Campbell. He was one of the few men whom I could at any time have walked half a dozen miles through the snow to spend an evening with; and I could no more do this with a penurious man, than I could with a sulky one. I know but of one fault he had, besides an extreme cautiousness in his writings, and that one was national, a matter of words, and amply overpaid by a stream of conversation, lively, piquant, and liberal, not the less interesting for occasionally betraying an intimacy with pain, and for a high and somewhat strained tone of voice, like a man speaking with suspended breath, and in the habit of subduing his feelings. No man felt more kindly towards his fellow-creatures, or took less credit for it. When he indulged in doubt and sarcasm, and spoke contemptuously of things in general, he did it partly, no doubt, out of actual dissatisfaction, but more, perhaps, than he suspected, out of a fear of being thought weak and sensitive; which is a blind that the best men very commonly practise. He professed to be hopeless and sarcastic, and took pains all the while to set up a university (the London).

When I first saw this eminent person, he gave me the idea of a French Virgil. Not that he was like a Frenchman, much less the French translator of Virgil. I found him as handsome as the Abbé Delille is said to have been ugly. But he seemed to me to embody a Frenchman's ideal notion of the Latin poet; something a little more cut and dry than I had looked for; compact and elegant, critical and acute, with a consciousness of authorship upon him; a taste overanxious not to commit itself, and refining and diminishing nature as in a drawing-room mirror. This fancy was strengthened in the course of conversation, by his expatiating on the greatness of Racine. I think he had a volume of the French poet in his hand. His skull was sharply cut and fine; with plenty, according to the phrenologists, both of the reflective and amative organs: and his poetry will bear them out. For a lettered solitude, and a bridal properly got up, both according to law and luxury, commend us to the lovely *Gertrude of Wyoming*. His face and person were rather on a small scale; his features regular; his eye lively and penetrating; and when he spoke, dimples played about his mouth, which, nevertheless, had something restrained and close in it. Some gentle puritan seemed to have crossed the breed, and to have left a stamp on his face, such as we often see in the female Scotch face rather than the male. But he appeared not at all grateful for this; and when his critiques and his Virgilianism were over, very unlike a puritan he talked! He seemed to spite his restrictions; and, out of the natural largeness of his sympathy with things high and low, to break at once out of Delille's Virgil into Cotton's, like a boy let loose from school. When I had the pleasure of hearing

11—2

him afterwards, I forgot his Virgilianisms, and thought only of the delightful companion, the unaffected philanthropist, and the creator of a beauty worth all the heroines in Racine.

Campbell tasted pretty sharply of the good and ill of the present state of society, and, for a bookman, had beheld strange sights. He witnessed a battle in Germany from the top of a convent (on which battle he has left us a noble ode); and he saw the French cavalry enter a town, wiping their bloody swords on the horses' manes. He was in Germany a second time,—I believe to purchase books; for in addition to his classical scholarship, and his other languages, he was a reader of German. The readers there, among whom he is popular, both for his poetry and his love of freedom, crowded about him with affectionate zeal; and they gave him, what he did not dislike, a good dinner. Like many of the great men in Germany—Schiller, Wieland, and others—he did not scruple to become editor of a magazine; and his name alone gave it a recommendation of the greatest value, and such as made it a grace to write under him.

I remember, one day at Sydenham, Mr. Theodore Hook coming in unexpectedly to dinner, and amusing us very much with his talent at extempore verse. He was then a youth, tall, dark, and of a good person, with small eyes, and features more round than weak; a face that had character and humour, but no refinement. His extempore verses were really surprising. It is easy enough to extemporize in Italian—one only wonders how, in a language in which everything conspires to render verse-making easy, and it is difficult to avoid rhyming, this talent should be so much cried up—but in English it is another matter. I have known but one other person besides Hook, who could extemporize in English, and he wanted the confidence to do it in public. Of course, I speak of rhyming. Extempore blank verse, with a little practice, would be found as easy in English as rhyming is in Italian. In Hook the faculty was very unequivocal. He could not have been pre-informed about all the visitors on the present occasion, still less of the subject of conversation when he came in, and he talked his full share till called upon; yet he ran his jokes and his verses upon us all in the easiest manner, saying something characteristic of everybody, or avoiding it with a pun; and he introduced so agreeably a piece of village scandal upon which the party had been rallying Campbell, that the poet, though not unjealous of his dignity, was, perhaps, the most pleased of us all. Theodore afterwards sat down to the pianoforte, and, enlarging upon this subject, made an extempore parody of a modern opera, introducing sailors and their clap-traps, rustics, &c., and making the poet and his supposed flame the hero and heroine. He parodied music as well as words, giving us the most received cadences and flourishes, and calling to mind (not without some hazard to his filial duties) the commonplaces of the pastoral songs and duets of the last half-century; so that if Mr. Dignum, the Damon of Vauxhall, had been present, he would have doubted whether to take it as an affront or a compliment. Campbell certainly took the theme of the parody as a compliment; for having drunk a little more wine than usual that evening, and happening to wear a wig on account of having lost his hair by a fever, he suddenly took off the wig, and dashed it at the head of the performer, exclaiming, " You dog! I'll throw my laurels at you."

I have since been unable to help wishing, perhaps not very wisely, that Campbell would have been a little less careful and fastidious in what he did for the public ; for, after all, an author may reasonably be supposed to do best that which he is most inclined to do. It is our business to be grateful for what a poet sets before us, rather than to be wishing that his peaches were nectarines, or his Falernian champagne. Campbell, as an author, was all for refinement and classicality, not, however, without a great deal of pathos and luxurious fancy. His merry *jongleur*, Theodore Hook, had as little propensity, perhaps, as can be imagined, to any of those niceties : yet in the pleasure of recollecting the evening which I passed with him, I was unable to repress a wish, as little wise as the other; to wit, that he had stuck to his humours and farces, for which he had real talent, instead of writing politics. There was ability in the novels which he subsequently wrote ; but their worship of high life and attacks on vulgarity were themselves of the vulgarest description.

Mathews, the comedian, I had the pleasure of seeing at Mr. Hill's several times, and of witnessing his imitations, which, admirable as they were on the stage, were still more so in private. His wife occasionally came with him, with her handsome eyes, and charitably made tea for us. Many years afterwards I had the pleasure of seeing them at their own table ; and I thought that while Time, with unusual courtesy, had spared the sweet countenance of the lady, he had given more force and interest to that of the husband in the very ploughing of it up. Strong lines had been cut, and the face stood them well. I had seldom been more surprised than on coming close to Mathews on that occasion, and seeing the bust which he possessed in his gallery of his friend Liston. Some of these comic actors, like comic writers, are as unfarcical as can be imagined in their interior. The taste for humour comes to them by the force of contrast. The last time I had seen Mathews, his face appeared to me insignificant to what it was then. On the former occasion, he looked like an irritable in-door pet; on the latter, he seemed to have been grappling with the world, and to have got vigour by it. His face had looked out upon the Atlantic, and said to the old waves, "Buffet on; I have seen trouble as well as you." The paralytic affection, or whatever it was, that twisted his mouth when young, had formerly appeared to be master of his face, and given it a character of indecision and alarm. It now seemed a minor thing; a twist in a piece of old oak. And what a bust was Liston's! The mouth and chin, with the throat under it, hung like an old bag; but the upper part of the head was as fine as possible. There was a speculation, a look-out, and even an elevation of character in it, as unlike the Liston on the stage, as Lear is to King Pippin. One might imagine Laberius to have had such a face.

The reasons why Mathews' imitations were still better in private than in public were, that he was more at his ease personally, more secure of his audience ("fit though few"), and able to interest them with traits of private character, which could not have been introduced on the stage. He gave, for instance, to persons who he thought could take it rightly, a picture of the manners and conversation of Sir Walter Scott, highly creditable to that celebrated person, and calculated to add regard to admiration. His commonest imitations were not superficial. Something of the mind and character of the individual was always insinuated, often with a dramatic dressing, and plenty of sauce piquante. At Sydenham he used to give us a dialogue among the actors, each of whom found fault with another for some defect or excess of his own— Kemble objecting to stiffness, Munden to grimace, and so on. His representation of Incledon was extraordinary: his nose seemed actually to become aquiline. It is a pity I cannot put upon paper, as represented by Mr. Mathews, the singular gabblings of that actor, the lax and sailor-like twist of mind, with which everything hung upon him; and his profane pieties in quoting the Bible; for which, and swearing, he seemed to have an equal reverence. He appeared to be charitable to everybody but Braham. He would be described as saying to his friend Holman, for instance, "My dear George, don't be abusive, George;—don't insult,—don't be indecent, by G—d! You should take the beam out of your own eye,—what the devil is it—you know—in the Bible? something" (the *a* very broad) "about *a* beam, my dear George! and—and—and *a* mote;—you'll find it in *any* part of the Bible: yes, George, my dear boy, the Bible, by G—d," (and then with real fervour and reverence,) "the Holy Scripture, G—d d— me!" He swore as dreadfully as a devout knight-errant. Braham, whose trumpet blew down his wooden walls, he could not endure. He is represented as saying one day, with a strange mixture of imagination and matter-of-fact, that "he only wished his beloved master, Mr. Jackson, could come down from heaven, and take the Exeter stage to London to hear that d—d Jew!"

As Hook made extempore verses on us, so Mathews one day gave an extempore imitation of us all round, with the exception of a young theatrical critic (*videlicet*, myself), in whose appearance and manner he pronounced that there was no handle for mimicry. This, in all probability, was intended as a politeness towards a comparative stranger, but it might have been policy; and the laughter was not missed by it. At all events, the critic was both good-humoured enough, and at that time self-satisfied enough, to have borne the mimicry; and no harm would have come of it.

One morning, after stopping all night at this pleasant house, I was getting up to breakfast, when I heard the noise of a little boy having his face washed. Our host was a merry bachelor, and to the rosiness of a priest might, for aught I knew, have added the paternity; but I had never heard of it, and still less expected to find a child in his house. More obvious and obstreperous proofs, however, of the existence of a boy with a dirty face could not have been met with. You heard the child crying and objecting; then the woman remonstrating; then the cries of the child snubbed and swallowed up in the hard towel; and at intervals out came his voice bubbling and deploring, and was again swallowed up. At breakfast, the child being pitied, I ventured to speak about it, and was laughing and sympathizing in perfect good faith,

when Mathews came in, and I found that the little urchin
was he.

The same morning he gave us his immortal imitation of
old Tate Wilkinson, patentee of the York Theatre. Tate had
been a little too merry in his youth, and was very melancholy
in old age. He had a wandering mind and a decrepit body;
and being manager of a theatre, a husband, and a ratcatcher,
he would speak, in his wanderings, "variety of wretchedness."
He would interweave, for instance, all at once, the subjects of
a new engagement at his theatre, the rats, a veal-pie, Garrick
and Mrs. Siddons, and Mrs. Tate and the doctor. I do not
pretend to give a specimen : Mathews alone could have done
it ; but one trait I recollect, descriptive of Tate himself, which
will give a good notion of him. On coming into the room,
Mathews assumed the old manager's appearance, and proceeded towards the window, to reconnoitre the state of the
weather, which was a matter of great importance to him.
His hat was like a hat worn the wrong way, side foremost,
looking sadly crinkled and old ; his mouth was desponding,
his eye staring, and his whole aspect meagre, querulous, and
prepared for objection. This miserable object, grunting and
hobbling, and helping himself with everything he can lay
hold of as he goes, creeps up to the window ; and, giving a
glance at the clouds, turns round with an ineffable look of
despair and acquiescence, ejaculating, "*Uh* Christ !"

Of James Smith, a fair, stout, fresh-coloured man, with
round features, I recollect little, except that he used to read to
us trim verses, with rhymes as pat as butter. The best of his
verses are in the *Rejected Addresses*—and they are excellent.
Isaac Hawkins Browne, with his *Pipe of Tobacco*, and all the
rhyming *jeux-d'esprit* in all the Tracts, are extinguished in
the comparison ; not excepting the *Probationary Odes*. Mr.
Fitzgerald found himself bankrupt in *non sequiturs ;* Crabbe
could hardly have known which was which, himself or his
parodist; and Lord Byron confessed to me, that the summing
up of his philosophy, to wit, that

"Nought is everything, and everything is nought,"

was very posing. Mr. Smith would sometimes repeat after
dinner, with his brother Horace, an imaginary dialogue,
stuffed full of incongruities, that made us roll with laughter.
His ordinary verse and prose were too full of the ridicule of

city pretensions. To be superior to anything, it should not always be running in one's head.

His brother Horace was delicious. Lord Byron used to say, that this epithet should be applied only to eatables; and that he wondered a friend of his (I forget who) that was critical in matters of eating, should use it in any other sense. I know not what the present usage may be in the circles, but classical authority is against his lordship, from Cicero downwards; and I am content with the modern warrant of another noble wit, the famous Lord Peterborough, who, in his fine, open way, said of Fénélon, that he was such a " delicious creature, he was forced to get away from him, else he would have made him pious!" I grant there is something in the word delicious which may be said to comprise a reference to every species of pleasant taste. It is at once a quintessence and a compound; and a friend, to deserve the epithet, ought, perhaps, to be capable of delighting us as much over our wine, as on graver occasions. Fénélon himself could do this, with all his piety; or rather he could do it because his piety was of the true sort, and relished of everything that was sweet and affectionate. A finer nature than Horace Smith's, except in the single instance of Shelley, I never met with in man; nor even in that instance, all circumstances considered, have I a right to say that those who knew him as intimately as I did the other, would not have had the same reasons to love him. Shelley himself had the highest regard for Horace Smith, as may be seen by the following verses, the initials in which the reader has here the pleasure of filling up :—

> " Wit and sense,
> Virtue and human knowledge, all that might
> Make this dull world a business of delight,
> Are all combined in H. S."

Horace Smith differed with Shelley on some points; but on others, which all the world agree to praise highly and to practise very little, he agreed so entirely, and showed unequivocally that he did agree, that with the exception of one person (Vincent Novello), too diffident to gain such an honour from his friends, they were the only two men I had then met with, from whom I could have received and did receive advice or remonstrance with perfect comfort, because I could be sure of the unmixed motives and entire absence of self-reflection, with which it would come from them.* Shelley said to me

---

* Notwithstanding his caprices of temper, I must add Hazlitt, who was quite capable, when he chose, of giving genuine advice, and

once, " I know not what Horace Smith must take me for sometimes : I am afraid he must think me a strange fellow : but is it not odd, that the only truly generous person I ever knew, who had money to be generous with, should be a stockbroker ? And he writes poetry too," continued Shelley, his voice rising in a fervour of astonishment—" he writes poetry and pastoral dramas, and yet knows how to make money, and does make it, and is still generous !" Shelley had reason to like him. Horace Smith was one of the few men, who, through a cloud of detraction, and through all that difference of conduct from the rest of the world which naturally excites obloquy, discerned the greatness of my friend's character. Indeed, he became a witness to a very unequivocal proof of it, which I shall mention by-and-by. The mutual esteem was accordingly very great, and arose from circumstances most honourable to both parties. " I believe," said Shelley on another occasion, " that I have only to say to Horace Smith that I want a hundred pounds or two, and he would send it me without any eye to its being returned; such faith has he that I have something within me beyond what the world supposes, and that I could only ask his money for a good purpose." And Shelley would have sent for it accordingly, if the person for whom it was intended had not said Nay. I will now mention the circumstance which first gave my friend a regard for Horace Smith. It concerns the person just mentioned, who is a man of letters. It came to Mr. Smith's knowledge, many years ago, that this person was suffering under a pecuniary trouble. He knew little of him at the time, but had met him occasionally ; and he availed himself of this circumstance to write him a letter as full of delicacy and cordiality as it could hold, making it a matter of grace to accept a bank-note of 100*l.*, which he enclosed. I speak on the best authority, that of the obliged person himself; who adds that he not only did accept the money, but felt as light and happy under the obligation, as he has felt miserable under the very report of being obliged to some ; and he says that nothing could induce him to withhold his name, but a reason which the generous, during his lifetime, would think becoming.

I have said that Horace Smith was a stockbroker. He left business with a fortune, and went to live in France, making you sensible of his disinterestedness. Lamb could have done it, too; but for interference of any sort he had an abhorrence.

where, if he did not increase, he did not seriously diminish it; and France added to the pleasant stock of his knowledge.

On returning to England, he set about exerting himself in a manner equally creditable to his talents and interesting to the public. I would not insult either the modesty or the understanding of my friend while he was alive, by comparing him with the author of *Old Mortality* and *Guy Mannering*: but I ventured to say, and I repeat, that the earliest of his novels, *Brambletye House*, ran a hard race with the novel of *Woodstock*, and that it contained more than one character not unworthy of the best volumes of Sir Walter. I allude to the ghastly troubles of the Regicide in his lone house; the outward phlegm and merry inward malice of Winky Boss (a happy name), who gravely smoked a pipe with his mouth, and laughed with his eyes; and, above all, to the character of the princely Dutch merchant, who would cry out that he should be ruined, at seeing a few nutmegs dropped from a bag, and then go and give a thousand ducats for an antique. This is hitting the high mercantile character to a nicety—minute and careful in its means, princely in its ends. If the ultimate effect of commerce (*permulti transibunt*, &c.) were not something very different from what its pursuers imagine, the character would be a dangerous one to society at large, because it throws a gloss over the spirit of money-getting; but, meanwhile, nobody could paint it better, or has a greater right to recommend it, than he who has been the first to make it a handsome portrait.

The personal appearance of Horace Smith, like that of most of the individuals I have met with, was highly indicative of his character. His figure was good and manly, inclining to the robust; and his countenance extremely frank and cordial; sweet without weakness. I have been told he was irascible. If so, it must have been no common offence that could have irritated him. He had not a jot of it in his appearance.

Another set of acquaintances which I made at this time used to assemble at the hospitable table of Mr. Hunter the bookseller, in St. Paul's Churchyard. They were the survivors of the literary party that were accustomed to dine with his predecessor, Mr. Johnson. They came, as of old, on the Friday. The most regular were Fuseli and Bonnycastle. Now and then, Godwin was present: oftener Mr. Kinnaird the magistrate, a great lover of Horace.

Fuseli was a small man, with energetic features, and a

white head of hair. Our host's daughter, then a little girl, used to call him the white-headed lion. He combed his hair up from the forehead ; and as his whiskers were large, his face was set in a kind of hairy frame, which, in addition to the fierceness of his look, really gave him an aspect of that sort. Otherwise, his features were rather sharp than round. He would have looked much like an old military officer, if his face, besides its real energy, had not affected more. There was the same defect in it as in his pictures. Conscious of not having all the strength he wished, he endeavoured to make up for it by violence and pretension. He carried this so far, as to look fiercer than usual when he sat for his picture. His friend and engraver, Mr. Houghton, drew an admirable likeness of him in this state of dignified extravagance. He is sitting back in his chair, leaning on his hand, but looking ready to pounce withal. His notion of repose was like that of Pistol :

"Now, Pistol, lay thy head in Furies' lap."

Agreeably to this over-wrought manner, he was reckoned, I believe, not quite so bold as he might have been. He painted horrible pictures, as children tell horrible stories ; and was frightened at his own lay-figures. Yet he would hardly have talked as he did about his terrors, had he been as timid as some supposed him. With the affected, impression is the main thing, let it be produced how it may. A student of the Academy told me, that Mr. Fuseli coming in one night, when a solitary candle had been put on the floor in a corner of the room, to produce some effect or other, he said it looked "like a damned soul." This was by way of being Dantesque, as Michael Angelo was. Fuseli was an ingenious caricaturist of that master, making great bodily displays of mental energy, and being ostentatious with his limbs and muscles, in proportion as he could not draw them. A leg or an arm was to be thrust down one's throat, because he knew we should dispute the truth of it. In the indulgence of this wilfulness of purpose, generated partly by impatience of study, partly by want of sufficient genius, and no doubt, also, by a sense of superiority to artists who could do nothing but draw correctly, he cared for no time, place, or circumstance in his pictures. A set of prints, after his designs, for Shakspeare and Cowper, exhibit a chaos of mingled genius and absurdity, such as, perhaps, was never before seen. He endeavoured to bring Michael Angelo's apostles and prophets, with their superhuman ponderousness of intention, into the commonplaces of modern life. A student reading in a garden, is all over intensity of muscle; and the quiet tea-table scene in Cowper, he has turned into a preposterous conspiracy of huge men and women, all bent on showing their thews and postures, with dresses as fantastical as their minds. One gentleman, of the existence of whose trousers you are not aware till you see the terminating line at the ankle, is sitting and looking grim on a sofa, with his hat on and no waistcoat. Yet there is real genius in his designs for Milton, though disturbed, as usual, by strainings after the energetic. His most extraordinary mistake, after all, is said to have been on the subject of his colouring. It was a sort of livid green, like brass diseased. Yet they say, that when praised for one of his pictures, he would modestly observe, " It is a pretty colour." This might have been thought a jest on his part, if remarkable stories were not told of the mistakes made by other people with regard to colour. Sight seems the least agreed upon of all the senses.

Fuseli was lively and interesting in conversation, but not without his usual faults of violence and pretension. Nor was he always as decorous as an old man ought to be; especially one whose turn of mind is not of the lighter and more pleasurable cast. The licences he took were coarse, and had not sufficient regard to his company. Certainly they went a great deal beyond his friend Armstrong; to whose account, I believe, Fuseli's passion for swearing was laid. The poet condescended to be a great swearer, and Fuseli thought it energetic to swear like him. His friendship with Bonnycastle had something childlike and agreeable in it. They came and went away together, for years, like a couple of old school-boys. They, also, like boys, rallied one another, and sometimes made a singular display of it,—Fuseli, at least; for it was he that was the aggressor.

Bonnycastle was a good fellow. He was a tall, gaunt, long-headed man, with large features and spectacles, and a deep internal voice, with a twang of rusticity in it; and he goggled over his plate, like a horse. I often thought that a bag of corn would have hung well on him. His laugh was equine, and showed his teeth upwards at the sides. Words-worth, who notices similar mysterious manifestations on the part of donkeys, would have thought it ominous. Bonny-castle was extremely fond of quoting Shakspeare and telling stories; and if the *Edinburgh Review* had just come out, would give us all the jokes in it. He had once a hypo-chondriacal disorder of long duration; and he told us, that he should never forget the comfortable sensation given him one night during this disorder, by his knocking a landlord, that was insolent to him, down the man's staircase. On the strength of this piece of energy (having first ascertained that the offender was not killed) he went to bed, and had a sleep of unusual soundness. Perhaps Bonnycastle thought more highly of his talents than the amount of them strictly war-ranted; a mistake to which scientific men appear to be more liable than others, the universe they work in being so large, and their universality (in Bacon's sense of the word) being often so small. But the delusion was not only pardonable, but desirable, in a man so zealous in the performance of his duties, and so much of a human being to all about him, as Bonnycastle was. It was delightful one day to hear him speak with complacency of a translation which had appeared of one of his books in Arabic, and which began by saying, on the part of the translator, that " it had pleased God, for the advancement of human knowledge, to raise us up a Bonny-castle." Some of his stories were a little romantic, and no less authentic. He had an anecdote of a Scotchman, who boasted of being descended from the Admirable Crichton; in proof of which, the Scotchman said he had " a grit quantity of table-leenen in his possassion, marked A. C., Admirable Creechton."

Kinnaird, the magistrate, was a sanguine man, under the middle height, with a fine lamping black eye, lively to the last, and a body that " had increased, was increasing, and ought to have been diminished; " which is by no means what he thought of the prerogative. Next to his bottle he was fond of his Horace; and, in the intervals of business at the police-office, would enjoy both in his arm-chair. Between the vulgar calls of this kind of magistracy, and the perusal of the urbane Horace, there must have been a gusto of con-tradiction, which the bottle, perhaps, was required to render quite palatable. Fielding did not love his bottle the less for being obliged to lecture the drunken. Nor did his son, who succeeded him in taste and office. I know not how a former poet-laureat, Mr. Pye, managed,—another man of letters, who was fain to accept a situation of this kind. Having been a man of fortune and a member of Parliament, and loving his Horace to boot, he could hardly have done

without his wine. I saw him once in a state of scornful
indignation at being interrupted in the perusal of a manuscript by the monitions of his police-officers, who were
obliged to remind him over and over again that he was a
magistrate, and that the criminal multitude were in waiting.
Every time the door opened, he threatened and implored.

> " Otium divos rogat in patenti
>   Prensus Ægæo."

Had you quoted this to Mr. Kinnaird, his eyes would have
sparkled with good-fellowship : he would have finished the
verse and the bottle with you, and proceeded to as many
more as your head could stand. Poor fellow ! the last time
I saw him, he was an apparition formidably substantial. The
door of our host's dining-room opened without my hearing
it, and, happening to turn round, I saw a figure in a great-
coat, literally almost as broad as it was long, and scarcely
able to articulate. He was dying of a dropsy, and was
obliged to revive himself, before he was fit to converse, by
the wine that was killing him. But he had cares besides,
and cares of no ordinary description; and, for my part, I will
not blame even his wine for killing him, unless his cares
could have done it more agreeably. After dinner that day,
he was comparatively himself again, quoted his Horace as
usual, talked of lords and courts with a relish, and begged
that *God save the King* might be played to him on the pianoforte; to which he listened, as if his soul had taken its hat
off. I believe he would have liked to die to *God save the
King,* and to have " waked and found those visions true."

CHAPTER XI.

POLITICAL CHARACTERS.

THE *Examiner* had been set up towards the close of the
reign of George the Third, three years before the appointment of the regency. Pitt and Fox had died two years
before; the one, in middle life, of constant ill-success, preying
on a sincere but proud, and not very large mind, and unwisely
supported by a habit of drinking ; the other, of older but
more genial habits of a like sort, and of demands beyond
his strength by a sudden accession to office. The king—a
conscientious but narrow-minded man, obstinate to a degree

(which had lost him America), and not always dealing ingenuously, even with his advisers — had lately got rid of Mr. Fox's successors, on account of their urging the Catholic claims. He had summoned to office in their stead Lords Castlereagh, Liverpool, and others, who had been the clerks of Mr. Pitt; and Bonaparte was at the height of his power as French Emperor, setting his brothers on thrones, and compelling our Russian and German allies to side with him under the most mortifying circumstances of tergiversation.

It is a melancholy period for the potentates of the earth when they fancy themselves obliged to resort to the shabbiest measures of the feeble; siding against a friend with his enemy; joining in accusations against him at the latter's dictation; believed by nobody on either side; returning to the friend, and retreating from him, according to the fortunes of war; secretly hoping that the friend will excuse them by reason of the pauper's plea, necessity; and at no time able to give better apologies for their conduct than those " mysterious ordinations of Providence " which are the last refuge of the destitute in morals, and a reference to which they contemptuously deny to the thief and the " king's evidence." It proves to them, " with a vengeance," the " something rotten in the state of Denmark;" and will continue to prove it, and to be despicable, whether in bad or good fortune, till the world find out a cure for the rottenness.

Yet this is what the allies of England were in the habit of doing, through the whole contest of England with France. When England succeeded in getting up a coalition against Napoleon, they denounced him for his ambition, and set out to fight him. When the coalition was broken by his armies, they turned round at his bidding, denounced England, and joined him in fighting against their ally. And this was the round of their history: a coalition and a tergiversation alternately; now a speech and a fight against Bonaparte, who beat them; then a speech and a fight against England, who bought them off; then, again, a speech and a fight against Bonaparte, who beat them again; and then, as before, a speech and fight against England, who again bought them off. Meanwhile, they took everything they could get, whether from enemy or friend, seizing with no less greediness whatever bits of territory Bonaparte threw to them for their meanness, than pocketing the millions of Pitt, for which we are paying to this day.

It becomes us to bow, and to bow humbly, to the "mysterious dispensations of Providence;" but in furtherance of those very dispensations, it has pleased Providence so to constitute us, as to render us incapable of admiring such conduct, whether in king's evidences or in kings; and some of the meanest figures that present themselves to the imagination, in looking back on the events of those times, are the Emperors of Austria and Russia, and the King of Prussia. It is salutary to bear this in mind, for the sake of royalty itself. What has since ruined Louis Philippe, in spite of all his ability, is his confounding royal privileges with base ones, and his not keeping his word as a gentleman.

If it be still asked, what are kings to do under such circumstances as those in which they were placed with Bonaparte? what is their alternative? it is to be replied, firstly, that the question has been answered already, by the mode in which the charge is put; and, secondly, that whatever they do, they must either cease to act basely, and like the meanest of mankind, or be content to be regarded as such, and to leave such stains on their order as tend to produce its downfall, and to exasperate the world into the creation of republics. Republics, in the first instance, are never desired for their own sakes. I do not think they will be finally desired at all; certainly not unaccompanied by curtly graces and good breeding, and whatever can tend to secure to them ornament as well as utility. I do not think it is in human nature to be content with a different settlement of the old question, any more than it is in nature physical to dispense with her pomp of flowers and colours. But sure I am, that the first cravings for republics always originate in some despair created by the conduct of kings.

It might be amusing to bring together a few of the exordiums of those same speeches, or state papers, of the allies of George the Third; but I have not time to look for them; and perhaps they would prove tiresome. It is more interesting to consider the "state" which Bonaparte kept in those days, and to compare it with his exile in St. Helena. There are more persons, perhaps, in the present generation who think of Bonaparte as the captive of Great Britain, defeated by Wellington, than as the maker of kings and queens, reigning in Paris, and bringing monarchs about his footstool.

But the fortunes of Napoleon were on the decline when they appeared to be at their height. The year 1808 beheld at once their culmination and their descent; and it was the feeblest of his vassals who, by the very excess of his servility, gave the signal for the change. Fortunately, too, for the interests of mankind, the change was caused by a violation of the most obvious principles of justice and good sense. It was owing to the unblushing seizure of Spain. It was owing to the gross and unfeeling farce of a pretended sympathy with the Spanish king's quarrel with his son; to the acceptance of a throne which the ridiculous father had no right to give away; and to the endeavour to force the accession on a country, which, instead of tranquilly admitting it on the new principles of indifference to religion and zeal for advancement (as he had ignorantly expected), opposed it with the united vehemence of dogged bigotry and an honest patriotism.

Spain was henceforth the millstone hung round the neck of the conqueror; and his marriage with a princess of Austria, which was thought such a wonderful piece of success, only furnished him with a like impediment; for it added to the weight of his unpopularity with all honest and prospective minds. It was well said by Cobbett, that he had much better have assembled a hundred of the prettiest girls in France, and selected the prettiest of them all for his wife. The heads and hearts of the "Young Continent" were henceforward against the self-seeker, ambitious of the old "shows of things," in contradiction to the honest "desires of the mind." Want of sympathy was prepared for him in case of a reverse; and when, partly in the confidence of his military pride, partly by way of making a final set-off against his difficulties in Spain, and partly in very ignorance of what Russian natures and Russian winters could effect, he went and ran his head against the great northern wall of ice and snow, he came back a ruined man, masterly and surprising as his efforts to reinstate himself might thereafter be. Nothing remained for him but to fume and fret in spirit, get fatter with a vitiated state of body, and see reverse on reverse coming round him, which he was to face to no purpose. The grandest thing he did was to return from Elba: the next, to fight the battle of Waterloo; but he went to the field, bloated and half asleep, in a carriage. He had already, in body, become one of the commonest of those "emperors" whom he had first laughed at and then leagued with: no great principle stood near him, as it did in the times of the republic, when armies of shoeless youths beat the veteran troops of Austria; and thus, deserted by everything but his veterans and his generalship, which came to nothing before the unyieldingness of English, and the advent of Prussian soldiers, he became a fugitive in the "belle France" which he had fancied his own, and died a prisoner in the hands of a man of the name of Lowe.

I do not believe that George the Third, or his minister, Mr. Pitt, speculated at all upon a catastrophe like this. I mean, that I do not believe they reckoned upon Napoleon's destroying himself by his own ambition. They looked, it is true, to the chance of "something turning up;" but it was to be of the ordinary kind. They thought to put him down by paid coalitions, and in the regular course of war. Hence, on repeated failures, the minister's broken heart, and probably the final extinguishment of the king's reason. The latter calamity, by a most unfortunate climax of untimeliness, took place a little before his enemy's reverses.

George the Third was a very brave and honest man. He feared nothing on earth, and he acted according to his convictions. But, unfortunately, his convictions were at the mercy of a will far greater than his understanding; and hence his courage became obstinacy, and his honesty the dupe of his inclinations. He was the son of a father with little brain, and of a mother who had a diseased blood: indeed, neither of his parents was healthy. He was brought up in rigid principles of morality on certain points, by persons who are supposed to have evaded them in their own conduct; he was taught undue notions of kingly prerogative; he was suffered to grow up, nevertheless, in homely as well as shy and moody habits; and while acquiring a love of power tending to the violent and uncontrollable, he was not permitted to have a taste of it till he became his own master. The consequences of this training were an extraordinary mixture of domestic virtue with official duplicity; of rustical, mechanical tastes and popular manners, with the most exalted ideas of authority; of a childish and self-betraying cunning, with the most stubborn reserves; of fearlessness with sordidness; good-nature with unforgivingness; and of the health and strength of temperance and self-denial, with the last weaknesses of understanding, and passions that exasperated it out of its reason. The English nation were pleased to see in him a crowning specimen of themselves—a royal John Bull. They did not discover till too late (perhaps have not yet discovered), how much of the objectionable, as well as the respectable, lies

hidden in the sturdy nickname invented for them by Arbuthnot; how much the animal predominates in it over the
intellectual; and how terribly the bearer of it may be over-
ridden, whether in a royal or a national shape. They had
much better get some new name for themselves, worthy of
the days of Queen Victoria and of the hopes of the world.

In every shape I reverence calamity, and would not be
thought to speak of it with levity, especially in connection
with a dynasty which has since become estimable, as well as
reasonable, in every respect.

If the histories of private as well as public families were
known, the race of the Guelphs would only be found, in the
person of one of their ancestors, to have shared, in common
perhaps with every family in the world, the sorrows of occasional deterioration. But in the greatest and most tragical
examples of human suffering, the homeliest, as well as the
loftiest images, are too often forced on the mind together.
George the Third, with all his faults, was a more estimable
man than many of his enemies, and, certainly, than any of
his wholesale revilers; and the memory of his last days is
sanctified by whatever can render the loss of sight and of
reason affecting.

Whatever of any kind has taken place in the world, may
have been best for all of us in the long run. Nature permits
us, retrospectively and for comfort's sake, though not in a different spirit, to entertain that conclusion among others. But
meantime, either because the world is not yet old enough to
know better, or because we yet live but in the tuning of its
instruments, and have not learned to play the harmonies of
the earth sweetly, men feel incited by what is good as well as
bad in them, to object and to oppose; and youth being the
season of inexperience and of vanity, as well as of enthusiasm
otherwise the most disinterested, the *Examiner*, which began
its career, like most papers, with thinking the worst of those
from whom it differed, and expressing its mind accordingly
with fearless sincerity (which was not equally the case with
those papers), speedily excited the anger of Government. It
did this the more, inasmuch as, according to what has been
stated of its opinions on foreign politics, and in matters of
church government, it did not fall into the common and half-
conciliating because degrading error of antagonists, by siding,
as a matter of course, with the rest of its enemies.

I need not reopen the questions of foreign and domestic

policy which were mooted with the ruling powers in those days, Reform in particular. The result is well known, and the details in general have ceased to be interesting. I would repeat none of them at all, if personal history did not give a new zest to almost any kind of relation. As such, however, is the case, I shall proceed to observe that the *Examiner* had not been established a year when Government instituted a prosecution against it, in consequence of some remarks on a pamphlet by a Major Hogan, who accused the Duke of York, as Commander-in-chief, of favouritism and corruption.

Major Hogan was a furious but honest Irishman, who had been in the army seventeen years. He had served and suffered bitterly; in the West Indies he possessed the highest testimonials to his character, had been a very active recruiting officer, had seen forty captains promoted over his head in spite of repeated applications and promises, and he desired, after all, nothing but the permission to purchase his advancement, agreeably to every custom.

Provoked out of his patience by these fruitless endeavours to buy what others who had done nothing obtained for nothing, and being particularly disgusted at being told, for the sixth time, that he had been " noted for promotion, and would be duly considered as favourable opportunities offered," the gallant Hibernian went straight, without any further ado, to the office of the Commander-in-chief, and there, with a vivacity and plain-speaking which must have looked like a scene in a play, addressed his Royal Highness in a speech that astounded him.

The Major explained to the royal Commander-in-chief how more than forty captains had been promoted without purchase, who had been his juniors when he was a captain, and how it had been suggested to him that he might obtain a majority without purchase by paying six hundred pounds as a bribe to certain persons. The Duke of York made no reply, asked no questions, but looked astounded. " *Vox faucibus hæsit.*" The Major proceeded to state his case in a pamphlet for publication. The day after his first advertisement, a lady in a barouche, with two footmen, called at the newspaper office for his address, and on the following evening an anonymous letter was left at his lodging, telling him that to maintain secrecy would benefit him with the royal family, and hoping that " the enclosed " (notes for 500*l*.) would pre-

vent the publication of his intended pamphlet. The receipt
of this letter was properly attested by several witnesses.
Major Hogan declined to be influenced by such agencies, and
instantly announced that the money should be returned.

The *Examiner* made comments on these disclosures, of a
nature that was to be expected from its ardour in the cause of
Reform; not omitting, however, to draw a distinction between
the rights of domestic privacy and the claims to indulgence
set up by traffickers in public corruption. The Government,
however, cared nothing for this distinction; neither would it
have had the corruption inquired into. Its prosecutions were
of a nature that did not allow truth to be investigated; and
one of these was accordingly instituted against us, when it
was unexpectedly turned aside by a member of Parliament,
Colonel Wardle, who was resolved to bring the female alluded
to by Major Hogan before the notice of that tribunal.

I say " unexpectedly," because neither then, nor at any
time, had I the least knowledge of Colonel Wardle. The
Examiner, so to speak, lived quite alone. It sought nobody;
and its principles in this respect had already become so well
understood that few sought it, and no one succeeded in
making its acquaintance. The colonel's motion for an investigation came upon us, therefore, like a god-send. The prosecution against the paper was dropped; and the whole
attention of the country was drawn to the strange spectacle of
a laughing, impudent woman, brought to the bar of the House
of Commons, and forcing them to laugh in their turn at the
effrontery of her answers. The poor Duke of York had
parted with her, and she had turned against him.

The upshot of the investigation was, that Mrs. Clarke had
evidently made money by the seekers of military promotion,
but that the duke was pronounced innocent of connivance.
His Royal Highness withdrew, however, from office for a
time (for he was not long afterwards reinstated), and public
opinion, as to his innocence or guilt, went meanwhile pretty
much according to that of party.

My own impression, at this distance of time, and after
better knowledge of the duke's private history and prevailing
character, is, that there was some connivance on his part, but
not of a systematic nature, or beyond what he may have
considered as warrantable towards a few special friends of his
mistress, on the assumption that she would carry her influence
no farther. His own letters proved that he allowed her to

talk to him of people with a view to promotion. He even let her recommend him a clergyman, who (as he phrased it) had an ambition to "preach before royalty." He said he would do what he could to bring it about ; probably thinking nothing whatsoever—I mean, never having the thought enter his head —of the secret scandal of the thing, or not regarding his consent as anything but a piece of good-natured patronizing acquiescence, after the ordinary fashion of the "ways of the world."

For, in truth, the Duke of York was as good-natured a man as he was far from being a wise one. The investigation gave him a salutary caution ; but I really believe, on the whole, that he had already been, as he was afterwards, a very good, conscientious war-office clerk. He was a brave man, though no general; a very filial, if not a very thinking politician (for he always voted to please his father); and if he had no idea of economy, it is to be recollected how easily princes' debts are incurred,—how often encouraged by the creditors who complain of them; and how often, and how temptingly to the debtor, they are paid off by governments.

As to his amours, the temptations of royalty that way are still greater: the duke seems to have regarded a mistress in a very tender and conjugal point of view, as long as the lady chose to be equally considerate; and if people wondered why such a loving man did not love his duchess—who appears to have been as good-natured as himself—the wonder ceased when they discovered that her Royal Highness was a lady of so whimsical a taste, and possessed such an overflowing amount of benevolence towards the respectable race of beings hight dogs, that in the constant occupation of looking after the welfare of some scores of her canine friends, she had no leisure to cultivate the society of those human ones that could better dispense with her attentions.

The ministers naturally grudged the *Examiner* its escape from the Hogan prosecution, especially as they gained nothing with the paper, in consequence of their involuntary forbearance. Accordingly, before another year was out, they instituted a second prosecution ; and so eager were they to bring it, that, in their haste, they again overleaped their prudence. Readers in the present times, when more libels have been written in a week by Toryism itself against royalty, in the most irreverent style, than appeared in those days in the course of a year from pens the most radical, and against princes the most provoking, are astonished to hear that the offence we had committed consisted of the following sentence:

" Of all monarchs since the Revolution, the successor of George the Third will have the finest opportunity of becoming nobly popular."

But the real offence was the contempt displayed towards the ministers themselves. The article in which the sentence appeared, was entitled " Change of Ministry ;" the Duke of Portland had just retired from the premiership ; and the *Examiner* had been long girding him and his associates on the score of general incompetency, as well as their particular unfitness for constitutional government. The ministers cared nothing for the king, in any sense of personal zeal, or of a particular wish to vindicate or exalt him. The tempers, caprices, and strange notions of sincerity and craft to which he was subject, by neutralizing in a great measure his ordinary good nature and somewhat exuberant style of intercourse on the side of familiarity and gossiping, did not render him a very desirable person to deal with, even among friends. But he was essentially a Tory king, and so far a favourite of Tories; he was now terminating the fiftieth year of his reign; there was to be a jubilee in consequence; and the ministers thought to turn the loyalty of the holiday into an instrument of personal revenge.

The passage in that article charged with being libellous was the following [reproduced now as a specimen of what was considered libel in those days]:—

"Whatever may be the truth of these statements, it is generally supposed that the mutilated administration, in spite of its tenacity of life, cannot exist much longer; and the Foxites, of course, are beginning to rally round their leaders, in order to give it the *coup de grace*. A more respectable set of men they certainly are,—with more general information, more attention to the encouragement of intellect, and altogether a more enlightened policy; and if his Majesty could be persuaded to enter into their conciliatory views with regard to Ireland, a most important and most necessary benefit would be obtained for this country. The subject of Ireland, next to the difficulty of coalition, is no doubt the great trouble in the election of his Majesty's servants; and it is this, most probably, which has given rise to the talk of a regency, a measure to which the court would never resort while it felt a possibility of acting upon its own principles. What a crowd of blessings rush upon one's mind, that might be bestowed upon the country in the event of such a change! Of all monarchs, indeed, since the revolution, the successor of George the Third will have the finest opportunity of becoming nobly popular."

The framers of the indictment evidently calculated on the

usual identification of a special with a Tory jury. They had reckoned, at the same time, so confidently on the effect to be produced with that class of persons, by any objection to the old king, that the proprietor of the *Morning Chronicle*, Mr. Perry, was prosecuted for having extracted only the two concluding sentences; and as the Government was still more angered with the Whigs who hoped to displace them, than with the Radicals who wished to see them displaced, Mr. Perry's prosecution preceded ours. This was fortunate; for though the proprietor of the *Morning Chronicle* pleaded his own cause, an occasion in which a man is said to have "a fool for his client" (that is to say, in the opinion of lawyers), he pleaded it so well, and the judge (Ellenborough), who afterwards showed himself so zealous a Whig, gave him a hearing and construction so favourable, that he obtained an acquittal, and the prosecution against the *Examiner* accordingly fell to the ground.

I had the pleasure of a visit from this gentleman while his indictment was pending. He came to tell me how he meant to conduct his defence. He was a lively, good-natured man, with a shrewd expression of countenance, and twinkling eyes, which he not unwillingly turned upon the ladies. I had lately married, and happened to be sitting with my wife. A chair was given him close to us; but as he was very near-sighted, and yet could not well put up his eyeglass to look at her (which purpose, nevertheless, he was clearly bent on effecting), he took occasion, while speaking of the way in which he should address the jury, to thrust his face close upon hers, observing at the same time, with his liveliest emphasis, and, as if expressly for her information, "I mean to be very modest."

The unexpectedness of this announcement, together with the equivocal turn given to it by the vivacity of his movement, had all the effect of a dramatic surprise, and it was with difficulty we kept our countenances.

Mr. Perry subsequently became one of my warmest friends, and, among other services, would have done me one of a very curious nature, which I will mention by-and-by.*

* [This is the first mention that the writer makes of his marriage, and it is a striking example of the manner in which, for various reasons, but principally out of delicacy to living persons, he felt himself bound to pass over, with very slight allusions, the greater part of his personal and private life. In the present instance there was no practical reason for this reserve, unless it was that if the

Of the ministers, whom a young journalist thus treated with contempt, I learned afterwards to think better. Not as ministers: for I still consider them, in that respect, as the luckiest, and the least deserving their luck, of any statesmen that have been employed by the House of Brunswick. I speak not only of the section at that moment reigning, but of the whole of what was called Mr. Pitt's successors. But with the inexperience and presumption of youth, I was too much in the habit of confounding difference of opinion with dishonest motives. I did not see (and it is strange how people, not otherwise wanting in common sense or modesty, can pass whole lives without seeing!) that if I had a right to have

author had entered upon domestic matters, he might, with his almost exaggerated sense of the active obligations which truth-speaking involved, have felt bound to enter into personal questions and perhaps judgments, which he thought it better to waive. The dominating motives for this characteristic reserve are treated in the closing chapter of the volume. Leigh Hunt was married in 1809, to Marianne, the daughter of Thomas and Ann Kent. Mr. Kent had died comparatively young. His widow had obtained an independent livelihood as a dressmaker in rather a "high" connection; amongst her acquaintance was the young editor, who fell in love with the eldest daughter, and married her after a long courtship. The bride was the reverse of handsome, and without accomplishments; but she had a pretty figure, beautiful black hair which reached down to her knees, magnificent eyes, and a very unusual natural turn for plastic art. She was an active and thrifty housewife, until the curious malady with which she was seized totally undermined her strength. Mrs. Kent, her mother, who had perhaps acquired some harshness of character in a very hard school of adversity, never quite succeeded in retaining the regard of her son-in-law,—one reason, perhaps, for the reserve which has been noticed. Mrs. Kent made, indeed, some fearful mistakes in her sternness; but she was really a very kind-hearted woman, only too anxious to please, and faithful in the attachments which she formed, even when disappointed. She subsequently married Mr. Rowland Hunter, a man of keen observation and simple mind, who has survived to a great age, and whose hearty friendship was cordially appreciated by Leigh Hunt, as they both advanced in years. Rowland Hunter was the nephew and successor of Johnson, the well-known bookseller in St. Paul's Churchyard, and the early patron of the poet Cowper. Johnson acquired celebrity for his success in business, his intelligence, and his peculiar hospitality; and Mr. Hunter continued his custom of keeping open house weekly for literary men, the friends of literature, and persons of any individual mark. At his house, the young author encountered a great variety of minds, and most unquestionably derived great advantage from the opportunity. His conversation frequently turned upon his recollections of these gatherings, and it was in this house that he formed many of his literary and personal acquaintances.]

good motives attributed to myself by those who differed with me in opinion, I was bound to reciprocate the concession. I did not reflect that political antagonists have generally been born and bred in a state of antagonism, and that for any one of them to demand identity of opinion from another on pain of his being thought a man of bad motives, was to demand that he should have had the antagonist's father and mother as well as his own—the same training, the same direction of conscience, the same predilections and very prejudices; not to mention, that good motives themselves might have induced a man to go counter to all these, even had he been bred in them; which, in one or two respects, was the case with myself.

Canning, indeed, was not a man to be treated with contempt under any circumstances, by those who admired wit and rhetoric; though, compared with what he actually achieved in either, I cannot help thinking that his position procured him an undue measure of fame. What has he left us to perpetuate the amount of it? A speech or two, and the *Ode on the Knife-Grinder*. This will hardly account, with the next ages, for the statue that occupies the highway in Westminster; a compliment, too, unique of its kind; monopolizing the parliamentary pavement, as though the original had been the only man fit to go forth as the representative of Parliament itself, and to challenge the admiration of the passengers. The liberal measures of Canning's last days renewed his claim on the public regard, especially as he was left, by the jealousy and resentment of his colleagues, to carry them by himself: jealousy, because, small as his wit was for a great fame, they had none of their own to equal it; and resentment, because in its indiscretions and inconsiderateness, it had nicknamed or bantered them all round,—the real cause, I have no doubt, of that aristocratical desertion of his ascendancy which broke his heart at the very height of his fortunes. But at the time I speak of, I took him for nothing but a great sort of impudent Eton boy, with an unfeelingness that surpassed his ability. Whereas he was a man of much natural sensibility, a good husband and father, and an admirable son. Canning continued, as long as he lived, to write a letter every week to his mother, who had been an actress, and whom he treated, in every respect, with a consideration and tenderness that may be pronounced to have been perfect. "Good son" should have been written under his statue. It would have given the somewhat pert look of his handsome face a pleasanter effect; and have done him a thousand times more good with the coming generations than his *Ode on the Knife-Grinder*.

The Earl of Liverpool, whom Madame de Staël is said to have described as having a "talent for silence," and to have asked, in company, what had become of "that dull speaker, Lord Hawkesbury" (his title during his father's lifetime), was assuredly a very dull minister; but I believe he was a very good man. His father had been so much in the confidence of the Earl of Bute at the accession of George III., as to have succeeded to his invidious reputation of being the secret adviser of the king; and he continued in great favour during the whole of the reign. The son, with little interval, was in office during the whole of the war with Napoleon; and after partaking of all the bitter draughts of disappointment which ended in killing Pitt, had the luck of tasting the sweets of triumph. I met him one day, not long afterwards, driving his barouche in a beautiful spot where he lived, and was so struck with the melancholy of his aspect, that, as I did not know him by sight, I asked a passenger who he was.

The same triumph did not hinder poor Lord Castlereagh from dying by his own hand. The long burden of responsibility had been too much, even for him; though, to all appearance, he was a man of a stronger temperament than Lord Liverpool, and had, indeed, a very noble aspect. He should have led a private life, and been counted one of the models of the aristocracy; for though a ridiculous speaker, and a cruel politician (out of impatience of seeing constant trouble, and not knowing otherwise how to end it), he was an intelligent and kindly man in private life, and could be superior to his position as a statesman.* He delighted in the political satire of the *Beggar's Opera;* has been seen applauding it from a stage box; and Lady Morgan tells us, would ask her in company to play him the songs on the pianoforte, and good-humouredly accompany them with a bad voice. How pleasant it is thus to find oneself reconciled to men whom we have ignorantly undervalued! and how fortunate to have lived long enough to say so!

* [The amount, and even existence, of the cruelty here attributed to Lord Castlereagh, have since been denied, and apparently not without reason.]

The *Examiner*, though it preferred the Whigs to the Tories, was not a Whig of the school then existing. Its great object was a reform in Parliament, which the older and more influential Whigs did not advocate, which the younger ones (the fathers of those now living) advocated but fitfully and misgivingly, and which had lately been suffered to fall entirely into the hands of those newer and more thorough-going Whigs, which were known by the name of Radicals, and have since been called Whig-Radicals, and Liberals. The opinions of the *Examiner*, in fact, both as to State and Church government, allowing, of course, for difference of position in the parties, and tone in their manifestation, were those that have since swayed the destinies of the country, in the persons of Queen Victoria and her ministers. I do not presume to give her Majesty the name of a partisan; or to imply that, under any circumstances, she would condescend to accept it. Her business, as she well knows and admirably demonstrates, is, not to side with any of the disputants among her children, but to act lovingly and dispassionately for them all, as circumstances render expedient. But the extraordinary events which took place on the Continent during her childhood, the narrow political views of most of her immediate predecessors, her own finer and more genial understanding, and the training of a wise mother, all these circumstances in combination have rendered her what no prince of her house has been before her,—equal to the demands not only of the nation and the day, but of the days to come, and the popular interests of the world. So, at least, I conceive. I do not pretend to any special knowledge of the court or its advisers. I speak from what I have seen of her Majesty's readiness to fall in with every great and liberal measure for the education of the country, the freedom of trade, and the independence of nations; and I spoke in the same manner, before I could be suspected of confounding esteem with gratitude. She knows how, and nobly dares, to let the reins of restriction in the hands of individuals be loosened before the growing strength and self-government of the many; and the royal house that best knows how to do this, and neither to tighten those reins in anger nor abandon them out of fear, will be the last house to suffer in any convulsion which others may provoke, and the first to be reassured in their retention, as long as royalty shall exist. May it exist, under the shape in which I can picture it to my imagination, as long as reasonableness can outlive envy, and ornament be known to be one of nature's desires! Excess, neither of riches nor poverty, would then endanger it. I am no republican, nor ever was, though I have lived during a period of history when kings themselves tried hard to make honest men republicans by their apparent unteachableness. But my own education, the love, perhaps, of poetic ornament, and the dislike which I had conceived at that time of an existing republic, even of British origin, kept me within the pale of the loyal. I might prefer, perhaps, a succession of queens to kings, and a simple fillet on their brows to the most gorgeous diadem. I think that men more willingly obey the one, and I am sure that nobody could mistake the cost of the other. But peaceful and reasonable provision for the progress of mankind towards all the good possible to their nature, from orderly good manners up to disinterested sentiments, is the great desideratum in government; and thinking this more securely and handsomely maintained in limited monarchies than republics, I am for English permanence in this respect, in preference to French mutability, and American electiveness; though, at the same time, I cannot but consider the two great nations of France and the United States as setting us enviable examples in regard to the more amiable sociality of the one and the special and constant consideration for women in the other.

The Tory Government having failed in its two attacks on the *Examiner*, could not be content, for any length of time, till it had failed in a third. For such was the case. The new charge was again on the subject of the army—that of military flogging. An excellent article on the absurd and cruel nature of that punishment, from the pen of the late Mr. John Scott (who afterwards fell in a duel with one of the writers in *Blackwood*), had appeared in a country paper, the *Stamford News*, of which he was editor. The most striking passages of this article were copied into the *Examiner*, and it is a remarkable circumstance in the history of juries, that after the journal which copied it had been acquitted in London, the journal which originated the copied matter was found guilty in Stamford; and this, too, though the counsel was the same in both instances—the present Lord Brougham.

The attorney-general at that time was Sir Vicary Gibbs; a name which it appears somewhat ludicrous to me to write at present, considering what a bugbear it was to politicians, and how insignificant it has since become. Sir Vicary was a little, irritable, sharp-featured, bilious-looking man (so at least he was described, for I never saw him); very worthy, I believe, in private; and said to be so fond of novels, that he would read them after the labours of the day, till the wax-lights guttered without his knowing it. I had a secret regard for him on this account, and wished he would not haunt me in a spirit so unlike Tom Jones. I know not what sort of lawyer he was; probably none the worse for imbuing himself with the knowledge of Fielding and Smollett; but he was a bad reasoner, and made half-witted charges. He used those edge-tools of accusation which cut a man's own fingers. He assumed that we could have no motives for writing but mercenary ones; and he argued, that because Mr. Scott (who had no more regard for Bonaparte than we had) endeavoured to shame down the practice of military flogging by pointing to the disuse of it in the armies of France, he only wanted to subject his native country to invasion. He also had the simplicity to ask, why we did not " speak privately on the subject to some member of Parliament," and get him to notice it in a proper manner, instead of bringing it before the public in a newspaper? We laughed at him; and the event of his accusations enabled us to laugh more.

The charge of being friends of Bonaparte against all who differed with Lord Castlereagh and Mr. Canning was a common, and, for too long a time, a successful trick, with such of the public as did not read the writings of the persons accused. I have often been surprised, much later in life, both in relation to this and to other charges, at the credulity into which many excellent persons had owned they had been thus beguiled, and at the surprise which they expressed in turn at finding the charges the reverse of true. To the readers of the *Examiner* they caused only indignation or merriment.

The last and most formidable prosecution against us remains to be told; but some intermediate circumstances must be related first.

CHAPTER XII.

LITERARY WARFARE.

The *Examiner* had been established between two and three years, when [in 1810] my brother projected a quarterly magazine of literature and politics, entitled the *Reflector*, which I edited. Lamb, Dyer, Barnes, Mitchell, the Greek Professor Scholefield (all Christ-Hospital men), together with Dr. Aikin and his family, wrote in it; and it was rising in sale every quarter, when it stopped at the close of the fourth number for want of funds. Its termination was not owing to want of liberality in the payments. But the radical reformers in those days were not sufficiently rich or numerous to support such a publication.

Some of the liveliest effusions of Lamb first appeared in this magazine; and in order that I might retain no influential class for my good wishers, after having angered the stage, dissatisfied the Church, offended the State, not very well pleased the Whigs, and exasperated the Tories, I must needs commence the maturer part of my verse-making with contributing to its pages the *Feast of the Poets*.

The *Feast of the Poets* was (perhaps, I may say, is) a *jeu d'esprit* suggested by the *Session of the Poets* of Sir John Suckling. Apollo gives the poets a dinner; and many verse-makers, who have no claim to the title, present themselves, and are rejected.

With this effusion, while thinking of nothing but showing my wit, and reposing under the shadow of my " laurels " (of which I expected a harvest as abundant as my self-esteem), I made almost every living poet and poetaster my enemy, and particularly exasperated those among the Tories. I speak of the shape in which it first appeared, before time and reflection had moderated its judgment. It drew upon my head all the personal hostility which had hitherto been held in a state of suspense by the vaguer daring of the *Examiner*, and I have reason to believe that its inconsiderate, and I am bound to confess, in some respects, unwarrantable levity, was the origin of the gravest, and far less warrantable attacks which I afterwards sustained from political antagonists, and which caused the most serious mischief to my fortunes. Let the young satirist take warning ; and consider how much self-love he is going to wound, by the indulgence of his own.

Not that I have to apologize to the memory of every one whom I attacked. I am sorry to have had occasion to differ with any of my fellow-creatures, knowing the mistakes to which we are all liable, and the circumstances that help to cause them. But I can only regret it, personally, in proportion to the worth or personal regret on the side of the enemy.

The *Quarterly Review*, for instance, had lately been set up, and its editor was Gifford, the author of the *Baviad and Mæviad*. I had been invited, nay, pressed by the publisher, to write in the new review ; which surprised me, considering its politics and the great difference of my own. I was not aware of the little faith that was held in the politics of any beginner of the world; and I have no doubt that the invitation had been made at the instance of Gifford himself, of whom, as the dictum of a " man of vigorous learning," and the " first satirist of his time," I had quoted in the *Critical Essays* the gentle observation, that " all the fools in the kingdom seemed to have risen up with one accord, and exclaimed, ' Let us write for the theatres !' "

Strange must have been Gifford's feelings, when, in the *Feast of the Poets*, he found his eulogizer falling as trenchantly on the author of the *Baviad and Mæviad* as the *Baviad and Mæviad* had fallen on the dramatists. The Tory editor discerned plainly enough, that if a man's politics were of no consideration with the *Quarterly Review*, provided the politician was his critical admirer, they were very different things with the editor Radical. He found also, that the new satirist had ceased to regard the old one as a " critical authority ;" and he might not have unwarrantably concluded that I had conceived some personal disgust against him as a man ; for such, indeed, was the secret of my attack.

The reader is, perhaps, aware, that George the Fourth, when he was Prince of Wales, had a mistress of the name of Robinson. She was the wife of a man of no great character, had taken to the stage for a livelihood, was very handsome, wrote verses, and is said to have excited a tender emotion in the bosom of Charles Fox. The prince allured her from the stage, and lived with her for some years. After their separation, and during her decline, which took place before she was old, she became afflicted with rheumatism; and as she solaced her pains, and perhaps added to her subsistence, by writing verses, and as her verses turned upon her affections, and she could not discontinue her old vein of love and sentiment, she fell under the lash of this masculine and gallant gentleman, Mr. Gifford, who, in his *Baviad and Mæviad*, amused himself with tripping up her " crutches," particularly as he thought her on her way to her last home. This he considered the climax of the fun.

" See," exclaimed he, after a hit or two at other women, like a boy throwing stones in the street—

> " See Robinson forget her state, and move
> *On crutches tow'rds the grave* to ' Light o' Love.' "

This is the passage which put all the gall into anything which I said, then or afterwards, of Gifford, till he attacked myself and my friends. At least, it disposed me to think the worst of whatever he wrote; and as reflection did not improve nor suffering soften him, he is the only man I ever attacked, respecting whom I have felt no regret.

It would be easy for me, at this distance of time, to own that Gifford possessed genius, had such been the case. It would have been easy for me at any time. But he had not a particle. The scourger of poetasters was himself a poetaster. When he had done with his whip, everybody had a right to take it up, and lay it over the scourger's shoulders; for though he had sense enough to discern glaring faults, he abounded in commonplaces. His satire itself, which at its best never went beyond smartness, was full of them.

The reader shall have a specimen or two, in order that Mr. Gifford may speak for himself; for his book has long ceased to be read. He shall see with how little a stock of his own a man may set up for a judge of others.

The *Baviad and Mæviad*—so called from two bad poets mentioned by Virgil—was a satire, imitated from Persius, on a set of fantastic writers who had made their appearance under the title of Della Cruscans. The coterie originated in the meeting of some of them at Florence, the seat of the famous Della-Cruscan Academy. Mr. Merry, their leader, who was a member of that academy, and who wrote under its signature, gave occasion to the name. They first published a collection of poems, called the *Florence Miscellany*, and then sent verses to the London newspapers, which occasioned an overflow of contributions in the like taste. The taste was as bad as can be imagined ; full of floweriness, conceits, and affectation; and, in attempting to escape from commonplace, it evaporated into nonsense :—

> " Was it the shuttle of the morn
> That wove upon the cobwebb'd thorn
>   Thy airy lay? "
>
> " Hang o'er his eye the gossamery tear."
>
> " Gauzy zephyrs, fluttering o'er the plain,
> On twilight's bosom drop their filmy rain."
>   &c. &c.

It was impossible that such absurdities could have had any lasting effect on the public taste. They would have died of inanition.

His satire consists, not in a critical exposure—in showing why the objects of his contempt are wrong—but in simply asserting that they are so. He turns a commonplace of his own in his verses, quotes a passage from his author in a note, expresses his amazement at it, and thus thinks he has proved his case, when he has made out nothing but an overweening assumption at the expense of what was not worth noticing. " I was born," says he,—

> " To *brand* obtrusive ignorance with scorn,
> On bloated pedantry to *pour my rage*,
> And *hiss preposterous fustian* from the stage."

What commonplace talking is that? Here is some more of the same stuff :—

> " Then let your style be brief, your meaning clear,
> Nor, like Lorenzo, tire the labouring ear
> With a wild waste of words; sound without sense,
> And all the florid glare of impotence.
> Still, with your characters your language change,—
> From grave to gay, *as nature dictates*, range;
> Now droop in all the plaintiveness of woe,—(!!)
> Now in glad numbers light and airy flow;
> Now shake the stage with guilt's alarming *tone*, (!!)
> And make the aching bosom *all your own*."

Was there ever a fonder set of complacent old phrases, such as any schoolboy might utter? Yet this is the man who undertook to despise Charles Lamb, and to trample on Keats and Shelley!

I have mentioned the Roxburgh sale of books. I was standing among the bidders with my friend the late Mr. Barron Field, when he jogged my elbow, and said, " There is Gifford over the way, looking at you with *such* a face ! " I met the eyes of my beholder, and saw a little man, with a warped frame and a countenance between the querulous and the angry, gazing at me with all his might. It was, truly enough, the satirist who could not bear to be satirized—the denouncer of incompetencies, who could not bear to be told of his own. He had now learnt, as I was myself to learn, what it was to taste of his own bitter medicaments; and he never profited by it, for his *Review* spared neither age nor sex as long as he lived. What he did at first out of a self-satisfied incompetence, he did at last out of an envious and angry one; and he was, all the while, the humble servant of power, and never expressed one word of regret for his inhumanity. The mixture of implacability and servility is the sole reason, as I have said before, why I still speak of him as I do. If he secretly felt regret for it, I am sorry—especially if he retained any love for his " Anna," whom I take to have been not only the good servant and friend he describes her, but such a one as he could wish that he had married. Why did he not marry her, and remain a humbler and a happier man? or how was it, that the power to have any love at all could not teach him that other people might have feelings as well as himself, especially women and the sick?

Such were the causes of my disfavour with the Tory critics in England.

To those in Scotland I gave, in like manner, the first cause of offence, and they had better right to complain of me; though they ended, as far as regards the mode of resentment, in being still more in the wrong. I had taken a dislike to Walter Scott, on account of a solitary passage in his edition of *Dryden*—nay, on account of a single word. The word, it must be allowed, was an extraordinary one, and such as he must have regretted writing; for a more dastardly or deliberate piece of wickedness than allowing a ship with its crew to go to sea, knowing the vessel to be leaky, believing it likely to founder, and on purpose to destroy one of the passengers, it is not so easy to conceive; yet, because this was done by a Tory king, the relator could find no severer term for it than " ungenerous." Here is the passage :—

" His political principles (the Earl of Mulgrave's) were those of a staunch Tory, which he maintained through his whole life; and he was zealous for the royal prerogative, although he had no small reason to complain of Charles the Second, who, to avenge himself of Mulgrave, for a supposed attachment to the Princess Anne, sent him to Tangiers, at the head of some troops, in a leaky vessel, *which it was supposed must have perished in the voyage.* Though Mulgrave was apprised of the danger, he scorned to shun it; and the Earl of Ply-

mouth, a favourite son of the king, generously insisted upon sharing
it along with him. This *ungenerous* attempt to destroy him in the
very act of performing his duty, with the refusal of a regiment, made
a temporary change in Mulgrave's conduct."—*Notes on Absalom and
Achithophel in Dryden's Works,* vol. ix. p. 304.

This passage was the reason why the future great novelist
was introduced to Apollo, in the *Feast of the Poets,* after a
very irreverent fashion.

I believe that with reference to high standards of poetry
and criticism, superior to mere description, however lively, to
the demands of rhyme for its own sake, to prosaical ground-
works of style, metaphors of common property, convention-
alities in general, and the prevalence of a material over a
spiritual treatment, my estimate of Walter Scott's then publications, making allowance for the manner of it, will still be
found not far from the truth, by those who have profited by
a more advanced age of æsthetical culture.

There is as much difference, for instance, poetically speaking, between Coleridge's brief poem, *Christabel,* and all the
narrative poems of Walter Scott, or, as Wordsworth called
them, " novels in verse," as between a precious essence and a
coarse imitation of it, got up for sale. Indeed, Coleridge, not
unnaturally, though not with entire reason (for the story and
characters in Scott were the real charm), lamented that an
endeavour, unavowed, had been made to catch his tone, and
had succeeded just far enough to recommend to unbounded
popularity what had nothing in common with it.

But though Walter Scott was no novelist at that time
except in verse, the tone of personal assumption towards him
in the *Feast of the Poets* formed a just ground of offence.
Not that I had not as much right to differ with any man on
any subject, as he had to differ with others ; but it would
have become me, especially at that time of life, and in speaking of a living person, to express the difference with modesty.
I ought to have taken care also not to fall into one of the very
prejudices I was reproving, and think ill or well of people in
proportion as they differed or agreed with me in politics.
Walter Scott saw the good of mankind in a Tory or retrospective point of view. I saw it from a Whig, a Radical, or
prospective one ; and though I still think he was mistaken,
and though circumstances have shown that the world think so
too, I ought to have discovered, even by the writings which I
condemned, that he was a man of a kindly nature ; and it

would have become me to have given him credit for the same
good motives, which I arrogated exclusively for my own side
of the question. It is true, it might be supposed, that I
should have advocated that side with less ardour, had I been
more temperate in this kind of judgment ; but I do not think
so. Or if I had, the want of ardour would probably have
been compensated by the presence of qualities, the absence of
which was injurious to its good effect. At all events, I am
now of opinion, that whatever may be the immediate impression, a cause is advocated to the most permanent advantage
by persuasive, instead of provoking manners; and certain I
am, that whether this be the case or not, no human being, be
he the best and wisest of his kind, much less a confident
young man, can be so sure of the result of his confidence, as
to warrant the substitution of his will and pleasure in that
direction, for the charity which befits his common modesty
and his participation of error.

It is impossible for me, in other respects, to regret the war
I had with the Tories. I rejoice in it as far as I can rejoice
at anything painful to myself and others, and I am paid for
the consequences in what I have lived to see; nay, in the
respect and regrets of the best of my enemies. But I am
sorry that in aiming wounds which I had no right to give, I
cannot deny that I brought on myself others which they had
still less right to inflict ; and I make the amends of this confession, not only in return for what they have expressed
themselves, but in justice to the feelings which honest men of
all parties experience as they advance in life, and when they
look back calmly upon their common errors.

" I shall put this book in my pocket," said Walter Scott to
Murray, after he had been standing a while at his counter,
reading the *Story of Rimini*.

" Pray do," said the publisher. The copy of the book was
set down to the author in the bookseller's account as a present
to Walter Scott. Walter Scott was beloved by his friends;
the author of the *Story of Rimini* was an old offender, personal as well as political ; and hence the fury with which they
fell on him in their new publication.

Every party has a right side and a wrong. The right side
of Whiggism, Radicalism, or the love of liberty, is the love
of justice—the wish to see fair play to all men, and the advancement of knowledge and competence. The wrong side is
the wish to pull down those above us, instead of the desire of

raising those who are below. The right side of Toryism is
the love of order and the disposition to reverence and personal
attachment ; the wrong side is the love of power for power's
sake, and the determination to maintain it in the teeth of all
that is reasonable and humane. A strong spice of superstition, generated by the habit of success, tended to confuse the
right and wrong sides of Toryism, in minds not otherwise
unjust or ungenerous. They seemed to imagine that heaven
and earth would " come together," if the supposed favourites
of Providence were to be considered as favourites no longer ;
and hence the unbounded licence which they gave to their
resentment, and the strange self-permission of a man like
Walter Scott, not only to lament over the progress of society,
as if the future had been ordained only to carry on the past,
but to countenance the Border-like forages of his friends into
provinces which they had no business to invade, and to
speculate upon still greater organizations of them, which circumstances, luckily for his fame, prevented. I allude to the
intended establishment of a journal, which, as it never existed,
it is no longer necessary to name.

Readers in these kindlier days of criticism have no conception of the extent to which personal hostility allowed itself to
be transported, in the periodicals of those times. Personal
habits, appearances, connections, domesticities, nothing was
safe from misrepresentations, begun, perhaps, in the gaiety of
a saturnalian licence, but gradually carried to an excess which
would have been ludicrous, had it not sometimes produced
tragical consequences. It threatened a great many more, and
scattered, meantime, a great deal of wretchedness among un-
offending as well as offending persons, sometimes in proportion
to the delicacy which hindered them from exculpating themselves, and which could only have vindicated one portion of a
family by sacrificing another. I was so caricatured, it seems,
among the rest, upon matters great and small (for I did not
see a tenth part of what was said of me), that persons, on
subsequently becoming acquainted with me, sometimes expressed their surprise at finding me no other than I was in
face, dress, manners, and very walk ; to say nothing of the
conjugality which they found at my fireside, and the affection
which I had the happiness of enjoying among my friends in
general. I never retaliated in the same way ; first, because I
had never been taught to respect it, even by the jests of
Aristophanes ; secondly, because I observed the sorrow which

it caused both to right and wrong; thirdly, because it is impossible to know the truth of any story related of a person,
without hearing all the parties concerned; and fourthly,
because, while people thought me busy with politics and contention, I was almost always absorbed in my books and verses,
and did not, perhaps, sufficiently consider the worldly consequences of the indulgence.

To return to the *Feast of the Poets*. I offended all the
critics of the old or French school by objecting to the monotony of Pope's versification, and all the critics of the new or
German school, by laughing at Wordsworth, with whose
writings I was then unacquainted, except through the medium
of his deriders. On reading him for myself, I became such
an admirer, that Lord Byron accused me of making him
popular upon town. I had not very well pleased Lord Byron
himself, by counting him inferior to Wordsworth. Indeed, I
offended almost everybody whom I noticed; some by finding
any fault at all with them; some, by not praising them on
their favourite points; some, by praising others on any point;
and some, I am afraid, and those amongst the most good-
natured, by needlessly bringing them on the carpet, and
turning their very good-nature into a subject of caricature.
Thus I introduced Mr. Hayley, whom I need not have noticed
at all, as he belonged to a bygone generation. He had been
brought up in the courtesies of the old school of manners,
which he ultra-polished and rendered caressing, after the
fashion of my Arcadian friends of Italy; and as the poetry of
the *Triumphs of Temper* was not as vigorous in style as it was
amiable in its moral and elegant in point of fancy, I chose to
sink his fancy and his amiableness, and to represent him as
nothing but an effeminate parader of phrases of endearment
and pickthank adulation. I looked upon him as a sort of
powder-puff of a man, with no real manhood in him, but fit
only to suffocate people with his frivolous vanity, and be struck
aside with contempt. I had not yet learned, that writers may
be very "strong" and huffing on paper, while feeble on other
points, and, *vice versâ*, weak in their metres, while they are
strong enough as regards muscle. I remember my astonishment, years afterwards, on finding that the "gentle Mr. Hayley," whom I had taken for

"A puny insect, shivering at a breeze,"

was a strong-built man, famous for walking in the snow

before daylight, and possessed of an intrepidity as a horseman amounting to the reckless. It is not improbable that the feeble Hayley, during one of his equestrian passes, could have snatched up the "vigorous" Gifford, and pitched him over the hedge into the next field.

Having thus secured the enmity of the Tory critics north and south, and the indifference (to say the least of it) of the gentlest lookers on, it fell to the lot of the better part of my impulses to lose me the only counteracting influence which was offered me in the friendship of the Whigs. I had partaken deeply of Whig indignation at the desertion of their party by the Prince Regent. The *Reflector* contained an article on his Royal Highness, bitter accordingly, which bantered, among other absurdities, a famous dinner given by him to "one hundred and fifty particular friends." There was a real stream of water running down the table at this dinner, stocked with golden fish. It had banks of moss and bridges of pasteboard; the salt-cellars were panniers borne by "golden asses;" everything, in short, was as unlike the dinners now given by the sovereign, in point of taste and good sense, as effeminacy is different from womanhood ; and the *Reflector*, in a parody of the complaint of the shepherd, described how

> " Despairing, beside a clear stream,
>   The bust of a cod-fish was laid;
> And while a false taste was his theme,
>   A drainer supported his head."

A day or two after the appearance of this article, I met in the street the late estimable Blanco White, whom I had the pleasure of being acquainted with. He told me of the amusement it had given at Holland House ; and added, that Lord Holland would be glad to see me among his friends there, and that he (Blanco White) was commissioned to say so.

I did not doubt for an instant that anything but the most disinterested kindness and good-nature dictated the invitation which was thus made to me. It was impossible, at any subsequent time, that I could speak with greater respect and admiration of his lordship, than I had been in the habit of doing already. Never had an unconstitutional or illiberal measure taken place in the House of Lords, but his protest was sure to appear against it ; and this, and his elegant literature and reputation for hospitality, had completely won my heart. At the same time, I did not look upon the invitation as any return for this enthusiasm. I considered his lordship (and now at this moment consider him) as having been as free from every personal motive as myself; and this absence of all suspicion, prospective or retrospective, enabled me to feel the more confident and consoled in the answer which I felt bound to make to his courtesy.

I said to Mr. Blanco White, that I could not sufficiently express my sense of the honour that his lordship was pleased to do me; and there was not a man in England at whose table I should be prouder or happier to sit; and I was fortunate in having a conveyer of the invitation, who would know how to believe what I said, and to make a true representation of it; and that with almost any other person, I should fear to be thought guilty of immodesty and presumption, in not hastening to avail myself of so great a kindness; but that the more I admired and loved the character of Lord Holland, the less I dared to become personally acquainted with him; that being a far weaker person than he gave me credit for being, it would be difficult for me to eat the mutton and drink the claret of such a man, without falling into any opinion into which his conscience might induce him to lead me; and that not having a single personal acquaintance, even among what was called my own party (the Radicals), his lordship's goodness would be the more easily enabled to put its kindest and most indulgent construction on the misfortune which I was obliged to undergo, in denying myself the delight of his society.

I do not say that these were the very words, but they convey the spirit of what I said to Mr. Blanco White; and I should not have doubted his giving them a correct report, even had no evidence of it followed. But there did; for Lord Holland courteously sent me his publications, and never ceased, while he lived, to show me all the kindness in his power.

Of high life in ordinary, it is little for me to say that I might have had a surfeit of it, if I pleased. Circumstances, had I given way to them, might have rendered half my existence a round of it. I might also have partaken no mean portion of high life extraordinary. And very charming is its mixture of softness and strength, of the manliness of its taste and the urbanity of its intercourse. I have tasted, if not much of it, yet some of its very essence, and I cherish, and am grateful for it at this moment. What I have said, therefore, of Holland House, is mentioned under no feelings, either of assumption or servility. The invitation was made, and declined, with an equal spirit of faith on both sides in better impulses.

Far, therefore, am I from supposing, that the silence of the Whig critics respecting me was owing to any hostile influence which Lord Holland would have condescended to exercise. Not being among the visitors at Holland House, I dare say I was not thought of; or if I was thought of, I was regarded as a person who, in shunning Whig connection, and, perhaps, in persisting to advocate a reform towards which they were cooling, might be supposed indifferent to Whig advocacy. And, indeed, such was the case, till I felt the want of it.

Accordingly, the *Edinburgh Review* took no notice of the *Feast of the Poets*, though my verses praised it at the expense of the *Quarterly*, and though some of the reviewers, to my knowledge, liked it, and it echoed the opinions of others. It took no notice of the pamphlet on the *Folly and Danger of Methodism*, though the opinions in it were, perhaps, identical with its own. And it took as little of the *Reformist's Answer to an Article in the Edinburgh Review*—a pamphlet which I wrote in defence of its own reforming principles, which it had lately taken it into its head to renounce as impracticable. Reform had been apparently given up for ever by its originators; the Tories were increasing in strength every day; and I was left to battle with them as I could. Little did I suppose, that a time would come when I should be an Edinburgh Reviewer myself; when its former editor, agreeably to the dictates of his heart, would be one of the kindest of my friends ; and when a cadet of one of the greatest of the Whig houses, too young at that time to possess more than a prospective influence, would carry the reform from which his elders recoiled, and gift the prince-opposing Whig-Radical with a pension, under the gracious countenance of a queen whom the Radical loves. I think the *Edinburgh Review* might have noticed my books a little oftener. I am sure it would have done me a great deal of worldly good by it, and itself no harm in these progressing days of criticism. But I said nothing on the subject, and may have been thought indifferent.

Of Mr. Blanco White, thus brought to my recollection, a good deal is known in certain political and religious quarters; but it may be new to many readers, that he was an Anglo-Spaniard, who was forced to quit the Peninsula for his liberal opinions, and who died in his adopted country not long ago, after many years' endeavour to come to some positive faith within the Christian pale. At the time I knew him he had not long arrived from Spain, and was engaged, or about to be engaged, as tutor to the present Lord Holland. Though English by name and origin, he was more of the Spaniard in appearance, being very unlike the portrait prefixed to his *Life and Correspondence.* At least, he must have greatly altered from what he was when I knew him, if that portrait ever resembled him. He had a long pale face, with prominent drooping nose, anxious and somewhat staring eyes, and a mouth turning down at the corners. I believe there was not an honester man in the world, or one of an acuter intellect, short of the mischief that had been done it by a melancholy temperament and a superstitious training. It is distressing, in the work alluded to, to see what a torment the intellect may be rendered to itself by its own sharpness, in its efforts to make its way to conclusions, equally unnecessary to discover and impossible to be arrived at.

But, perhaps, there was something naturally self-tormenting in the state of Mr. White's blood. The first time I met him at a friend's house, he was suffering under the calumnies of his countrymen; and though of extremely gentle manners in ordinary, he almost startled me by suddenly turning round, and saying, in one of those incorrect foreign sentences which force one to be relieved while they startle, " If they proceed more, I will go mad."

In like manner, while he was giving me the Holland-House invitation, and telling me of the amusement derived from the pathetic cod's head and shoulders, he looked so like the piscatory bust which he was describing, that with all my respect for his patriotism and his sorrows, I could not help partaking of the unlucky tendency of my countrymen to be amused, in spite of myself, with the involuntary burlesque.

Mr. White, on his arrival in England, was so anxious a student of the language, that he noted down in a pocket-book every phrase which struck as remarkable. Observing the words " Cannon Brewery" on premises then standing in Knightsbridge, and taking the figure of a cannon which was over them, as the sign of the commodity dealt in, he put down as a nicety of speech, " The English *brew* cannon."

Another time, seeing maid-servants walking with children in a nursery-garden, he rejoiced in the progeny-loving character of the people among whom he had come, and wrote down, "Public garden provided for nurses, in which they take the children to walk."

This gentleman, who had been called "Blanco" in Spain—which was a translation of his family name "White," and who afterwards wrote an excellent English book of entertaining letters on the Peninsula, under the Græco-Spanish appellation of Don Leucadio Doblado (White Doubled)—was author of a sonnet which Coleridge pronounced to be the best in the English language. I know not what Mr. Wordsworth said on this judgment. Perhaps he wrote fifty sonnets on the spot to disprove it. And in truth it was a bold sentence, and probably spoken out of a kindly, though not conscious, spirit of exaggeration. The sonnet, nevertheless, is truly beautiful.*

CHAPTER XIII.

THE REGENT AND THE "EXAMINER."

EVERYTHING having been thus prepared, by myself as well as by others, for a good blow at the *Examiner*, the ministers did not fail to strike it.

There was an annual dinner of the Irish on Saint Patrick's Day, at which the Prince of Wales's name used to be the reigning and rapturous toast, as that of the greatest friend they possessed in the United Kingdom. He was held to be the jovial advocate of liberality in all things, and sponsor in particular for concession to the Catholic claims. But the Prince of Wales, now become Prince Regent, had retained the Tory ministers of his father; he had broken life-long engagements; had violated his promises, particular as well as general, those to the Catholics among them; and led *in toto* a different political life from what had been expected. The name, therefore, which used to be hailed with rapture, was now, at the dinner in question, received with hisses.

An article appeared on the subject in the *Examiner*; the attorney-general's eye was swiftly upon the article; and the result to the proprietors was two years' imprisonment, with a fine, to each, of five hundred pounds. I shall relate the story of my imprisonment a few pages onward. Much as it injured me, I cannot wish that I had evaded it, for I believe that it

---

* It is the one beginning—

"Mysterious night! when our first parent knew."

did good, and I should have suffered far worse in the self-abasement.   Neither have I any quarrel, at this distance of time, with the Prince Regent; for though his frivolity, his tergiversation, and his treatment of his wife, will not allow me to respect his memory, I am bound to pardon it as I do my own faults, in consideration of the circumstances which mould the character of every human being.   Could I meet him in some odd corner of the Elysian fields, where charity had room for both of us, I should first apologize to him for having been the instrument in the hand of events for attacking a fellow-creature, and then expect to hear him avow as hearty a regret for having injured myself, and unjustly treated his wife.

[The author repeated the article in the first edition of his *Autobiography;* but in revising the present edition he marked the whole of it for omission.   The greater portion, indeed, is completely out of date, as so often happens with political writing ; the facts, the allusions, the very turn of the phrases, belong to circumstances long since forgotten; and the effect of the composition, even as a work of art, could not now be appreciated.   But since so much has turned upon the purport of this paper, and especially upon one passage, it may be as well to preserve that portion.   The occurrence which prompted the article was a public dinner on Saint Patrick's Day, at which the Chairman, Lord Moira, a generous man, made not the slightest allusion to the Prince Regent, and Mr. Sheridan, who manfully stood up for his royal friend, declaring that he still sustained the principles of the Prince Regent, was saluted by angry shouts and cries of "Change the subject!"   The Whig *Morning Chronicle* moralized this theme; and the *Morning Post,* which then affected to be the organ of the Court, in a strain of unqualified admiration, replied to the *Chronicle,* partly in vapid prose objurgation, and partly in a wretched poem, graced with epithets intended to be extravagantly flattering to the Prince. To this reply the *Examiner* rejoined in a paper of considerable length, analyzing the whole facts, and translating the language of adulation into that of truth.   The close of the article shows its spirit and purpose, and is a fair specimen of Leigh Hunt's political writing at that time.]

" What person, unacquainted with the true state of the case, would imagine, in reading these astounding eulogies, that this 'Glory of the people' was the subject of millions of shrugs and reproaches !—that this 'Protector of the arts' had named a wretched foreigner his historical painter, in disparagement or in ignorance of the merits of his own countrymen!—that this ' Mecænas of the age' patronized not a single deserving writer!—that this ' Breather of eloquence' could not say a few decent extempore words, if we are to judge, at least, from what he said to his regiment on its embarkation for Portugal!—that this ' Conqueror of hearts' was the disappointer of hopes!—that this ' Exciter of desire' [bravo! Messieurs of the *Post!*]—this ' Adonis in loveliness,' was a corpulent man of fifty!—in short, this *delightful, blissful, wise, pleasurable, honourable, virtuous, true,* and *immortal* prince, was a violator of his word, a libertine over head and ears in disgrace, a despiser of domestic ties, the companion of gamblers and demireps, a man who has just closed half a century without one single claim on the gratitude of his country, or the respect of posterity!

" These are hard truths; but are they *not* truths? And have we not suffered enough—are we not now suffering bitterly—from the disgusting flatteries of which the above is a repetition? The ministers may talk of the shocking boldness of the press, and may throw out their wretched warnings about interviews between Mr. Percival and Sir Vicary Gibbs; but let us inform them, that such vices as have just been enumerated are shocking to all Englishmen who have a just sense of the state of Europe; and that he is a bolder man, who, in times like the present, dares to afford reason for the description. Would to God, the *Examiner* could ascertain that difficult, and perhaps undiscoverable, point which enables a public writer to keep clear of an appearance of the love of scandal, while he is hunting out the vices of those in power! Then should one paper, at least, in this metropolis help to rescue the nation from the charge of silently encouraging what it must publicly rue; and the Sardanapalus who is now afraid of none but informers, be taught to shake, in the midst of his minions, in the very drunkenness of his heart, at the voice of honesty. But if this be impossible, still there is one benefit which truth may derive from adulation—one benefit which is favourable to the former in proportion to the grossness of the latter, and of which none of his flatterers seem to be aware—the opportunity of contradicting its assertions. Let us never forget this advantage, which adulation cannot help giving us; and let such of our readers as are inclined to deal insincerely with the great from a false notion of policy and of knowledge of the world, take warning from what we now see of the miserable effects of courtly disguise, paltering, and profligacy. Flattery in any shape is unworthy a man and a gentleman; but political flattery is almost a request to be made slaves. If we would have the great to be what they ought, we must find some means or other to speak of them as they are."

This article, no doubt, was very bitter and contemptuous; therefore, in the legal sense of the term, very libellous; the more so, inasmuch as it was very true. There will be no question about the truth of it, at this distance of time, with any class of persons, unless, possibly, with some few of the old Tories, who may think it was a patriotic action in the Prince to displace the Whigs for their opponents. But I believe, that under all the circumstances, there are few persons indeed nowadays, of my class, who will not be of opinion that, bitter as the article was, it was more than sufficiently avenged by two years' imprisonment and a fine of a thousand pounds. For it did but express what all the world were feeling, with the exception of the Prince's once bitterest enemies, the Tories themselves, then newly become his friends; and its very sincerity and rashness, had the Prince possessed greatness of mind to think so, might have furnished him such a ground for pardoning it, as would have been the best proof he could have given us of our having mistaken him, and turned us into blushing and grateful friends. An attempt to bribe us on the side of fear did but further disgust us. A free and noble waiving of the punishment would have bowed our hearts into regret. We should have found in it the evidence of that true generosity of nature paramount to whatsoever was frivolous or appeared to be mean, which his flatterers claimed for him, and which would have made us doubly blush for the formal virtues to which we seemed to be attached, when, in reality, nothing would have better pleased us than such a combination of the gay and the magnanimous. I say doubly blush, for I now blush at ever having been considered, or rather been willing to be considered, an advocate of any sort of conventionality, unqualified by liberal exceptions and prospective enlargement; and I am sure that my brother, had he been living, who was one of the best-natured and most indulgent of men, would have joined with me in making the same concession; though I am bound to add that, with all his indulgence of others, I have no reason to believe that he had ever stood in need of that pardon for even conventional licence, from the necessity of which I cannot pretend to have been exempt.

I have spoken of an attempt to bribe us. We were given to understand, through the medium of a third person, but in a manner emphatically serious and potential, that if we would abstain in future from commenting upon the actions of the royal personage, means would be found to prevent our going to prison. The same offer was afterwards repeated, as far as the payment of a fine was concerned, upon our going thither. I need not add that we declined both.

The expectation of a prison was, in one respect, very formidable to me; for I had been a long time in a bad state of health. I was suffering under the worst of those hypochondriacal attacks which I have described in a former chapter; and when notice was given that we were to be brought up for judgment, I had just been advised by the physician to take exercise every day on horseback, and go down to the sea-side. I was resolved, however, to do no disgrace either to the courage which I really possessed, or to the example set me by my excellent brother. I accordingly put my countenance in its best trim; I made a point of wearing my best apparel; and descended into the legal arena to be sentenced gallantly. As an instance of the imagination which I am accustomed to mingle with everything, I was at that time reading a little work, to which Milton is indebted, the *Comus* of Erycius Puteanus; and this, which is a satire on "Bacchuses and their revellers," I pleased myself with having in my pocket.

It is necessary, on passing sentence for a libel, to read over again the words that composed it. This was the business of Lord Ellenborough, who baffled the attentive audience in a very ingenious manner by affecting every instant to hear a noise, and calling upon the officers of the court to prevent it. Mr. Garrow, the attorney-general (who had succeeded Sir Vicary Gibbs at a very cruel moment, for the indictment had been brought by that irritable person, and was the first against us which took effect), behaved to us with a politeness that was considered extraordinary. Not so Mr. Justice Grose, who delivered the sentence. To be didactic and old-womanish seemed to belong to his nature; but to lecture us on pandering to the public appetite for scandal was what we could not so easily bear. My brother, as I had been the writer, expected me, perhaps, to be the spokesman; and speak I certainly should have done, had I not been prevented by the dread of that hesitation in my speech to which I had been subject when a boy, and the fear of which (perhaps, idly, for I hesitated at that time least among strangers, and very rarely do so at all) has been the main cause why I have appeared and acted in public less than any other public man. There is reason to think that Lord Ellenborough was still less easy than ourselves. He knew that we were acquainted with his visits to Carlton-house and Brighton (sympathies not eminently decent in a judge), and with the good things which he had obtained for his kinsmen; and we could not help preferring our feelings at the moment to those which induced him to keep his eyes fixed on his papers, which he did almost the whole time of our being in court, never turning them once to the place

14

on which we stood. There were divers other points too, on which he had some reason to fear that we might choose to return the lecture of the bench. He did not even look at us when he asked, in the course of his duty, whether it was our wish to make any remarks? I answered, that we did not wish to make any *there;* and Mr. Justice Grose proceeded to pass sentence. At the sound of two years' imprisonment in separate gaols, my brother and myself instinctively pressed each other's arm. It was a heavy blow; but the pressure that acknowledged it encouraged the resolution to bear it; and I do not believe that either of us interchanged a word afterwards on the subject. We knew that we had the respect of each other, and that we stood together in the hearts of the people.

Just before our being brought up for judgment, the friendly circumstance took place on the part of Mr. Perry, of the *Morning Chronicle*, to which allusion has been made in the eleventh chapter, and which I forgot to supply in the first edition of this work. It was an offer made us to give Whig sanction, and therefore certain and immediate influence, to the announcement of a manuscript for publication, connected with some important state and court secrets, and well known and dreaded by the Regent, under the appellation of *The Book.* I forget whether Mr. Perry spoke of its appearance, or of its announcement only; but the offer was made for the express purpose of saving us from going to prison. We heartily thanked the kind man; but knowing that what it is very proper sometimes, and handsome for persons to offer, it may not be equally so for other persons to accept, and not liking to owe our deliverance to a threat or a *ruse de guerre*, we were "romantic," and declined the favour.

CHAPTER XIV.

IMPRISONMENT.

WE parted in hackney-coaches to our respective abodes, accompanied by two tipstaves apiece, and myself by my friend Barron Field.

The tipstaves prepared me for a singular character in my gaoler. His name was Ives. I was told he was a very self-willed personage, not the more accommodating for being in a bad state of health; and that he called everybody *Mister*. "In short," said one of the tipstaves, "he is one as may be led, but he'll never be *druv*."

The sight of the prison-gate and the high wall was a dreary business. I thought of my horseback and the downs of Brighton; but congratulated myself, at all events, that I had come thither with a good conscience. After waiting in the prison-yard as long as if it had been the anteroom of a minister, I was ushered into the presence of the great man. He was in his parlour, which was decently furnished, and he had a basin of broth before him, which he quitted on my appearance, and rose with much solemnity to meet me. He seemed about fifty years of age. He had a white night-cap on, as if he was going to be hanged, and a great red face, which looked as if he had been hanged already, or were ready to burst with blood. Indeed, he was not allowed by his physician to speak in a tone above a whisper.

The first thing which this dignified person said was, "Mister, I'd ha' given a matter of a hundred pounds, that you had not come to this place—a hundred pounds!" The emphasis which he had laid on the word "hundred" was ominous.

I forgot what I answered. I endeavoured to make the best of the matter; but he recurred over and over again to the hundred pounds; and said he wondered, for his part, what the Government meant by sending me there, for the prison was not a prison fit for a gentleman. He often repeated this opinion afterwards, adding, with a peculiar nod of his head, "And, Mister, they knows it."

I said, that if a gentleman deserved to be sent to prison, he ought not to be treated with a greater nicety than any one else: upon which he corrected me, observing very properly (though, as the phrase is, it was one word for the gentleman and two for the letter of prison-lodgings), that a person who had been used to a better mode of living than "low people" was not treated with the same justice, if forced to lodge exactly as they did.

I told him his observation was very true; which gave him a favourable opinion of my understanding; for I had many occasions of remarking, that he looked upon nobody as his superior, speaking even of members of the royal family as persons whom he knew very well, and whom he estimated at no higher rate than became him. One royal duke had lunched in his parlour, and another he had laid under some polite obligation. "They knows me," said he, "very well, Mister; and, Mister, I knows them." This concluding sentence he uttered with great particularity and precision.

He was not proof, however, against a Greek Pindar, which he happened to light upon one day among my books. Its unintelligible character gave him a notion that he had got somebody to deal with, who might really know something which he did not. Perhaps the gilt leaves and red morocco binding had their share in the magic. The upshot was, that he always showed himself anxious to appear well with me, as a clever fellow, treating me with great civility on all occasions but one, when I made him very angry by disappointing him in a money amount. The Pindar was a mystery that staggered him. I remember very well, that giving me a long account one day of something connected with his business, he happened to catch with his eye the shelf that contained it, and, whether he saw it or not, abruptly finished by observing, "But, Mister, you knows all these things as well as I do."

Upon the whole, my new acquaintance was as strange a person as I ever met with. A total want of education, together with a certain vulgar acuteness, conspired to render him insolent and pedantic. Disease sharpened his tendency to fits of passion, which threatened to suffocate him; and then in his intervals of better health he would issue forth, with his cock-up-nose and his hat on one side, as great a fop as a jockey. I remember his coming to my rooms, about the middle of my imprisonment, as if on purpose to insult over my ill health with the contrast of his convalescence, putting his arms in a gay manner a-kimbo, and telling me I should never live to go out, whereas he was riding about as stout as ever, and had just been in the country. He died before I left prison.

The word *jail*, in deference to the way in which it is sometimes spelt, this accomplished individual pronounced *gole;* and Mr. Brougham he always spoke of as Mr. *Bruffam.* He one day apologized for this mode of pronunciation, or rather gave a specimen of vanity and self-will, which will show the reader the high notions a jailer may entertain of himself. " I find," said he, " that they calls him *Broom;* but, Mister" (assuming a look from which there was to be no appeal), " *I* calls him *Bruffam !*"

Finding that my host did not think the prison fit for me, I asked if he could let me have an apartment in his house. He

pronounced it impossible; which was a trick to enhance the
price. I could not make an offer to please him; and he
stood out so long, and, as he thought, so cunningly, that he
subsequently overreached himself by his trickery, as the
reader will see. His object was to keep me among the
prisoners, till he could at once sicken me of the place, and
get the permission of the magistrates to receive me into his
house; which was a thing he reckoned upon as a certainty.
He thus hoped to secure himself in all quarters; for his
vanity was almost as strong as his avarice. He was equally
fond of getting money in private, and of the approbation of
the great men whom he had to deal with in public; and it so
happened, that there had been no prisoner, above the poorest
condition, before my arrival, with the exception of Colonel
Despard. From abusing the prison, he then suddenly fell to
speaking well of it, or rather of the room occupied by the
colonel; and said, that another corresponding with it would
make me a capital apartment. "To be sure," said he, "there
is nothing but bare walls, and I have no bed to put in it." I
replied, that of course I should not be hindered from having
my own bed from home. He said, "No; and if it rains,"
observed he, "you have only to put up with want of light
for a time." "What!" exclaimed I, "are there no windows?" "Windows, Mister!" cried he; "no windows in a
prison of this sort; no glass, Mister: but excellent shutters."

It was finally agreed, that I should sleep for a night or two
in a garret of the gaoler's house, till my bed could be got
ready in the prison and the windows glazed. A dreary evening followed, which, however, let me completely into the
man's character, and showed him in a variety of lights, some
ludicrous, and others as melancholy. There was a full-length
portrait in the room, of a little girl, dizened out in her best.
This, he told me, was his daughter, whom he had disinherited
for her disobedience. I tried to suggest a few reflections,
capable of doing her service; but disobedience, I found, was
an offence doubly irritating to his nature, on account of his
sovereign habits as a gaoler; and seeing his irritability likely
to inflame the plethora of his countenance, I desisted. Though
not allowed to speak above a whisper, he was extremely willing to talk; but at an early hour I pleaded my own state of
health, and retired to bed.

On taking possession of my garret, I was treated with a
piece of delicacy, which I never should have thought of find-

ing in a prison. When I first entered its walls, I had been received by the under-gaoler, a man who seemed an epitome of all that was forbidding in his office. He was short and very thick, had a hook-nose, a great severe countenance, and a bunch of keys hanging on his arm. A friend stopped short at sight of him, and said, in a melancholy tone, " And this is the gaoler !"

Honest old *Cave!* thine outside would have been unworthy of thee, if upon further acquaintance I had not found it a very hearty outside—ay, and in my eyes, a very good-looking one, and as fit to contain the milk of human kindness that was in thee, as the husk of a cocoa. To show by one specimen the character of this man—I could never prevail on him to accept any acknowledgment of his kindness, greater than a set of tea-things, and a piece or two of old furniture, which I could not well carry away. I had, indeed, the pleasure of leaving him in possession of a room which I had papered; but this was a thing unexpected, and which neither of us had supposed could be done. Had I been a prince, I would have forced on him a pension; being a journalist, I made him accept an *Examiner* weekly, which he lived for some years to relish his Sunday pipe with.

This man, in the interval between my arrival and my introduction to the head-gaoler, had found means to give me further information respecting my condition, and to express the interest he took in it. I thought little of his offers at the time. He behaved with the greatest air of deference to his principal; moving as fast as his body would allow him, to execute his least intimation; and holding the candle to him while he read, with an obsequious zeal. But he had spoken to his wife about me, and his wife I found to be as great a curiosity as himself. Both were more like the romantic gaolers drawn in some of our modern plays, than real Horsemonger-lane palpabilities. The wife, in her person, was as light and fragile as the husband was sturdy. She had the nerves of a fine lady, and yet went through the most unpleasant duties with the patience of a martyr. Her voice and look seemed to plead for a softness like their own, as if a loud reply would have shattered her. Ill-health had made her a Methodist, but this did not hinder her from sympathizing with an invalid who was none, or from loving a husband who was as little of a saint as need be. Upon the whole, such an extraordinary couple, so apparently unsuitable, and yet so fitted for one another; so apparently vulgar on one side, and yet so naturally delicate on both; so misplaced in their situation, and yet for the good of others so admirably put there, I have never met with before or since.

It was the business of this woman to lock me up in my garret; but she did it so softly the first night, that I knew nothing of the matter. The night following, I thought I heard a gentle tampering with the lock. I tried it, and found it fastened. She heard me as she was going down-stairs, and said the next day, " Ah, sir, I thought I should have turned the key so as for you not to hear it; but I found you did." The whole conduct of this couple towards us, from first to last, was of a piece with this singular delicacy.

My bed was shortly put up, and I slept in my new room. It was on an upper story, and stood in a corner of the quadrangle, on the right hand as you enter the prison-gate. The windows (which had now been accommodated with glass, in addition to their " excellent shutters ") were high up, and barred; but the room was large and airy, and there was a fireplace. It was intended to be a common room for the prisoners on that story; but the cells were then empty. The cells were ranged on either side of the arcade, of which the story is formed, and the room opened at the end of it. At night-time the door was locked; then another on the top of the staircase, then another on the middle of the staircase, then a fourth at the bottom, a fifth that shut up the little yard belonging to that quarter, and how many more, before you got out of the gates, I forget: but I do not exaggerate when I say there were ten or eleven. The first night I slept there, I listened to them, one after the other, till the weaker part of my heart died within me. Every fresh turning of the key seemed a malignant insult to my love of liberty. I was alone, and away from my family; I, who to this day have never slept from home above a dozen weeks in my life. Furthermore, the reader will bear in mind that I was ill. With a great flow of natural spirits, I was subject to fits of nervousness, which had latterly taken a more continued shape. I felt one of them coming on, and having learned to anticipate and break the force of it by exercise, I took a stout walk by pacing backwards and forwards for the space of three hours. This threw me into a state in which rest, for rest's sake, became pleasant. I got hastily into bed, and slept without a dream till morning.

By the way, I never dreamt of prison but twice all the time I was there, and my dream was the same on both occasions. I fancied I was at the theatre, and that the whole house looked at me in surprise, as much as to say, "How could he get out of prison?"

I saw my wife for a few minutes after I entered the gaol, but she was not allowed on that day to stop longer. The next day she was with me for some hours. To say that she never reproached me for these and the like taxes upon our family prospects, is to say little. A world of comfort for me was in her face. There is a note in the fifth volume of my *Spenser*, which I was then reading, in these words:— "February 4th, 1813." The line to which it refers is this:—

"Much dearer be the things which come through hard distresse."

I now applied to the magistrates for permission to have my wife and children constantly with me, which was granted. Not so my request to move into the gaoler's house. Mr. Holme Sumner, on occasion of a petition from a subsequent prisoner, told the House of Commons that my room had a view over the Surrey hills, and that I was very well content with it. I could not feel obliged to him for this postliminous piece of enjoyment, especially when I remembered that he had done all in his power to prevent my removal out of the room, precisely (as it appeared to us) because it looked upon nothing but the felons, and because I was *not* contented. In fact, you could not see out of the windows at all, without getting on a chair; and then, all that you saw was the miserable men whose chains had been clanking from daylight. The perpetual sound of these chains wore upon my spirits in a manner to which my state of health allowed me reasonably to object. The yard, also, in which I took exercise, was very small. The gaoler proposed that I should be allowed to occupy apartments in his house, and walk occasionally in the prison garden; adding, that I should certainly die if I did not; and his opinion was seconded by that of the medical man. Mine host was sincere in this, if in nothing else. Telling us, one day, how warmly he had put it to the magistrates, and how he insisted that I should not survive, he turned round upon me, and, to the doctor's astonishment, added, "Nor, Mister, will you." I believe it was the opinion of many; but Mr. Holme Sumner argued otherwise; perhaps from his own sensations, which were sufficiently iron.

Perhaps he concluded, also, like a proper old Tory, that if I did not think fit to flatter the magistrates a little, and play the courtier, my wants could not be very great. At all events, he came up one day with the rest of them, and after bowing to my wife, and piteously pinching the cheek of an infant in her arms, went down and did all he could to prevent our being comfortably situated.

The doctor then proposed that I should be removed into the prison infirmary ; and this proposal was granted. Infirmary had, I confess, an awkward sound, even to my ears. I fancied a room shared with other sick persons, not the best fitted for companions ; but the good-natured doctor (his name was Dixon) undeceived me. The infirmary was divided into four wards, with as many small rooms attached to them. The two upper wards were occupied, but the two on the floor had never been used : and one of these, not very providently (for I had not yet learned to think of money), I turned into a noble room. I papered the walls with a trellis of roses; I had the ceiling coloured with clouds and sky; the barred windows I screened with Venetian blinds ; and when my bookcases were set up with their busts, and flowers and a pianoforte made their appearance, perhaps there was not a handsomer room on that side the water. I took a pleasure, when a stranger knocked at the door, to see him come in and stare about him. The surprise on issuing from the Borough, and passing through the avenues of a gaol, was dramatic. Charles Lamb declared there was no other such room, except in a fairy tale.

But I possessed another surprise; which was a garden. There was a little yard outside the room, railed off from another belonging to the neighbouring ward. This yard I shut in with green palings, adorned it with a trellis, bordered it with a thick bed of earth from a nursery, and even contrived to have a grass-plot. The earth I filled with flowers and young trees. There was an apple-tree, from which we managed to get a pudding the second year. As to my flowers, they were allowed to be perfect. Thomas Moore, who came to see me with Lord Byron, told me he had seen no such heart's-ease. I bought the *Parnaso Italiano* while in prison, and used often to think of a passage in it, while looking at this miniature piece of horticulture :—

" Mio picciol orto,
A me sei vigna, e campo, e selva, e prato."—BALDI.

" My little garden,
To me thou'rt vineyard, field, and meadow, and wood,"

Here I wrote and read in fine weather, sometimes under an awning. In autumn, my trellises were hung with scarlet-runners, which added to the flowery investment. I used to shut my eyes in my arm-chair, and affect to think myself hundreds of miles off.

But my triumph was in issuing forth of a morning. A wicket out of the garden led into the large one belonging to the prison. The latter was only for vegetables; but it contained a cherry-tree, which I saw twice in blossom. I parcelled out the ground in my imagination into favourite districts. I made a point of dressing myself as if for a long walk; and then, putting on my gloves, and taking my book under my arm, stepped forth, requesting my wife not to wait dinner if I was too late. My eldest little boy, to whom Lamb addressed some charming verses on the occasion, was my constant companion, and we used to play all sorts of juvenile games together. It was, probably, in dreaming of one of these games (but the words had a more touching effect on my ear) that he exclaimed one night in his sleep, "No: I'm not lost; I'm found." Neither he nor I were very strong at that time; but I have lived to see him a man of eight and forty; and wherever he is found, a generous hand and a great understanding will be found together.*

I entered prison the 3rd of February, 1813, and removed to my new apartments the 16th of March, happy to get out of the noise of the chains. When I sat amidst my books, and saw the imaginary sky overhead, and my paper roses about me, I drank in the quiet at my ears, as if they were thirsty. The little room was my bedroom. I afterwards made the two

* [A kind relative supplies an anecdote of this period. " Mrs. Leigh Hunt, having occasion to make some purchases in town, went, accompanied by her sister, and by this little boy, then in petticoats. She returned in a coach; and when it stopped at the prison gates, the driver opened the coach-door, and, apologizing for the liberty he was taking, said that, as it seemed unlikely that ladies should be visiting any one *else* in that prison, he presumed we came to see Mr. Leigh Hunt. When answered that he spoke to Mrs. Hunt, he became agitated, asked her if that was her child, and, learning that it was, he caught the child up in his arms and kissed it passionately. He explained his agitation by saying, that what Mr. Leigh Hunt had said about military flogging, had been the means of saving his son from the infliction; and that he should for ever bless his name. He would not hear of taking any payment. This circumstance was naturally most grateful to Mr. Leigh Hunt's feelings. He had suffered for his advocacy of the soldier's cause; but he had not suffered in vain."]

rooms change characters, when my wife lay in. Permission
for her continuance with me at that period was easily obtained
of the magistrates, among whom a new-comer made his appearance. This was another good-natured man, Lord Leslie,
afterwards Earl of Rothes.* He heard me with kindness; and
his actions did not belie his countenance. My eldest girl
(now, alas! no more) was born in prison. She was beautiful,
and for the greatest part of an existence of thirty years, she
was happy. She was christened Mary after my mother, and
Florimel after one of Spenser's heroines. But Mary we called
her. Never shall I forget my sensations when she came into
the world ; for I was obliged to play the physician myself, the
hour having taken us by surprise. But her mother found
many unexpected comforts: and during the whole time of her
confinement, which happened to be in very fine weather, the
garden door was set open, and she looked upon trees and
flowers. A thousand recollections rise within me at every
fresh period of my imprisonment, such as I cannot trust myself with dwelling upon.

These rooms, and the visits of my friends, were the bright
side of my captivity. I read verses without end, and wrote
almost as many. I had also the pleasure of hearing that my
brother had found comfortable rooms in Coldbath-fields, and
a host who really deserved that name as much as a gaoler
could. The first year of my imprisonment was a long pull
up-hill; but never was metaphor so literally verified, as by
the sensation at the turning of the second. In the first year,
all the prospect was that of the one coming : in the second,
the days began to be scored off, like those of children at school
preparing for a holiday. When I was fairly settled in my new
apartments, the gaoler could hardly give sufficient vent to his
spleen at my having escaped his clutches, his astonishment
was so great. Besides, though I treated him handsomely, he
had a little lurking fear of the *Examiner* upon him ; so he
contented himself with getting as much out of me as he could,
and boasting of the grand room which he would fain have prevented my enjoying.

My friends were allowed to be with me till ten o'clock at
night, when the under-turnkey, a young man with his lantern,
and much ambitious gentility of deportment, came to see them
out. I believe we scattered an urbanity about the prison, till

* George William, twelfth earl of that name. He died a few years
afterwards.

then unknown. Even William Hazlitt, who there first did me
the honour of a visit, would stand interchanging amenities at
the threshold, which I had great difficulty in making him pass.
I know not which kept his hat off with the greater pertinacity
of deference, I to the diffident cutter-up of Tory dukes and
kings, or he to the amazing prisoner and invalid who issued
out of a bower of roses.   There came my old friends and
school-fellows, Pitman, whose wit and animal spirits have still
kept him alive ; Mitchell, now no more, who translated Aristophanes; and Barnes, gone too, who always reminded me of
Fielding. It was he that introduced me to the late Mr. Thomas
Alsager, the kindest of neighbours, a man of business, who
contrived to be a scholar and a musician. Alsager loved his
leisure, and yet would start up at a moment's notice to do the
least of a prisoner's biddings.

My now old friend, Cowden Clarke, with his ever young
and wise heart, was good enough to be his own introducer,
paving his way, like a proper visitor of prisons, with baskets
of fruit.

The Lambs came to comfort me in all weathers, hail or sunshine, in daylight and in darkness, even in the dreadful frost
and snow of the beginning of 1814.

My physician, curiously enough, was Dr. Knighton (afterwards Sir William), who had lately become physician to the
prince. He, therefore, could not, in decency, visit me under
the circumstances, though he did again afterwards, never failing in the delicacies due either to his great friend or to his
small. Meantime, another of his friends, the late estimable
Dr. Gooch, came to me as his substitute, and he came often.

Great disappointment and exceeding viciousness may talk
as they please of the badness of human nature. For my part,
I am now in my seventy-fourth year, and I have seen a good
deal of the world, the dark side as well as the light, and I say
that human nature is a very good and kindly thing, and capable
of all sorts of virtues. Art thou not a refutation of all that
can be said against it, excellent Sir John Swinburne? another
friend whom I made in prison, and who subsequently cheered
some of my greatest passes of adversity. Health, as well as
sense and generosity, has blessed him; and he retains a young
heart at the age of ninety-four.

To evils I have owed some of my greatest blessings. It was
imprisonment that brought me acquainted with my friend of
friends, Shelley. I had seen little of him before; but he wrote

to me, making me a princely offer, which at that time I stood in no need of.

Some other persons, not at all known to us, offered to raise money enough to pay the fine of 1,000*l.* We declined it, with proper thanks; and it became us to do so. But, as far as my own feelings were concerned, I have no merit; for I was destitute, at that time, of even a proper instinct with regard to money. It was not long afterwards that I was forced to call upon friendship for its assistance; and nobly (as I shall show by and by) was it afforded me.

To some other friends, near and dear, I may not even return thanks in this place for a thousand nameless attentions, which they make it a business of their existence to bestow on those they love. I might as soon thank my own heart. But one or two others, whom I have not seen for years, and who by some possibility (if, indeed, they ever think it worth their while to fancy anything on the subject) might suppose themselves forgotten, I may be suffered to remind of the pleasure they gave me. M. S. [Michael Slegg?], who afterwards saw us so often near London, has long, I hope, been enjoying the tranquillity he so richly deserved; and so, I trust, is C. S. [Caroline Scott?], whose face, or rather something like it (for it was not easy to match her own), I continually met with afterwards in the land of her ancestors. Her veil, and her baskets of flowers, used to come through the portal, like light.

I must not omit a visit from the venerable Bentham, who was justly said to unite the wisdom of a sage with the simplicity of a child. I had had the honour of one from him before my imprisonment, when he came, he said, to make my acquaintance, because the *Examiner* had spoken well of a new weekly paper. On the present occasion he found me playing at battledore, in which he took a part; and, with his usual eye towards improvement, suggested an amendment in the constitution of shuttlecocks. I remember the surprise of the governor at his local knowledge and his vivacity. "Why, Mister," said he, "his eye is everywhere at once."

All these comforts were embittered by unceasing ill-health, and by certain melancholy reveries, which the nature of the place did not help to diminish. During the first six weeks the sound of the felons' chains, mixed with what I took for horrid execrations or despairing laughter, was never out of my ears. When I went into the infirmary, which stood between the gaol and the prison walls, gallowses were occasionally put in order by the side of my windows, and afterwards set up over the prison gates, where they remained visible. The keeper one day, with an air of mystery, took me into the upper ward, for the purpose, he said, of gratifying me with a view of the country from the roof. Something prevented his showing me this; but the spectacle he did show me I shall never forget. It was a stout country girl, sitting in an absorbed manner, her eyes fixed on the fire. She was handsome, and had a little hectic spot in either cheek, the effect of some gnawing emotion. He told me, in a whisper, that she was there for the murder of her bastard child. I could have knocked the fellow down for his unfeelingness in making a show of her; but, after all, she did not see us. She heeded us not. There was no object before her but what produced the spot in her cheek. The gallows, on which she was executed, must have been brought out within her hearing; but, perhaps, she heard that as little.

To relieve the reader's feelings I will here give him another instance of the delicacy of my friend the under-gaoler. He always used to carry up her food to this poor girl himself; because, as he said, he did not think it a fit task for younger men.

This was a melancholy case. In general, the crimes were not of such a staggering description, nor did the criminals appear to take their situation to heart. I found by degrees that fortune showed fairer play than I had supposed to all classes of men, and that those who seemed to have most reason to be miserable were not always so. Their criminality was generally proportioned to their want of thought. My friend Cave, who had become a philosopher by the force of his situation, said to me one day when a new batch of criminals came in, " Poor ignorant wretches, sir!" At evening, when they went to bed, I used to stand in the prison garden, listening to the cheerful songs with which the felons entertained one another. The beaters of hemp were a still merrier race. Doubtless the good hours and simple fare of the prison contributed to make the blood of its inmates run better, particularly those who were forced to take exercise. At last, I used to pity the debtors more than the criminals ; yet even the debtors had their gay parties and jolly songs. Many a time (for they were my neighbours) have I heard them roar out the old ballad in Beaumont and Fletcher:—

> "He that drinks, and goes to bed sober,
> Falls as the leaves do, and dies in October."

To say the truth, there was an obstreperousness in their mirth that looked more melancholy than the thoughtlessness of the lighter-feeding felons.

On the 3rd of February, 1815, I was free. When my family, the preceding summer, had been obliged to go down to Brighton for their health, I felt ready to dash my head against the wall at not being able to follow them. I would sometimes sit in my chair with this thought upon me, till the agony of my impatience burst out at every pore. I would not speak of it if it did not enable me to show how this kind of suffering may be borne, and in what sort of way it terminates. I learnt to prevent it by violent exercise. All fits of nervousness ought to be anticipated as much as possible with exercise. Indeed, a proper healthy mode of life would save most people from these effeminate ills, and most likely cure even their inheritors.

It was now thought that I should dart out of my cage like a bird, and feel no end in the delight of ranging. But, partly from ill-health, and partly from habit, the day of my liberation brought a good deal of pain with it. An illness of a long standing, which required very different treatment, had by this time been burnt in upon me by the iron that enters into the soul of the captive, wrap it in flowers as he may; and I am ashamed to say, that after stopping a little at the house of my friend Alsager, I had not the courage to continue looking at the shoals of people passing to and fro, as the coach drove up the Strand. The whole business of life seemed a hideous impertinence. The first pleasant sensation I experienced was when the coach turned into the New Road, and I beheld the old hills of my affection standing where they used to do, and breathing me a welcome.

It was very slowly that I recovered anything like a sensation of health. The bitterest evil I suffered was in consequence of having been confined so long in one spot. The habit stuck to me on my return home in a very extraordinary manner; and, I fear, some of my friends thought me ungrateful. They did me an injustice; but it was not their fault; nor could I wish them the bitter experience which alone makes us acquainted with the existence of strange things. This weakness I outlived; but I have never thoroughly recovered the shock given my constitution. My natural spirits, however, have always struggled hard to see me reasonably treated. Many things give me exquisite pleasure which seem to affect other men in a very minor degree; and I enjoyed, after all, such happy moments with my friends, even in prison, that in the midst of the beautiful climate which I afterwards visited, I was sometimes in doubt whether I would not rather have been in gaol than in Italy.

CHAPTER XV.

FREE AGAIN.—SHELLEY IN ENGLAND.

On leaving prison I went to live in the Edgeware Road, because my brother's house was in the neighbourhood. When we met, we rushed into each other's arms, and tears of manhood bedewed our cheeks.

Not that the idea of the Prince Regent had anything to do with such grave emotions. His Royal Highness continued to affect us with anything but solemnity, as we took care to make manifest in the *Examiner*. We had a hopeful and respectful word for every reigning prince but himself; and I must say, that with the exception of the Emperor Alexander, not one of them deserved it.

The lodging which my family occupied (for the fine, and the state of my health, delayed my resumption of a house) was next door to a wealthy old gentleman, who kept a handsome carriage, and spoke very bad grammar. My landlord, who was also a dignified personage after his fashion, pointed him out to me one day as he was getting into his carriage; adding, in a tone amounting to the awful, " He is the greatest plumber in London." The same landlord, who had a splendid turn for anti-climax, and who had gifted his children with names proportionate to his paternal sense of what became him, called out to one of them from his parlour window, " You, sir, there—Maximilian—come out of the gutter." He was a good-natured sort of domineering individual; and would say to his wife, when he went out, " Damn it, my love, I insist on having the pudding."

In this house Lord Byron continued the visits which he made me in prison. Unfortunately, I was too ill to return them. He pressed me very much to go to the theatre with him; but illness, and the dread of committing my critical independence, alike prevented me. His lordship was one of a management that governed Drury-lane Theatre at that time, and that were not successful. He got nothing by it but petty vexations and a good deal of scandal.

Lord Byron's appearance at that time was the finest I ever saw it. He was fatter than before his marriage, but only just enough so to complete the elegance of his person; and the turn of his head and countenance had a spirit and elevation in it which, though not unmixed with disquiet, gave him altogether a very noble look. His dress, which was black, with white trousers, and which he wore buttoned close over the body, completed the succinctness and gentlemanliness of his appearance. I remember one day, as he stood looking out of the window, he resembled, in a lively manner, the portrait of him by Phillips, by far the best that has appeared: I mean, the best of him at his best time of life, and the most like him in features as well as expression. He sat one morning so long that Lady Byron sent up twice to let him know she was waiting. Her ladyship used to go on in the carriage to Henderson's nursery-ground, to get flowers. I had not the honour of knowing her, nor ever saw her but once, when I caught a glimpse of her at the door. I thought she had a pretty, earnest look, with her "pippin" face; an epithet by which she playfully designated herself.

I had a little study overlooking the fields to Westbourne— a sequestered spot at that time embowered in trees. The study was draperied with white and green, having furniture to match; and as the noble poet had seen me during my imprisonment in a bower of roses, he might here be said, with no great stretch of imagination, to have found me in a box of lilies. I mention this, because he took pleasure in the look of the little apartment. Also, because my wife's fair cousin, Virtue Kent, now, alas! no more, who was as good as she was intelligent, and as resolute as gentle, extinguished me there one morning when my dressing-gown had caught fire. She was all her life, indeed, taking painful tasks on herself, to save trouble to others.

In a room at the end of the garden to this house was a magnificent rocking-horse, which a friend had given my little boy; and Lord Byron, with a childish glee becoming a poet, would ride upon it. Ah! why did he ever ride his Pegasus to less advantage? Poets should never give up their privilege of surmounting sorrow with joy.

It was here also I had the honour of a visit from Mr.

Wordsworth. He came to thank me for the zeal I had shown in advocating the cause of his genius. I had the pleasure of showing him his book on my shelves by the side of Milton; a sight which must have been the more agreeable, inasmuch as the visit was unexpected. He favoured me, in return, with giving his opinion of some of the poets his contemporaries, who would assuredly not have paid him a visit on the same grounds on which he was pleased to honour myself. Nor do I believe, that from that day to this, he thought it becoming in him to reciprocate the least part of any benefit which a word in good season may have done for him. Lord Byron, in resentment for my having called him the " prince of the bards of his time," would not allow him to be even the " one-eyed monarch of the blind." He said he was the " blind monarch of the one-eyed." I must still differ with his lordship on that point; but I must own, that, after all which I have seen and read, posterity, in my opinion, will differ not a little with one person respecting the amount of merit to be ascribed to Mr. Wordsworth ; though who that one person is, I shall leave the reader to discover.

Mr. Wordsworth, whom Mr. Hazlitt designated as one that would have had the wide circle of his humanities made still wider, and a good deal more pleasant, by dividing a little more of his time between his lakes in Westmoreland and the hotels of the metropolis, had a dignified manner, with a deep and roughish but not unpleasing voice, and an exalted mode of speaking. He had a habit of keeping his left hand in the bosom of his waistcoat; and in this attitude, except when he turned round to take one of the subjects of his criticism from the shelves (for his contemporaries were there also), he sat dealing forth his eloquent but hardly catholic judgments. In his " father's house" there were not " many mansions." He was as sceptical on the merits of all kinds of poetry but one, as Richardson was on those of the novels of Fielding.

Under the study in which my visitor and I were sitting was an archway, leading to a nursery-ground; a cart happened to go through it while I was inquiring whether he would take any refreshment; and he uttered, in so lofty a voice, the words, " Anything which is *going forward*," that I felt inclined to ask him whether he would take a piece of the cart. Lamb would certainly have done it. But this was a levity which would neither have been so proper on my part, after so short an acquaintance, nor very intelligible, perhaps, in any sense of the word, to the serious poet. There are good-humoured warrants for smiling, which lie deeper even than Mr. Wordsworth's thoughts for tears.

I did not see this distinguished person again till thirty years afterwards; when, I should venture to say, his manner was greatly superior to what it was in the former instance; indeed, quite natural and noble, with a cheerful air of animal as well as spiritual confidence; a gallant bearing, curiously reminding me of the Duke of Wellington, as I saw him walking some eighteen years ago by a lady's side, with no unbecoming oblivion of his time of life. I observed, also, that the poet no longer committed himself in scornful criticisms, or, indeed, in any criticisms whatever, at least as far as I knew. He had found out that he could, at least, afford to be silent. Indeed, he spoke very little of anything. The conversation turned upon Milton, and I fancied I had opened a subject that would have "brought him out," by remarking, that the most diabolical thing in all *Paradise Lost* was a feeling attributed to the angels. "Ay!" said Mr. Wordsworth, and inquired what it was. I said it was the passage in which the angels, when they observed Satan journeying through the empyrean, let down a set of steps out of heaven, on purpose to add to his misery—to his despair of ever being able to re-ascend them; they being angels in a state of bliss, and he a fallen spirit doomed to eternal punishment. The passage is as follows:—

> "Each stair was meant mysteriously, nor stood
> There always, but, drawn up to heaven, sometimes
> Viewless; and underneath a bright sea flow'd
> Of jasper, or of liquid pearl, whereon
> Who after came from earth sailing arriv'd
> Wafted by angels, or flew o'er the lake
> Rapt in a chariot drawn by fiery steeds.
> The stairs were then let down, whether to dare
> The fiend by easy ascent, *or aggravate*
> *His sad exclusion from the doors of bliss.*"

Mr. Wordsworth pondered, and said nothing. I thought to myself, what pity for the poor devil would not good uncle Toby have expressed! Into what indignation would not Burns have exploded! What knowledge of themselves would not have been forced upon those same coxcombical and malignant angels by Fielding or Shakspeare!

Walter Scott said, that the eyes of Burns were the finest he ever saw. I cannot say the same of Mr. Wordsworth's; that is, not in the sense of the beautiful, or even of the pre-found.   But certainly I never beheld eyes that looked so inspired or supernatural.   They were like fires half burning, half smouldering, with a sort of acrid fixture of regard, and seated at the further end of two caverns.   One might imagine Ezekiel or Isaiah to have had such eyes.   The finest eyes, in every sense of the word, which I have ever seen in a man's head (and I have seen many fine ones) are those of Thomas Carlyle.

It was for a good while after leaving prison that I was unable to return the visits of the friends who saw me there. Two years' confinement, and illness in combination, had acted so injuriously upon a sensitive temperament, that for many months I could not leave home without a morbid wish to return, and a fear of being seized with some fit or other in the streets, perhaps with sudden death; and this was one of the periods when my hypochondria came back.   In company, however, or at the sight of a friend, animal spirits would struggle even with that; and few people, whatever ill-health I showed in my face, had the slightest idea of what I suffered. When they thought I was simply jaundiced, I was puzzling myself with the cosmogony.   When they fancied me wholly occupied in some conversation on a poem or a pot of flowers, I would be haunted with the question respecting the origin of evil.   What agonies, to be sure—what horrible struggles between wonder and patience—I suffered then! and into what a heaven of reliance and of gladness have I been since brought by a little better knowledge of the tuning of the in- struments of this existence, whether bodily or mental, taking right healthy spirits as the key-note, and harmonizing every- thing else with those!   But I have treated this point already. Let me again, however, advise any one who may be suffering melancholy of the same sort, or of any sort, to take this recol- lection of mine to heart, and do his best to derive comfort from it.   I thought I should die early, and in suffering; and here I am still, forty-two years afterwards, writing these words.

> "For thilkè ground, that beareth the weeds wick,
>   Beareth also these wholesome herbs as oft;
> And next to the foul nettle, rough and thick,
>   The rose ywaxeth sweet, and smooth, and soft;
> And next the valley is the hill aloft;
>   And next the darkè night is the glad morrow,
> And also joy is next the fine of sorrow."—CHAUCER.

In the spring of the year 1816 I went to reside again in

Hampstead, for the benefit of the air, and of my old field walks; and there I finished the *Story of Rimini*, which was forthwith published. I have spoken of a masque on the downfall of Napoleon, called the *Descent of Liberty*, which I wrote while in prison. Liberty descends in it from heaven, to free the earth from the burden of an evil magician. It was a compliment to the Allies, which they deserved well enough, inasmuch as it was a failure; otherwise they did not deserve it all; for it was founded on a belief in promises which they never kept. There was a vein of something true in the *Descent of Liberty*, particularly in passages where the domestic affections were touched upon; but the poetry was too much on the surface. Fancy (encouraged by the allegorical nature of the masque) played her part too entirely in it at the expense of imagination. I had not yet got rid of the self-sufficiency caused by my editorial position, or by the credit, better deserved, which political courage had obtained for me. I had yet to learn in what the subtler spirit of poetry consisted.

Nor had I discovered it when I wrote the *Story of Rimini*. It was written in what, perhaps, at my time of life, and after the degree of poetical reputation which had been conceded me, I may be allowed, after the fashion of painters, to call my " first manner;" not the worst manner conceivable, though far from the best; as far from it (or at whatever greater distance modesty may require it to be put) as Dryden's *Flower and the Leaf*, from the story in Chaucer which Dryden imitated. I must take leave, however, to regard it as a true picture, painted after a certain mode ; and I can never forget the comfort I enjoyed in painting it, though I think I have since executed some things with a more inward perception of poetical requirement.

This poem, the greater part of which was written in prison, had been commenced a year or two before, while I was visiting the sea-coast at Hastings, with my wife and our first child. I was very happy; and looking among my books for some melancholy theme of verse, by which I could steady my felicity, I unfortunately chose the subject of Dante's famous episode. I did not consider, indeed at the time was not critically aware, that to enlarge upon a subject which had been treated with exquisite sufficiency, and to his immortal renown, by a great master, was not likely, by any merit of detail, to save a tyro in the art from the charge of presumption, especially one who had not yet even studied poetical mastery itself, except in a subordinate shape. Dryden, at that time, in spite of my sense of Milton's superiority, and my early love of Spenser, was the most delightful name to me in English poetry. I had found in him more vigour, and music too, than in Pope, who had been my closest poetical acquaintance; and I could not rest till I had played on his instrument. I brought, however, to my task a sympathy with the tender and the pathetic, which I did not find in my pattern; and there was also an impulsive difference now and then in the style, and a greater tendency to simplicity of words. My versification was far from being so vigorous as his. There were many weak lines in it. It succeeded best in catching the variety of his cadences; at least so far as they broke up the monotony of Pope. But I had a greater love for the beauties of external nature; I think also I partook of a more southern insight into the beauties of colour, of which I made abundant use in the procession which is described in the first canto; and if I invested my story with too many circumstances of description, especially on points not essential to its progress, and thus took leave *in toto* of the brevity, as well as the force of Dante, still the enjoyment which led me into the superfluity was manifest, and so far became its warrant. I had the pleasure of supplying my friendly critic, Lord Byron, with a point for his *Parisina* (the incident of the heroine talking in her sleep); of seeing all the reigning poets, without exception, break up their own heroic couplets into freer modulation (which they never afterwards abandoned) and being paid for the resentment of the Tory critics in one single sentence from the lips of Mr. Rogers, who told me, when I met him for the first time at Lord Byron's house, that he had " just left a beautiful woman sitting over my poem in tears."

I was then between twenty and thirty. Upwards of thirty years afterwards I was told by a friend, that he had just heard one of the most distinguished of living authoresses say she had shed " tears of vexation" on finding that I had recast the conclusion of the poem, and taken away so much of the first matter. Let it be allowed me to boast of tears of this kind, and to say what balm they have given me for many a wound. The portion of the poem taken away I have since restored, under a separate title, in the edition of my *Poetical Works*, which has appeared in America. By the other alteration I have finally thought it best to abide; and I have thus reconciled as well as I could the friends of the first form of the poem and those of the new.

I need hardly advert, at the present time of day, to the objections which were made to this production when it first appeared, by the wrath of the Tory critics. In fact, it would have met with no such hostility, or indeed any hostility at all, if politics had not judged it. Critics might have differed about it, of course, and reasonably have found fault; but had it emanated from the circles, or been written by any person not obnoxious to political objection, I believe there is nobody at this time of day, who will not allow, that the criticism in all quarters would have been very good-natured, and willing to hail whatever merit it possessed. I may, therefore, be warranted in having spoken of it without any greater allusion to quarrels which have long been over, and to which I have confessed that I gave the first cause of provocation.

The *Story of Rimini* had not long appeared when I received a copy of it, which looked like witchcraft. It was the identical poem, in type and appearance, bound in calf, and sent me without any explanation; but it was a little smaller. I turned it over a dozen times, wondering what it could be, and how it could have originated. The simple solution of the puzzle I did not consider, till I had summoned other persons to partake my astonishment. At length we consulted the title-page, and there saw the names of "Wells and Lilly, Boston; and M. Carey, Philadelphia."—I thought how the sight would have pleased my father and mother.

I now returned the visits which Lord Byron had made me in prison. His wife's separation from him had just taken place, and he had become ill himself; his face was jaundiced with bile; he felt the attacks of the public severely; and, to crown all, he had an execution in his house. I was struck with the real trouble he manifested, compared with what the public thought of it. The adherence of his old friends was also touching. I saw Mr. Hobhouse, now Lord Broughton, and Mr. Scrope Davies (college friends of his) almost every time I called. Mr. Rogers was regular in his daily visits; and Lord Holland, he told me, was very kind.

Lord Byron, at this juncture, took the blame of the quarrel upon himself. He even enlisted the self-love of his new visitor so far on the lady's side, as to tell him " that she liked my poem, and had compared his temper to that of Giovanni, the heroine's consort." He also showed me a letter which she had written him after her departure from the house, and when she was on her way to the relations who persuaded her not to return. It was signed with the epithet before mentioned; and was written in a spirit of good-humour, and even of fondness, which, though containing nothing but what a wife ought to write, and is the better for writing, was, I thought, almost too good to show. But a certain over-communicativeness was one of those qualities of his lordship, which, though it sometimes became the child-like simplicity of a poet, startled you at others in proportion as it led to disclosures of questionable propriety.

I thought I understood the circumstances of this separation at the time, and still better some time afterwards; but I have since been convinced, and the conviction grows stronger every day, that no domestic dispute, even if it were desirable or proper to investigate it, can ever be thoroughly understood unless you hear both parties, and know their entire relative situations, together with the interests and passions of those about them. You must also be sure of their statements, and see whether the statements on all sides themselves are prejudiced or the reverse. Indeed you cannot know individuals themselves truly, unless you have lived with them; at all events, unless you have studied them long enough to know whether appearances are realities; and although you may, and to a certain degree must, draw your own conclusions respecting people from statements which they give to the world, whether for or against themselves, yet it is safer, as well as pleasanter, to leave that question as much as possible in the place where it ought ever to abide, unless brought forward on the highest and noblest grounds; namely, in the silence of the heart that has most suffered under its causes.

I shall, therefore, say nothing more of a business which nobody ought to have heard of. Lord Byron soon afterwards left England, and I did not see him again, or hear from him, scarcely of him, till he proposed my joining him in Italy. I take my leave of him, therefore, till that period, and proceed to speak of the friends with whom I became intimate in the meanwhile—Shelley and Keats.

I first saw Shelley during the early period of the *Examiner*, before its indictment on account of the Regent; but it was only for a few short visits, which did not produce intimacy. [It was indeed Mr. Rowland Hunter who first brought Leigh Hunt and his most valued friend personally together. Shelley had brought a manuscript poem which proved by no means suited to the publishing house in St. Paul's Churchyard. But Mr. Hunter sent the young reformer to seek the counsel of Leigh Hunt.] He was then a youth, not come to his full growth ; very gentlemanly, earnestly gazing at every object that interested him, and quoting the Greek dramatists. Not long afterwards he married his first wife ; and he subsequently wrote to me while I was in prison, as I have before mentioned. I renewed the correspondence a year or two afterwards, during which period one of the earliest as well as most beautiful of his lyric poems, the *Hymn to Intellectual Beauty*, had appeared in the *Examiner*. Meantime, he and his wife had parted ; and now he re-appeared before me at Hampstead, in consequence of the calamity which I am about to mention.

But this circumstance it will be proper to introduce with some remarks, and a little previous biography.

It is hardly necessary to inform the reader at this present day, that Percy Bysshe Shelley was the eldest son of Sir Timothy Shelley, Bart., of Castle-Goring, in Sussex. He was born at Field Place, in that county, the 4th of August, 1792.

It is difficult, under any circumstances, to speak with proper delicacy of the living connections of the dead ; but it is no violation of decorum to observe, that the family connections of Mr. Shelley belonged to a small party in the House of Commons, itself belonging to another party. They were Whig Aristocrats, voting in the interest of the Duke of Norfolk. To a man of genius, endowed with a metaphysical acuteness to discern truth and falsehood, and a strong sensibility to give way to his sense of it, such an origin, however respectable in the ordinary point of view, was not the very luckiest that could have happened for the purpose of keeping him within ordinary bounds. With what feelings is Truth to open its eyes upon this world among the most respectable of our mere party gentry ? Among licensed contradictions of all sorts ? among the Christian doctrines and the worldly practices ? Among fox-hunters and their chaplains ? among beneficed loungers, rakish old gentlemen, and more startling young ones, who are old in the folly of *knowingness ?* people not indeed bad in themselves ; not so bad as their wholesale and unthinking decriers, much less their hypocritical decriers ; many excellent by nature, but spoilt by those professed demands of what is right and noble, and those inculcations, at the same time, of what is false and wrong, which have been so admirably exposed by a late philosopher (Bentham), and which he has fortunately helped some of our best living statesmen to leave out of the catalogue of their ambitions.

Shelley began to think at a very early age, and to think, too, of these anomalies. He saw that at every step in life some compromise was expected between a truth which he was told not to violate, and a colouring and double-meaning of it which forced him upon the violation.

With this jumble, then, of truth and falsehood in his head, and a genius born to detect it, Shelley was sent to Eton, and afterwards to the University of Oxford. At Eton a Reviewer recollected him setting trees on fire with a burning-glass; a proceeding which the critic set down to his natural taste for destruction. Perhaps the same Reviewer (if we are not mistaken as to the person) would now, by the help of his own riper faculties, attribute it to the natural curiosity of genius. At the same school, the young reformer rose up in opposition to the system of fagging. Against this custom he formed a conspiracy; and for a time he made it pause, at least as far as his own person was concerned. His feelings at this period of his life are touchingly and powerfully described in the dedication of the *Revolt of Islam* :—

"Thoughts of great deeds were mine, dear friend, when first
    The clouds which wrap this world from youth did pass.
I do remember well the hour which burst
    My spirit's sleep: a fresh May day it was,
    When I walk'd forth upon the glittering grass,
And wept, I know not why, until there rose,
    From the near schoolroom, voices that, alas!
Were but one echo from a world of woes—
The harsh and grating strife of tyrants and of foes.

"And then I clasp'd my hands, and look'd around,—
    But none was near to mock my streaming eyes,
Which pour'd their warm drops on the sunny ground:
    So without shame I spake: 'I will be wise,
    And just, and free, and mild, if in me lies
Such power; for I grow weary to behold
    The selfish and the strong still tyrannize
Without reproach or check.' I then controll'd
My tears; my heart grew calm, and I was meek and bold.

"And from that hour did I, with earnest thought,
    Heap knowledge from forbidden mines of lore;
Yet nothing that my tyrants knew or taught
    I cared to learn; but from that secret store
    Wrought linkèd armour for my soul, before
It might walk forth to war among mankind."

Shelley, I believe, was taken from Eton before the regular period for leaving school. His unconventional spirit—penetrating, sincere, and demanding the reason and justice of things—was found to be inconvenient. At Oxford it was worse. Logic was there put into his hands; and he used it in the most uncompromising manner. The more important the proposition, the more he thought himself bound to investigate it : the greater the demand upon his assent, the less, upon their own principle of reasoning, he thought himself bound to grant it : for the university, by its ordinances, invited scholars to ask questions which they found themselves unable to answer. Shelley did so ; and the answer was expulsion. It is true, the question he asked was a very hard one. It was upon the existence of God. But could neither Faith, Hope, nor Charity find a better answer than that ? and in the teeth, too, of their own challenge to inquiry ? Could not some gentle and loving nature have been found to speak to him in private, and beg him at least to consider and pause over the question, for reasons which might have had their corresponding effect ? The Church of England has been a blessing to mankind, inasmuch as it has discountenanced the worst superstitions, and given sense and improvement leave to grow; but if it cannot learn still further to sacrifice letter to spirit, and see the danger of closing its lips on the greatest occasions and then proceeding to open them on the smallest, and dispute with its very self on points the most " frivolous and vexatious," it will do itself an injury it little dreams of with the new and constantly growing intelligence of the masses; who are looking forward to the noblest version of Christianity, while their teachers are thus fighting about the meanest.

Conceive a young man of Mr. Shelley's character, with no better experience of the kindness and sincerity of those whom he had perplexed, thus thrown forth into society, to form his own judgments, and pursue his own career. It was *Emilius out in the World*, but formed by his own tutorship. There is a novel, under that title, written by the German La Fontaine, which has often reminded me of him. The hero of another, by the same author, called the *Reprobate*, still more resembles him. His way of proceeding was entirely after the fashion of those guileless, but vehement hearts, which not being well replied to by their teachers, and finding them hostile to inquiry, add to a natural love of truth all the passionate ardour of a generous and devoted protection of it. Shelley had met with Godwin's *Political Justice*, and he seemed to breathe, for the first time, in an open and bright atmosphere. He resolved to square all his actions by what he conceived to be the strictest justice, without any consideration for the opinions of those whose little exercise of that virtue towards himself ill fitted them, he thought, for better teachers, and as ill warranted him in deferring to the opinions of the world whom they guided. That he did some extraordinary things in consequence is admitted: that he did many noble ones, and all with sincerity, is well known to his friends, and will be admitted by all sincere persons. Let those who are so fond of exposing their own natures, by attributing every departure from ordinary conduct to bad motives, ask themselves what conduct could be more extraordinary in their eyes, and at the same time less attributable to a bad motive, than the rejection of an estate for the love of a principle? Yet Shelley rejected one. He had only to become a yea and nay man in the House of Commons, to be one of the richest men in Sussex. He declined it, and lived upon a comparative pittance. Even the fortune that he would ultimately have inherited, as secured to his person, was petty in the comparison.

So he went up to town. Had he now behaved himself pardonably in the eyes of the conventional in those days (for it is wonderful in how short a time honest discussion may be advanced by a court at once correct and unbigoted, and by a succession of calmly progressing ministries; and all classes are now beginning to permit the wisdom of every species of abuse to be doubted), Shelley would have gone to London with the resolution of sowing his wild oats, and becoming a decent member of society; that is to say, he would have seduced a few maid-servants, or at least haunted the lobbies of the theatre, and then bestowed the remnant of his constitution upon some young lady of his own rank in life, and settled into a proper church-and-king man of the old leaven, perhaps a member of the Society for the Suppression of Vice. This used to be the proper routine, and gave one a right to be didactic. Alas! Shelley did not do so ; and bitterly had he to repent, not that he did not do it, but that he married while yet a stripling, and that the wife whom he took was not of a nature to appreciate his understanding, or, perhaps, to come from contact with it uninjured in what she had of her own. They separated by mutual consent, after the birth of two children. To this measure his enemies would hardly have demurred ; especially as the marriage was disapproved by the husband's family, and the lady was of inferior rank. It might have been regarded even as something like making amends. But to one thing they would strongly have objected. He proceeded, in the spirit of Milton's doctrines, to pay his court to another lady. I wish I could pursue the story in the same tone ; but now came the greatest pang of his life. He was residing at Bath, when news came to him that his wife had destroyed herself. It was a heavy blow to him, and he never forgot it. For a time it tore his being to pieces ; nor is there a doubt that, however deeply he was accustomed to reason on the nature and causes of evil, and on the steps necessary to b taken for opposing it, he was not without remorse for having no better exercised his judgment with regard to the degree of intellect he had allied himself with, and for having given rise to a premature independence of conduct in one unequal to the task. The lady was greatly to be pitied; so was the survivor. Let the collegiate refusers of argument, and the conventional sowers of their wild oats, with myriads of unhappy women behind them, rise up in judgment against him ! Honester men will not be hindered from doing justice to sincerity wherever they find it ; nor be induced to blast the memory of a man of genius and benevolence, for one painful passage in his life, which he might have avoided had he been no better than his calumniators.

On the death of his unfortunate lady, Shelley married the daughter of Mr. Godwin, and resided at Great Marlow, in Buckinghamshire, where my family and myself paid him a visit, and where he was a blessing to the poor. His charity, though liberal, was not weak. He inquired personally into the circumstances of his petitioners, visited the sick in their beds (for he had gone the round of the hospitals on purpose to be able to practise on occasion), and kept a regular list of industrious poor, whom he assisted with small sums to make up their accounts.

Here he wrote the *Revolt of Islam* and *A Proposal for putting Reform to the Vote through the Country*. He offered to give a tenth part of his income for a year towards the advancement of the project. He used to sit in a study adorned with casts, as large as life, of the Vatican Apollo and the celestial Venus. Betweenwhiles he would walk in the garden, or take strolls about the country, or a sail in a boat, a diversion of which he was passionately fond. Flowers, or the sight of a happy face, or the hearing of a congenial remark, would make his eyes sparkle with delight. At other times he would suddenly droop into an aspect of dejection, particularly when a wretched face passed him, or when he saw the miserable-looking children of a lace-making village near him, or when he thought of his own children, of whom he had been deprived by the Court of Chancery. He once said to me during a walk in the Strand, "Look at all these worn and miserable faces that pass us, and tell me what is to be thought of the world they appear in?" I said, "Ah, but these faces are not all worn with grief. You must take the wear and tear of pleasure into the account; of secret joys as well as sorrows; of merry-makings and sittings-up at night." He owned that there was truth in the remark. This was the sort of consolation which I was in the habit of giving him, and for which he was thankful, because I was sincere.

As to his children, the reader, perhaps, is not aware that in this country of England, so justly called free on many accounts, and so proud of its "Englishman's castle"—of the house which nothing can violate—a man's offspring can be taken from him to-morrow, who holds a different opinion from the Lord Chancellor in faith and morals. Hume's, if he had any, might have been taken. Gibbon's might have been taken. The virtuous Condorcet, if he had been an Englishman and a father, would have stood no chance. Plato, for his *Republic*, would have stood as little; and Mademoiselle de Gournay might have been torn from the arms of her adopting father, Montaigne, convicted beyond redemption of seeing farther than the walls of the Court of Chancery. That such things are not done often, I believe: that they may be done oftener than people suspect, I believe also; for they are transacted with closed doors, and the details are forbidden to transpire.

Queen Mab, Shelley's earliest poetical production, written before he was out of his teens, and regretted by him as a crude production, was published without his consent. Yet he was convicted from it of holding the opinion which his teachers at the University had not thought fit to reason him out of. He was also charged with not being of the received opinions with regard to the intercourse of the sexes; and his children, a girl and a boy, were taken from him. They were transferred to the care of a clergyman of the Church of England. The circumstance deeply affected Shelley: so much so, that he never afterwards dared to trust himself with mentioning their names in my hearing, though I had stood at his side throughout the business ; probably for that reason.* Shelley's manner of life suffered greatly in its repute from this circumstance. He was said to be keeping a seraglio at Marlow ; and his friends partook of the scandal. This keeper of a seraglio, who, in fact, was extremely difficult to be pleased in such matters, and who had no idea of love unconnected with sentiment, passed his days like a hermit. He rose early in the morning, walked and read before breakfast, took that meal sparingly, wrote and studied the greater part of the morning, walked and read again, dined on vegetables (for he took neither meat nor wine), conversed with his friends (to whom his house was ever open), again walked out, and usually finished with reading to his wife till ten o'clock, when he went to bed. This was his daily existence. His book was generally Plato, or Homer, or one of the Greek tragedians, or the Bible, in which last he took a great, though peculiar, and often admiring interest. One of his favourite parts was the book of Job. The writings attributed to Solomon he thought too Epicurean, in the modern sense of the word ; and in his notions of St. Paul he agreed with the writer of the work entitled, *Not Paul but Jesus*. For his Christianity, in the proper sense of the word, he went to the Epistle of St. James, and to the Sermon on the Mount by Christ himself, for whose beneficent intentions he entertained the greatest reverence. There was nothing which embittered his enemies against him more than the knowledge of this fact. His want of faith, indeed, in the letter, and his exceeding faith in the spirit, of Christianity, formed a comment, the one on the other, very formidable to those who chose to forget what Scripture itself observes on that point.†

As an instance of Shelley's extraordinary generosity, a

* The boy is since dead; and Shelley's son by his second wife, the daughter of Godwin, has succeeded to the baronetcy. It seldom falls to the lot of a son to have illustrious descent so heaped upon him; his mother a woman of talents; his father a man of genius; his grandfather, Godwin, a writer secure of immortality; his grandmother, Godwin's wife, the celebrated Mary Wollstonecraft: and on the side of his father's ancestors he partakes of the blood of the intellectual as well as patrician family of the Sackvilles. But, what is best of all, his own intelligent and liberal nature makes him worthy of all this lustre.

† "For the letter killeth, but the spirit giveth life."

friend of his, a man of letters, enjoyed from him at that period a pension of a hundred a year, though he had but a thousand of his own; and he continued to enjoy it till fortune rendered it superfluous. But the princeliness of his disposition was seen most in his behaviour to another friend, the writer of this memoir, who is proud to relate, that with money raised by an effort, Shelley once made him a present of fourteen hundred pounds, to extricate him from debt. I was not extricated, for I had not yet learned to be careful: but the shame of not being so, after such generosity, and the pain which my friend afterwards underwent when I was in trouble and he was helpless, were the first causes of my thinking of money matters to any purpose. His last sixpence was ever at my service, had I chosen to share it. In a poetical epistle written some years afterwards, and published in the volume of *Posthumous Poems*, Shelley, in alluding to his friend's circumstances, which for the second time were then straitened, only made an affectionate lamentation that he himself was poor; never once hinting that he had already drained his purse for his friend.

To return to Hampstead.—Shelley often came there to see me, sometimes to stop for several days. He delighted in the natural broken ground, and in the fresh air of the place, especially when the wind set in from the north-west, which used to give him an intoxication of animal spirits. Here also he swam his paper boats on the ponds, and delighted to play with my children, particularly with my eldest boy, the seriousness of whose imagination, and his susceptibility of a "grim" impression (a favourite epithet of Shelley's), highly interested him. He would play at "frightful creatures" with him, from which the other would snatch "a fearful joy," only begging him occasionally "not to do the horn," which was a way that Shelley had of screwing up his hair in front, to imitate a weapon of that sort. This was the boy (now the man of forty-eight, and himself a fine writer) to whom Lamb took such a liking on similar accounts, and addressed some charming verses as his "favourite child." I have already mentioned him during my imprisonment.

As an instance of Shelley's playfulness when he was in good spirits, he was once going to town with me in the Hampstead stage, when our only companion was an old lady, who sat silent and still after the English fashion. Shelley was fond of quoting a passage from *Richard the Second*, in

the commencement of which the king, in the indulgence of
his misery, exclaims—

> "For Heaven's sake! let us sit upon the ground,
> And tell sad stories of the death of kings."

Shelley, who had been moved into the ebullition by something objectionable which he thought he saw in the face of
our companion, startled her into a look of the most ludicrous
astonishment, by suddenly calling this passage to mind, and,
in his enthusiastic tone of voice, addressing me by name with
the first two lines.   "Hunt!" he exclaimed,—

> "For Heaven's sake! let us sit upon the ground,
> And tell sad stories of the death of kings."

The old lady looked on the coach-floor, as if expecting to see
us take our seats accordingly.

But here follows a graver and more characteristic anecdote.
Shelley was not only anxious for the good of mankind in
general. We have seen what he proposed on the subject of
Reform in Parliament, and he was always very desirous of the
national welfare. It was a moot point when he entered your
room, whether he would begin with some half-pleasant, half-
pensive joke, or quote something Greek, or ask some question
about public affairs. He once came upon me at Hampstead,
when I had not seen him for some time ; and after grasping
my hands with both his, in his usual fervent manner, he sat
down, and looked at me very earnestly, with a deep, though
not melancholy, interest in his face. We were sitting with
our knees to the fire, to which we had been getting nearer and
nearer, in the comfort of finding ourselves together. The
pleasure of seeing him was my only feeling at the moment ;
and the air of domesticity about us was so complete, that I
thought he was going to speak of some family matter, either
his or my own, when he asked me, at the close of an intensity
of pause, what was "the amount of the national debt."

I used to rally him on the apparent inconsequentiality of his
manner upon those occasions, and he was always ready to carry
on the jest, because he said that my laughter did not hinder
my being in earnest.

But here follows a crowning anecdote, with which I shall
close my recollections of him at this period. We shall meet
him again in Italy, and there, alas! I shall have to relate
events graver still.

I was returning home one night to Hampstead after the

opera. As I approached the door, I heard strange and alarming shrieks, mixed with the voice of a man. The next day it was reported by the gossips that Mr. Shelley, no Christian (for it was he who was there), had brought some "very strange female" into the house, no better, of course, than she ought to be. The real Christian had puzzled them. Shelley, in coming to our house that night, had found a woman lying near the top of the hill, in fits. It was a fierce winter night, with snow upon the ground; and winter loses nothing of its fierceness at Hampstead. My friend, always the promptest as well as most pitying on these occasions, knocked at the first houses he could reach, in order to have the woman taken in. The invariable answer was, that they could not do it. He asked for an outhouse to put her in, while he went for a doctor. Impossible! In vain he assured them she was no impostor. They would not dispute the point with him; but doors were closed, and windows were shut down. Had he lit upon worthy Mr. Park, the philologist, that gentleman would assuredly have come, in spite of his Calvinism. But he lived too far off. Had he lit upon my friend Armitage Brown, who lived on another side of the Heath; or on his friend and neighbour Dilke; they would either of them have jumped up from amidst their books or their bed-clothes, and have gone out with him. But the paucity of Christians is astonishing, considering the number of them. Time flies; the poor woman is in convulsions; her son, a young man, lamenting over her. At last my friend sees a carriage driving up to a house at a little distance. The knock is given; the warm door opens; servants and lights pour forth. Now, thought he, is the time. He puts on his best address, which anybody might recognize for that of the highest gentleman as well as of an interesting individual, and plants himself in the way of an elderly person, who is stepping out of the carriage with his family. He tells his story. They only press on the faster. "Will you go and see her?" "No, sir; there's no necessity for that sort of thing, depend on it. Impostors swarm everywhere: the thing cannot be done; sir, your conduct is extraordinary." "Sir," cried Shelley, assuming a very different manner, and forcing the flourishing householder to stop out of astonishment, "I am sorry to say that *your* conduct is *not* extraordinary; and if my own seems to amaze you, I will tell you something which may amaze you a little more, and I hope will frighten you. It is such men as you who madden the spirits and the patience of the poor and wretched ; and if ever a convulsion comes in this country (which is very probable), recollect what I tell you :—you will have your house, that you refuse to put the miserable woman into, burnt over your head." " God bless me, sir ! Dear me, sir !" exclaimed the poor, frightened man, and fluttered into his mansion. The woman was then brought to our house, which was at some distance, and down a bleak path (it was in the Vale of Health); and Shelley and her son were obliged to hold her till the doctor could arrive. It appeared that she had been attending this son in London, on a criminal charge made against him, the agitation of which had thrown her into the fits on her return. The doctor said that she would have perished, had she lain there a short time longer. The next day my friend sent mother and son comfortably home to Hendon, where they were known, and whence they returned him thanks full o gratitude.

CHAPTER XVI.

KEATS, LAMB, AND COLERIDGE.

AND now to speak of Keats, who was introduced to me by his schoolmaster's son, Charles Cowden Clarke, a man of a most genial nature and corresponding poetical taste, admirably well qualified to nourish the genius of his pupil.

I had not known the young poet long, when Shelley and he became acquainted under my roof. Keats did not take to Shelley as kindly as Shelley did to him. Shelley's only thoughts of his new acquaintance were such as regarded his bad health, with which he sympathized, and his poetry, of which he has left such a monument of his admiration in *Adonais*. Keats, being a little too sensitive on the score of his origin, felt inclined to see in every man of birth a sort of natural enemy. Their styles in writing also were very different ; and Keats, notwithstanding his unbounded sympathies with ordinary flesh and blood, and even the transcendental cosmopolitics of *Hyperion*, was so far inferior in universality to his great acquaintance, that he could not accompany him in his dædal rounds with nature, and his Archimedean endeavours to move the globe with his own hands. I am bound to state thus much; because, hopeless of recovering his health, under circumstances that made the feeling extremely bitter,

16—2

an irritable morbidity appears even to have driven his suspicions to excess; and this not only with regard to the acquaintance whom he might reasonably suppose to have had some advantages over him, but to myself, who had none; for I learned the other day, with extreme pain, such as I am sure so kind and reflecting a man as Mr. Monckton Milnes would not have inflicted on me could he have foreseen it, that Keats at one period of his intercourse with us suspected both Shelley and myself of a wish to see him undervalued! Such are the tricks which constant infelicity can play with the most noble natures. For Shelley, let *Adonais* answer. For myself, let every word answer which I uttered about him, living and dead, and such as I now proceed to repeat. I might as well have been told that I wished to see the flowers or the stars undervalued, or my own heart that loved him.

But it was sickness, and passed away. It appears, by Mr. Milnes' book, that all his friends dissatisfied him in the course of those trials of his temper; and my friend, Mr. Milnes, will allow me to say, that those Letters and Remains of the young poet were not among his happiest effusions, nor wanting to supply a certain force of character to his memory. That memory possessed force enough already for those who were qualified to discern it; and those who were not, hardly deserved to have their own notions of energy flattered at the poet's expense. Keats was already known to have personally chastised a blackguard, and to have been the author of *Hyperion*:

"That large utterance of the early gods."

What more could have been necessary to balance the trembling excess of sensibility in his earlier poems? The world has few enough incarnations of poets themselves in Arcadian shapes, to render necessary any deterioration of such as it has the luck to possess.

But perhaps my own personal feelings induce me to carry this matter too far. In the publication alluded to is a contemptuous reference (not by Mr. Milnes) to a paper in the *Examiner* on the season of Christmas. I turned to it with new feelings of anxiety; and there I found no warrant for such reference, unless a certain tone of self-complacency, so often regretted in this autobiography, can have justified it.

Keats appears to have been of opinion that I ought to have taken more notice of what the critics said against him. And perhaps I ought. My notices of them may not have been sufficient. I may have too much contented myself with panegyrizing his genius, and thinking the objections to it of no ultimate importance. Had he given me a hint to another effect, I should have acted upon it. But in truth, as I have before intimated, I did not see a twentieth part of what was said against us; nor had I the slightest notion, at that period, that he took criticism so much to heart. I was in the habit, though a public man, of living in a world of abstractions of my own; and I regarded him as of a nature still more abstracted, and sure of renown. Though I was a politician (so to speak), I had scarcely a political work in my library. Spensers and Arabian Tales filled up the shelves; and Spenser himself was not remoter, in my eyes, from all the common-places of life, than my new friend. Our whole talk was made up of idealisms. In the streets we were in the thick of the old woods. I little suspected, as I did afterwards, that the hunters had struck him; and never at any time did I suspect that he could have imagined it desired by his friends. Let me quit the subject of so afflicting a delusion.

In everything but this reserve, which was to a certain extent encouraged by my own incuriousness (for I have no reserve myself with those whom I love)—in every other respect but this, Keats and I might have been taken for friends of the old stamp, between whom there was no such thing even as obligation, except the pleasure of it. I could not love him as deeply as I did Shelley. That was impossible. But my affection was only second to the one which I entertained for that heart of hearts. Keats, like Shelley himself, enjoyed the usual privilege of greatness with all whom he knew, rendering it delightful to be obliged by him, and an equal, but not greater, delight to oblige. It was a pleasure to his friends to have him in their houses, and he did not grudge it. When *Endymion* was published, he was living at Hampstead with his friend, Charles Armitage Brown, who attended him most affectionately through a severe illness, and with whom, to their great mutual enjoyment, he had taken a journey into Scotland. The lakes and mountains of the north delighted him exceedingly. He beheld them with an epic eye. Afterwards, he went into the south, and luxuriated in the Isle of Wight. On Brown's leaving home a second time, to visit the same quarter, Keats, who was too ill to accompany him, came to reside with me, when his last and best volume of poems appeared, containing *Lamia, Isabella,* the *Eve of St. Agnes,*

and the noble fragment of *Hyperion*. I remember Lamb's
delight and admiration on reading this book; how pleased he
was with the designation of Mercury as " the star of Lethe "
(rising, as it were, and glittering as he came upon that pale
region); and the fine daring anticipation in that passage of
the second poem—

> " So the two brothers and *their murdered man*
> Rode past fair Florence."

So also the description, at once delicate and gorgeous, of Agnes
praying beneath the painted window. The public are now well
acquainted with those and other passages, for which Persian
kings would have filled a poet's mouth with gold. I remember
Keats reading to me with great relish and particularity, conscious of what he had set forth, the lines describing the supper,
and ending with the words,

> " Lucent syrops tinct with cinnamon."

Mr. Wordsworth would have said that the vowels were not
varied enough; but Keats knew where his vowels were *not* to
be varied. On the occasion above alluded to, Wordsworth
found fault with the repetition of the concluding sound of the
participles in Shakspeare's line about bees:—

> " The *singing* masons *building* roofs of gold."

This, he said, was a line which Milton would never have
written. Keats thought, on the other hand, that the repetition
was in harmony with the continued note of the singers, and
that Shakspeare's negligence (if negligence it was) had instinctively felt the thing in the best manner. The assertion
about Milton is startling, considering the tendency of that
great poet to subject his nature to art; yet I have dipped,
while writing this, into *Paradise Lost*, and at the second
chance have lit on the following:—

> " The gray
> Dawn, and the Pleiades before him danced,
> Shedding sweet influence. Less bright the moon,
> But opposite, *in levelled west, was set*
> His mirrour, with full force borrowing her light."

The repetition of the *e* in the fourth line is an extreme case in
point, being monotonous in order to express oneness and even-
ness.

Keats had felt that his disease was mortal, two or three
years before he died. He had a constitutional tendency to
consumption; a close attendance on the deathbed of a belovèd

brother, when he ought to have been nursing himself in bed, gave it a blow which he felt for months. Despairing love (that is to say, despairing of living to enjoy it, for the love was returned) added its hourly torment; and, meanwhile, the hostile critics came up, and roused an indignation in him, both against them and himself, which on so many accounts he could ill afford to endure.

When I was in Italy, Lord Byron showed me in manuscript the well-known passage in *Don Juan*, in which Keats's death is attributed to the *Quarterly Review*; the couplet about the "fiery particle," that was "snuffed out by an article." I told him the real state of the case, proving to him that the supposition was a mistake, and therefore, if printed, would be a misrepresentation. But a stroke of wit was not to be given up.

At length Keats was persuaded by his friends to try the milder climate of Italy. He thought it better for others as well as himself, that he should go. He was accompanied by Mr. Severn, then a young artist of a promise equal to his subsequent repute, who possessed all that could recommend him for a companion — old acquaintanceship, great animal spirits, active tenderness, and a mind capable of appreciating that of the poet. They went first to Naples, and afterwards to Rome; where, on the 23rd of February, 1821, our author died in the arms of his friend, completely worn out, and longing for the release. He suffered so much in his lingering, that he used to watch the countenance of the physician for the favourable and fatal sentence, and express his regret when he found it delayed. Yet no impatience escaped him. He was manly and gentle to the last, and grateful for all services. A little before he died, he said that he "felt the daisies growing over him." But he made a still more touching remark respecting his epitaph. "If any," he said, "were put over him, he wished it to consist of nothing but these words: 'Here lies one whose name was writ in water:'"—so little did he think of the more than promise he had given;—of the fine and lasting things he had added to the stock of poetry! The physicians expressed their astonishment that he had held out so long, the lungs turning out, on inspection, to have been almost obliterated. They said he must have lived upon the mere strength of the spirit within him. He was interred in the English burying-ground at Rome, near the monument of Caius Cestius, where his great mourner, Shelley, was shortly to join him.

Keats, when he died, had just completed his four-and-twentieth year. He was under the middle height; and his lower limbs were small in comparison with the upper, but neat and well turned. His shoulders were very broad for his size: he had a face in which energy and sensibility were remarkably mixed up; an eager power, checked and made patient by ill-health. Every feature was at once strongly cut, and delicately alive. If there was any faulty expression, it was in the mouth, which was not without something of a character of pugnacity. His face was rather long than otherwise; the upper lip projected a little over the under; the chin was bold, the cheeks sunken; the eyes mellow and glowing; large, dark, and sensitive. At the recital of a noble action, or a beautiful thought, they would suffuse with tears, and his mouth trembled. In this, there was ill-health as well as imagination, for he did not like these betrayals of emotion; and he had great personal as well as moral courage. He once chastised a butcher, who had been insolent, by a regular stand-up fight. His hair, of a brown colour, was fine, and hung in natural ringlets. The head was a puzzle for the phrenologists, being remarkably small in the skull; a singularity which he had in common with Byron and Shelley, whose hats I could not get on. Keats was sensible of the disproportion above noticed, between his upper and lower extremities; and he would look at his hand, which was faded, and swollen in the veins, and say it was the hand of a man of fifty. He was a seven months' child. His mother, who was a lively woman, passionately fond of amusement, is supposed to have hastened her death by too great an inattention to hours and seasons. Perhaps she hastened that of her son. His father died of a fall from his horse in the year 1804.

I have endeavoured, in another publication,* to characterize the poetry of Keats, both in its merits and defects. It is not necessary to repeat them here. The public have made up their minds on the subject; and such of his first opponents as were men of genius themselves, but suffered their perceptions to be obscured by political prejudice, (as who has not in such time?) have long agreed with, or anticipated the verdict. Sir Walter Scott confessed to Mr. Severn at Rome, that the truth respecting Keats had prevailed; and it would have been strange, indeed, when the heat of the battle was over, had not Christopher North stretched out his large and

* *Imagination and Fancy*, p. 312.

warm hand to his memory. Times arrive, under the hallowing influences of thought and trouble, when genius is as sure to acknowledge genius, as it is to feel its own wants, and to be willing to share its glory. A man's eyes, the manlier they are, perceive at last, that there is nothing nobler in them than their tears.

It was during my intimacy with Keats that I published a hasty set of miscellaneous poems, under the title of *Foliage*, and wrote the set of essays that have since become popular under that of the *Indicator*. About this time also, I translated the *Aminta* of Tasso, a poem (be it said with the leave of so great a name) hardly worth the trouble, though the prologue is a charming presentment of love in masquerade, and the *Ode on the Golden Age*, a sigh out of the honestest part of the heart of humanity. But I translated it to enable me to meet some demands, occasioned by the falling off in the receipts of the *Examiner*, now declining under the twofold vicissitude of triumphant ascendancy in the Tories, and the desertion of reform by the Whigs. The *Indicator* assisted me still more, though it was but published in a corner, owing to my want of funds for advertising it, and my ignorance of the best mode of circulating such things—an ignorance so profound, that I was not even aware of its very self; for I had never attended, not only to the business part of the *Examiner*, but to the simplest money matter that stared at me on the face of it. I could never tell anybody who asked me, what was the price of its stamp!

Do I boast of this ignorance? Alas! I have no such respect for the pedantry of absurdity as that. I blush for it; and I only record it out of a sheer painful movement of conscience, as a warning to those young authors who might be led to look upon such folly as a fine thing; which at all events is what I never thought it myself. I did not think about it at all, except to avoid the thought; and I only wish that the strangest accidents of education, and the most inconsiderate habit of taking books for the only ends of life, had not conspired to make me so ridiculous. I am feeling the consequences at this moment, in pangs which I cannot explain, and which I may not live long enough, perhaps, to escape.

Let me console myself a little by remembering how much Hazlitt and Lamb, and others, were pleased with the *Indicator*. I speak most of them, because they talked most to me about it. Hazlitt's favourite paper (for they liked it enough to have favourite papers) was the one on *Sleep;* perhaps because there is a picture in it of a sleeping despot; though he repeated, with more enthusiasm than he was accustomed to do, the conclusion about the parent and the bride. Lamb preferred the paper on *Coaches and their Horses,* that on the *Deaths of Little Children,* and (I think) the one entitled *Thoughts and Guesses on Human Nature.* Shelley took to the story of the *Fair Revenge;* and the paper that was most liked by Keats, if I remember, was the one on a hot summer's day, entitled *A Now.* He was with me while I was writing and reading it to him, and contributed one or two of the passages. Keats first published in the *Indicator* his beautiful poem *La Belle Dame sans Mercy,* and the *Dream after reading Dante's Episode of Paulo and Francesca.* Lord Holland, I was told, had a regard for the portraits of the *Old Lady* and the *Old Gentleman,* &c., which had appeared in the *Examiner;* and a late gallant captain in the navy was pleased to wonder how I became so well acquainted with seamen (in the article entitled *Seamen on Shore*). They had "sat to me" for their portraits. The common sailor was a son of my nurse at school, and the officer a connection of my own by marriage.

Let me take this opportunity of recording my recollections in general of my friend Lamb; of all the world's friend, particularly of his oldest friends, Coleridge and Southey; for I think he never modified or withheld any opinion (in private or bookwards) except in consideration of what he thought they might not like.

Charles Lamb had a head worthy of Aristotle, with as fine a heart as ever beat in human bosom, and limbs very fragile to sustain it. There was a caricature of him sold in the shops, which pretended to be a likeness. Proctor went into the shop in a passion, and asked the man what he meant by putting forth such a libel. The man apologized, and said that the artist meant no offence. There never was a true portrait of Lamb. His features were strongly yet delicately cut: he had a fine eye as well as forehead; and no face carried in it greater marks of thought and feeling. It resembled that of Bacon, with less worldly vigour and more sensibility.

As his frame, so was his genius. It was as fit for thought as could be, and equally as unfit for action; and this rendered him melancholy, apprehensive, humorous, and willing to make the best of everything as it was, both from tenderness of heart and abhorrence of alteration. His understanding was too great to admit an absurdity; his frame was not strong enough to deliver it from a fear. His sensibility to strong contrasts was the foundation of his humour, which was that of a wit at once melancholy and willing to be pleased. He would beard a superstition, and shudder at the old phantasm while he did it. One could have imagined him cracking a jest in the teeth of a ghost, and then melting into thin air himself, out of sympathy with the awful. His humour and his knowledge both, were those of Hamlet, of Molière, of Carlin, who shook a city with laughter, and, in order to divert his melancholy, was recommended to go and hear himself. Yet he extracted a real pleasure out of his jokes, because good-heartedness retains that privilege when it fails in everything else. I should say he condescended to be a punster, if condescension had been a word befitting wisdom like his. Being told that somebody had lampooned him, he said, " Very well, I'll Lamb-pun him." His puns were admirable, and often contained as deep things as the wisdom of some who have greater names; such a man, for instance, as Nicole, the Frenchman, who was a baby to him. Lamb would have cracked a score of jokes at Nicole, worth his whole book of sentences; pelted his head with pearls. Nicole would not have understood him, but Rochefoucault would, and Pascal too ; and some of our old Englishmen would have understood him still better. He would have been worthy of hearing Shakspeare read one of his scenes to him, hot from the brain. Commonplace found a great comforter in him, as long as it was good-natured; it was to the ill-natured or the dictatorial only that he was startling. Willing to see society go on as it did, because he despaired of seeing it otherwise, but not at all agreeing in his interior with the common notions of crime and punishment, he " *dumbfounded* " a long tirade against vice one evening, by taking the pipe out of his mouth, and asking the speaker, " Whether he meant to say that a thief was not a good man ? " To a person abusing Voltaire, and indiscreetly opposing his character to that of Jesus Christ, he said admirably well (though he by no means overrated Voltaire, nor wanted reverence in the other quarter), that " Voltaire was a very good Jesus Christ *for the French*." He liked to see the church-goers continue to go to church, and wrote a tale in his sister's admirable little book (*Mrs. Leicester's School*) to encourage the rising generation to do so ; but to a

conscientious deist he had nothing to object; and if an atheist
had found every other door shut against him, he would
assuredly not have found his. I believe he would have had
the world remain precisely as it was, provided it innovated no
farther; but this spirit in him was anything but a worldly
one, or for his own interest. He hardly contemplated with
patience the new buildings in the Regent's Park: and, privately speaking, he had a grudge against *official* heaven-
expounders, or clergymen. He would rather, however, have
been with a crowd that he disliked, than felt himself alone.
He said to me one day, with a face of great solemnity,
" What must have been that man's feelings, who thought himself *the first deist?*" Finding no footing in certainty, he
delighted to confound the borders of theoretical truth and
falsehood. He was fond of telling wild stories to children,
engrafted on things about them; wrote letters to people
abroad, telling them that a friend of theirs [Mr. Alsager, the
commercial editor of the *Times*] had come out in genteel
comedy; and persuaded George Dyer that *Lord Castlereagh*
was the author of *Waverley!* The same excellent person
walking one evening out of his friend's house into the New
River, Lamb (who was from home at the time) wrote a paper
under his signature of Elia, stating, that common friends
would have stood dallying on the bank, have sent for neighbours, &c., but that *he,* in his magnanimity, jumped in, and
rescued his friend after the old noble fashion. He wrote in
the same magazine two lives of Liston and Munden, which
the public took for serious, and which exhibit an extraordinary jumble of imaginary facts and truth of bye-painting.
Munden he made born at " Stoke Pogis : " the very sound of
which was like the actor speaking and digging his words. He
knew how many false conclusions and pretensions are made
by men who profess to be guided by facts only, as if facts
could not be misconceived, or figments taken for them; and
therefore, one day, when somebody was speaking of a person
who valued himself on being a matter-of-fact man, " Now,"
said he, " I value myself on being a matter-of-lie man."
This did not hinder his being a man of the greatest veracity,
in the ordinary sense of the word; but " truth," he said,
" was precious, and not to be wasted on everybody." Those
who wish to have a genuine taste of him, and an insight into
his modes of life, should read his essays on *Hogarth* and
King Lear, his *Letters*, his article on the *London Streets*, on

Whist-Playing, which he loves, and on *Saying Grace before Meat*, which he thinks a strange moment to *select* for being grateful. He said once to a brother whist-player, whose hand was more clever than clean, and who had enough in him to afford the joke, " M., if dirt were trumps, what hands you would hold." [Another anecdote of Lamb his friend would relate with great gusto. While Leigh Hunt was living at Highgate, he used sometimes to be visited by his old school-fellow; and Coleridge, who, it will be remembered, was Lamb's contemporary at Christ's Hospital, would sometimes supervene, and join for a short space in the walk and the con-versation, the talk being, as usual, chiefly appropriated by himself. One day the soliloquy thus poured into the ears of the two friends turned upon the blessings of faith, and it was both in tone and phraseology marked by the accepted dialect of the most "regenerated" orthodoxy: in short, what un-courteous or invidious persons might call canting. After the illustrious poet had taken his leave, Leigh Hunt exclaimed, in a tone of perplexed vexation, " What makes Coleridge talk in that way about heavenly grace, and the holy church, and that sort of thing ? " " Ah," replied Lamb, with the hearty tone of a man uttering an obvious truism, but struggling with his habitual stammer, " there is a g-g-reat deal of fun in Coleridge ! "]

Lamb had seen strange faces of calamity ; but they did not make him love those of his fellow-creatures the less. Few persons guessed what he had suffered in the course of his life, till his friend Talfourd wrote an account of it, and showed the hapless warping that disease had given to the fine brain of his sister.

I will append to this account of Lamb, though I had not the good fortune to know much of him personally, my im-pression respecting his friend Coleridge.

Coleridge was as little fitted for action as Lamb, but on a different account. His person was of a good height, but as sluggish and solid as the other's was light and fragile. He had, perhaps, suffered it to look old before its time, for want of exercise. His hair was white at fifty ; and as he generally dressed in black, and had a very tranquil demeanour, his ap-pearance was gentlemanly, and for several years before his death was reverend. Nevertheless, there was something in-vincibly young in the look of his face. It was round and fresh-coloured, with agreeable features, and an open, indolent, good-natured mouth. This boy-like expression was very becoming in one who dreamed and speculated as he did when he was really a boy, and who passed his life apart from the rest of the world, with a book, and his flowers. His forehead was prodigious—a great piece of placid marble; and his fine eyes, in which all the activity of his mind seemed to concentrate, moved under it with a sprightly ease, as if it was pastime to them to carry all that thought.

And it was pastime. Hazlitt said that Coleridge's genius appeared to him like a spirit, all head and wings, eternally floating about in etherealities. He gave me a different impression. I fancied him a good-natured wizard, very fond of earth, and conscious of reposing with weight enough in his easy chair, but able to conjure his etherealities about him in the twinkling of an eye. He could also change them by thousands, and dismiss them as easily when his dinner came. It was a mighty intellect put upon a sensual body; and the reason why he did little more with it than talk and dream was, that it is agreeable to such a body to do little else. I do not mean that Coleridge was a sensualist in an ill sense. He was capable of too many innocent pleasures to take any pleasure in the way that a man of the world would take it. The idlest things he did would have had a warrant. But if all the senses, in their time, did not find lodging in that humane plenitude of his, never believe that they did in Thomson or in Boccaccio. Two affirmatives in him made a negative. He was very metaphysical and very corporeal; so in mooting everything, he said (so to speak) nothing. His brains pleaded all sorts of questions before him, and he heard them with too much impartiality (his spleen not giving him any trouble), that he thought he might as well sit in his easy chair and hear them for ever, without coming to a conclusion. It has been said (indeed, he said himself) that he took opium to deaden the sharpness of his cogitations. I will venture to affirm, that if he ever took anything to deaden a sensation within him, it was for no greater or more marvellous reason than other people take it; which is, because they do not take enough exercise, and so plague their heads with their livers. Opium, perhaps, might have settled an uneasiness of this sort in Coleridge, as it did in a much less man with a much greater body —the Shadwell of Dryden. He would then resume his natural ease, and sit, and be happy, till the want of exercise must be again supplied. The vanity of criticism, like all other vanities, except that of dress (which, so far, has an involuntary philosophy in it), is always forgetting that we are half made up of body. Hazlitt was angry with Coleridge for not being as zealous in behalf of progress as he used to be when young. I was sorry for it, too; and if other men as well as Hazlitt had not kept me in heart, should have feared that the world was destined to be for ever lost, for want either of perseverance or calmness. But Coleridge had less right to begin his zeal in favour of liberty than he had to leave it off. He should have bethought himself, first, whether he had the courage not to get fat.

As to the charge against him, of eternally probing the depths of his own mind, and trying what he could make of them beyond the ordinary pale of logic and philosophy, surely there was no harm in a man taking this new sort of experiment upon him, whatever little chance there may have been of his doing anything with it. Coleridge, after all, was but one man, though an extraordinary man : his faculties inclined him to the task, and were suitable to it ; and it is impossible to say what new worlds may be laid open, some day or other, by this apparently hopeless process. The fault of Coleridge, like that of all thinkers indisposed to action, was, that he was too content with things as they were,—at least, too fond of thinking that old corruptions were full of good things, if the world did but understand them. Now, here was the dilemma; for it required an understanding like his own to refine upon and turn them to good as he might do ; and what the world requires is not metaphysical refinement, but a hearty use of good sense. Coleridge, indeed, could refine his meaning so as to accommodate it with great good-nature to every one that came across him; and, doubtless, he found more agreement of intention among people of different opinions, than they themselves were aware of; which it was good to let them see. But when not enchained by his harmony, they fell asunder again, or went and committed the greatest absurdities for want of the subtle connecting tie ; as was seen in the books of Mr. Irving, who, eloquent in one page, and reasoning in a manner that a child ought to be ashamed of in the next, thought to avail himself, in times like these, of the old menacing tones of damnation, without being considered a quack or an idiot, purely because Coleridge had shown him, last Friday, that damnation was not what its preachers took it for. With the same subtlety and good-nature of interpretation, Coleridge would persuade a deist that he was a Christian, and an atheist that he believed in God: all which would be very good, if the world could get on by it, and not remain stationary; but, meanwhile, millions are wretched with having too little to eat, and thousands with having too much; and these subtleties are like people talking in their sleep, when they should be up and helping.

However, if the world is to remain always as it is, give me to all eternity new talk of Coleridge, and new essays of Charles Lamb. They will reconcile it beyond all others: and that is much.

Coleridge was fat, and began to lament, in very delightful verses, that he was getting infirm. There was no old age in his verses. I heard him one day, under the Grove at High-gate, repeat one of his melodious lamentations, as he walked up and down, his voice undulating in a stream of music, and his regrets of youth sparkling with visions ever young. At the same time, he did me the honour to show me that he did not think so ill of all modern liberalism as some might sup-pose, denouncing the pretensions of the money-getting in a style which I should hardly venture upon, and never could equal; and asking with a triumphant eloquence what chastity itself were worth, if it were a casket, not to keep love in, but hate, and strife, and worldliness? On the same occasion, he built up a metaphor out of a flower, in a style surpassing the famous passage in Milton; deducing it from its root in reli-gious mystery, and carrying it up into the bright, consum-mate flower, "the bridal chamber of reproductiveness." Of all "the Muse's mysteries," he was as great a high-priest as Spenser; and Spenser himself might have gone to Highgate to hear him talk, and thank him for his *Ancient Mariner*. His voice did not always sound very sincere; but perhaps the humble and deprecating tone of it, on those occasions, was out of consideration for the infirmities of his hearers, rather than produced by his own. He recited his *Kubla Khan* one morning to Lord Byron, in his lordship's house in Piccadilly, when I happened to be in another room. I remember the other's coming away from him, highly struck with his poem, and saying how wonderfully he talked. This was the impres-sion of everybody who heard him.

It is no secret that Coleridge lived in the Grove at Highgate with a friendly family, who had sense and kindness enough to know that they did themselves honour by looking after the comfort of such a man. His room looked upon a delicious prospect of wood and meadow, with coloured gardens under the window, like an embroidery to the mantle. I thought, when I first saw it, that he had taken up his dwelling-place like an abbot. Here he cultivated his flowers, and had a set of birds for his pensioners, who came to breakfast with him. He might have been seen taking his daily stroll up and down, with his black coat and white locks, and a book in his hand; and was a great acquaintance of the little children. His main occupation, I believe, was reading. He loved to read old folios, and to make old voyages with Purchas and Marco Polo; the seas being in good visionary condition, and the vessel well stocked with botargoes.*

CHAPTER XVII.

VOYAGE TO ITALY.

It was not at Hampstead that I first saw Keats. It was in York Buildings, in the New Road (No. 8), where I wrote part of the *Indicator*—and he resided with me while in Mortimer Terrace, Kentish Town (No. 13), where I concluded it. I mention this for the curious in such things; among whom I am one.

I proceed to hasten over the declining fortunes of the *Examiner*. Politics different from ours were triumphing all over Europe; public sympathy (not the most honourable circumstance of its character) is apt to be too much qualified by fortune. Shelley, who had been for some time in Italy, had often invited me abroad; and I had as repeatedly declined going, for the reason stated in my account of him. That reason was done away by a proposal from Lord Byron to go and set up a liberal periodical publication in conjunction with them both. I was ill; it was thought by many I could not live; my wife was very ill too; my family was numerous; and it was agreed by my brother John, that while a struggle was made in England to reanimate the *Examiner*, a simultaneous endeavour should be made in Italy to secure new aid to

* For a more critical summary of my opinions respecting Coleridge's poetry (which I take upon the whole to have been the finest of its time; that is to say, the most quintessential, the most purely emanating from imaginative feeling, unadulterated by "thoughts" and manner), the reader may, if he pleases, consult *Imagination and Fancy*, p. 276.

our prospects, and new friends to the cause of liberty. My family, therefore, packed up such goods and chattels as they had a regard for, my books in particular, and we took, with strange new thoughts and feelings, but in high expectation, our journey by sea.

It was not very discreet to go many hundred miles by sea in winter-time with a large family; but a voyage was thought cheaper than a journey by land. Even that, however, was a mistake. It was by Shelley's advice that I acted; and, I believe, if he had recommended a balloon, I should have been inclined to try it. "Put your music and your books on board a vessel" (it was thus that he wrote to us), "and you will have no more trouble." The sea was to him a pastime; he fancied us bounding over the waters, the merrier for being tossed; and thought that our will would carry us through anything, as it ought to do, seeing that we brought with us nothing but good things,—books, music, and sociality. It is true, he looked to our coming in autumn, and not in winter; and so we should have done, but for the delays of the captain. We engaged to embark in September, and did not set off till November the 16th.

I have often thought that a sea-voyage, which is generally the dullest thing in the world, both in the experiment and the description, might be turned to different account on paper, if the narrators, instead of imitating the dulness of their predecessors, and recording that it was four o'clock P.M. when they passed Cape St. Vincent, and that on such-and-such-a-day they beheld a porpoise or a Dutchman, would look into the interior of the floating-house they inhabited, and tell us about the seamen and their modes of living; what adventures they have had,—their characters and opinions,—how they eat, drink, and sleep, &c.; what they do in fine weather, and how they endure the sharpness, the squalidness, and inconceivable misery of bad. With a large family around me to occupy my mind, I did not think of this till too late: but I am sure that this mode of treating the subject would be interesting; and what I remember to such purpose, I will set down.

Our vessel was a small brig of a hundred and twenty tons burden, a good tight sea-boat, nothing more. Its cargo consisted of sugar; but it took in also a surreptitious stock of gunpowder, to the amount of fifty barrels, which was destined for Greece. Of this intention we knew nothing, till the barrels were sent on board from a place up the river; otherwise, so touchy a companion would have been objected to, my wife, who was in a shattered state of health, never ceasing to entertain apprehensions on account of it, except when the storms that came upon us presented a more obvious peril. There were nine men to the crew, including the mate. We numbered almost as many souls, though with smaller bodies, in the cabin, which we had entirely to ourselves; as well we might, for it was small enough.

On the afternoon of the 15th of November (1821), we took leave of some friends, who accompanied us on board; and next morning were awakened by the motion of the vessel making its way through the shipping in the river. The new life in which we thus, as it were, found ourselves enclosed, the clanking of iron, and the cheerly cries of the seamen, together with the natural vivacity of the time of day, presented something animating to our feelings; but while we thus moved off, not without encouragement, we felt that the friend whom we were going to see was at a great distance, while others were very near, whose hands it would be a long while before we should touch again, perhaps never. We hastened to get up and busy ourselves; and great as well as small found a novel diversion in the spectacle that presented itself from the deck, our vessel threading its way through the others with gliding bulk.

The next day it blew strong from the south-east, and even in the river (the navigation of which is not easy) we had a foretaste of the alarms and bad weather that awaited us at sea. The pilot, whom we had taken in over-night (and who was a jovial fellow with a whistle like a blackbird, which, in spite of the dislike that sailors have to whistling, he was always indulging), thought it prudent to remain at anchor till two in the afternoon; and at six, a vessel meeting us carried away the jib-boom, and broke in one of the bulwarks. My wife, who had had a respite from the most alarming part of her illness, and whom it was supposed that a sea-voyage, even in winter, might benefit, again expectorated blood with the fright; and I began to regret that I had brought my family into this trouble.—Even in the river we had a foretaste of the sea; and the curse of being at sea to a landsman is, that you know nothing of what is going forward, and can take no active part in getting rid of your fears. You cannot "lend a hand." The business of these small vessels is not carried on with the orderliness and tranquillity of greater ones, or of men-of-war.

The crew are not very wise; the captain does not know how to make them so; the storm roars; the vessel pitches and reels; the captain, over your head, stamps and swears, and announces all sorts of catastrophes. Think of a family hearing all this, and parents in alarm for their children!

On Monday, the 19th, we passed the Nore, and proceeded down Channel amidst rains and squalls. We were now out at sea; and a rough taste we had of it. I had been three times in the Channel before, once in hard weather; but I was then a bachelor, and had only myself to think of. Let the reader picture to his imagination the little back-parlour of one of the shops in Fleet Street or the Strand, attached or let into a great moving vehicle, and tumbling about the waves from side to side, now sending all the things that are loose this way, and now that. This will give him an idea of a cabin at sea, such as we occupied. It had a table fastened down in the middle; places let into the walls on each side, one over the other, to hold beds; a short, wide, sloping window, carried off over a bulk, and looking out to sea, closed in bad weather, and a skylight, also closed in the worst storms; a bench, or locker, running under the bulk from one side of the cabin to the other; and a little fireplace opposite, in which it was impossible to keep a fire on account of the wind. The weather, at the same time, was bitterly cold, as well as wet. On one side of the fireplace was the door, and on the other a door leading into a petty closet dignified with the title of the state-room. In this room we put our servant, the captain sleeping in another closet outside. The berths were occupied by the children, and my wife and myself lay, as long as we could manage to do so, on the floor. Such was the trim, with boisterous wet weather, cold days, and long evenings, on which we set out on our sea-adventure.

At six o'clock in the evening of the 19th, we came to in the Downs, on a line with Sandown Castle. The wind during the night increasing to a gale, the vessel pitched and laboured considerably; and the whole of the next day it blew a strong gale, with hard squalls from the westward. The day after, the weather continuing bad, the captain thought proper to run for Ramsgate, and took a pilot for that purpose.

We stopped for a change of weather nearly three weeks at Ramsgate, where we had visits from more than one London friend, to whom I only wish we could give a tenth part of the consolation when they are in trouble, which they afforded to us. At Ramsgate I picked up Condorcet's *View of the Progress of Society*, which I read with a transport of gratitude to the author, though it had not entered so deeply into the matter as I supposed. But the very power to persevere in hopes for mankind, at a time of life when individuals are in the habit of reconciling their selfishness and fatigue by choosing to think ill of them, is a great good to any man, and achieves a great good if it act only upon one other person. Such instances of perseverance beget more; and it is these that alter the world.

For some days we remained on board, as it was hoped that we should be able to set sail again. Ramsgate harbour is very shallow; and though we lay in the deepest part of it, the vessel took to a new and ludicrous species of dance, grinding and thumping upon the chalky ground. The consequence was, that the metal pintles of the rudder were all broken, and new ones obliged to be made; which the sailors told us was very lucky, as the rudder was thus proved not to be in a good condition, and it might have deserted us at sea.

We lay next a French vessel, smaller than our own, the crew of which became amusing subjects of remark. They were always whistling, singing, and joking. The men shaved themselves elaborately, cultivating heroic whiskers; and they strutted up and down, when at leisure, with their arms folded, and the air of naval officers. A woman or two, with kerchiefs and little curls, completed the picture. They all seemed very merry and good-humoured.

At length, tired of waiting on board, we took a quiet lodging at the other end of the town, and were pleased to find ourselves sitting still, and secure of a good rest at night. It is something, after being at sea, to find oneself not running the fork in one's eye at dinner, or suddenly sliding down the floor to the other end of the room. My wife was in a very weak state; but the rest she took was deep and tranquil, and I resumed my walks.

Few of the principal bathing-places have anything worth looking at in the neighbourhood, and Ramsgate has less than most. Pegwell Bay is eminent for shrimps. Close by was Sir William Garrow, and a little farther on was Sir William Curtis. The sea is a grand sight, but it becomes tiresome and melancholy—a great monotonous idea; at least one thinks so, when not happy. I was destined to see it grander, and dislike it more. With great injustice; for all the works of nature are beautiful, and their beauty is not to be subjected to our petty vicissitudes.

On Tuesday, the 11th of December, we set forth again, in company with nearly a hundred vessels, the white sails of which, as they shifted and presented themselves in different quarters, made an agreeable spectacle, exhibiting a kind of noble minuet. My wife was obliged to be carried down to the pier in a sedan; and the taking leave, a second time, of a dear friend, rendered our new departure a melancholy one. I would have stopped and waited for summer-time, had not circumstances rendered it advisable for us to persevere; and my wife herself fully agreed with me, and even hoped for benefit, as well as a change of weather.

Unfortunately, the promise to that effect lasted us but a day. The winds recommenced the day following, and there ensued such a continuity and vehemence of bad weather as rendered the winter of 1821 memorable in the shipping annals. It strewed the whole of the north-western coast of Europe with wrecks. Some readers may remember that winter. It was the one in which Mount Hecla burst out into flame, and Dungeness Lighthouse was struck with lightning. The mole at Genoa was dilapidated. Next year there were between fourteen and fifteen hundred sail less upon Lloyd's books; which, valued at an average at 1,500l., made a loss of two millions of money—the least of all the losses, considering the feelings of survivors. Fifteen hundred sail (colliers) were wrecked on the single coast of Jutland. Of this turmoil we were destined to have a sufficient experience.

Two days after we left Ramsgate, the wind blowing violently from the south-west, we were under close-reefed topsails; but on its veering to westward, the captain was induced to persevere, in hopes that by coming round to the north-west, it would enable him to clear the Channel. The ship laboured very much, the sea breaking over her; and the pump was constantly going.

The next day, the 14th, we shipped a great deal of water, the pump going as before. The fore-topsail and foresail were taken in; the storm-staysail set; and the captain said we were " in the hands of God." We now wore ship to southward.

On the 15th, the weather was a little moderated, with fresh gales and cloudy. The captain told us to-day how his hair turned white in a shipwreck; and the mate entertained us with an account of the extraordinary escape of himself and some others from an American pirate, who seized their vessel, plundered and made it a wreck, and confined them under the hatches, in the hope of their going down with it. They escaped in a rag of a boat, and were taken up by a Greek vessel, which treated them with the greatest humanity. The pirate was afterwards taken and hanged at Malta, with five of his men. This story, being tragical without being tempestuous, and terminating happily for our friend, was very welcome, and occupied us agreeably. I tried to elicit some ghost stories of vessels, but could hear of nothing but the *Flying Dutchman;* nor did I succeed better on another occasion. This dearth of supernatural adventure is remarkable, considering the superstition of sailors. But their wits are none of the liveliest; the sea blunts while it mystifies ; and the sailor's imagination, driven in, like his body, to the vessel he inhabits, admits only the petty wonders that come directly about him in the shape of storm-announcing fishes and birds. His superstition is that of a blunted and not of an awakened ignorance. Sailors had rather sleep than see visions.

On the 16th, the storm was alive again, with strong gales and heavy squalls. We set the fore storm-staysail anew, and at night the jolly-boat was torn from the stern.

The afternoon of the 17th brought us the gale that lasted fifty-six hours, "one of the most tremendous," the captain said, " that he had ever witnessed." All the sails were taken in, except the close-reefed topsail and one of the trysails. At night, the wind being at south-west, and Scilly about fifty miles north by east, the trysail sheet was carried away, and the boom and sail had a narrow escape. We were now continually wearing ship. The boom was unshipped, as it was; and it was a melancholy sight to see it lying next morning, with the sail about it, like a wounded servant who had been fighting. The morning was occupied in getting it to rights. At night we had hard squalls with lightning.

We lay-to under main-topsail until the next morning, the 19th, when at ten o'clock we were enabled to set the reefed foresail, and the captain prepared to run for Falmouth; but finding he could not get in till night, we hauled to the wind, and at three in the afternoon, wore ship to south-westward. It was then blowing heavily; and the sea, breaking over the vessel, constantly took with it a part of the bulwark. I believe we had long ceased to have a duck alive. Our poor goat had contrived to find itself a corner in the long-boat, and lay frightened and shivering under a piece of canvas. I afterwards took it down in the cabin to share our lodging; but not having a berth to give it, it passed a sorry time, tied up and slipping about the floor. At night we had lightning again, with hard gales, the wind being west and north-west, and threatening to drive us on the French coast. It was a grand thing, through the black and turbid atmosphere, to see the great fiery eye of the lighthouse at the Lizard Point: it looked like a good genius with a ferocious aspect. Ancient mythology would have made dragons of these noble structures,—dragons with giant glare, warning the seaman off the coast.

The captain could not get into Falmouth: so he wore ship, and stood to the westward with fresh hopes, the wind having veered a little to the north; but, after having run above fifty miles to the south and west, the wind veered again in our teeth, and at two o'clock on the 20th, we were reduced to a close-reefed main-topsail, which, being new, fortunately held, the wind blowing so hard that it could not be taken in without the greatest risk of losing it. The sea was very heavy, and the rage of the gale tremendous, accompanied with lightning. The children on these occasions slept, unconscious of their danger. My wife slept, too, from exhaustion. I remember, as I lay awake that night, looking about to see what help I could get from imagination, to furnish a moment's respite from the anxieties that beset me, I cast my eyes on the poor goat; and recollecting how she devoured some choice biscuit I gave her one day, I got up, and going to the cupboard took out as much as I could find, and occupied myself in seeing her eat. She munched the fine white biscuit out of my hand, with equal appetite and comfort; and I thought of a saying of Sir Philip Sidney's, that we are never perfectly miserable when we can do a good-natured action.

"A large vessel is coming right down upon us;—lights—lights!" This was the cry at eleven o'clock at night, on the 21st December, the gale being tremendous, and the sea to match. Lanthorns were handed up from the cabin, and, one after the other, put out. The captain thought it was owing to the weather; but it was the drunken steward, who jolted them out as he took them up the ladder. We furnished more, and contrived to see them kept in; and the captain afterwards told me that we had saved his vessel. The ship, discerning us just in time, passed ahead, looking very huge and terrible. Next morning, we saw her about two miles on our lee-bow, lying-to under trysails. It was an Indiaman. There was another vessel, a smaller, near us in the night. I thought the Indiaman looked very comfortable, with its spacious and powerful body: but the captain said we were better off a great deal in our own sea-boat; which turned out to be too true, if this was the same Indiaman, as some thought it, which was lost the night following off the coast of Devonshire. The crew said, that in one of the pauses of the wind they heard a vessel go down. We were at that time near land. While drinking tea, the keel of our ship grated against something, perhaps a shoal. The captain afterwards very properly made light of it; but at the time, being in the act of raising a cup to his mouth, I remember he turned very grave, and, getting up, went upon deck.

Next day, the 22nd, we ran for Dartmouth, and succeeding this time, found ourselves, at twelve o'clock at noon, in the middle of Dartmouth harbour,—

> "Magno telluris amore
> Egressi, optata potiuntur Troës arena."

We left Dartmouth, where no ships were in the habit of sailing for Italy, and went to Plymouth; intending to set off again with the beginning of spring, in a vessel bound for Genoa. But the mate of it, who, I believe, grudged us the room we should deprive him of, contrived to tell my wife a number of dismal stories, both of the ship and its captain, who was an unlucky fellow that seemed marked by fortune. Misery had also made him a Calvinist,—the most miserable of all ways of getting comfort; and this was no additional recommendation. To say the truth, having a pique against my fears on the former occasion, I was more bent on allowing myself to have none on the present; otherwise, I should not have thought of putting forth again till the fine weather was complete. But the reasons that prevailed before, had now become still more imperative; my wife being confined to her bed, and undergoing repeated bleedings; so, till summer we waited.

The sea upon the whole had done me good, and I found myself able to write again, though by driblets. We lived very quietly at Stonehouse, opposite Mount-Edgecumbe, nursing our hopes for a new voyage, and expecting one of a very different complexion, in sailing towards an Italian summer. My wife kept her bed almost the whole time, and lost a great deal of blood; but the repose, together with the sea-air, was of service to her, and enabled her to receive benefit on resuming our journey.

Thus quietly we lived, and thus should have continued, agreeably to both of our inclinations; but some friends of the *Examiner* heard of our being in the neighbourhood, and the privatest of all public men (if I may be ranked among the number) found himself complimented by his readers, face to face, and presented with a silver cup. I then had a taste of the Plymouth hospitality, and found it friendly and cordial to the last degree, as if the seamen's atmosphere gave a new spirit to the love of books and liberty. Nor, as the poet would say, was music wanting; nor fair faces, the crown of welcome. Besides the landscapes in the neighbourhood, I had the pleasure of seeing some beautiful ones in the painting-room of Mr. Rogers, a very clever artist and intelligent man, who has travelled, and can think for himself. But my great *Examiner* friend, who afterwards became a personal one, was Mr. Hine, subsequently master of an academy near the metropolis, and the most attentive and energetic person of his profession that I ever met with. My principal visitors, indeed, at Plymouth consisted of schoolmasters;—one of those signs of the times which has not been so ill regarded since the accession of a lettered and liberal minister to the government of this country, as they were under the supercilious ignorance, and (to say the truth) well-founded alarm of some of his predecessors.

The Devonshire people, as far as I had experience of them, were pleasant and good-humoured. Queen Elizabeth said of their gentry, that they were "all born courtiers with a becoming confidence." I know not how that may be, though she had a good specimen in Sir Walter Raleigh. But the private history of modern times might exhibit instances of natives of Devonshire winning their way into regard and power by the force of a well-constituted mixture of sweet and strong; and it is curious that the milder climate of that part of England should have produced more painters, perhaps, of a superior kind, than any other two counties can show. Drake, Jewel, Hooker, and old Fortescue, were also Devonshire-men; William Browne, the most genuine of Spenser's disciples; and Gay, the enjoying and the good-hearted, the natural man in the midst of the sophisticate.

We left Plymouth on the 13th of May, 1822, accompanied by some of our new friends who would see us on board; and set sail in a fresh vessel, on our new summer voyage, a very different one from the last. Short acquaintances sometimes cram as much into their intercourse, as to take the footing of long ones; and our parting was not without pain. Another shadow was cast on the female countenances by the observation of our boatman, who, though an old sailor who ought to have known better, bade us remark how heavily laden our ship was, and how deep she lay in the water: so little can ignorance afford to miss an opportunity of being important.

Our new captain, and, I believe, all his crew, were Welsh, with the exception of one sailor, an unfortunate Scotchman, who seemed pitched among them to have his nationality put to the torture. Jokes were unceasingly cracked on the length of his person, the oddity of his dialect, and the uncouth manner in which he stood at the helm. It was a new thing to hear Welshmen cutting up the barbarism of the "Modern Athens;" but they had the advantage of the poor fellow in wit, and he took it with a sort of sulky patience, that showed he was not destitute of one part of the wisdom of his countrymen. To have made a noise would have been to bring down new shouts of laughter; so he pocketed the affronts as well as he might, and I could not help fancying that his earnings lay in the same place more securely than those of the others about him. The captain was choleric and *brusque*, a temperament which was none the better for an inclination to plethora; but his enthusiasm in behalf of his brother tars, and the battles they had fought, was as robust as his frame; and he surprised us with writing verses on the strength of it. Very good *heart* and *impart* verses they were, too, and would cut as good a figure as any in the old magazines. While he read them, he rolled the *r*'s in the most rugged style, and looked as if he could have run them down the throats of the enemy. The objects of his eulogy he called " our gallant *herroes*."

We took leave of Plymouth with a fine wind at north-east; and next day, on the confines of the Channel, spoke the *Two Sisters* of Guernsey, from Rio Janeiro. On a long voyage ships lose their longitude; and our information enabled the vessel to enter the Channel with security. Ships approaching and parting from one another present a fine spectacle, shifting in the light, and almost looking conscious of the grace of their movements.

We were now on the high Atlantic, with fresh health and hopes, and the prospect of an easy voyage before us. Next night, the 15th, we saw, for the first time, two grampuses, who interested us extremely with their unwieldy gambols. They were very large—in fact, a small kind of whale; but they played about the vessel like kittens, dashing round, and even under it, as if in scorn of its progress. The swiftness of fish is inconceivable. The smallest of them must be enormously strong: the largest are as gay as the least. One of these grampuses fairly sprang out of the water, bolt upright.

The same day, we were becalmed in the Bay of Biscay— a pleasant surprise. A calm in the Bay of Biscay, after what we had read and heard of it, sounded to us like repose in a boiling cauldron. But a calm, after all, is not repose: it is a very unresting and unpleasant thing, the ship taking a great gawky motion from side to side, as if playing the buffoon; and the sea heaving in huge oily-looking fields, like a carpet lifted. Sometimes it appears to be striped into great ribbons; but the sense of it is always more or less unpleasant, and to impatient seamen is torture.

The next day we were still becalmed. A small shark played all day long about the vessel, but was shy of the bait. The sea was swelling, and foul with putrid substances, which made us think what it would be if a calm continued a month. Coleridge has touched upon that matter, with the hand of a master, in his *Ancient Mariner*. (Here are three words in one sentence beginning with *m* and ending with *r*, to the great regret of fingers that cannot always stop to make corrections. But the compliment to Coleridge shall be the greater, since it is at my own expense.) During a calm, the seamen, that they may not be idle, are employed in painting the vessel— an operation that does not look well, amidst the surrounding aspect of sickness and faintness. The favourite colours are black and yellow; I believe, because they are the least expensive. The combination is certainly the most ugly. There are shades of darkness and yellowness that look well together in certain materials and under certain circumstances, as in the case of dark-haired beauties attired in garments of daffodil or jonquil; but in great broad stripes upon ships, the effect is nothing but a coarse combination of the glaring and the sombre.

On the 17th, we had a fine breeze at north-east. There is great enjoyment in a beautiful day at sea. You quit all the discomforts of your situation for the comforts; interchange congratulations with the seamen, who are all in good humour; seat yourself at ease on the deck, enjoy the motion, the getting on, the healthiness of the air; watch idly for new sights; read a little, or chat, or give way to a day-dream; then look up again, and expatiate on the basking scene around you, with its ripples of blue and green, or of green and gold —what the old poet beautifully calls *the innumerable smile* of the waters.

" Πόντιών τε κύματων
Ἀνηρίθμον γέλασμα."
PROMETHEUS VINCTUS.

The appearance of another vessel sets conjecture alive: it is " a Dane," " a Frenchman," " a Portuguese;" and these words have a new effect upon us, as though we suddenly became intimate with the country to which they belong. A more striking effect of the same sort is produced by the sight of a piece of land; it is Flamborough Head, Ushant, Cape Ortegal:—you see a part of another country, one perhaps on which you have never set foot; and even this is a great thing: it gives you an advantage; others have *read* of Spain or Portugal; you have *seen* it, and are a grown man and a tra-veller, compared with those little children of books. These novelties affect the dullest; but to persons of any imagination, and such as are ready for any pleasure or consolation that nature offers them, they are like pieces of a new morning of life. The world seems begun again, and our stock of know-ledge recommencing on a new plan.

Then at night-time, there are those beautiful fires on the water. In a fine blue sea, the foam caused by the ship at night seems full of stars. The white fermentation, with golden sparkles in it, is beautiful beyond conception. You look over the side of the vessel, and devour it with your eyes, as you would so much ethereal syllabub. Finally, the stars in the firmament issue forth, and the moon; always the more lovely the farther you get south. Or when there is no moon on the sea, the shadows at a little distance become grander and more solemn, and you watch for some huge fish to lift himself in the middle of them—a darker mass, breathing and spouting water.

On the 21st, after another two days of calm, and one of rain, we passed Cape Finisterre. There was a heavy swell and rolling. Being now on the Atlantic, with not even any other name for the part of it that we sailed over to interrupt the widest association of ideas, I thought of America, and Columbus, and the chivalrous squadrons that set out from

Lisbon, and the old Atlantis of Plato, formerly supposed to exist
off the coast of Portugal. It is curious that the Portuguese
have a tradition to this day that there is an island occasionally
seen off the coast of Lisbon. The story of the Atlantis looks
like some old immemorial tradition of a country that has
really existed; nor is it difficult to suppose that there was
formerly some great tract of land, or even continent, occupying these now watery regions, when we consider the fluctua-
tion of things, and those changes of dry to moist, and of lofty
to low, which are always taking place all over the globe.
Off the coast of Cornwall, the mariner, it has been said, now
rides over the old country of Lyones, or whatever else it was
called, if that name be fabulous; and there are stories of
doors and casements, and other evidences of occupation,
brought up from the bottom. These, indeed, have lately
been denied, or reduced to nothing: but old probabilities
remain. In the eastern seas the gigantic work of creation is
visibly going on by means of those little creatures, the coral
worms; and new lands will as assuredly be inhabited there
after a lapse of centuries, as old ones have vanished in the west.

> " So, in them all, raignes mutabilitie."

22nd. Fine breeze to-day from the N.E. A great shark
went by. One longs to give the fellow a great dig in the
mouth. Yet he is only going " on his vocation." Without
him, as without the vultures on land, something would be
amiss. It is only moral pain and inequality which it is
desirable to alter—that which the mind of man has an
invincible tendency to alter.

To-day the seas reminded me of the " marmora pelagi " of
Catullus (the " marbles of the ocean "). They looked, at a
little distance, like blue water petrified. You might have
supposed, that by some sudden catastrophe the mighty main
had been turned into stone; and the huge animals, whose
remains we find in it, fixed there for ever.

A shoal of porpoises broke up the fancy. Waves might be
classed, as clouds have been; and more determination given
to pictures of them. We ought to have waves and wavelets,
billows, fluctuosities, &c., a marble sea, a sea weltering. The
sea varies its look at the immediate side of the vessel, according as the progress is swift or slow. Sometimes it is a crisp
and rapid flight, hissing; sometimes an interweaving of the
foam in snake-like characters; sometimes a heavy weltering

shouldering the ship on this side and that. In what is called "the trough of the sea," which is a common state to be in during violent weather, the vessel literally appears stuck and labouring in a trough, the sea looking on either side like a hill of yeast. This was the gentlest sight we used to have in the Channel; very different from our summer amenities. I never saw what are called waves "mountains high." It is a figure of speech; and a very violent one.

23rd. A strong breeze from the N. and N.E., with clouds and rain. The foam by the vessel's side was full of those sparkles I have mentioned, like stars in clouds of froth. On the 24th the breeze increased, but the sky was fairer, and the moon gave a light. We drank the health of a friend in England, whose birthday it was; being great observers of that part of religion. The 25th brought us beautiful weather, with a wind right from the north, so that we ran down the remainder of the coast of Portugal in high style. Just as we desired it, too, it changed to N.W., so as to enable us to turn the Strait of Gibraltar merrily. Cape St. Vincent (where the battle took place), just before you come to Gibraltar, is a beautiful lone promontory jutting out upon the sea, and crowned with a convent. It presented itself to my eyes the first thing when I came upon deck in the morning, clear, solitary, blind-looking; feeling, as it were, the sea air and the solitude for ever, like something between stone and spirit. It reminded me of a couplet, written not long before, of

"Ghastly castle, that eternally
    Holds its blind visage out to the lone sea."

Such things are beheld in one's day-dreams, and we are almost startled to find them real.

Gibraltar has a noble look, tall, hard, and independent. But you do not wish to live there: it is a fortress, and an insulated rock; and such a place is but a prison. The inhabitants feed luxuriously with the help of their fruits and smugglers.

The first sight of Africa is an achievement. Voyagers in our situation are obliged to be content with a mere sight of it; but that is much. They have seen another quarter of the globe. "Africa!" They look at it, and repeat the word, till the whole burning and savage territory, with its black inhabitants and its lions, seems put into their possession. Ceuta and Tangier bring the old Moorish times before you; "Ape's Hill," which is pointed out, sounds fastastic and remote, "a wilderness of monkeys;" and as all shores on which you do not clearly distinguish objects have a solemn and romantic look, you get rid of the petty effect of those vagabond Barbary States that occupy the coast, and think at once of Africa, the country of deserts and wild beasts, the "dry-nurse of lions," as Horace, with a vigour beyond himself, calls it.

At Gibraltar you first have a convincing proof of the rarity of the southern atmosphere in the near look of the Straits, which seem but a few miles across, though they are thirteen.

But what a crowd of thoughts face one on entering the Mediterranean! Grand as the sensation is in passing through the classical and romantic memories of the sea off the western coast of the Peninsula, it is little compared with this. Countless generations of the human race, from three quarters of the world, with all the religions, and the mythologies, and the genius, and the wonderful deeds, good and bad, that have occupied almost the whole attention of mankind, look you in the face from the galleries of that ocean-floor, rising one above another, till the tops are lost in heaven. The water at your feet is the same water that bathes the shores of Europe, of Africa, and of Asia—of Italy and Greece, and the Holy Land, and the lands of chivalry and romance, and pastoral Sicily, and the Pyramids, and Old Crete, and the Arabian city of Al Cairo, glittering in the magic lustre of the Thousand and One Nights. This soft air in your face comes from the grove of "Daphne by Orontes;" these lucid waters, that part from before you like oil, are the same from which Venus arose, pressing them out of her hair. In that quarter Vulcan fell—

> "Dropt from the zenith like a falling star:"

and there is Circe's Island, and Calypso's, and the promontory of Plato, and Ulysses wandering, and Cymon and Miltiades fighting, and Regulus crossing the sea to Carthage, and

> "Damasco and Morocco, and Trebisond;
> And whom Biserta sent from Afric shore,
> When Charlemagne with all his peerage fell
> By Fontarabia."

The mind hardly separates truth from fiction in thinking of all these things, nor does it wish to do so. Fiction is Truth in another shape, and gives as close embraces. You may shut a door upon a ruby, and render it of no colour; but the colour shall not be the less enchanting for that, when the sun, the poet of the world, touches it with his golden pen. What we glow at and shed tears over, is as real as love and pity.

27th. Almost a calm. We proceeded at no greater rate than a mile an hour. I kept repeating to myself the word " Mediterranean;" not the word in prose, but the word in verse, as it stands at the beginning of the line:

> " And the sea
> Mediterranean."

We saw the mountains about Malaga, topped with snow. Velez Malaga is probably the place at which Cervantes landed on his return from captivity at Algiers. (See *Don Quixote*, vol. ii.) I had the pleasure of reading the passage, while crossing the line betwixt the two cities. It is something to sail by the very names of Granada and Andalusia. There was a fine sunset over the hills of Granada. I imagined it lighting up the Alhambra. The clouds were like great wings of gold and yellow and rose-colour, with a smaller minute sprinkle in one spot, like a shower of glowing stones from a volcano. You see very faint imitations of such lustre in England. A heavy dew succeeded; and a contrary wind at south-east, but very mild. At night, the reflection of the moon on the water was like silver snakes.

30th. Passed Cape de Gata. My wife was very ill, but observed that illness itself was not illness, compared to what she experienced in the winter voyage. She never complained, summer or winter. It is very distressing not to be able to give perfect comfort to patients of this generous description. The Mediterranean Sea, after the Channel, was like a basin of gold fish ; but when the winds are contrary, the waves of it have a short uneasy motion, that fidget the vessel, and make one long for the nobler billows of the Atlantic. The wind, too, was singularly unpleasant,—moist and feverish. It continued contrary for several days, but became more agreeable, and sank almost into a calm on the 3rd of June.

The books with which I chiefly amused myself in the Mediterranean, were *Don Quixote* (for reasons which will be obvious to the reader), *Ariosto* and *Berni* (for similar reasons, their heroes having to do with the coasts of France and Africa), and Bayle's admirable *Essay on Comets*, which I picked up at Plymouth. It is the book that put an end to the superstition about comets. It is full of amusement, like

all his dialectics; and holds together a perfect chain-armour
of logic, the handler of which may cut his fingers with it at
every turn, almost every link containing a double edge. A
generation succeeds quietly to the good done it by such
works, and its benefactor's name is sunk in the washy pretensions of those whom he has enriched. As to what seems
defective in Bayle on the score of natural piety, the reader
may supply that. A benevolent work, tending to do away
real dishonour to things supernatural, will be no hindrance to
any benevolent addition which others can bring it; nor would
Bayle, with his good-natured face, and the scholarly simplicity of his life, have found fault with it. But he was a
soldier, after his fashion, with qualities, both positive and
negative, fit to keep him one; and some things must be dispensed with on the side of what is desirable, for the sake of
the part that is taken in the overthrow of what is detestable.
Him whom inquisitors hate, angels may love.

7th. Saw the Colombrettes, and the land about Tortosa.
Here commences the ground of Italian romance. It was on
this part of the west of Spain, that the Paynim chivalry used
to land, to go against Charlemagne. Here Orlando played
him the tricks that got him the title of Furioso; and from the
port of Barcelona, Angelica and Medoro took ship for her
dominion of Cathay. I confess I looked at these shores with
a human interest, and could not help fancying that the keel of
our vessel was crossing a real line, over which knights and
lovers had passed. And so they have, both real and fabulous;
the former not less romantic, the latter scarcely less real; to
thousands, indeed, much more so; for who knows of hundreds
of real men and women that have crossed these waters, and
suffered actual passion on those shores and hills? And who
knows not Orlando and all the hard blows he gave, and the
harder blow than all given him by two happy lovers; and the
lovers themselves, the representatives of all the young love
that ever was. I had a grudge of my own against Angelica,
looking upon myself as jilted by those fine eyes which the
painter has given her in the English picture; for I took her
for a more sentimental person; but I excused her, seeing her
beset and tormented by all those knights, who thought they
earned a right to her by hacking and hewing; and I more
than pardoned her, when I found that Medoro, besides being
young and handsome, was a friend and a devoted follower.
But what of that? They were both young and handsome;

and love, at that time of life, goes upon no other merits, taking all the rest upon trust in the generosity of its wealth and as willing to bestow a throne as a ribbon, to show the all-sufficiency of its contentment. Fair speed your sails over the lucid waters, ye lovers, on a lover-like sea! Fair speed them, yet never land; for where the poet has left you, there ought ye, as ye are, to be living for ever—for ever gliding about a summer-sea, touching at its flowery islands, and reposing beneath its moon.

9th. Completely fair wind at south-west. Saw Montserrat. The sunshine, reflected on the water from the lee studding-sail, was like shot silk. At half-past seven in the evening, night was risen in the east, while the sun was setting opposite. "Black night has come up already," said our poetical captain. A fair breeze all night and all next day, took us on at the rate of about five miles an hour, very refreshing after the calms and foul winds. We passed the Gulf of Lyons still more pleasantly than we did the Bay of Biscay, for in the latter there was a calm. In both of these places a little rough handling is generally looked for.

13th. The ALPS! It was the first time I had seen mountains. They had a fine sulky look, up aloft in the sky,—cold, lofty, and distant. I used to think that mountains would impress me but little; that by the same process of imagination reversed, by which a brook can be fancied a mighty river, with forests instead of verdure on its banks, a mountain could be made a molehill, over which we step. But one look convinced me to the contrary. I found I could elevate better than I could pull down; and I was glad of it. It was not that the sight of the Alps was necessary to convince me of "the being of a God," as it is said to have done somebody, or to put me upon any reflections respecting infinity and first causes, of which I have had enough in my time; but I seemed to meet for the first time a grand poetical thought in a material shape,—to see a piece of one's book-wonders realized,—something very earthly, yet standing between earth and heaven, like a piece of the antediluvian world looking out of the coldness of ages. I remember reading in a Review a passage from some book of travels, which spoke of the author standing on the sea-shore, and being led by the silence and the abstraction, and the novel grandeur of the objects around him, to think of the earth, not in its geographical relations, but as a planet in connection with other planets, and rolling in the immensity of space. With these thoughts I have been familiar, as I suppose every one has been who knows what solitude is, and has an imagination, and perhaps not the best health. But we grow used to the mightiest aspects of thought, as we do to the immortal visages of the moon and stars: and therefore the first sight of the Alps, though much less things than any of these, and a toy, as I had fancied, for imagination to recreate itself with after their company, startles us like the disproof of a doubt, or the verification of an early dream,—a ghost, as it were, made visible by daylight, and giving us an enormous sense of its presence and materiality.

In the course of the day, we saw the table-land about Monaco. It brought to my mind the ludicrous distress of the petty prince of that place, when on his return from interchanging congratulations with his new masters and the legitimates, he suddenly met his old master, Napoleon, on his return from Elba. Or did he meet him when going to Elba? I forget which; but the distresses and confusion of the prince were at all events as certain as the superiority and amusement of the great man. In either case, this was the natural division of things, and the circumstances would have been the same. A large grampus went by, heaping the water into clouds of foam. Another time, we saw a shark with his fin above water. The Alps were now fully and closely seen, and a glorious sunset took place. There was the greatest grandeur and the loveliest beauty. Among others was a small string of clouds, like rubies with facets, a very dark tinge being put here and there, as if by a painter, to set off the rest. Red is certainly the colour of beauty, and ruby the most beautiful of reds. It was in no commonplace spirit that Marlowe, in his list of precious stones, called them "beauteous rubies," but with exquisite gusto:

> " Bags of fiery opals, sapphires, amethysts,
>   Jacinths, hard topaz, grass-green emeralds,
>   *Beauteous* rubies, sparkling diamonds," &c.

They come upon you, among the rest, like the women of gems. All these colours we had about us in our Mediterranean sunsets; and as if fortune would add to them by a freak of fancy, a little shoal of fish, sparkling as silver, leaped out of the water this afternoon, like a sprinkle of shillings. They were the anchovies, or Sardinias that we eat. They give a burlesque

title to the sovereign of these seas, whom the Tuscans call
" King of the Sardinias."*

We were now sailing up the angle of the Gulf of Genoa,
its shore looking as Italian as possible, with groves and white
villages. The names, too, were alluring,—Oneglia, Albenga,
Savona; the last, the birthplace of a sprightly poet (Frugoni),
whose works I was acquainted with. The breeze was the strongest we had had yet, and not quite fair, but we made good
head against it; the queen-like city of Genoa, crowned with
white palaces, sat at the end of the gulf, as if to receive us in
state; and at two o'clock, the waters being as blue as the sky,
and all hearts rejoicing, we entered our Italian harbour, and
heard Italian words.

Luckily for us, these first words were Tuscan. A pilot boat
came out. Somebody asked a question which we did not hear,
and the captain replied to it. "VA BENE," said the pilot, in a
fine open voice, and turned the head of the boat with a tranquil
dignity. "Va bene," thought I, indeed. "All goes well"
truly. The words are delicious, and the omen good. My family
have arrived so far in safety; we have but a little more voyage
to make, a few steps to measure back in this calm Mediterranean; the weather is glorious; Italy looks like what we expected; in a day or two we shall hear of our friends: health
and peace are before us, pleasure to others and profit to ourselves; and it is hard if we do not enjoy again, before long,
the society of all our friends, both abroad and at home. In a
day or two we received a letter from Shelley, saying that
winds and waves, he hoped, would never part us more.—
Alas! for that saying.

On the 28th of June, we set sail for Leghorn. The weather
was still as fine as possible, and our concluding trip as agreeable; with the exception of a storm of thunder and lightning
one night, which was the completest I ever saw. Our newspaper friend, "the oldest man living," ought to have been
there to see it. The lightning fell in all parts of the sea, like
pillars ; or like great melted fires, suddenly dropped from a
giant torch. Now it pierced the sea like rods; now fell like
enormous flakes or tongues, suddenly swallowed up. At one
time, it seemed to confine itself to a dark corner of the ocean,
making formidable shows of gigantic and flashing lances (for
it was the most perpendicular lightning I ever saw) : then it

* Not, however, I suppose, the King now reigning; who has given
despots other fish to fry.

dashed broadly at the whole sea, as if it would sweep us away in flame; and then came in random portions about the vessel, treading the waves hither and thither, like the legs of fiery spirits descending in wrath.

I now had a specimen (and confess I was not sorry to see it) of the fear which could enter even into the hearts of our "gallant *herroes*," when thrown into an unusual situation. The captain, almost the only man unmoved, or apparently so (and I really believe he was as fearless on all occasions, as his native valour, to say nothing of his brandy and water, could make him), was so exasperated with the alarm depicted in the faces of some of his crew, that he contemptuously knocked down the poor fellow at the helm [his brother, an apprentice seaman] and cried, "You are afraid, sir!" For our parts, having no fear of thunder and lightning, and not being fully aware perhaps of the danger to which vessels are exposed on these occasions, particularly if, like our Channel friend, they carry gunpowder (as most of them do, more or less), we were quite at our ease compared with our inexperienced friends about us, who had never witnessed anything of the like before, even in books. Besides, we thought it impossible for the Mediterranean to play us any serious trick,—that sunny and lucid basin, which we had beheld only in its contrast with a northern and a winter sea. Little did we think, that in so short a space of time, and somewhere about this very spot, a catastrophe would take place, that should put an end to all sweet thoughts, both of the Mediterranean and of the south.

CHAPTER XVIII.

RETURN TO FIRST ACQUAINTANCE WITH LORD BYRON AND THOMAS MOORE.

LORD BYRON was at Leghorn; the bad weather has disappeared; the vessel is about to enter port; and as everything concerning the noble lord is interesting, and the like may be said of his brother wit and poet, Thomas Moore, who introduced me to him, I will take this opportunity of doing what had better, perhaps, have been done when I first made his lordship's acquaintance; namely, state when it was that I first *saw* the one, and how I became acquainted with the other. My intimacy with Lord Byron is about to become closer; the results of it are connected both with him and his friend, and as these results are on the eve of commencing, my own interest in the subject is strengthened, and I call things to mind which I had suffered to escape me.

The first time I saw Lord Byron, he was rehearsing the part of Leander, under the auspices of Mr. Jackson, the prize-fighter. It was in the river Thames, before his first visit to Greece. There used to be a bathing-machine stationed on the eastern side of Westminster Bridge ; and I had been bathing, and was standing on this machine adjusting my clothes, when I noticed a respectable-looking manly person, who was eyeing something at a distance. This was Mr. Jackson waiting for his pupil. The latter was swimming with somebody for a wager. I forgot what his tutor said of him ; but he spoke in terms of praise. I saw nothing in Lord Byron at that time, but a young man who, like myself, had written a bad volume of poems ; and though I had a sympathy with him on this account, and more respect for his rank than I was willing to suppose, my sympathy was not an agreeable one ; so, contenting myself with seeing his lordship's head bob up and down in the water, like a buoy, I came away.

Lord Byron, when he afterwards came to see me in prison, was pleased to regret that I had not stayed. He told me, that the sight of my volume at Harrow had been one of his incentives to write verses, and that he had had the same passion for friendship which I had displayed in it. To my astonishment he quoted some of the lines, and would not hear me speak ill of them. His harbinger in the visit was Moore. Moore told me, that, besides liking my politics, his lordship liked the *Feast of the Poets*, and would be glad to make my acquaintance. I said I felt myself highly flattered, and should be proud to entertain his lordship as well as a poor patriot could. He was accordingly invited to dinner. His friend only stipulated that there should be "fish and vegetables for the noble bard ;" his lordship at that time being anti-carnivorous in his eating. He came, and we passed a very pleasant afternoon, talking of books, and school, and of their friend and brother poet the late Rev. Mr. Bowles, whose sonnets were among the early inspirations of Coleridge.

Lord Byron, as the reader has seen, subsequently called on me in the prison several times. He used to bring books for the *Story of Rimini*, which I was then writing. He would not let the footman bring them in. He would enter with a

couple of quartos under his arm; and give you to understand
that he was prouder of being a friend and a man of letters,
than a lord. It was thus that by flattering one's vanity he
persuaded us of his own freedom from it; for he could see
very well, that I had more value for lords than I supposed.

The noble poet was a warm politician, earnest in the cause
of liberty. His failure in the House of Lords is well known.
He was very candid about it; said he was much frightened,
and should never be able to do anything that way. Lords of
all parties came about him, and consoled him. He particularly mentioned Lord Sidmouth, as being unexpectedly kind.

It was very pleasant to see Lord Byron and Moore together. They harmonized admirably: though their knowledge
of one another began in talking of a duel, in consequence of
his lordship attacking the licence of certain early verses.
Moore's acquaintance with myself (as far as concerned correspondence by letter) originated in the mention of him in the
Feast of the Poets. He subsequently wrote an opera called the
Blue Stocking, respecting which he sent me a letter, at once
deprecating, and warranting, objection to it. I was then
editor of the *Examiner:* I did object to it, though with all
acknowledgment of his genius. He came to see me, saying
I was very much in the right; and an intercourse took place
which was never ostensibly interrupted till I thought myself
aggrieved by his opposition to the periodical work proposed
to me by his noble friend. I say "thought myself aggrieved,"
because I have long since acquitted him of any intention
towards me, more hostile than that of zeal in behalf of what
he supposed best for his lordship. He was desirous of pre-
venting his friend from coming before the Tory critics under
a new and irritating aspect, at a time when it might be
considered prudent to keep quiet, and propitiate objections
already existing. The only thing which remained for me to
complain of, was his not telling me so frankly; for this would
have been a confidence which I deserved; and it would either
have made me, of my own accord, object to the project at
once, without the least hesitation, or, at all events, have been
met by me with such a hearty sense of the objector's plain
dealing, and in so friendly a spirit of difference, that no ill-
will, I think, could have remained on either side. Moore, at
least, was of too generous a spirit for it; and I was of too
grateful a one.

Unfortunately, this plan was not adopted by his lordship's

friends; and hence a series of bitter feelings on both sides, which, as I was the first to express them, so I did not hesitate to be the first to regret publicly, when on both sides they had tacitly been done away.

Moore fancied, among other things, that I meant to pain him by speaking of his small stature; and perhaps it was wrong to hazard a remark on so delicate a subject, however inoffensively meant; especially as it led to other personal characteristics, which might have seemed of less doubtful intention. But I felt only a painter's pleasure in taking the portrait; and I flattered myself that, as far as externals went, I abundantly evinced my good-will, not only by doing justice to all that was handsome and poetical in his aspect, and by noticing the beauty reported of his childhood, but by the things which I said of the greatness observable in so many little men in history, especially as recorded by Clarendon. In fact, this had been such a favourite subject with me, that some journalists concluded I must be short myself; which is not the case. Men of great action, I suspect, including the most heroical soldiers, have been for the most part of short stature, from the fabulous Tydeus, to Alexander and Agesilaus, and so downwards to Wellington and Napoleon. Nor have sages and poets, or any kind of genius, been wanting to the list; from the ancient philosopher who was obliged to carry lead in his pockets lest he should be blown away, down to Michael Angelo, and Montaigne, and Barrow, and Spenser himself, and the Falklands and Haleses of Clarendon, and Pope, and Steele, and Reynolds, and Mozart.

Moore's forehead was bony and full of character, with " bumps " of wit, large and radiant enough to transport a phrenologist; Sterne had such another. His eyes were as dark and fine as you would wish to see under a set of vine-leaves; his mouth generous and good-humoured, with dimples; and his manner as bright as his talk, full of the wish to please and be pleased. He sang, and played with great taste on the pianoforte, as might be supposed from his musical compositions. His voice, which was a little hoarse in speaking (at least I used to think so), softened into a breath, like that of the flute, when singing. In speaking, he was emphatic in rolling the letter r, perhaps out of a despair of being able to get rid of the national peculiarity. The structure of his versification, when I knew him, was more artificial than it was afterwards; and in his serious compositions it suited him better. He had hardly faith enough in the sentiments of which he treated to give way to his impulses in writing, except when they were festive and witty; and artificial thoughts demand a similar embodiment. Both patriotism and personal experience, however, occasionally inspired him with lyric pathos; and in his naturally musical perception of the right principles of versification, he contemplated the fine, easy-playing, muscular style of Dryden, with a sort of perilous pleasure. I remember his quoting with delight a couplet of Dryden's, which came with a particular grace from his lips:—

"Let honour and preferment go for gold;
But glorious beauty isn't to be sold."

Beside the pleasure I took in Moore's society as a man of wit, I had a great esteem for him as a man of candour and independence. His letters were full of all that was pleasant in him. As I was a critic at that time, and in the habit of giving my opinion of his works in the *Examiner*, he would write me his *opinion* of the *opinion*, with a mixture of good humour, admission, and deprecation, so truly delightful, and a sincerity of criticism on my own writings so extraordinary for so courteous a man, though with abundance of balm and eulogy, that never any subtlety of compliment could surpass it; and with all my self-confidence I never ceased to think that the honour was on my side, and that I could only deserve such candour of intercourse by being as ingenuous as himself. This admiring regard for him he completed by his behaviour to an old patron of his, who, not thinking it politic to retain him openly by his side, proposed to facilitate his acceptance of a place under the Tories; an accommodation which Moore rejected as an indignity. I thought, afterwards, that a man of such a spirit should not have condescended to attack Rousseau and poor foolish Madame de Warens, out of a desire to right himself with polite life, and with the memory of some thoughtless productions of his own. Polite life was only too happy to possess him in his graver days; and the thoughtless productions, however to be regretted on reflection, were reconcileable to reflection itself on the same grounds on which Nature herself and all her exuberance is to be reconciled. At least, without presuming to judge nature in the abstract, an ultra-sensitive and enjoying poet is himself a production of nature; and we may rest assured, that she will no more judge him with harshness ultimately, than she will condemn the excess of her own vines and fig-trees.

CHAPTER XIX.

LORD BYRON IN ITALY—SHELLEY—PISA.

As I am now about to re-enter into the history of my connection with Lord Byron, I will state in what spirit I mean to do it.

It is related of an Italian poet (Alamanni), that having in his younger days bitterly satirized the house of Austria, he found himself awkwardly situated in more advanced life, when, being in exile, and employed by Francis the First, the king sent him on an embassy to the court of Charles the Fifth. One of his sarcasms, in particular, had been very offensive. Alluding to the Austrian crest, the two-headed eagle, he had described the imperial house as a monstrous creature,

> Which bore two beaks, the better to devour.
> (" Che per più divorar, due becchi porta.")

Charles had treasured this passage in his mind; and when the ambassador, perhaps forgetting it altogether, or trusting to its being forgotten, had terminated a fine oration, full of compliments to the power which he had so angrily painted, the Emperor, without making any other observation, calmly said—

> " Which bore two beaks, the better to devour."

" Sir," said Alamanni, not hesitating, or betraying any confusion (which shows that he was either prepared for the rebuke, or was a man of great presence of mind), " when I wrote that passage I spoke as a poet, to whom it is permitted to use fictions; but now I speak as an ambassador, who is bound to utter truth. I spoke then as a young man; but I now speak as a man advanced in years. I spoke as one who was agitated by grief and passion at the wretched condition of my country; but now I am calm, and free from passion." Charles rose from his seat, and laying his hand on the shoulder of the ambassador, said, in the kindest manner, that the loss of his country ought not to grieve him, since he had found such a patron in Francis; and that to an honest man every place was his country.

I would apply this anecdote to some things which I have formerly said of Lord Byron. I do not mean that I ever wrote any fictions about him. I wrote nothing which I did not feel to be true, or think so. But I can say with Alamanni, that I was then a young man, and that I am now advanced in years. I can say, that I was agitated by grief and anger, and that I am now free from anger. I can say, that I was far more alive to other people's defects than to my own, and that I am now sufficiently sensible of my own to show to others the charity which I need myself. I can say, moreover, that apart from a little allowance for provocation, I do not think it right to exhibit what is amiss, or may be thought amiss, in the character of a fellow-creature, out of any feeling but unmistakeable sorrow, or the wish to lessen evils which society itself may have caused.

Lord Byron, with respect to the points on which he erred and suffered (for on all others, a man like himself, poet and wit, could not but give and receive pleasure), was the victim of a bad bringing up, of a series of false positions in society, of evils arising from the mistakes of society itself, of a personal disadvantage (which his feelings exaggerated), nay, of his very advantages of person, and of a face so handsome as to render him an object of admiration. Even the lameness, of which he had such a resentment, only softened the admiration with tenderness.

But he did not begin life under good influences. He had a mother, herself, in all probability, the victim of bad training, who would fling the dishes from table at his head, and tell him he would be a scoundrel like his father. His father, who was cousin to the previous lord, had been what is called a man upon town, and was neither rich nor very respectable. The young lord, whose means had not yet recovered themselves, went to school, noble but poor, expecting to be in the ascendant with his title, yet kept down by the inconsistency of his condition. He left school to put on the cap with the gold tuft, which is worshipped at college:—he left college to fall into some of the worst hands on the town:—his first productions were contemptuously criticized, and his genius was thus provoked into satire:—his next were over-praised, which increased his self-love:—he married when his temper had been soured by difficulties, and his will and pleasure pampered by the sex:—and he went companionless into a foreign country, where all this perplexity could repose without being taught better, and where the sense of a lost popularity could be drowned in licence.

Should we not wonder that he retained so much of the grand and beautiful in his writings?—that the indestructible tendency of the poetical to the good should have struggled to so much purpose through faults and inconsistencies?—

rather than quarrel with his would-be misanthropy and his effeminate wailings? The worst things which he did were to gird resentfully at women, and to condescend to some other pettiness of conduct which he persuaded himself were self-defences on his own part, and merited by his fellow-creatures. But he was never incapable of generosity : he was susceptible of the tenderest emotions; and though I doubt, from a certain proud and stormy look about the upper part of his face, whether his command of temper could ever have been quite relied on, yet I cannot help thinking, that had he been properly brought up, there would have been nobody capable of more lasting and loving attachments. The lower part of the face was a model of beauty.

I am sorry I ever wrote a syllable respecting Lord Byron which might have been spared. I have still to relate my connection with him, but it will be related in a different manner. Pride, it is said, will have a fall: and I must own, that on this subject I have experienced the truth of the saying. I had prided myself—I should pride myself now if I had not been thus rebuked—on not being one of those who talk against others. I went counter to this feeling in a book; and to crown the absurdity of the contradiction, I was foolish enough to suppose that the very fact of my so doing would show that I had done it in no other instance! that having been thus public in the error, credit would be given me for never having been privately so! Such are the delusions inflicted on us by self-love. When the consequence was represented to me as characterized by my enemies, I felt, enemies though they were, as if I blushed from head to foot. It is true I had been goaded to the task by misrepresentations:—I had resisted every other species of temptation to do it:—and, after all, I said more in his excuse, and less to his disadvantage, than many of those who reproved me. But enough. I owed the acknowledgment to him and to myself; and I shall proceed on my course with a sigh for both, and I trust in the good-will of the sincere.

To return, then, to my arrival at Leghorn.

In the harbour of Leghorn I found Mr. Trelawny, of the old Cornish family of that name, since known as the author of the *Younger Brother*. He was standing with his knight-errant aspect, dark, handsome, and mustachioed, in Lord Byron's boat, the *Bolivar*, of which he had taken charge for his lordship. In a day or two I went to see my noble ac-

quaintance, who was in what the Italians call villeggiatura at
Monte Nero; that is to say, enjoying a country house for the
season. I there became witness to a singular adventure,
which seemed to make me free of Italy and stilettos before
I had well set foot in the country.

The day was very hot; the road to Monte Nero was very
hot, through dusty suburbs; and when I got there, I found
the hottest looking house I ever saw. It was salmon colour.
Think of this, flaring over the country in a hot Italian sun!

But the greatest of all the heats was within. Upon seeing
Lord Byron, I hardly knew him, he was grown so fat; and he
was longer in recognising me, I had grown so thin. He took
me into an inner room, and introduced me to Madame Guiccioli, then very young as well as handsome, who was in a state
of great agitation. Her face was flushed, her eyes lit up, and
her hair (which she wore hanging loose), streaming as if in
disorder. The Conte Pietro, her brother, came in presently,
also in a state of agitation, and having his arm in a sling. I
then learned that a quarrel having taken place among the
servants, the young Count had interfered, and been stabbed.
He was very angry; Madame Guiccioli was more so, and could
not admit the charitable comments of Lord Byron, who was
for making light of the matter. They seemed to think the
honour of their nation at stake. Indeed, there was a look in
the business not a little formidable; for though the stab was
not much, the inflictor of it threatened more, and was at that
minute keeping watch outside, with the avowed intention of
assaulting the first person that issued forth. I looked out of
the window, and met his eye glaring upwards like a tiger. He
had a red cap on like a sansculotte, and a most sinister aspect,
dreary and meagre—that of a proper caitiff.

How long things had continued in this state I cannot say;
but the hour was come when Lord Byron and his friend took
their evening drive, and the thing was to be put an end to
somehow. A servant had been despatched for the police, and
was not returned.

At length we set out, the lady earnestly entreating his lordship to keep back, and all of us uniting to keep in advance of
Conte Pietro, who was exasperated.

It was a curious moment for a stranger from England. I
fancied myself pitched into one of the scenes in the *Mysteries
of Udolpho*. Everything was new, foreign, and vehement.
There was the lady, flushed and dishevelled, exclaiming against

the " scelerato ;" the young Count, wounded and threatening;
and the assassin waiting for us with his knife. Nobody, however, could have put a better face on the matter than Lord
Byron did,—composed, and endeavouring to compose: and as
to myself, I was so occupied with the whole scene, that I had
not time to be frightened. Forth we issue at the house door,
all squeezing to have the honour of being first, when a termination is put to the tragedy by the man's throwing himself on
a bench, extending his arms, and bursting into tears. His cap
was half over his eyes ; his face gaunt, ugly, and unshaved ;
his appearance altogether more squalid and miserable than
an Englishman would conceive it possible to find in such an
establishment. This blessed figure reclined weeping and wailing, and asking pardon for his offence ; and to crown all, he
requested Lord Byron to kiss him.

The noble lord conceived such an excess of charity superfluous. He pardoned him, but said he must not think of
remaining in his service ; upon which the man renewed his
weeping and wailing, and continued kissing his hand. I
was then struck with the footing on which the gentry and
their servants stand with each other in Italy, and the good-
nature with which the strongest exhibitions of anger can be
followed up. Conte Pietro, who was full of good qualities (for
though he was here with his sister's lover, we must not judge
of Italian customs by English), accepted the man's hand, and
even shook it heartily ; and Madame Guiccioli, though unable
to subside so quickly from her state of indignant exaltation,
looked in relenting sort, and speedily accorded him her grace
also, seeing my lord had forgiven him. The man was all
penitence and wailing, but he was obliged to quit. The police
would have forced him, if he had not been dismissed. He left
the country, and called in his way on Shelley, who was shocked
at his appearance, and gave him some money out of his very
antipathy ; for he thought nobody would help such an ill-look-
ing fellow, if he did not.

The unpleasant part of the business did not end here. It
was, remotely, one of the causes of Lord Byron's leaving Italy;
for it increased the awkwardness of his position with the
Tuscan government, and gave a further unsteadiness to his
proceedings. His friends, the Gambas, were already only
upon sufferance in Tuscany. They had been obliged to quit
their native country Romagna, on account of their connection
with the Carbonari ; and Lord Byron, who had identified him-

self with their fortunes, became a party to their wanderings, and to the footing on which they stood wherever they were permitted to abide. The Grand Duke's government had given him to understand that they were at liberty to reside in Tuscany, provided they were discreet. A *fracas* which happened in the streets of Pisa, a little before I came, had given a shock to the tranquillity of this good understanding; the retinue of the Gambas having been the foremost persons concerned in it : and now, another of their men having caused a disturbance, the dilemma was completed. Lord Byron's residence in Tuscany was made uneasy to him. It was desired that he should separate himself from the Gambas : and though it was understood that a little courtesy on his part towards the Grand Duke and Duchess, the latter of whom was said to be particularly desirous of seeing him at court, would have produced a *carte-blanche* for all parties, yet he chose to take neither of those steps; he therefore returned to his house at Pisa, only to reside there two or three months longer ; after which he quitted the grand-ducal territory, and departed for Genoa.

From Monte Nero I returned to Leghorn ; and, taking leave of our vessel, we put up at an hotel. Mr. Shelley then came to us from his *villeggiatura* at Lerici. His town abode, as well as Lord Byron's, was at Pisa. I will not dwell upon the moment.

Leghorn is a polite Wapping, with a square and a theatre. The country around is uninteresting when you become acquainted with it; but to a stranger the realization of anything he has read about is a delight, especially of such things as vines hanging from trees, and the sight of Apennines. It is pleasant, too, to a lover of books, when at Leghorn, to think that Smollett once lived there ; not, indeed, happily, for he was very ill, and besides living there, died there. But genius gives so much pleasure (and must also have received so much in the course of its life) that the memory of its troubles is overcome by its renown. Smollett once lived, as Lord Byron did, at Monte Nero ; and he was buried in the Leghorn cemetery.

Mr. Shelley accompanied us from Leghorn to Pisa, in order to see us fixed in our new abode. Lord Byron left Monte Nero at the same time, and joined us. We occupied the ground-floor of his lordship's house, the Casa Lanfranchi, on the river Arno, which runs through the city. Divided tenancies of this kind are common in Italy, where few houses are in possession of one family. The families in this instance, as in others, remained distinct. The ladies at the respective heads of them never exchanged even a word. It was set to the account of their want of acquaintance with their respective languages; and the arrangement, I believe, which in every respect thus tacitly took place, was really, for many reasonable considerations, objected to by nobody.

The Casa Lanfranchi, which had been the mansion of the great Pisan family whose ancestors figure in Dante, is said to have been built by Michael Angelo, and is worthy of him. It is in a bold and broad style throughout, with those harmonious graces of proportion which are sure to be found in an Italian mansion. The outside is of rough marble.

We had not been in the house above an hour or two, when my friend brought the celebrated surgeon, Vaccà, to see Mrs. Hunt. He had a pleasing, intelligent face, and was the most gentlemanlike Italian I ever saw. Vaccà pronounced his patient to be in a decline; and little hope was given us by others that she would survive beyond the year. She lived till the year 1857, and Vaccà had been dead many years before. I do not say this to his disparagement, for he was very skilful, and deserved his celebrity. But it appears to me, from more than one remarkable instance, that there is a superstition about what are called declines and consumptions, from which the most eminent of the profession are not free. I suspect, indeed I may say I know, that many people of this tendency, or at least supposed to be of it, may reach, with a proper mode of living, to as good a period of existence as most others. The great secret in this as in all other cases, and, indeed, in almost all moral as well as physical cases of ill, seems to be in diet and regimen. If some demi-god could regulate for mankind what they should eat and drink, and by what bodily treatment circulate their blood, he would put an end to half the trouble which the world undergo, some of the most romantic sorrows with which they flatter themselves not excepted. The case, however, in the present instance was perhaps peculiar, and may not before have been witnessed by Vaccà. The expectoration, at all events, of blood itself, and this too sometimes in alarming quantities, and never entirely without recurrence, lasted throughout a life of no ordinary duration.

The next day, while in the drawing-room with Lord Byron, I had a curious specimen of Italian manners. It was like a scene in an opera. One of his servants, a young man, suddenly came in smiling, and was followed by his sister, a handsome brunette, in a bodice and sleeves, and her hair uncovered. She advanced to his lordship to welcome him back to Pisa, and present him with a basket of flowers. In doing this, she took his hand and kissed it; then turned to the stranger, and kissed his hand also. I thought we ought to have struck up a quartett.

It is the custom of Italy, as it used to be in England, for inferiors to kiss your hand in coming and going. There is an air of good-will in it that is very agreeable, though the implied sense of inferiority is hardly so pleasant. Servants have a custom also of wishing you a " happy evening" (*felice sera*) when they bring in lights. To this you may respond in like manner; after which it seems impossible for the sun to "go down on the wrath," if there is any, of either party.

In a day or two Shelley took leave of us to return to Lerici for the rest of the season, meaning, however, to see us more than once in the interval. I spent one delightful afternoon with him, wandering about Pisa, and visiting the cathedral. On the night of the same day he took a postchaise for Leghorn, intending next morning to depart with his friend Captain Williams for Lerici. I entreated him, if the weather were violent, not to give way to his daring spirit and venture to sea. He promised me he would not; and it seems that he did set off later than he otherwise would have done, apparently at a more favourable moment.* I never beheld him more.

The same night there was a tremendous storm of thunder and lightning, which made us very anxious; but we hoped our friend had arrived before then. When, some days later, Trelawny came to Pisa, and told us he was missing, I underwent one of the sensations which we read of in books, but seldom experience: I was tongue-tied with horror.

A dreadful interval took place of more than a week, during which, every inquiry and every fond hope were exhausted. At the end of that period our worst fears were confirmed. A body had been washed on shore, near the town of Via Reggio, which, by the dress and stature, was known to be our friend's. Keats's last volume also (the *Lamia*, &c.), was found open in

* [This is a mistake. Shelley set off *earlier* than he intended, his departure being hastened by a desponding note which he received from his wife.]

the jacket pocket. He had probably been reading it when surprised by the storm. It was my copy. I had told him to keep it till he gave it me with his own hands. So I would not have it from any other. It was burnt with his remains. The body of his friend Mr. Williams was found near a tower, four miles distant from its companion. That of the third party in the boat, Charles Vivian, the seaman, was not discovered till nearly three weeks afterwards.*

The remains of Shelley and Mr. Williams were burnt after the good ancient fashion, and gathered into coffers [those of Williams on the 15th of August, of Shelley on the 16th]. Those of Mr. Williams were subsequently taken to England. Shelley's were interred at Rome, in the Protestant burial-ground, the place which he had so touchingly described in recording its reception of Keats. The ceremony of the burning was alike beautiful and distressing. Trelawny, who had been the chief person concerned in ascertaining the fate of his friends, completed his kindness by taking the most active part on this last mournful occasion. He and his friend Captain Shenley were first upon the ground, attended by proper assistants. Lord Byron and myself arrived shortly afterwards. His lordship got out of his carriage, but wandered away from the spectacle, and did not see it. I remained inside the carriage, now looking on, now drawing back with feelings that were not to be witnessed.

None of the mourners, however, refused themselves the little comfort of supposing, that lovers of books and antiquity, like Shelley and his companion, Shelley in particular with his Greek enthusiasm, would not have been sorry to foresee this part of their fate. The mortal part of him, too, was saved from corruption; not the least extraordinary part of his history. Among the materials for burning, as many of the gracefuller and more classical articles as could be procured—frankin-

---

* [A story was current in Leghorn which conjecturally helped to explain the shipwreck of Shelley's boat. It went out to sea in rough weather, and *yet* was followed by a native boat. When Shelley's yacht was raised, a large hole was found stove in the stern. Shelley had on board a sum of money in dollars; and the supposition is, that the men in the other boat had tried to board Shelley's piratically, but had desisted because the collision caused the English boat to sink; and they abandoned it because the men saved would have become their accusers. The only facts in support of this conjectural story are the alleged following of the native boat, and the damage to the stern of Shelley's boat, otherwise not very accountable.]

cense, wine, &c.—were not forgotten; and to these Keats's
volume was added. The beauty of the flame arising from the
funeral pile was extraordinary. The weather was beautifully
fine. The Mediterranean, now soft and lucid, kissed the
shore as if to make peace with it. The yellow sand and blue
sky were intensely contrasted with one another: marble
mountains touched the air with coolness; and the flame of
the fire bore away towards heaven in vigorous amplitude,
waving and quivering with a brightness of inconceivable
beauty. It seemed as though it contained the glassy essence
of vitality. You might have expected a seraphic countenance
to look out of it, turning once more before it departed, to
thank the friends that had done their duty.

Yet, see how extremes can appear to meet even on occasions
the most overwhelming; nay, even by reason of them; for as
cold can perform the effect of fire, and burn us, so can despair
put on the monstrous aspect of mirth. On returning from
one of our visits to this sea-shore, we dined and drank; I
mean, Lord Byron and myself;—dined little, and drank too
much. Lord Byron had not shone that day, even in his cups,
which usually brought out his best qualities. As to myself, I
had bordered upon emotions which I have never suffered myself to indulge, and which, foolishly as well as impatiently,
render calamity, as somebody termed it, "an affront, and not
a misfortune." The barouche drove rapidly through the
forest of Pisa. We sang, we laughed, we shouted. I even
felt a gaiety the more shocking, because it was real and a
relief. What the coachman thought of us, God knows; but
he helped to make up a ghastly trio. He was a good-
tempered fellow, and an affectionate husband and father; yet
he had the reputation of having offered his master to kill a
man. I wish to have no such waking dream again. It was
worthy of a German ballad.

Shelley, when he died, was in his thirtieth year. His
figure was tall and slight, and his constitution consumptive.
He was subject to violent spasmodic pains, which would
sometimes force him to lie on the ground till they were over;
but he had always a kind word to give to those about him,
when his pangs allowed him to speak. In this organization,
as well as in some other respects, he resembled the German
poet, Schiller. Though well-turned, his shoulders were bent
a little, owing to premature thought and trouble. The same
causes had touched his hair with gray; and though his habits

of temperance and exercise gave him a remarkable degree of strength, it is not supposed that he could have lived many years. He used to say that he had lived three times as long as the calendar gave out; which he would prove, between jest and earnest, by some remarks on Time,

> " That would have puzzled that stout Stagyrite."

Like the Stagyrite's, his voice was high and weak. His eyes were large and animated, with a dash of wildness in them; his face small, but well shaped, particularly the mouth and chin, the turn of which was very sensitive and graceful. His complexion was naturally fair and delicate, with a colour in the cheeks. He had brown hair, which, though tinged with gray, surmounted his face well, being in considerable quantity, and tending to a curl. His side-face, upon the whole, was deficient in strength, and his features would not have told well in a bust; but when fronting and looking at you attentively his aspect had a certain seraphical character that would have suited a portrait of John the Baptist, or the angel whom Milton describes as holding a reed "tipt with fire." Nor would the most religious mind, had it known him, have objected to the comparison; for, with all his scepticism, Shelley's disposition was truly said to have been anything but irreligious. A person of much eminence for piety in our times has well observed, that the greatest want of religious feeling is not to be among the greatest infidels, but among those who never think of religion except as a matter of course. The leading feature of Shelley's character may be said to have been a natural piety. He was pious towards nature, towards his friends, towards the whole human race, towards the meanest insect of the forest. He did himself an injustice with the public in using the popular name of the Supreme Being inconsiderately. He identified it solely with the most vulgar and tyrannical notions of a God made after the worst human fashion; and did not sufficiently reflect that it was often used by a juster devotion to express a sense of the great Mover of the universe. An impatience in contradicting worldly and pernicious notions of a supernatural power led his own aspirations to be misconstrued; for though, in the severity of his dialectics, and particularly in moments of despondency, he sometimes appeared to be hopeless of what he most desired—and though he justly thought that a Divine Being would prefer the increase of benevolence and good before any praise, or even recognition of himself (a reflection worth thinking of by the intolerant), yet there was in reality no belief to which he clung with more fondness than that of some great pervading " Spirit of Intellectual Beauty;" as may be seen in his aspirations on that subject. He assented warmly to an opinion which I expressed in the cathedral at Pisa, while the organ was playing, that a truly divine religion might yet be established, if charity were really made the principle of it, instead of faith.

Music affected him deeply. He had also a delicate perception of the beauties of sculpture. It is not one of the least evidences of his conscientious turn of mind that, with the inclination and the power to surround himself in Italy with all the graces of life, he made no sort of attempt that way; finding other uses for his money, and not always satisfied with himself for indulging even in the luxury of a boat. When he bought elegancies of any kind it was to give them away. Boating was his great amusement. He loved the mixture of action and repose which he found in it; and delighted to fancy himself gliding away to Utopian isles and bowers of enchantment. But he would give up any pleasure to do a deed of kindness. Indeed, he may be said to have made the whole comfort of his life a sacrifice to what he thought the wants of society.

Temperament and early circumstances conspired to make him a reformer, at a time of life when few begin to think for themselves; and it was his misfortune, as far as immediate reputation was concerned, that he was thrown upon society with a precipitancy and vehemence which rather startled others with fear for themselves, than allowed them to become sensible of the love and zeal that impelled him. He was like a spirit that had darted out of its orb, and found itself in another world. I used to tell him that he had come from the planet Mercury. When I heard of the catastrophe that overtook him it seemed as if this spirit, not sufficiently constituted like the rest of the world to obtain their sympathy, yet gifted with a double portion of love for all living things, had been found dead in a solitary corner of the earth, its wings stiffened, its warm heart cold; the relics of a misunderstood nature, slain by the ungenial elements.

We remained but three months at Pisa subsequently to this calamitous event. We then went to Genoa, where we received the first number of the periodical work, the *Liberal*, which Lord Byron had invited me to set up, and in which Shelley was to have assisted. He did assist; for his beautiful translation of the *May Day Night*, from Goethe, appeared in the first number.

But more of this publication when I come to Genoa. I will first say a few words respecting the way in which we passed our time at Pisa, and then speak of the city itself and its highly interesting features, which are not so well known as they should be.

Our manner of life was this. Lord Byron, who used to sit up at night writing *Don Juan* (which he did under the influence of gin and water), rose late in the morning. He breakfasted; read; lounged about, singing an air, generally out of Rossini; then took a bath, and was dressed; and coming down stairs, was heard, still singing, in the court-yard, out of which the garden ascended, by a few steps, at the back of the house. The servants, at the same time, brought out two or three chairs. My study, a little room in a corner, with an orange-tree at the window, looked upon this court-yard. I was generally at my writing when he came down, and either acknowledged his presence by getting up and saying something from the window, or he called out "Leontius!" (a name into which Shelley had pleasantly converted that of "Leigh Hunt") and came up to the window with some jest or other challenge to conversation. His dress, as at Monte Nero, was a nankin jacket, with white waistcoat and trousers, and a cap, either velvet or linen, with a shade to it. In his hand was a tobacco-box, from which he helped himself occasionally to what he thought a preservative from getting too fat. Perhaps, also, he supposed it good for the teeth. We then lounged about, or sat and talked, Madame Guiccioli, with her sleek tresses, descending after her toilet to join us. The garden was small and square, but plentifully stocked with oranges and other shrubs; and, being well watered, it looked very green and refreshing under the Italian sky. The lady generally attracted us up into it, if we had not been there before. Her appearance might have reminded an English spectator of Chaucer's heroine—

> " Yclothed was she, fresh for to devise.
> Her yellow hair was braided in a tress
> Behind her back, a yardè long, I guess:
> And in the garden (as the sun uprist)
> She walketh up and down, where as her list :"

and then, as Dryden has it:—

"At every turn she made a little stand,
    And thrust among the thorns her lily hand."

Madame Guiccioli, who was at that time about twenty, was handsome and lady-like, with an agreeable manner, and a voice not partaking of the Italian fervour too much to be gentle. She had just enough of it to give her speaking a grace. None of her graces appeared entirely free from art; nor, on the other hand, did they betray enough of it to give you an ill opinion of her sincerity and good humour. I was told that her Romagnese dialect was observable; but to me, at that time, all Italian in a lady's mouth was Tuscan pearl; and she trolled it over her lip, pure or not, with that sort of conscious grace which seems to belong to the Italian language as a matter of right. I amused her with speaking bad Italian out of Ariosto, and saying *speme* for *speranza;* in which she good-naturedly found something pleasant and *pellegrino;* keeping all the while that considerate countenance for which a foreigner has so much to be grateful. Her hair was what the poet has described, or rather *blond*, with an inclination to yellow; a very fair and delicate yellow, at all events, and within the limits of the poetical. She had regular features, of the order properly called handsome, in distinction to prettiness or to piquancy; being well proportioned to one another, large rather than otherwise, but without coarseness, and more harmonious than interesting. Her nose was the handsomest of the kind I ever saw; and I have known her both smile very sweetly, and look intelligently, when Lord Byron has said something kind to her.

In the evening we sometimes rode or drove out, generally into the country. The city I first walked through in company with Shelley, but speedily, alas! explored it by myself, or with my children. The state of my wife's health would not suffer her to quit her apartment.

Let the reader imagine a small white city, with a tower leaning at one end of it, trees on either side, and blue mountains for the background; and he may fancy he sees Pisa, as the traveller sees it in coming from Leghorn. Add to this, in summer-time, fields of corn on all sides, bordered with hedgerow trees, and the festoons of vines, of which he has so often read, hanging from tree to tree; and he may judge of the impression made upon an admirer of Italy, who is in Tuscany for the first time.

In entering the city, the impression is not injured. What looked white in the distance, remains as pure and fair on closer acquaintance. You cross a bridge, and cast your eye up the whole extent of the city one way, the river Arno (the river of Dante, Petrarch, and Boccaccio) winding through the middle of it under two more bridges; and fair, elegant houses of good size bordering the white pavement on either side. This is the Lung'Arno, or street "Along the Arno." The mountains, in which you fancy you see the marble veins (for it is from these that the marble of Carrara comes), tower away beautifully at the further end, and, owing to the clear atmosphere, seem to be much nearer than they are. The Arno, which is about as wide perhaps as the Isis at Oxford, is sandy-coloured, and in the summer-time shrunken ; but still it is the river of the great Tuscan writers, the visible possessor of the name we have all heard a thousand times ; and we feel what a true thing is that which is called ideal.

The first novelty that strikes you, after your dreams and matter-of-fact have recovered from the surprise of their introduction to one another, is the singular fairness and new look of houses that have been standing hundreds of years. This is owing to the dryness of the Italian atmosphere. Antiquity refuses to look ancient in Italy. It insists upon retaining its youthfulness of aspect. The consequence at first is a mixed feeling of admiration and disappointment; for we miss the venerable. The houses seem as if they ought to have sympathized more with humanity, and were as cold and as hard-hearted as their materials. But you discover that Italy is the land, not of the venerable, but the beautiful; and cease to look for old age in the chosen country of the Apollo and the Venus. The only real antiquities are those in Dante and the oldest painters, who treat of the Bible in an ancient style. Among the mansions on the Lung'Arno is one entirely fronted with marble, and marble so pure and smooth that you can see your face in it. It is in a most graceful style of architecture; and over the door has a mysterious motto and symbol. The symbol is an actual fetter, attached with great nicety to the middle stone over the doorway: the motto, *Alla Giornata* (By the Day, or the Day's Work). The allusion is supposed to be to some captivity undergone by one of the Lanfreducci family, the proprietors : but nobody knows. Further up on the same side of the way, is the old ducal palace, said to be the scene of the

murder of Don Garcia by his father, which is the subject
of one of Alfieri's tragedies: and between both, a little before you come to the old palace, is the mansion before mentioned, in which he resided, and which still belongs to the
family of the Lanfranchi, formerly one of the most powerful
in Pisa. They were among the nobles who conspired against
the ascendancy of Count Ugolino, and who were said, but not
truly, to have wreaked that revenge on him and his children,
recorded without a due knowledge of the circumstances by
Dante. The tower in which Ugolino perished was subsequently called the Tower of Famine. Chaucer, who is supposed to have been in Italy, says that it stood "a littel out"
of Pisa; Villani says, in the Piazza of the Anziani. It is understood to be no longer in existence, and even its site is disputed.

It is curious to feel oneself sitting quietly in one of the old
Italian houses, and to think of all the passions that have
agitated the hearts of so many generations of its tenants; all
the revels and the quarrels that have echoed along its wall;
all the guitars that have tinkled under its windows: all the
scuffles that have disputed its doors. Along the great halls,
how many feet have hurried in alarm! how many stately
beauties have drawn their trains! how many torches have
ushered magnificence up the staircases! how much blood
perhaps been shed! The ground-floors of all the great
houses in Pisa, as in other Italian cities, have iron bars at
the windows. They were for security in time of trouble.
The look is at first very gloomy and prison-like, but you get
used to it. The bars are round, and painted white, and the
interstices are large; and if the windows look towards a garden, and are bordered with shrubs and ivy, as those at the
back were in the Casa Lanfranchi, the imagination makes a
compromise with their prison-like appearance, and persuades
itself they are but comforts in times of war, and trellises
during a peace establishment. All the floors are made for
separate families, it having been the custom in Italy from
time immemorial for fathers and mothers, sons and daughters-
in-law, or *vice versa*, with as many other relations as might
be "agreeable," to live under the same roof. Spaciousness and
utility were the great objects with the builder; and a stranger
is sometimes surprised with the look of the finest houses
outside, particularly the arrangement of the ground-floor.
The stables used often to be there, and their place is now as
often occupied by shops. In the inside of the great private

houses there is always a certain majestic amplitude; but the entrances of the rooms, and the staircase on the ground floor, are often placed irregularly, so as to sacrifice everything to convenience. In the details there is sure to be a noble eye to proportion. You cannot look at the elevation of the commonest doorway, or the ceiling of a room appropriated to the humblest purposes, but you recognise the land of the fine arts. You think Michael Angelo has been at the turning of those arches—at the harmonizing of those beautiful varieties of shade, which, by the secret principles common to all arts and sciences, affect the mind like a sort of inaudible music. The very plasterer who is hired to give the bare walls of some old disused apartment an appearance of ornament, paints his door-ways, his pilasters, and his borders of leaves, in a bold style of relief and illusion, which would astonish the doubtful hand of many an English student " in the higher walks of art." It must be observed, however, that this is a piece of good taste which seems to have survived most others, and to have been kept up by the objects on which it works; for the arts are at present lying fallow in Italy, waiting for better times.

I was so taken up, on my arrival at Pisa, with friends and their better novelties, that I forgot even to look about me for the Leaning Tower. You lose sight of it on entering the town, unless you come in at the Lucca gate. On the Sunday following, however, I went to see it, and the spot where it stands, in illustrious company. Forsyth, a late traveller of much shrewdness and pith (though a want of ear, and an affectation of ultra good sense, rendered him in some respects extremely unfit for a critic on Italy—as when he puts music and perfumery on a level!), had been beforehand with me in putting this idea in my head. " Pisa," says he, " while the capital of a republic, was celebrated for its profusion of marble, its patrician towers, and its grave magnificence. It still can boast some marble churches, a marble palace, and a marble bridge. Its towers, though no longer a mark of nobility, may be traced in the walls of modernized houses. Its gravity pervades every street; but its magnificence is now confined to one sacred corner. There stand the Cathedral, the Baptistery, the Leaning Tower, and the Campo Santo; all built of the same marble, all varieties of the same architecture, all venerable with years, and fortunate both in their society and in their solitude."

I know not whether my first sensation at the sight of the Leaning Tower, was admiration of its extreme beauty, or astonishment at its posture. Its beauty has never been sufficiently praised. Its overhanging seems to menace the houses beneath it with destruction. The inclination is fourteen feet out of the perpendicular. We are amazed that people should build houses underneath it, till we recollect that it has probably stood thus ever since it was built, that is to say, for nearly six hundred and fifty years; and that habit reconciles us to anything. Something of a curve backwards is given to it. The structure was begun by a German artist, William of Inspruck, and finished by Italians. Several other towers in Pisa, including the Observatory, have a manifest inclination, owing to the same cause,—the sinking of the soil, which is light, sandy, and full of springs.*

With regard to the company in which it stands, let the reader imagine a broad grass-walk, standing in the solitary part of a country town. Let him suppose at one end of this walk the Leaning Tower, with a row of small but elegant houses right under the inclination, and looking down the grass-plot; the Baptistery, a rotunda, standing by itself at the opposite end; the public hospital, an extremely neat and quiet building, occupying the principal length of the road which borders the grass-plot on one side; on the other side, and on the grass itself, the cathedral, stretching between the Leaning Tower and the Baptistery; and lastly, at the back of the cathedral, and visible between the openings at its two ends, the Campo Santo (Holy Field) or burial-ground, walled in with marble cloisters full of the oldest paintings in Italy. All these buildings are detached; they all stand in a free, open situation; they all look as if they were built but a year ago; they are all of marble; the whole place is kept extremely clean,—the very grass in a state of greenness not common to turf in the south; and there are trees looking upon it over a wall next the Baptistery. Let the reader add to this scene a few boys playing about, all ready to answer your questions in pure Tuscan,—women occasionally passing with veils or bare

* Upon reflection, since the appearance of the first edition of this book, I cannot help thinking, after all, that the inclination of this famous tower so much out of the perpendicular, must have taken place long after it was completed; that it was left standing as it does, after long and anxious watching for the consequences; and that anything which architecture may have done by way of counteraction, could only have ensued upon experience of the tower's safety.

heads, or now and then a couple of friars; and though finer individual sights may be found in the world, it will be difficult to come upon an assemblage of objects more rich in their combination.

The Baptistery is a large rotunda, richly carved, and appropriated solely to the purpose after which it was christened. It is in a mixed style, and was built in the twelfth century. Forsyth, who is deep in arches and polygons, objects to the crowd of unnecessary columns; to the " hideous tunnel which conceals the fine swell of the cupola;" and to the appropriation of so large an edifice to a christening. The " tunnel" may deserve his " wrath;" but his architectural learning sometimes behaves as ill as the tunnel. It obscures his better taste. A christening, in the eyes of a good Catholic, is at least as important an object as a rotunda; and there is a religious sentiment in the profusion with which ornament is heaped upon edifices of this nature. It forms a beauty of itself, and gives even mediocrity a sort of abundance of intention that looks like the wealth of genius. The materials take leave of their materiality, and crowd together into a worship of their own. It is no longer " let everything" only " that has *breath* praise the Lord;" but let everything else praise him, and take a meaning and life accordingly. Let column obscure column, as in a multitude of men; let arch strain upon arch, as if to ascend to heaven; let there be infinite details, conglomerations, mysteries, lights, darknesses; and let the birth of a new soul be celebrated in the midst of all.

The cathedral is in the Greek style of the middle ages, a style which this writer thinks should rather be called the Lombard, " as it appeared in Italy first under the Lombard princes." He says, that it includes " whatever was grand or beautiful in the works of the middle ages; " and that " this was perhaps the noblest of them all." He proceeds to find fault with certain incongruities, amongst which are some remains of Pagan sculpture left standing in a Christian church; but he enthusiastically admires the pillars of oriental granite that support the roof. The outside of the building consists of mere heaps of marble, mounting by huge steps to the roof; but their simplicity as well as size gives them a new sort of grandeur ; and Mr. Forsyth has overlooked the extraordinary sculpture of the bronze doors, worthy of the same hand that made those others at Florence, which Michael Angelo said were fit to be the gates of Paradise. It is divided into compartments, the subjects of which are taken from Scripture. The relief is the most graceful and masterly conceivable; the perspective astonishing, as if in drawing; and equal justice is done to the sharp monstrosities of the devil with his bat-wings, and to the gentle graces of Jesus. There is a great number of pictures in the cathedral, good enough to assist rather than spoil the effect, but not remarkable. I never was present when the church-service was at its best; but the leader did not seem to rely much on his singers, by the noise which he made in beating time. His vehement roll of paper sounded like the lashing of a whip.

One evening, in August, I saw the whole inside of the cathedral lit up with wax in honour of the Assumption. The lights were disposed with much taste, but produced a great heat. There was a gigantic picture of the Virgin displayed at the upper end, who was to be supposed sitting in heaven, sur-rounded with the celestial ardours; but she was " dark with excess of bright." It is impossible to see this profusion of lights, especially when one knows their symbolical meaning, without being struck with the source from which Dante took his idea of the beatified spirits. His heaven, filled with lights, and lights too, arranged in figures, which glow with lustre in proportion to the beatitude of the souls within them, is the sublimation of a Catholic church. And so far it is heavenly indeed, for nothing escapes the look of materiality like fire. It is so airy, joyous, and divine a thing, when separated from the idea of pain and an ill purpose, that the language of happiness naturally adopts its terms, and can tell of nothing more rapturous than burning bosoms and sparkling eyes. The Seraph of the Hebrew theology was a fire. But then the materials of heaven and hell are the same? Yes; and a very fine piece of moral theology might be made out of their sameness, always omitting the brute injustice of eternal punishment. Is it not by our greater or less cultivation of health and benevolence, that we all make out our hells and heavens upon earth? by a turning of the same materials and passions of which we are all composed to different accounts; burning now in the horrors of hell with fear, hatred, and un-charitableness, and now in the joys, or at least the happiest sympathies of heaven, with good effort and courage, with gratitude, generosity, and love?

The crowning glory of Pisa is the Campo Santo. I entered for the first time at twilight, when the indistinct shapes, colours, and antiquity of the old paintings wonderfully harmonized with the nature of the place. I chose to go towards evening, when I saw it again; and though the sunset came upon me too fast to allow me to see all the pictures as minutely as I could have wished, I saw enough to warrant my giving an opinion of them; and I again had the pleasure of standing in the spot at twilight. It is an oblong enclosure, about the size of Stratford Place, and surrounded with cloisters wider and lighter than those of Westminster. At least, such was my impression. The middle is grassed earth, the surface of which, for some depth, is said to have been brought from Palestine at the time of the crusades, and to possess the virtue of decomposing bodies in the course of a few hours. The tradition is, that Ubaldo Lanfranchi, Archbishop of Pisa, who commanded the forces contributed by his countrymen, brought the earth away with him in his ships; but though such a proceeding would not have been impossible, the story is now, I believe, regarded as a mere legend. The decomposition of the bodies might have been effected by other means. Persons are buried both in this enclosure and in the cloisters, but only persons of rank or celebrity. Most of the inscriptions for instance (of which there are some hundreds, all on marble, and mixed with busts and figures), are to the memory of Pisans in the rank of nobility; but there are several also to artists and men of letters. The most interesting grave is that of Benozzo, one of the old painters, who lies at the feet of his works.

The paintings on the walls, the great glory of Pisa, are by Orgagna, Simon Memmi, Giotto, Buffalmacco, Benozzo, and others—all more or less renowned by illustrious pens; all, with more or less gusto, the true and reverend harbingers of the greatest painters of Italy. Simon Memmi is the artist celebrated by Petrarch for his portrait of Laura; Buffalmacco is the mad wag (grave enough here) who cuts such a figure in the old Italian novels; and Giotto, the greatest of them all, is the friend of Dante, the hander down of his likeness to posterity, and himself the Dante of his art, without the drawbacks of satire and sorrow. His works have the same real character, the imaginative mixture of things familiar with things unearthly, the same strenuous and (when they choose) gentle expression,—in short, the same true discernment of the " differences of things," now grappling with a fiend or a fierce thought, now sympathising with fear and sorrow, now setting hard the teeth of grim warriors, now dissolving in the looks

and flowing tresses of women, or putting a young gallant in
an attitude to which Raphael might have traced his cavaliers.
And this is more or less the character of the very oldest pictures in the Campo Santo. They have the germs of beauty
and greatness, however obscured and stiffened ; the struggle
of true pictorial feeling with the inexperience of art. As you
proceed along the walls, you see gracefulness and knowledge
gradually helping one another, and legs and arms, lights,
shades, and details of all sorts taking their proper measures
and positions, as if every separate thing in the world of painting had been created with repeated efforts, till it answered the
fair idea. They are like a dream of humanity during the
twilight of creation.

I have already mentioned that the pictures are painted on
the walls of the four cloisters. They occupy the greater part
of the elevation of these walls, beginning at top and finishing
at a reasonable distance from the pavement. The subjects
are from the Old Testament up to the time of Solomon, from
the legends of the middle ages, particularly St. Ranieri (the
patron saint of Pisa) and from the history of the Crucifixion,
Resurrection, &c., with the Day of Judgment. There is also
a Triumph of Death. The colours of some of them, especially of the sky and ship in the voyage of St. Ranieri, are
wonderfully preserved. The sky looks as blue as the finest
out of doors. But others are much injured by the sea air,
which blows into Pisa ; and it is a pity that the windows of
the cloisters in these quarters are not glazed, to protect them
from further injury. The best idea, perhaps, which I can
give an Englishman of the general character of the paintings,
is by referring him to the engravings of Albert Durer, and
the serious parts of Chaucer. There is the same want of proper costume—the same intense feeling of the human being,
both in body and soul—the same bookish, romantic, and retired character—the same evidences, in short, of antiquity
and commencement, weak (where it is weak) for want of a
settled art and language, but strong for that very reason in first
impulses, and in putting down all that is felt. An old poet,
however, always has the advantage of an old painter, because
he is not bound to a visible exhibition of arms, legs, and attitudes, and thus escapes the artistical defects of the time. But
they truly illustrate one another. Chaucer's Duke Theseus,
clothed and behaving accordingly—his yawning courtiers,
who thank King Cambuscan for dismissing them to bed—his

god Janus keeping Christmas with his fireside and his dish of brawn, &c.—exhibit the same fantastic mixtures of violated costume and truth of nature. The way in which the great old poet mingles together personages of all times, nations, and religions, real and fictitious, Samson and Turnus with Socrates, Ovid with St. Augustin, &c., and his descriptions of actual "purtreyings on a wall," in which are exhibited, in one and the same scene, Narcissus, Solomon, Venus, Crœsus, and "the porter Idleness," resemble the manner in which some of the painters in the Campo Santo defy all perspective, and fill one picture with twenty different solitudes. There is a painting, for instance, devoted to the celebrated anchorites, or hermits of the desert. They are represented according to their several legends—reading, dying, undergoing temptations, assisted by lions, &c. At first they all look like fantastic actors in the same piece; but you dream, and are reconciled.

The contempt of everything like interval, and of all which may have happened in it, makes the ordinary events of life seem of as little moment; and the mind is exclusively occupied with the sacred old men and their solitudes, all at the same time, and yet each by himself. The manner in which some of the hoary saints in these pictures pore over their books, and carry their decrepit old age, full of a bent and absorbed feebleness—the set limbs of the warriors on horseback—the sidelong unequivocal looks of some of the ladies playing on harps, and conscious of their ornaments—the people of fashion, seated in rows, with Time coming up unawares to destroy them—the other rows of elders and doctors of the church, forming part of the array of heaven—the uplifted hand of Christ denouncing the wicked at the Day of Judgment—the daring satires occasionally introduced against monks and nuns—the profusion of attitudes, expressions, incidents, broad draperies, ornaments of all sorts, visions, mountains, ghastly-looking cities, fiends, angels, sibylline old women, dancers, virgin brides, mothers and children, princes, patriarchs, dying saints;—it would be a simply blind injustice to the superabundance and truth of conception in all this multitude of imagery not to recognise the real inspirers as well as harbingers of Raphael and Michael Angelo, instead of confining the honour to the Masaccios and Peruginos. The Masaccios and Peruginos, for all that ever I saw, meritorious as they are, are no more to be compared with them than the sonneteers of Henry the Eighth's time are to be compared with Chaucer. Even in the very rudest of the pictures, where the souls of the dying are going out of their mouths in the shape of little children, there are passages not unworthy of Dante or Michael Angelo—angels trembling at the blowing of trumpets; men in vain attempting to carry their friends into heaven; and saints who have lived ages of temperance, sitting in calm air upon hills far above the progress of Death, who goes bearing down the great, the luxurious, and the young. The picture by Titian (or Giorgione), in which he has represented the three great stages of existence, bubble-blowing childhood, love-making manhood, and death-contemplating old age, is not better conceived, and hardly better made out, than some of the designs of Orgagna and Giotto.

Since I have beheld the Campo Santo I have enriched my day-dreams and my stock of the admirable, and am thankful that I have names by heart to which I owe homage and gratitude. Giotto, be thou one to me hereafter, of a kindred brevity, solidity, and stateliness, with that of thy friend Dante, and far happier! Tender and noble Orgagna, be thou blessed for ever beyond the happiness of thine own heaven!

The air of Pisa is soft and balmy to the last degree. A look out upon the Lung 'Arno at noon is curious. A blue sky is overhead—dazzling stone underneath—the yellow Arno gliding along, generally with nothing upon it, sometimes a lazy sail; the houses on the opposite side, with their green blinds down, appear to be asleep; and nobody passes but a few labourers, carmen, or countrywomen in their veils and handkerchiefs, hastening with bare feet, but never too fast to lose a certain air of strut and stateliness. Dante, in one of his love poems praises his mistress for walking like a peacock; nay, even like a crane, *straight above herself*:—

> "Soave a guisa va di un bel pavone,
>   Diritta sopra se, coma una grua."

> Sweetly she goes, like the bright peacock; straight
>   Above herself, like to the lady crane.

This is the common walk of Italian women, rich and poor. To an English eye, at first it seems wanting in a certain modesty and moral grace; but you see what the grave poet thinks of it, and it is not associated in an Italian mind with any such deficiency. That it has a beauty of its own is certain.

Solitary as Pisa may look at noon, it is only by comparison with what you find in very populous cities. Its desolate aspect is much exaggerated. The people, for the most part, sit in shade at their doors in the hottest weather, so that it cannot look so solitary as many parts of London at the same time of the year; and though it is true that grass grows in some of the streets, it is only in the remotest. The streets, for the most part, are kept very neat and clean, not excepting the poorest alleys; a benefit arising not only from the fine pavement which is everywhere to be found, but from the wise use to which criminals are put. The punishment of death is not kept up in Tuscany. Robbers, and even murderers, are made to atone for the ill they have done by the good works of sweeping and keeping clean. A great murderer on the English stage used formerly to be dressed in a suit of brick-dust. In Tuscany, or at least in Pisa, robbers condemned to this punishment are clothed in a red livery, and murderers in a yellow. A stranger looks with a feeling more grave than curiosity at these saffron-coloured anomalies quietly doing their duty in the streets, and not seeming to avoid observation. But, in fact, they look just like other men. They are either too healthy by temperance and exercise to exhibit a conscience, or think they make up by their labour for so trifling an ebullition of animal spirits. And they have a good deal to say for themselves, considering that circumstances modify all men, and that the labour is in chains and for life.

The inhabitants of Pisa, in general, are not reckoned a favourable specimen of Tuscan looks. You are sure to meet fine faces in any large assembly, but the common run is bad enough. They are hard, prematurely aged, and what expression there is, is worldly. Some of them have no expression whatever, but are as destitute of speculation and feeling as masks. The bad Italian face and the good Italian face are the extremes of insensibility and the reverse. But it is rare that the eyes are not fine; and the females have a profusion of good hair. Lady Morgan has remarked the promising countenances of Italian children, compared with what they turn out to be as they grow older; and she adds, with equal justice, that it is an evident affair of government and education. You doubly pity the corruptions of a people who, besides their natural genius, preserve in the very midst of their sophistication a frankness distinct from it, and an entire freedom from affectation. An Italian annoys you neither with his pride like an Englishman, nor with his vanity like a Frenchman. He is quiet and natural, self-possessed without wrapping himself up in a corner, and ready for cheerfulness without grimace. His frankness sometimes takes the air of a simplicity, at once misplaced and touching. A young man, who exhibited a taste for all good and generous sentiments, and who, according to the representation of his friends, was a very worthy as well as ingenious person, did not scruple to tell me one day, as a matter of course, that he made a point of getting acquainted with rich families, purely to be invited to their houses and partake of their good things. Many an Englishman would do this, but he would hardly be so frank about it, especially to a stranger ; nor would an Englishman of the same tastes in other respects be easily found to act so. But it is the old story of " following the multitude to do evil," and is no doubt accounted a matter of necessity and common sense.

There seems a good deal of talent for music among the Pisans, which does not know how to make its way. You never hear the poorest melody, but somebody strikes in with what he can muster up of a harmony. Boys go about of an evening, and parties sit at their doors, singing popular airs, and hanging as long as possible on the last chord. It is not an uncommon thing for gentlemen to play their guitars as they go along to a party. I heard one evening a voice singing past a window, that would not have disgraced an opera ; and I once walked behind a common post-boy, who, in default of having another to help him to a harmony, contrived to make chords of all his notes, by rapidly sounding the second and the treble, one after the other. The whole people are bitten with a new song, and hardly sing anything else till the next. There were two epidemic airs of this kind when I was there, which had been imported from Florence, and which the inhabitants sang from morning till night, though they were nothing remarkable. Yet Pisa is said to be the least fond of music of any city in Tuscany.

Pisa is a tranquil, an imposing, and even now a beautiful and stately city. It looks like what it is, the residence of an university : many parts of it seem made up of colleges ; and we feel as if we ought to " walk gowned." It possesses the Campo Santo ; its river is the river of Tuscan poetry, and furnished Michael Angelo with the subject of his cartoon ; and it disputes with Florence the birth of Galileo. Here, at all events, the great astronomer studied and taught : here his mind was born, and another great impulse given to the progress of philosophy and liberal opinion.

CHAPTER XX.

GENOA.

Towards the end of September, Lord Byron and myself, in different parties, left Pisa for Genoa. Tuscany had been rendered uncomfortable to him by the misadventures both there and at Leghorn; and at Genoa he would hover on the borders of his inclination for Greece. Perhaps he had already made arrangements for going thither.

On our way to Genoa we met at Lerici. He had an illness at that place; and all my melancholy was put to its height by seeing the spot which my departed friend had lived in, and his solitary mansion on the sea-shore. Lerici is wild and retired, with a bay and rocky eminences; the people suited to it, something between inhabitants of sea and land. In the summer time they will be up all night dabbling in the water and making wild noises. Here Trelawny joined us. He took me to the Villa Magni (the house just alluded to); and we paced over its empty rooms and neglected garden. The sea fawned upon the shore, as though it could do no harm.

At Lerici we had an earthquake. The shock was the smartest we experienced in Italy. At Pisa there had been a dull intimation of one, such as happens in that city about once in three years. In the neighbourhood of Florence we had another, less dull, but lasting only for an instant. It was exactly as if somebody with a strong hand had jerked a pole up against the ceiling of the lower room right under one's feet. This was at Maiano, among the Fiesolan hills. People came out of their rooms, and inquired of one another what was the matter. At Lerici I awoke at dawn with an extraordinary sensation, and directly afterwards the earthquake took place. It was strong enough to shake the pictures on the wall; and it lasted a sufficient time to resemble the rolling of a waggon under an archway, which it did both in noise and movement. I got up and went to the window. The people were already collecting in the open place beneath it; and I heard, in the clear morning air, the word *Terremoto* (earthquake) repeated from one to another. The sensation for the next ten minutes or so was very distressing. You expected the shock to come again, and to be worse. However, we had no more of it. We congratulated ourselves the more, because there was a tower on a rock just above our heads, which would have stood upon no ceremony with our inn. They told us, if I remember, that they had an earthquake on this part of the coast of Italy about once every five years. Italy is a land of volcanoes, more or less subdued. It is a great grapery, built over a flue. If the earthquake did not come, it was thought the crops were not so good.

From Lerici we proceeded part of our way by water, as far as Sestri. Lord Byron went in a private boat; Trelawny in another; myself and family in a felucca. It was pretty to see the boats with their white sails, gliding by the rocks over that blue sea. A little breeze coming on, our seamen were afraid, and put into Porto Venere, a deserted town a short distance from Lerici.

After resting a few hours, we put forth again, and had a lazy, sunny passage to Sestri, where a crowd of people assailed us, like savages at an island, for our patronage and portmanteaux. They were robust, clamorous, fishy fellows, like so many children of the Tritons in Raphael's pictures; as if those plebeian gods of the sea had been making love to Italian chambermaids. Italian goddesses have shown a taste not unsimilar, and more condescending; and English ones, too, in Italy, if scandal is to be believed. But Naples is the headquarters of this overgrowth of wild luxury. Marino, a Neapolitan, may have had it in his eye when he wrote that fine sonnet of his, full of gusto, brawny and bearded, about Triton pursuing Cymothoe. (See *Parnaso Italiano*, tom. 41, p. 10.)

From Sestri we proceeded over the maritime part of the Apennines to Genoa. Their character is of the least interesting sort of any mountains, being neither distinct nor wooded; but undulating, barren, and coarse; without any grandeur but what arises from an excess of that appearance. They lie in a succession of great doughy billows, like so much enormous pudding, or petrified mud.

Genoa again!—With what different feelings we beheld it from those which enchanted us the first time! Mrs. Shelley, who preceded us, had found houses both for Lord Byron's family and my own at Albaro, a neighbouring village on a hill. We were to live in the same house with her; and in the Casa Negrotto we accordingly found an English welcome. There were forty rooms in it, some of them such as would be considered splendid in England, and all neat and new, with borders and arabesques. The balcony and staircase were of marble; and there was a little flower-garden. The rent of this house was twenty pounds a year. Lord Byron paid four-and-twenty for his, which was older and more imposing, and a good piece of ground. It was called the Casa Saluzzi.* Mr. Landor and his family had occupied a house in the same village—the Casa Pallavicini. He has recorded an interesting dialogue that took place in it.† Of Albaro, and the city itself, I shall speak more at large in the course of the chapter.

The Genoese post brought us the first number of our new quarterly, the *Liberal*, accompanied both with hopes and fears, the latter of which were too speedily realized. Living now in a separate house from Lord Byron, I saw less of him than before; and, under all the circumstances, it was as well: for though we had always been on what are called "good terms," the cordiality did not increase. His friends in England, who, after what had lately taken place there in his instance, were opposed, naturally enough, to his opening new fields of publicity, did what they could to prevent his taking a hearty interest in the *Liberal*; and I must confess that I did not mend the matter by my own inability to fall in cordially with his ways, and by a certain jealousy of my position, which prevented me, neither very wisely nor justly, from manifesting the admiration due to his genius, and reading the manuscripts he showed me with a becoming amount of thanks and good words. I think he had a right to feel this want of accord in a companion, whatever might be its value. A dozen years later, reflection would have made me act very differently. At the same time, though the *Liberal* had no mean success, he unquestionably looked to its having a far greater; and the result of all these combined circumstances was, that the interest he took in it cooled in proportion as it should have grown warm, and after four numbers it ceased. They were all published during our residence in this part of Italy. Lord Byron contributed some poems, to which his customary publisher had objected on account of their fault-finding in Church and State, and their critical attacks on acquaintances. Among

* Are the Saluzzi family from Chaucer's *Country of Saluces*, whose "Markis" married the patient Griselda? Saluces was in the maritime Apennines, by Piedmont, and might have originated a family of Genoese nobles. Classical and romantic associations meet us in such abundance at every turn in Italy, that upon the least hint a book speaketh.

Imaginary Conversations, vol. i. p. 179, second edition.

them was the *Vision of Judgment*, the best satire since the days of Pope. Churchill's satires, compared with it, are bludgeons compared with steel of Damascus. Hazlitt contributed some of the most entertaining of his vigorous essays; and Shelley had left us his masterly translation of the *May-Day Night* in *Faust*. As to myself, if I may speak of my own articles after these, I wrote by far the greater number,— perhaps nearly half the publication; but I was ill; and with the exception of one or two, I hope they were not among my best. This, however, did not hinder great puzzlement among the critics of that day. I say it with not the slightest intention of self-compliment; and I should think him a very dull fellow who supposed it.

Puzzlement and posement of various sorts awaited many readers of the *Liberal*. A periodical work which is understood to be written by known authors, whose names are, nevertheless, unaffixed to their contributions, has the disadvantage of hazarding uneasiness to the minds of such readers as pique themselves on knowing a man's style without really being sure of it. They long to assign the articles to this and that author, but they fear to be mistaken. The perplexity irritates them; they are forced to wait the judgments of others; and they willingly comfort the wound given to their self-love by siding with such as are unfavourable, and pronouncing the articles to be of an undistinguishable mediocrity. I do not know how far this kind of dilemma may have injured the *Liberal*. I suspect it had no little effect. But what must have exasperated, while it consoled it, critics of an opposite kind were sometimes as much in the wrong as the former were afraid of being. A signal instance occurred in the case of a writer not disesteemed in his day, whose name I suppress, because the mention of it might disconcert some relation. One of the poems in the *Liberal* is entitled the *Book of Beginnings*. Its subject is poetical exordiums. The writer in question attributed it to Lord Byron; and after denouncing the "atheists and scoffers," by whom, he said, his lordship had been "led into defiance of the sacred writings," thus proceeded to notice a religious passage from Dryden, which was quoted with admiration in the notes to the poem :—

"In vain was Lord Byron led into the defiance of the sacred writings; there are passages in his letters and in his works which show that religion might have been in his soul. Could he recite the following lines and resist the force of them? It is true that he marks them for the beauty of the verse, but no less for the sublimity of the conception; and I cannot but hope that, had he lived, he would have proved another instance of genius bowing to the power of truth."

Now the poem in question, and the notes to it, were written by myself, one of those " atheists and scoffers" (according to this gentleman), by whom the supposed writer of the poem had been " led into defiance of the sacred writings."

This person knew as little of my religion as he knew of an author's manner. Among these same notes of mine is the following passage :—

"What divine plays would not Beaumont and Fletcher have left us, if they had not been fine gentlemen about town, and ambitious to please a perishing generation! Their muse is like an accomplished country beauty, of the most exquisite kind, seduced up to town, and made familiar with the most devilish parts of it, yet retaining, through all her debauchery, a sweet regret and an adoring fondness for nature. She has lilies about her paint and patch-boxes, and loves them almost as much as when she was a child."

I do not think that the author of *Don Juan* was accustomed to make critical reflections of that sort. I do not allude, of course, to the writing, but to the sentiment. But the poem was written in the stanza of *Don Juan*, and, therefore, his Lordship was to be complimented with the religion of it, at the expense of his *Juanity*.

I will take this opportunity of recording some more anecdotes as they occur to me. My neighbour and myself used to walk in the grounds of the Casa Saluzzi; talking for the most part of indifferent things, and endeavouring to joke away the consciousness of our position. We joked even upon our differences of opinion. It was a jest between us, that the only book that was a thorough favourite on both sides, was Boswell's *Life of Johnson.* I used to talk of Johnson when I saw him disturbed, or when I wished to avoid other subjects. He asked me one day how I should have felt in Johnson's company. I said it was difficult to judge; because, living in other times, and one's character being modified by them, I could not help thinking of myself as I was now, and Johnson as he was in times previous : so that it appeared to me that I should have been somewhat " Jacobinical" in his company, and not disposed to put up with his *ipse dixits*. He said that " Johnson would have awed him, he treated lords with so much respect." The reader, after what I have lately said, will see what was at the bottom of these remarks on both sides. Had the question been asked me now, I should have said, that I loved Johnson, and hope I should have shown him all due homage ; though I think I should have been inclined sometimes to contest his conclusions more than they are contested by his interlocutors in Boswell. Lord Byron liked to imitate Johnson, and say, " Why, sir," in a high mouthing way, rising, and looking about him. His imitation was very pleasant.

It is a credit to my noble friend, that he was by far the pleasantest when he had got a little wine in his head. The only time I invited myself to dine with him, I told him I did it on that account, and that I meant to push the bottle so that he should intoxicate me with his good company. He said he would have a set-to ; but he never did. It was a little before he left Italy ; and there was a point in contest between us (not regarding myself) which he thought perhaps I should persuade him to give up. When in his cups, which was not often nor immoderately, he was inclined to be tender ; but not weakly so, nor lachrymose. I know not how it might have been with everybody, but he paid me the compliment of being excited to his very best feelings; and when I rose late to go away, he would hold me down, and say with a look of entreaty, " Not yet." Then it was that I seemed to talk with the proper natural Byron as he ought to have been ; and I used to think there was not a sacrifice which I could not have made to keep him in that temper, and see his friends love him as much as the world admired. But I ought to have made the sacrifice at once. I should have broken the ice between us which had been generated on points of literary predilection; and admired, and shown that I admired, as I ought to have done, his admirable genius. It was not only an oversight in me; it was a want of friendship. Friendship ought to have made me discover what less cordial feelings had kept me blind to. Next morning the happy moment had gone, and nothing remained but to despair and joke.

In his wine he would volunteer an imitation of somebody, generally of Incledon. He was not a good mimic in the detail, but he could give a lively broad sketch; and over his cups his imitations were good-natured, which was not always the case at other times. His Incledon was vocal. I made pretensions to the oratorical part; and between us we boasted that we made up the entire phenomenon. He would sometimes, however, give a happy comprehensive idea of a person's manner and turn of mind by the utterance of a single phrase, or even word. Thus he would pleasantly pretend that Braham called "enthusiasm" *entoozymoozy ;* and in the extraordinary combination of lightness, haste, indifference, and fervour with which he would pitch out that single word from his lips, accompanied with a gesture to correspond, he would really set before you the admirable singer in one of his (then) characteristic passages of stage dialogue. He did not live to see Braham become an exception in his dialogue as in his singing.

Lord Byron left Italy for Greece, and our conversation was at an end. I will, therefore, request the reader's company in a walk with me about Genoa.

Genoa is truly "Genoa the Superb." Its finest aspect is from the sea, and from the sea I first beheld it. Imagine a glorious amphitheatre of white houses, with mountains on each side and at the back. The base is composed of the city with its churches and shipping; the other houses are country seats, looking out, one above the other, up the hill. To the left are the Alps with their snowy tops : to the right, and for the back, are the Apennines. This is Genoa. It is situate at the very angle of the pointed gulf, which is called after its name, and which presents on either side, as you sail up it, white villages, country seats, and olive groves.

When we first saw Genoa, which was the first Italian city we beheld, our notions of the Italian countenance were formidably startled by the pilot-boat, which came out to offer its assistance in conducting us by the mole. The mole had been injured greatly by the storms of the preceding winter. The boat contained, I thought, as ugly a set of faces as could well have been brought together. It was a very neat boat, and the pilots were singularly neat and clean in their persons; but their faces ! My wife looked at me as much as to say, "Are these our fine southern heads ?" The children looked at me : we all looked at one another : and what was very inhospitable, the pilots all looked at us. The sun was in their eyes; and there they sat on their oars, grinning up at us, and bargaining with the captain. The older ones were like monkeys; the younger like half-withered masks — hard, stony, and pale.

The first sight of Italian women disappointed us almost as much as Italian men, because we expected still more of them. Of course, had we seen them first, they would have disappointed us more. But I afterwards found, that as you ascended

among the more educated classes, the faces improved; and I
have reason to believe, that most of the women whom we saw
in boats, deceived us as to their rank in this respect.   In
Italy, gentlemen do not look so much like gentlemen as in
England, but there are greater numbers of women who look
like ladies.   This is partly owing to their dress.   In Genoa
particularly, the out-of-door head-dress for women of all
ranks is a white veil; and an Englishman, unaccustomed to
see this piece of drapery upon common heads, and observing,
besides, the stateliness with which female Italians carry themselves, thinks he is oftener looking at gentlewomen than he is.

We had not been long in harbour before we inquired, with
all the eagerness of voyagers, for our fresh provisions.   In
Italy, we also looked for our fresh heaps of fruit; and we had
them—in all the luxury of baskets and vine-leaves, and a
cheapness that made us laugh.   Grapes were not in season;
but there were figs, apricots, fresh almonds, oranges, pears,
and gigantic cherries, as fine as they were large.   We also
took leave of our biscuit for excellent bread; and had milk
brought to us in bottles, which were stopped with vine-leaves.
The mutton turned out to be kid, and lean enough; but it
was a novelty, and we ate it upon a principle of inquiry.
An excellent light wine accompanied our repast, drunk, not
in little cautious glasses, like our " hot intoxicating liquor,"
but out of tumblers.   It was just threepence English a quart.
It had, notwithstanding its lightness, a real vinous body, and
both looked and tasted like a sort of claret; but we were
sorry to find it was French, and not Italian.   As to the fruit,—
to give a specimen in one word,—the apricots, very fine ones,
were twopence a gallon.

The quay of Genoa is a handsome one, profuse of good
pavement, gate, &c.; and the abundance of stone everywhere,
the whiteness of the houses, and the blueness of the sky, cast,
at first sight, an extraordinary look of lightness and cleanli-
ness upon everything.   Nor are you disappointed in Genoa,
as people are at Lisbon, between the fairness of the look outside and the dirt within.   The large wrinkled features of the
old women, with their uncapped gray hair, strike you at first
as singularly plain: so do the people in general: but everything looks clean and neat, and full of the smart bustle of a
commercial city.   What surprises you is the narrowness of
the streets.   As soon as you have passed the gate, you think
you have entered upon a lane, remarkably good indeed for a

lane,—a sort of Bond Street of an alley,—but you have no
suspicion that it is a street, and of the ordinary dimensions.
The shops also, though neat, are entirely open, like English
potato shops, or at best like some of the little comb shops now
rarely to be seen in London. I mean, they have no windows,
or such walls as would hold them. After entering this street,
you soon come upon the public place, or exchange, which is a
very fair one. You cross over this into the principal street,
or street of goldsmiths, full of shops in which trinkets are
sold, including a world of crosses and other Christian emblems,
and huge ear-rings. It is the custom in several parts of Italy
for girls to carry their marriage portion about with them, in
the shape of gold ear-rings and crosses; and no maid-servant
thinks herself properly dressed on mass-days without an-
nouncing, in this way, that she is equally fit for heaven and a
husband. The gold is very thin, but solidity is made up for
by the length and width of the ornaments; and the ear-rings
are often heavy enough to tear through the lobes of the ears.
Imagine a brown, black-eyed girl, with her thick hair done
up in combs, a white veil over it, a coloured, sometimes a
white gown, large dangling gold ornaments at her ears and
bosom, and perhaps bare feet or tattered shoes, and you have
the complete portrait of a Genoese maid-servant or peasant
girl, issuing forth to church or to a dance. The men of all
classes dress more like the same classes in other countries,
with an exception, however, as before noticed, in favour of
the humbler ones. Yet you often see the old Genoese cap,
and you notice a set of porters from Bergamo, who wear a
puckered kilt. They are a good-looking race, and are esteemed
for their honesty. The burdens they carry are enormous.
The labourer of Italy often shows his propensity to a piece of
drapery, by hanging his jacket over his shoulders with the
sleeves dangling; a custom naturally prompted by the heat.

In England we have delicate names for some of our streets
and alleys. There is Love Lane, Maiden Lane, Garden Court,
Green Arbour Court, &c., but in Italy they beat us hollow.
Pisa has not only Love Street and Lily Street, but Beautiful
Ladies' Lane, and the Lane of the Beautiful Towers. In
Genoa, after passing through Goldsmith Street, and another
that leads up from it, you came out by the post-office upon
the Piazza delle Fontane Amorose,—the Place of the Amorous
Fountains. There is a magnificent mansion in it, containing
baths; and another, adorned on the outside with paintings of

festive women. But here all the houses begin to be magnificent mansions, and you again recognise " Genova la Superba."
From the Piazza delle Fontane Amorose you turn into the
Strada Nuova, which leads round through another sumptuous
street into the Strada Balbi, fit, says Madame de Staël, for a
congress of kings. The three streets are literally a succession
of palaces on each side of the way; and these palaces are of
costly architecture, and are adorned inside with the works
of the Italian masters. Marble is lavished everywhere. It
is like a street raised by Aladdin, to astonish his father-in-
law, the Sultan. Yet there is one lamentable deficiency.
Even these streets are narrow. I do not think the Strada
Nuova is wider than Bond Street *without* the pavements. " A
lane ! " you cry. Yes, a lane of Whitehalls, encrusted with
the richest architecture. Imagine how much the buildings
lose by this confinement, and then wonder how it could have
taken place. The alleged reason is, that in a hot country
shade is wanted, and therefore beauty is sacrificed to utility.
But the reason is a bad one: for porticos might have been
used, as at Bologna, and the street made so wide as to render
the disadvantage to the architecture a comparative nothing.
The circumstance probably originated in some reasons connected with the ground, or the value of it, and the pressure
of the population within the then city walls. Some other
magnificent streets, built subsequently, are wider, though still
a good deal too narrow. The Genoese have found out, before
ourselves, the folly of calling a street New Street; but they
have not very wisely corrected it by naming one of their last,
Newest Street,—Strada Nuovissima. Upon this principle,
they must call the next street they build, Newer-than-all-
street, or Extremely-new-street, or New-of-the-very-newest-
description-street. They seem to have no idea of calling
their streets, as we do, after the names of obscure builders
and proprietors; a very dull custom, and idle piece of vanity;
especially in a country which abounds in great names. The
streets of a metropolis ought to exhaust the whole nomenclature of great men, national or otherwise, before it begins
with bricklayers. Nay, it would be handsome to see the
names of illustrious foreigners mingled with those of the
nation; and I have no doubt, that as nations become fused
together by intercourse, such compliments will take place.
They will be regarded, indeed, as discharges of debts: for who
does not feel grateful to the wise and good of all countries ?

In Genoa I first had the pleasure of seeing a religious procession. I found chairs brought out in one of the streets, and well-dressed company seated on each side, as in a music-room. In Genoa, some of the streets are paved all over. In the rest, the flat pavement is in the middle, and used both for traffic and walking. This, I suppose, originated in a vile custom which they have in several cities of Italy,—the same which Smollett speaks of in the Edinburgh of his time. Accidents frequently occur in consequence; but anything is sooner mended than a habit originating in idleness or moral indifference; and the inhabitants and the mules go on in their old way. But to return to the procession.—The reader must imagine a narrow street, with the company as above mentioned, and an avenue left for the passage of the spectacle. The curiosity expressed in the company's faces was of a very mild description, the next thing to indifference. The music was heard at a little distance, then came a bustling sound of feet, and you saw the friars advancing. Nearly at the head of the procession was a little live Virgin, about four years old, walking in much state, with a silver-looking crown on her head, and a sceptre in her hand. A pleased relation helped her along, occasionally righting the crown and sceptre, which she bore with all that dignified gravity which children so soon imitate. By her side was another grown person, equally pleased, supporting a still smaller St. John, dressed in a lamb-skin, and apparently selected for his office on account of his red little waxen cheeks and curly flaxen hair. He did not seem quite as much *au fait* in the matter as the Virgin, but was as grave as need be, and not a little heated. A string of clergy followed in their gowns, carrying large lighted wax candles, and each one assisted by a personage whose appearance was singularly striking to a foreigner from a Protestant country.

These coadjutors were neither more nor less than the very raggedest and dirtiest fellows, old and young, in all Genoa. There was one to every light. His object was to collect the wax that fell from the candles, which he did in a piece of paper; and the candle seemed to be made to gutter on purpose, in order to oblige him with as much of it as possible. The wax is sold by the gainer. I dare say this accompaniment of pauperism has a reference to the best doctrines of the Christian religion; but it is a singular mistake, and has a most unedifying appearance. Poverty should not be in this

squalid condition, especially by the side of comfortable clergymen. The faces, too, of the poor fellows had, for the most
part, all the signs of bad education. Now and then there was
a head like the beggar who sat for Sir Joshua's Ugolino,—a
fine head, but still a beggar. Some were of a portentous
raffishness.

As to the priests and friars (for there followed a variety), I
could not help observing, that, with very few exceptions, the
countenances grew indifferent and worldly as they grew old.
A few of the young ones were worthy of the heads in Raphael.
One young man had a saint-like manner with him, casting
down his eyes, and appearing absorbed in meditation; but I
thought, when he did cast them up (which he instantly followed by casting them down again), it was in approaching the
young ladies. He had certainly a head fit for an Abelard.

I spoke just now of a bustle of feet. You do not know at
first to what the loudness of it is owing, but the secret is
explained as a large machine approaches, preceded by music.
This is a group of wax-work as large as life, carried on the
shoulders of ambling friars; for they are obliged to shuffle
into that step on account of the weight. It represented, on
the present occasion, St. Antonio kneeling before the Virgin,
around whom were little angels fluttering like Cupids. It is
impossible not to be reminded of Paganism by these spectacles. Indeed, as the Jupiter of the Capitol still sits there
under his new name of St. Peter, so there is no doubt that
the ancients, under other names, had these identical processions. The Cupids remain unaltered. The son of Myrrha
himself could not look more lover-like than Sant' Antonio,
nor Venus more polite than the Virgin; and the flowers stuck
all about (the favourite emblem of the Cyprian youth), completed the likeness to an ancient festival of Adonis. So also
would the priests have looked in their ancient garments; so
would have come the music and the torches (paupers excepted);
and so would the young priests have looked, in passing by the
young ladies. To see the grandeurs of the Catholic religion,
you must consult its rarest and most serious festivals, its
pictures, and its poet Dante. I must not forget, that among
the musical instruments were violins. One set of friars wore
cowls over their faces, having holes only to see through, and
looking extremely hideous,—like executioners. Or were they
brethren of the benevolent order of the Misericordia, who
disguise themselves, only the more nobly to attend to any

disaster that calls upon them for aid? If so, observe how people may be calumniated merely in consequence of a spectator's ignorance. Among the persons who showed their faces, and who did not seem at all ashamed of them, was one good-natured, active individual, who ran back, with great vivacity, to encourage the machine-bearers. He looked as much as to say, "It is hot enough for you, Heaven knows!" and so it was.

Somebody has said, that in the south all the monks look like soldiers, and all the soldiers like monks. I dare say this might have been the case before the spread of liberal opinions; but it is so no longer. In Spain and Portugal it cannot be so; though the troops quartered in Genoa were for the most part under-grown and poor-looking men. The officers, however, were better. They had a propensity, common, I am told, in the south, to overgrown caps and epaulets; but they had otherwise a manly aspect, and looked more like gentlemen than any one else. This, indeed, is always the case where there is any difference—military habits begetting an air of self-possession. The Genoese soldiery were remarkably well-dressed. They had a bad way of learning their exercise. They accompanied every motion—the whole set of men—with a loud Ho! just as if a multitude of quick paviors were at work. This, besides encouraging noise, must take away from a ready dependence on the eye.

I used often to go to the churches in Genoa and elsewhere. I liked their quiet, their coolness, and their richness. Besides, I find my own religion in some part or other of all imaginative religions. In one of the churches are pillars of porphyry, and several are very imposing; but they struck me upon the whole as exhibiting the genius of a commercial rather than a tasteful country; as being more weighty and expensive than beautiful. There are some good pictures; but by far the greater number adorn the houses of the nobility. In all Catholic churches, there is an unfortunate mixture of petty ornaments with great, of dusty artificial flowers with fine altar-pieces, and of wretched little votive pictures, and silver hearts and legs, stuck up by the side of the noblest pieces of art.

This is another custom handed down from antiquity. I was reminded of Horace's *Ode to Pyrrha*, by a painting of a shipwreck, in which the wind blew one way and the sails another. If a man has got rid of a pain in the pericardium, he dedicates a little silver heart to the saint whose assistance he prayed for. If a toe has been the complaining part, he hangs up a toe. The general feeling is good, but not so the detail. It is affecting, however, to think that many of the hearts hung up (and they are by far the most numerous) have been owing to pangs of the spirit.

The most interesting thing I met with in the Genoese churches, next to a picture by Raphael and Giulio Romano in that of St. Stephen, was a sermon by a friar on Weeping. He seemed a popular preacher, and held the attention of his audience for a good hour. His exordium was in a gentle and restrained voice, but he warmed as he went on, and became as loud and authoritative as the tenderness of his subject could well permit. He gave us an account of all sorts of tears—of the tears of joy and the tears of sorrow, of penitent tears, tears of anger, spite, ill-temper, worldly regret, love, patience, &c.; and from what I could collect, with an ear unaccustomed to hear Italian spoken, a very true, as well as full and particular account it was. The style was more florid than in our northern sermons. He spoke of murmuring rills and warbling nightingales, and admitted all the merits of poetical luxury; but in denouncing luxury in general, it was curious to hear a stout, jovial-looking friar exhorting his auditors to value above all other enjoyments that of weeping in solitude. The natives are not likely to be too much softened by injunctions of this description.

The houses in Genoa are very high as well as large. Many of them are painted on the outside, not only with pictures, but with imitations of architecture; and whatever we may think of such a taste, these displays must have looked magnificent when the paintings were first executed. Some of them look so now; colours in this beautiful climate retaining their vividness for centuries out of doors. But in some instances, the paintings being done upon stucco, the latter has partly crumbled away, and this gives a shabby, dilapidated appearance to houses otherwise excellent. Nobody seems to think of repairing them. It is the same with many of the houses unpainted, and with common garden walls, most of which must have once made a splendid appearance. The mere spirit of commerce has long succeeded to its ancient inclusion of a better one; or Genoa would not be what it is in many respects. But a Genoese must nevertheless have grand notions of houses; especially as in this city, as well as the rest of Italy, shop-keepers sometimes occupy the ground floors of the finest mansions. You shall see a blacksmith or a carpenter looking out of a window where you might expect a duchess.

Neither Genoa nor even the country around it abounds in trees. It is a splendid sea-port of stone and marble, and the mountains in the neighbourhood are barren, though they soon begin to be clothed with olive-trees. But among the gigantic houses and stone walls you now and then detect a garden, with its statues and orange-trees; some of the windows have vines trailed over them, not in the scanty fashion of our creepers, but like great luxuriant green hair hanging over the houses' eyes; and sometimes the very highest stories have a terrace along the whole length of the house embowered with them. Calling one day upon a gentleman who resided in an elevated part of the suburbs, and to get at whose abode I had walked through a hot sun and a city of stone, I was agreeably surprised, when the door opened, with a long yellow vista of an arcade of vines, at once basking in the sun and defending from it. In the suburbs there are some orchards in all the southern luxuriance of leaves and fruit. In one of these, I walked among heaps of vines, olives, cherry, orange, and almond-trees, and had the pleasure of plucking fresh lemons from the bough, a merry old brown gardener, with a great straw hat and bare legs, admiring all the while my regard for those commonplaces, and encouraging me with a good-natured paternity to do what I pleased. The cherries were Brobdignagian, and bursting with juice. Next the orchard was a *wine-garden*, answering to our *tea-gardens*, with vine-arbours and seats as with us, where people drink wine and play at their games. Returning through the city, I saw a man in one of the bye-streets alternately singing and playing on a pipe, exactly as we conceive of the ancient shepherds.

One night I went to the opera, which was indifferent enough, but I understand it is a good deal better sometimes. The favourite composer here and all over Italy, is Rossini, a truly national genius, full of the finest animal spirits, yet capable of the noblest gravity. My northern faculties were scandalized at seeing men in the pit with *fans!* Effeminacy is not always incompatible with courage, but it is a very dangerous help towards it; and I wondered what Doria would have said had he seen a captain of one of his galleys indulging his cheeks in this manner. Yet perhaps they did so in his own times. What would be effeminate in a man of the north, unaccustomed to it, may be a harmless trifle to a southern.

One night, on our first arrival in Genoa, the city was illuminated, and bonfires and rockets put in motion, in honour of St. John the Baptist. The effect from the harbour was beautiful; fire, like the stars, having a brilliancy in this pure atmosphere, of which we have no conception. The scent of the perfumes employed in the bonfires was very perceptible on board ship.

You learn for the first time in this climate, what colours really are. No wonder it produces painters. An English artist of any enthusiasm might shed tears of vexation, to think of the dull medium through which blue and red come to him in his own atmosphere, compared with this. One day we saw a boat pass us, which instantly reminded us of Titian, and accounted for him: and yet it contained nothing but an old boatman in a red cap, and some women with him in other colours, one of them in a bright yellow petticoat. But a red cap in Italy goes by you, not like a mere cap, much less anything vulgar or butcher-like, but like what it is, an intense specimen of the colour of red. It is like a scarlet bud in the blue atmosphere. The old boatman, with his brown hue, his white shirt, and his red cap, made a complete picture; and so did the women and the yellow petticoat. I have seen pieces of orange-coloured silk hanging out against a wall at a dyer's, which gave the eye a pleasure truly sensual. Some of these boatmen are very fine men. I was rowed to shore one day by a man the very image of Kemble. He had nothing but his shirt on, and it was really grand to see the mixed power and gracefulness with which all his limbs came into play as he pulled the oars, occasionally turning his heroic profile to give a glance behind him at other boats. They generally row standing, and pushing from them.

The most interesting sight, after all, in Genoa, was the one we first saw—the Doria palace. Bonaparte lodged there when he was in Genoa; but this, which would have been one of its greatest praises, had he done all he could for liberty, is one of its least. Andrew Doria dwelt there after a long life, which he spent in giving security and glory to his country, and which he crowned by his refusal of power. "I know the value," said he, "of the liberty I have earned for my country, and shall I finish by taking it from her?" When upwards of eighty, he came forward and took the command of an armament in a rough season. His friends remonstrated. "Excuse me," said he; "I have never yet stopped for anything when my duty was in the way, and at my time of life one cannot get rid of one's old habits." This is the very perfection of a speech—a mixture of warrantable self-esteem, modesty, energy, pathos, and pleasantry; for it contains them all. He died upwards of ninety.

I asked for Doria's descendants, and was told they were rich. The Pallavicini, with whom the Cromwell family were connected, are extant. I could ascertain nothing more of the other old families, except that they had acquired a considerable dislike of the English; which, under all circumstances at that time, was in their favour. I found one thing, however, which they *did*; and I must correct, in favour of this one thing, what I have said about the Doria palace; for the sight of it upon the whole gave me still greater satisfaction. This was, the overthrow of the Genoese Inquisition. There was a wish to rebuild it; but this the old families opposed; and the last ruins of it were being cleared away. It was pleasant to see the workmen crashing its old marble jaws.

Genoa has shown how much and how little can be done by mere commerce. A great man here and there in former times is an exception; and the princely mansions, the foundations of schools and hospitals, and the erection of costly churches, attest that in similar periods money-getting had not degenerated into miserliness. But the Genoese did not cultivate mind enough to keep up the breed of patriots; and it remained for an indignant spirit to issue out of a neighbouring arbitrary monarchy and read them lectures on their absorption in money-getting. Alfieri, in his *Satire on Commerce*, ranks them with their mules. It avails nothing to a people to be merely acquiring money, while the rest of the world are acquiring ideas;—a truth which England has gloriously understood, and, it is to be trusted, will still more gloriously illustrate. It turns out, that Genoa and its neighbourhood have no pretensions to Columbus; which is lucky for her. He was born at Cuccaro, in the province of Aqui, not far from Asti—Alfieri's birth-place. Chiabrera, who is sometimes called the Italian Pindar, was born near Genoa, at Savona. I have read little of him; but he must have merit to be counted an Italian classic; and it says little for the Genoese, that I could not find a copy of his works at their principal bookseller's. I have since become better acquainted with him. He was a bigot in his religion, and of so violent a temper, as to have been guilty, twice over, of what he calls manslaughter in self-vindication: yet he had not only force and expression in his graver lyrics, but a light and gay turn for Anacreontics. He tried to introduce a Greek turn of writing into the language, especially in compound words; but the practice did not obtain. Frugoni, their other poet, was born, I believe, in the same place. He is easy and lively, but wrote a great deal too much, probably for bread. There is a pleasant petition of his in verse to the Genoese senate, about some family claims, in which he gives an account of his debts that must have startled the faculties of that prudent and opulent body. A few more Frugonis, however, and a few less rich men, would have been better for Genoa. The best production I ever met with from a Genoese pen, is a noble sonnet by Giambattista Pastorini, a Jesuit; written after the bombardment of the city by the troops of Louis XIV. The poet glories in the resistance made by Genoa, and kisses the ruins caused by the bombardment with transport. What must have been his mortification, when he saw the Doge and a number of senators set out for France, to go and apologize to Louis XIV. for having been so erroneous as to defend their country!

There is a proverb which says of Genoa, that it has a sea without fish, land without trees, men without faith, and women without modesty. Ligurian trickery is a charge as old as Virgil. But M. Millin very properly observes (*Voyage en Savoie*, &c.) that accusations of this description are generally made by jealous neighbours, and that the Genoese have most likely no more want of good faith than other Italians who keep shops. I must confess, at the same time, that the most barefaced trick ever attempted to be practised on myself, was by a Genoese. The sea, it is said, has plenty of fish, only the duty on it is very high, and the people prefer butchers' meat. This is hardly a good reason why fish is not eaten at a seaport. Perhaps it is naturally scarce at the extreme point of a gulf like that of Genoa. The land is naked enough, certainly, in the immediate vicinity, though it soon begins to be otherwise. As to the women, they have fine eyes and figures, but by no means appear destitute of modesty; and modesty has much to do with appearance. Wholesale charges of want of modesty are, at all times and in all places, most likely to be made by those who have no modesty themselves.

The Governor of Genoa, at that time, was a Savoyard Marquis of the name of D'Yennes, and he is said to have related with much glee a current anecdote about himself.

As he was coming to take possession of his appointment, he stopped at a town not far from Genoa, the inhabitants of which were ambitious of doing him honour. They accordingly gave him an entertainment, at which was an allegorical picture containing *a hyæna surrounded with Cupids.* The hyæna was supposed to be a translation of his name. Upon requesting an explanation of the compliment, he received the following smiling reply:—" *Les Amours, Monsieur, sont nous: et vous êtes la bête.*" (" The loves, sir, are ourselves: the beast is you.")

CHAPTER XXI.

FLORENCE—BACCHUS IN TUSCANY—THE VENUS DE' MEDICI
—AND ITALY IN GENERAL.

RESOLVING to remain a while in Italy, though not in Genoa, we took our departure from that city in the summer of the year 1823, and returned into Tuscany in order to live at Florence. We liked Genoa on some accounts, and none the less for having a son born there, who, from that hour to this, has been a comfort to us.* But in Florence there were more conveniences for us, more books, more fine arts, more illustrious memories, and a greater concourse of Englishmen; so that we might possess, as it were, Italy and England together. In Genoa we no longer possessed a companion of our own country; for Mrs. Shelley had gone to England; and we felt strange enough at first, thus seeking a home by ourselves in a foreign land.

Unfortunately, in the first instance, the movement did us no good; for it was the height of summer when we set out, and in Italy this is not the time for being in motion. The children, however, living temperately, and not yet being liable to cares which temperance could not remove, soon recovered. It was otherwise with the parents; but there is a habit in being ill, as in everything else; and we disposed ourselves to go through our task of endurance as cheerfully as might be.

In Genoa you heard nothing in the streets but the talk of money. I hailed it as a good omen in Florence, that the

---

* This was written in the year 1849, and held good till the year 1852, when, alas! he died.

first two words which caught my ears were flowers and women (*Fiori* and *Donne*). The night of our arrival we put up at an hotel in a very public street, and were kept awake (as agreeably as illness would let us be) by songs and guitars. It was one of our pleasantest experiences of the south; and, for the moment, we lived in the Italy of books. One performer to a jovial accompaniment sang a song about somebody's fair wife, which set the street in roars of laughter.

From the hotel we went to a lodging in the street of Beautiful Women—Via delle Belle Donne—a name which it is a sort of tune to pronounce. We there heard one night a concert in the street; and looking out, saw music-stands, books, &c. in regular order, and amateurs performing as in a room. Opposite our lodgings was an inscription on a house, purporting that it was the hospital of the Monks of Vallombrosa. Wherever you turned was music or a graceful memory.

From the Via delle Belle Donne we went to live in the Piazza Santa Croce, in a corner house on the left side of it, near to the church of that name, which contains the ashes of Galileo, Michael Angelo, Boccaccio, Macchiavelli, Alfieri, and others. Englishmen call it the Florentine Westminster Abbey, but it has not the venerable look of the Abbey, nor, indeed, any resemblance at all—but that of a building half finished; though it is several hundred years old. There are so many of these unfinished old edifices in Florence, owing to decline in the funds left for their completion, that they form a peculiar feature in this otherwise beautiful city, and a whole volume has been devoted to the subject. On the other side of this sepulchre of great men is the monastery in which Pope Sixtus the Fifth went stooping as if in decrepitude— "looking," as he said afterwards, "for the keys of St. Peter." We lodged in the house of a Greek, who came from the island of Andros, and was called Dionysius; a name which has existed there, perhaps, ever since the god who bore it. Our host was a proper Bacchanalian, always drunk, and spoke faster than I ever heard. He had a "fair Andrian" for his mother, old and ugly, whose name was Bella.

The church of Santa Croce would disappoint you as much inside as out, if the presence of the remains of great men did not always cast a mingled shadow of the awful and beautiful over one's thoughts. Any large space, also, devoted to the purposes of religion disposes the mind to the loftiest of speculations. The vaulted sky out of doors appears small, compared with the opening into immensity represented by that very enclosure—that larger dwelling than common, entered by a little door. The door is like a grave, and the enclosure like a vestibule of heaven.

Agreeably to our old rustic propensities, we did not stop long in the city. We left Santa Croce to live at Maiano, a village on the slope of one of the Fiesolan hills, about two miles off. It gives its name to one of the earliest of the Italian poets, precursor of the greater Dante, called Dante of Maiano. He had a namesake living on the spot, in the person of a little boy—a terrible rover out of bounds, whom his parents were always shouting for with the apostrophe of " O Dante !" He excelled in tearing his clothes and getting a dirty face and hands. I heard his mother one evening hail his return home with the following welcome :—" O Dante, what a brute beast you are !" I thought how probable it was, that the Florentine adversaries of the great poet, his namesake, would have addressed their abuser in precisely the same terms, after reading one of his infernal flayings of them in the Lakes of Tartarus. Dante and Alfieri were great favourites with a Hebrew family (jewellers, if I remember), who occupied the ground-floor of the house we lived in, the Villa Morandi, and who partook the love of music in common with their tribe. Their little girls declaimed out of Alfieri in the morning, and the parents led concerts in the garden of an evening. They were an interesting set of people, with marked characters ; and took heartily to some specimens which I endeavoured to give them of the genius of Shakspeare. They had a French governess, who, though a remarkably good speaker of English in general, told me one day, in eulogizing the performance of one of the gentlemen who was a player on the bassoon, that " his excellence lay in the *bason*." It was the grandfather of this family whom I have described in another work (*Men, Women, and Books*), as hailed one May morning by the assembled merry-makers of the hamlet, in verses which implied that he was the efficient cause of the exuberance of the season.

The manners of this hamlet were very pleasant and cheerful. The priest used to come of an evening, and take a Christian game at cards with his Hebrew friends. A young Abate would dance round a well with the daughters of the vine-growers, the whole party singing as they footed. I remember the burden of one of the songs—

"Ne di giorno, ne di sera,
Non passiamo la selva nera."
(Night and morn be it understood,
Nobody passes the darksome wood.)

One evening all the young peasantry in the neighbourhood assembled in the hall of the village, by leave of the proprietor (an old custom), and had the most energetic ball I ever beheld. The walls of the room seemed to spin round with the waltz, as though it would never leave off—the whirling faces all looking grave, hot, and astonished at one another. Among the musicians I observed one of the apprentices of my friend the bookseller, an evidence of a twofold mode of getting money not unknown in England. I recollected his face the more promptly, inasmuch as not many days previous he had accompanied me to my abode with a set of books, and astonished me by jumping on a sudden from one side of me to the other. I asked what was the matter, and he said, " A viper, sir" (una vipera, signore). He seemed to think that an Englishman might as well settle the viper as the bill.

Notwithstanding these amusements at Maiano, I passed a very disconsolate time; yet the greatest comfort I experienced in Italy (next to writing a book which I shall mention) was living in that neighbourhood, and thinking, as I went about, of Boccaccio. Boccaccio's father had a house at Maiano, supposed to have been situated at the Fiesolan extremity of the hamlet. That many-hearted writer (whose sentiment outweighed his levity a hundredfold, as a fine face is oftener serious than it is merry) was so fond of the place, that he has not only laid the two scenes of the *Decameron* on each side of it, with the valley which his company resorted to in the middle, but has made the two little streams that embrace Maiano, the Affrico and the Mensola, the hero and heroine of his *Nimphale Fiesolano*. A lover and his mistress are changed into them, after the fashion of Ovid. The scene of another of his works is on the banks of the Mugnone, a river a little distant; and the *Decameron* is full of the neighbouring villages. Out of the windows of one side of our house we saw the turret of the Villa Gherardi, to which, according to his biographers, his "joyous company" resorted in the first instance. A house belonging to the Macchiavelli was nearer, a little to the left; and farther to the left, among the blue hills, was the white village of Settignano, where Michael Angelo was born. The house is still in possession of the family. From our windows on the other side we saw, close to us, the Fiesole of antiquity and of Milton, the site of the Boccaccio-house before mentioned still closer, the *Decameron's* Valley of Ladies at our feet; and we looked over towards the quarter of the Mugnone and of a house of Dante, and in the distance beheld the mountains of Pistoia. Lastly, from the terrace in front, Florence lay clear and cathedralled before us, with the scene of Redi's *Bacchus* rising on the other side of it, and the Villa of Arcetri, illustrious for Galileo. Hazlitt, who came to see me there (and who afterwards, with one of his felicitous images, described the state of mind in which he found me, by saying that I was " moulting"), beheld the scene around us with the admiration natural to a lover of old folios and great names, and confessed, in the language of Burns, that it was a sight to enrich the eyes.

But I stuck to my Boccaccio haunts, as to an old home. I lived with the true human being, with his friends of the *Falcon* and the *Basil,* and my own not unworthy melancholy; and went about the flowering lanes and hills, solitary indeed, and sick to the heart, but not unsustained. In looking back to such periods of one's existence, one is surprised to find how much they surpass many seasons of mirth, and what a rich tone of colour their very darkness assumes, as in some fine old painting. My almost daily walk was to Fiesole, through a path skirted with wild myrtle and cyclamen; and I stopped at the cloister of the Doccia, and sat on the pretty melancholy platform behind it, reading or looking through the pines down to Florence. In the Valley of Ladies I found some English trees (trees, not vine and olive), and even a meadow; and these, while I made them furnish me with a bit of my old home in the north, did no injury to the memory of Boccaccio, who is of all countries, and who finds his home wherever we do ourselves, in love, in the grave, in a desert island.

But I had other friends, too, not far off, English, and of the right sort. My friend, Charles Armitage Brown (Keats's friend, and the best commentator on Shakspeare's Sonnets), occupied for a time the little convent of San Baldassare, near Maiano, where he represented the body corporate of the former possessors, with all the joviality of a comfortable natural piety. The closet in his study, where it is probable the church treasures had been kept, was filled with the

humanities of modern literature, not the less Christian for
being a little sceptical: and we had a zest in fancying that we
discoursed of love and wine in the apartments of the Lady
Abbess.   I remember I had the pleasure of telling an Italian
gentleman there the joke attributed to Sydney Smith, about
sitting next a man at table, who possessed a " seven-parson
power;" and he understood it, and rolled with laughter, crying out—" Oh, ma bello! ma bellissimo!" (Beautiful! exquisite!)   There, too, I had the pleasure of dining in company with an English beauty (Mrs. W.), who appeared to be
such as Boccaccio might have admired, capable both of mirth
and gravity ; and she had a child with her that reflected her
graces.   The appearance of one of these young English
mothers among Italian women, looks (to English eyes at least)
like domesticity among the passions.   It is a pity when you
return to England, that the generality of faces do not keep up
the charm.   You are then too apt to think, that an Italian
beauty among English women would look like poetry among
the sullens.

Our friend Brown removed to Florence, and, together with
the books and newspapers, made me a city visitor.   I there
became acquainted with Landor, to whose genius I had made
the *amende honorable* the year before ; and with Mr. Kirkup,
an English artist, who was not poor enough, I fear, either in
purse or accomplishment, to cultivate his profession as he
ought to have done; while at the same time he was so
beloved by his friends, that they were obliged to get at a
distance from him before they could tell him of it.   Yet I
know not why they should; for a man of a more cordial
generosity, with greater delicacy in showing it, I never met
with: and such men deserve the compliment of openness.
They know how to receive it.

To the list of my acquaintances, I had the pleasure of adding Lord Dillon ; who, in the midst of an exuberance of
temperament more than national, concealed a depth of understanding, and a genuine humanity of knowledge, to which
proper justice was not done in consequence.   The luxuriant
vegetation and the unstable ground diverted suspicion from
the ore beneath it.   I remember him saying something one
evening about a very ill-used description of persons in the
London streets, for which Shakspeare might have taken him
by the hand ; though the proposition came in so startling a
shape, that the company were obliged to be shocked in self-

defence. The gallant Viscount was a cavalier of the old school of the Meadowses and Newcastles, with something of the O'Neal superadded; and instead of wasting his words upon tyrants or Mr. Pitt, ought to have been eternally at the head of his brigade, charging mercenaries on his war horse, and meditating romantic stories.

When the *Liberal* was put an end to, I had contributed some articles to a new work set up by my brother, called the *Literary Examiner*. Being too ill at Florence to continue those, I did what I could, and had recourse to the lightest and easiest translation I could think of, which was that of Redi's *Bacco in Toscana*.* The *Bacco in Toscana* (Bacchus in Tuscany), is a mock-heroical account of the Tuscan wines, put into the mouth of that god, and delivered in dithyrambics. It is ranked among the Italian classics, and deserves to be so for its style and originality. Bacchus is represented sitting on a hill outside the walls of Florence, in company with Ariadne and his usual attendants, and jovially giving his opinion of the wines, as he drinks them in succession. He gets drunk after a very mortal fashion ; but recovers, and is borne away into ecstasy by a draught of Montepulciano, which he pronounces to be the King of Wines.

I was the more incited to attempt a version of this poem, inasmuch as it was thought a choke-pear for translators. English readers asked me how I proposed to render the "famous"

" Mostra aver poco giudizio "—

(a line much quoted); and Italians asked what I meant to do with the " compound words" (which are very scarce in their language). I laughed at the famous " mostra aver," which it required but a little animal spirits to "give as good as it brought; " and I had the pleasure of informing Italians, that the English language abounded in compound words, and could make as many more as it pleased.

At Maiano, I wrote the articles which appeared in the *Examiner*, under the title of the *Wishing Cap*. Probably the reader knows nothing about them; but they contained

---

* [In 1824 or 1825 Redi was physician to the Grand Duke Cosmo of Tuscany; his love of wine was ideal, for he was himself a water-drinker. The autobiographer had met with a copy of it in the Sion College Library, while he was yet in prison; and he found in the poem mention of Maiano, and of persons, friends of Redi, whose families still remained at Maiano, the Bellini and the Salviati.]

some germs of a book he may not be unacquainted with, called *The Town*, as well as some articles since approved of in the volume entitled *Men, Women, and Books*. The title was very genuine.

When I put on my cap, and pitched myself in imagination into the thick of Covent Garden, the pleasure I received was so vivid,—I turned the corner of a street so much in the ordinary course of things, and was so tangibly present to the pavement, the shop-windows, the people, and a thousand agreeable recollections which looked me naturally in the face,—that sometimes when I walk there now, the impression seems hardly more real. I used to feel as if I actually pitched my soul there, and that spiritual eyes might have seen it shot over from Tuscany into York Street, like a rocket. It is much pleasanter, however, on waking up, to find soul and body together in one's native land :—yes, even than among thy olives and vines, Boccaccio! I not only missed "the town" in Italy; I missed my old trees—oaks and elms. Tuscany, in point of wood, is nothing but olive-ground and vineyard. I saw there, how it was, that some persons when they return from Italy say it has no wood, and some, a great deal. The fact is, that many parts of it, Tuscany included, has no wood to *speak of*; and it wants larger trees interspersed with the small ones, in the manner of our hedge-row elms. A tree of a reasonable height is a godsend. The olives are low and hazy-looking, like dry sallows. You have plenty of these; but to an Englishman, looking from a height, they appear little better than brushwood. Then, there are no meadows, no proper green lanes (at least, I saw none), no paths leading over field and stile, no hayfields in June, nothing of that luxurious combination of green and russet, of grass, wild flowers, and woods, over which a lover of Nature can stroll for hours with a foot as fresh as the stag's; unvexed with chalk, dust, and an eternal public path; and able to lie down, if he will, and sleep in clover. In short (saving, alas ! a finer sky and a drier atmosphere, great ingredients in good spirits), we have the best part of Italy in books; and this we can enjoy in England. Give me Tuscany in Middlesex or Berkshire, and the Valley of Ladies between Harrow and Jack Straw's Castle. The proud names and flinty ruins above the Mensola may keep their distance. Boccaccio shall build a bower for us out of his books, of all that we choose to import; and we will have daisies and fresh meadows besides. An Italian may prefer his own country after the same fashion; and he is right. I knew a young English-woman, who, having grown up in Tuscany, thought the land-scapes of her native country insipid, and could not imagine how people could live without walks in vineyards. To me, Italy had a certain hard taste in the mouth. Its mountains were too bare, its outlines too sharp, its lanes too stony, its voices too loud, its long summer too dusty. I longed to bathe myself in the grassy balm of my native fields. But I was ill, unhappy, in a perpetual low fever ; and critics, in such con-dition, or in any condition which is not laudatory, should give us a list of the infirmities under which they sit down to esti-mate what they differ with. What a comfort, by the way, that would be to many an author ! What uncongenialities, nay, what incompetencies we should discover ! What a relief to us to find that it was " only A's opinion !" or " only B's !" and how we should laugh at him while giving it in his own person, *vivâ voce*, instead of the mysterious body corporate of " We." Nay, how we do laugh,—provided the bookseller's account will let us, provided omissions of notice, or commis-sions of it, have not been the ruin of our " edition !" Thus may Italians laugh at me, should they read my English criti-cisms on their beautiful country.

Disappointed of transplanting Redi's Italian vines into England, I thought I would try if I could bring over some literature of modern English growth into Italy. I proposed to a Florentine bookseller to set up a quarterly compila-tion from the English magazines. Our periodical publica-tions are rarely seen in Italy, though our countrymen are numerous. In the year 1825, two hundred English families were said to be resident in Florence. In Rome, visitors, though not families, were more numerous; and the publica-tion, for little cost, might have been sent all over the Penin-sula. The plan was to select none but the very best articles, and follow them with an original one commenting upon their beauties, so as to make readers in Italy well acquainted with our living authors. But the Tuscan authorities were frightened.

" You must submit the publication " (said my bookseller) " to a censorship."

" Be it so."

" But you must let them see every sheet before it goes to press, in order that there may be no religion or politics."

" Very well :—to please the reverend censors, we will have no religion. Politics also are out of the question."

"Ay, but politics may creep in."

"They shall not."

"Ah, but they may creep in" (say the authorities) "without your being aware; and then what is to be done?"

"Why, if neither the editor nor the censors are aware, I do not see how any very vivid impression need be apprehended with regard to the public."

"That has a very plausible sound; but how if the censors do not understand English?"

"There, indeed, they confound us. All I can say is, that the English understand the censors, and I see we must drop our intended work."

This was the substance of a discourse which I had with the bookseller, in answer to the communications which he brought me from his Government. The prospectus had been drawn out; the bookseller had rubbed his hands at it, thinking of the money which the best writers in England were preparing for him; but he was forced to give up the project. "Ah," said he to me in his broken English, as he sat in winter-time with cold feet and an irritable face, pretending to keep himself warm by tantalizing the tips of his fingers over a little bason of charcoal, "Ah, you are vere happee in England. You can get so much money as you please."

I know not what the Tuscan Government would have said to another book which I wrote at Maiano, and which English readers have not yet heard of, at least not publicly; for, though intended for publication, and the least faulty book, perhaps, which I have written, it has hitherto been only privately circulated. [A warmhearted friend, of admirable taste, who has subsequently achieved for himself a high place in literature, requested, and obtained, leave to print it at his own expense.] It is entitled, *Christianism, or Belief and Unbelief Reconciled;* and contains, among other matters, the conclusions which the author had then come to on points of religious belief and practice. I wrote it because I was in a state of health which I thought might terminate fatally, and I was anxious before I died to do what good I could, as far as my reflections on those points had, in my opinion, enabled me. I shall say more of it towards the end of this volume. I had the consolation—I hope not the unchristian one—of writing it at a window opposite the dissolved convent of the Doccia; for though I contemplated with pleasure that image of departing superstition—then a lay abode, beautifully overlooking the country—the book had any design in the world but that of grieving one gentle heart.*

Attached, however, as associations of this nature, and those with Boccaccio and Redi, contributed to make me to my country walks, I often varied them by going into Florence; or rather, I went there whenever the graver part of them became too much for me. I loved Florence, and saw nothing in it but cheerfulness and elegance. I loved the name; I loved the fine arts and the old palaces; I loved the memories of Pulci and Lorenzo de' Medici, the latter of whom I could never consider in any other light than that of a high-minded patron of genius, himself a poet; I loved the good-natured, intelligent inhabitants, who saw fair play between industry and amusement; nay, I loved the Government itself, however afraid it was of English periodicals; for at that time it was good-natured also, and could "live and let live," after a certain quiet fashion, in that beautiful bye-corner of Europe, where there were no longer any wars, nor any great regard for the parties that had lately waged them, illegitimate or legitimate. The reigning family were Austrians, but with a difference, long Italianized, and with no great family affection. One good-natured Grand Duke had succeeded another for several generations; and the liberalism of that extraordinary prince, the first Leopold, was still to be felt, in a general way, very sensibly, though it lost in some particulars after the triumph of the allies, and the promises broken to the Carbonari;† nor, indeed, has the reigning Grand Duke in his old age and his fright about Mazzini, bettered them.

* This book has been since enlarged and systematized, and is now entitled the *Religion of the Heart.*

† The sixth volume of the *Florentine History* of the late Captain Henry Edward Napier is almost entirely occupied by a full and excellent account of the reign of this admirable and indeed wonderful prince, Leopold the First, Grand Duke of Tuscany, afterwards Emperor of Germany. He was not only a reformer, but a reformer of the noblest and most liberal kind, and this, too, notwithstanding opposition the most harassing from the priests, from his own ministers, nay, actually from the very nation for whom he reformed, and who had not yet been well taught enough to understand him. Such readers as are not acquainted with him, are earnestly recommended to become so; and they cannot do it better than in the pages of Captain Napier, who was himself a worthy member of a remarkable family, and a writer as honest as he was painstaking. I have the honour to possess a copy of his work, given me by himself; and I regret that I had not time to make that thorough intimacy with it before he died, which would have enabled me to say of it what I say

Talking of Grand Dukes and de' Medicis, be it known, before I forget to mention it (so modest am I by nature), that on one of these visits to Florence, and in the house of a Medici himself, I had the happiness of folding to my bosom, with reciprocal pleasure in our faces, no less a personage than a certain lovely Maddalena de' Medici, daughter of said distinguished individual, and now, at this moment, in all probability, lovelier than ever; seeing, alas! that she was then little more than a baby, just able to express her satisfaction at being noticed by her admirers.

I wish I could equally have admired the famous Venus de' Medici, in whom I expected to find the epitome of all that was charming; for I had been led, by what I thought the popular misrepresentations of her, to trust almost as little to plaster casts as to engravings. But how shall I venture to express what I felt? how own the disappointment which I shared with the "Smellfungus" of Sterne, instead of the raptures which I had looked for in unison with Sterne himself, and Thomson, and, perhaps, all the travelled connoisseurs of the earth, Smollett alone and Hazlitt excepted?

When the intelligent traveller approaches Florence, when he ascends the top of the gentle mountains that surround it, and sees the beautiful city lying in a plain full of orchards— what are the anticipations and ideas in which he indulges? Not surely images of a Grand Duke, however grand or even good he may be, nor of divers other Grand Dukes that preceded him, nor of the difference between *tables-d'hôte*, nor any such local phenomena, eminent in the eyes of the postilion :— he thinks of the old glories of Florence: of Lorenzo de' Medici, of Dante, of Boccaccio, of Michael Angelo, of Galileo, of the river Arno and Fiesole, of the rank which that small city has challenged, by the sole power of wit, among the greatest names of the earth; of the lively and clever generation that have adorned it, playing their music, painting their pictures, and pouring forth a language of pearls; and last, but not least, he thinks of the goddess who still *lives* there— the far-famed Venus de' Medici, triumphing in her worshippers as if no such thing as a new religion had taken place, and attracting adoration from all parts of the earth.

now. I do not agree with some of his conclusions respecting what is finally desirable in the nature of government; but I do not wonder at them, considering what a set of iniquitous princes he had for the most part to describe.

He enters, and worships likewise. I, too, entered and worshipped, prepared to be the humblest of her admirers. I did not even hurry to the gallery as soon as I arrived. I took a respectful time for going properly. When I entered the room, I retained my eyes a little on the objects around her, willing to make my approaches like a devout lover, and to prepare myself for that climax of delight. It seemed too great a pleasure to be vulgarly and abruptly taken. At length I look. I behold, and I worship indeed; but not for the old reasons. How shall I venture to state the new ones? I must make a little further preface, and will take the opportunity of noticing the gallery itself.

The celebrated Florentine Gallery is an oblong, occupying the upper story of a whole street of government offices. The street is joined at the end, though opening into a portico underneath on the river Arno, so that the gallery runs almost entirely round the three sides. The longer corridor is 430 feet long (French), the intermediate one 97 feet. They are 11 feet broad, 20 feet high, floored with variegated stucco, and painted on the roof *in fresco*.

The windows are ample, curtained from the sun, and generally opened to admit the air. The whole forms a combination of neatness and richness, of clear and soft light, of silence, firmness, and grace, worthy to be the cabinet of what it contains. These contents are statues, busts, pictures, sarcophagi; the paintings filling the interstices between the sculptures, and occupying the continued space over their heads. The first things you behold on entering the gallery are busts of Roman emperors and their kindred.

But these more obvious portions of the gallery are not *all*. These illustrious corridors present certain tempting-looking doors, which excite curiosity, and these doors open into rooms which are the very boudoirs of connoisseurship. They contain specimens of the different schools, collections of gems and medals, and select assemblages from the whole artistic treasure. One of them, called the Tribune, little more perhaps than 20 feet in diameter, is a concentration of beauty and wealth. It is an octagon, lighted from above, floored with precious marble, and over-arched with a cupola adorned with mother-o'-pearl. But I knew nothing of all this till I read it in a book. I saw only the pictures and the statues. Here, among other wonderful things, is the more wonderful Venus of Titian. Here is the Fornarina of Raphael; his

Julius the Second, with four other pictures, showing the progress of his hand; the adoring Virgin of Correggio; the Epiphany of Albert Durer; a masterpiece of Vandyke; another of Paul Veronese; another by Domenichino; another by Leonardo da Vinci. In the middle of the room, forming a square, stand the famous Apollo, with his arm over his head, leaning on a tree; the Grinder, or Listening Slave; the Wrestlers; and the Faun Playing the Cymbals. And as the climax of attraction to all this, with the statues and paintings in attendance, elevated by herself, opposite the doorway, and approached by a greater number of pilgrims than are now drawn to Italy by the Virgin herself, presides the goddess of the place, the ancient deity restored and ever young—the far-famed Venus de' Medici.

" So stands the statue which enchants the world."

Seeing what I saw, and feeling as I did, when I first beheld this renowned production, glittering with the admiration of ages as well as its own lustre, it was easy to conceive the indignation which the Florentines displayed when they saw it take its departure for France, and the vivacity with which Bonaparte broke out when he spoke of its acquisition. (See page 78 of this volume.)

After this second preface, which is another genuine transcript of my feelings on entering the room, I should again be at a loss how to venture upon the opinion I am about to express, if I did not recollect that the *entire* statue is acknowledged not to be antique, and that the very important part which called forth my disappointment is by some *supposed* not to be so. The statue was originally dug up near Tivoli, at Hadrian's Villa, and was then in a broken as well as in a mutilated state. Luckily the divisions were such as to refit easily; but it is confessed that the whole right arm was wanting, and so was part of the left arm from the elbow downwards.

" With the exception of a little bit of the body or so," says the French editor of the *Guide*, " all the rest is evidently antique."*

This, it appears, is disputable; but nobody doubts the greater part of the body, and the body is certainly divine. Luckily for me, I approached the statue on the left as you enter the door, so that I first saw it from the point of view

* [The work of Praxiteles has undoubtedly been pieced by restorations in the head, and some part of the arms; but the restoration itself is supposed to be antique.]

which shows it to most advantage.   The timid praises which
cold northern criticism ventures to bestow upon naked beauty,
are not calculated to do it justice.   The good faith with which
I speak must warrant me in resorting to the more pictorial
allowances and swelling words of the Italians.   The really
modest will forgive me, at all events; and I am only afraid
that the prudish will be disappointed at not having enough to
blame.   *Hips* and *sides*, however (if they understand such
words), will do.   We first vulgarize our terms with a coarse
imagination, and then are afraid to do justice to what they
express.   It was not so with our ancient admirers of beauty,
the Spensers and Philip Sidneys; and they, I believe, were
not worse men than ourselves.   It would be difficult nowadays to convey, in English, the impression of the Italian word
fianchi (flanks) with the requisite delicacy, in speaking of the
naked human figure.   We use it to mean only the sides of an
army, of a fortified place, or of a beast.   Yet the words *rile-
vati fianchi* (flanks in relief) are used by the greatest Italian
poets to express a beauty, eminent among all beautiful females
who are not pinched and spoilt by modern fashions; and this
is particularly the case with the figure which the sculptor presented to his mind in forming the Venus de' Medici.   Fielding,
in one of his passages about Sophia, would help me out with
the rest.   But to those who have seen the Venus of Canova, it
is sufficient to say, that in all which constitutes the loveliness
of the female figure, the Venus de' Medici is the reverse of
that lank and insipid personage.   Venus, above all goddesses,
ought to be a woman; whereas the statue of Canova, with its
straight sides and Frenchified head of hair, is the image (if
of anything at all) of Fashion affecting Modesty.   The finest
view of the Venus de' Medici is a three-quarter one, looking
towards the back of the head.   Let the statue rest its fame
on this.   It is perfection; if, indeed, the shoulders are not a
thought too broad.   But the waist, and all thereunto belonging—I would quote Sir Philip Sidney at once, if I were sure
I had none but an audience worthy of him.   The feet are very
beautiful—round, light, and tender.   It is justly said, that there
is no cast of the Venus which gives a proper idea of the original.
Perhaps the nature of the marble is one of the reasons.   It
has warmth, and a polish that swims away with the eye; such
as what Horace speaks of in the countenance of his mistress—

" Vultus nimium lubricus aspici."
" Looks too slippery to be looked upon."—Creech,

Alas! not so the face, nor the gesture. When I saw the *face*, all the charms of the body vanished. Thomson thought otherwise—

> " Bashful she bends ; her well-taught look aside
> Turns in enchanting guise, where dubious mix
> Vain conscious beauty, a dissembled sense
> Of modest shame, and slippery looks of love.
> The gazer grows enamour'd ; and the stone,
> As if exulting in its conquest, smiles."

See the poem of *Liberty*, part the fourth. But Thomson writes like a poet who made what he went to find. I was not so lucky. I do not remember what it was that Smollett, in his morbid spleen, said of the Venus. Something, if Sterne is to be believed, not very decent. I hope I am not going to behave myself as ill. With all my admiration of Smollett and his masterly writing, I would rather err with the poetical Scotchman, than be right with the prose one ; but setting aside the body (which, if Smollett said anything indecent against, I say he spoke in a manner worthy of his friend Peregrine Pickle), I must make bold to say, that I think neither the gesture of the figure modest, nor the face worthy even of the gesture. Yes; perhaps it is worthy of the gesture, for affected modesty and real want of feeling go together; and, to my mind, the expression of the face (not to mince the matter, now I must come to it) is pert, petty, insolent, and fastidious. It is the face of a foolish young woman, who thinks highly of herself, and is prepared to be sarcastic on all her acquaintance.

I cling eagerly to the supposition that the head is not an antique; and, I must add, that, if artists are warranted (as they very probably are) in deducing a necessity of the present position of the hands from the turn of the shoulders, the hands were certainly not in their present finical taste. A different character given to them would make a world of difference in the expression of the figure. It is not to be supposed that the sculptor intended to make a sophisticate pert Venus, such as nobody could admire. It is out of all probability. There is too much sentiment in the very body. On the other hand, the expression is neither graceful and good enough for the diviner aspect of the Goddess of Love, nor sufficiently festive and libertine for the other character under which she was worshipped. It might be said, that the Greek women, in consequence of the education they received, were more famous for the beauty of their persons than for the expression of their faces; that the artist, therefore, copied this peculiarity of his countrywomen; that it might not have been his object to excel in expression of countenance; or that he could not, perhaps, have made a face equal to the figure, his talent not being equally turned for both. But it is said, on the other hand, that the women of Greece, owing to moral causes of some kind, were inferior to the other sex in beauty, so that artists took their models from among those of a certain licensed order, who, strange to say, were the only females that received a good education; and certainly it is *possible* that the Venus de' Medici may have been a portrait of one of those anomalous personages. The face, however, has the very worst look of meretriciousness, which is want of feeling; and this, we are bound to suppose, would at least have been veiled under a pleasant and more winning aspect. That it may not have been the sculptor's object to render the face worthy of the figure, it is hardly possible to conceive; though it may be conceded that he would have found it difficult to do so, especially in marble. But the question lies, not between a figure divine and a face unequal to it, but between a figure divine and a face altogether unworthy. Apuleius has said, that if Venus herself were bald, she would no longer be Venus. It is difficult not to agree with him. And yet with much more truth might he have said, that Venus could not be Venus without attractiveness of expression. A beautiful figure is not all, nor even half. It is far more requisite to have beauty in the eyes, beauty in the smile, and that graceful and affectionate look of *approach*, or of meeting the approacher half way, which the Latins expressed by a word taken from the same root as her name, *Venustas*. The cestus was round the waist; but what gave it its power? Winning looks, tenderness, delightful discourse, the whole power of seduction and entertainment, such as Homer has described it, in verses rich as the girdle. Now, there is nothing of all this in the Venus de' Medici. Her face seems to vilify and to vulgarize all which her person inspires. Even the countenance of Titian's Venus, which hangs on the wall behind the statue, just over its head, as if on purpose to out-do it, succeeds in so doing; and yet this naked figure, though called a Venus, is nothing more, I believe, than the portrait of somebody's mistress, not romantically delicate, and waiting till an old woman in the background brings her her clothes to get up. But not to mention that it is an excellent painting, the expression of the face is at least genuine and to the purpose, and the whole figure worthy to be adored in the temple of the Venus Pandemos, if not of the diviner one.

Upon the whole, I found the busts of the Roman emperors far more interesting than this renowned statue. Julius Cesar leads them, with a thin face, traversed in all directions with wrinkles. I thought I had never beheld such a care-worn countenance. Such was the price he paid for ruling his happier fellow-creatures. Augustus, on the contrary, has quite a prosperous aspect,—healthy, elegant, and composed,— though, if I remember rightly, the expression was hard. You thought he could easily enough put his sign-manual to the proscription. His daughter Julia (I speak on all these points from memory) has a fat, voluptuous face, and (I think) wore a wig; at all events, her hair was dressed in some high, artificial manner. I think also she had a double chin, though she was far from old. You could well enough fancy her letting Ovid out, at a back staircase. Somebody—Hazlitt, I think—said that the Roman emperors in this gallery had more of an ordinary English look than what we conceive of the Roman ; and, if I am not mistaken at this distance of time, I agreed with him. There was the good English look with the good, the dull with the dull, and so on. Domitian had exactly the pert aspect of a footman peering about him in a doorway. The look, however, of the glutton Vitellius was something monstrous. His face was simply vulgar, but he had a throat like that of a pelican. Nero's face it was sad to contemplate. There is a series of busts of him at different periods of his life ; one, that of a charming happy little boy ; another, that of a young man growing uneasy ; and a third, that of the miserable tyrant. You fancied that he was thinking of having killed his mother, and was trying to bully his conscience into no care about it.

After all, I know not whether the most interesting sight in Florence is not a little mysterious bit of something looking like parchment, which is shown you under a glass case in the principal public library. It stands pointing towards heaven, and is one of the fingers of Galileo. The hand to which it belonged is supposed to have been put to the torture by the Inquisition, for ascribing motion to the earth; and the finger is now worshipped for having proved the motion. After this, let no suffering reformer's pen misgive him. If his cause be good, justice will be done it some day,

But I must return to Maiano, in order to take leave of it for England; for the fortunes of the *Examiner*, as far as its then proprietors were concerned, had now come to their crisis; and constant anxiety in a foreign land for the very subsistence of my family was not to be borne any longer. I need not enter into some private matters which had tended to produce this aggravation of a public result. Suffice to say, that the author's customary patron—the bookseller—enabled me to move homewards; and that I did so with joy, which almost took away half my cares.

My last day in Italy was jovial. I had a proper Bacchanalian parting with Florence. A stranger and I cracked a bottle together in high style. He ran against me with a flask of wine in his hand, and divided it gloriously between us. My white waistcoat was drenched into rose colour. It was impossible to be angry with his good-humoured face; so we complimented one another on our joviality, and parted on the most flourishing terms. In the evening I cracked another flask, with equal abstinence of inside. Mr. Kirkup made me a present of a vine-stick. He came to Maiano with Brown, to take leave of us; so we christened the stick as they do a seventy-four, and he stood *rod*-father.

We set off next morning at six o'clock. I took leave of Maiano with a dry eye, Boccaccio and the Valley of Ladies notwithstanding. But the grave face of Brown (who had stayed all night, and who was to continue doing us service after we had gone, by seeing to our goods and chattels) was not so easily to be parted with. I was obliged to gulp down a sensation in the throat, such as men cannot very well afford to confess " in these degenerate days," though Achilles and old Lear made nothing of owning it.

But before I quit Italy altogether, I will describe some of our further impressions about it, both physical and moral, and general as well as particular.

You find yourself in Virgil's country the moment you see the lizards running up the walls, and hear the *cicadæ* (now *cicale*) " bursting the bushes with their song." This famous " grasshopper " of Anacreon, as the translators call it, which is not a grasshopper but a beetle, sitting on the trees, produces his " song " by scraping a hollow part of his chest with certain muscles. The noise is so loud, as well as incessant during the heats of the summer-days, as to resemble that of a stocking-manufactory. Travellers in Sicily declare, that

while conversing with a friend along a wood, you sometimes
cannot be heard for them.

All the insect tribes, good and bad, acquire vigour and size
as they get southward. We found, however, but one scorpion
in-doors, and he was young. We were looking on him with
much interest, and speculating upon his turn of mind, when a
female servant quietly took out her scissors, and cut him in
two. Her bile, with eating oil and minestra, was as much
exalted as his. Scorpions, however, are no very dangerous
things in Italy. The gnats are bad enough without them, and
even the flies are almost as bad as the gnats. The zanzaliere
(the bed-net against the gnats) appeared almost as necessary
against the flies, as against the enemy from whom it is named.

But there is one insect which is equally harmless and beautiful. It succeeds the noisy cicala of an evening ; and is of so
fairy-like a nature and lustre, that it would be almost worth
coming into the south to look at it, if there were no other attraction. I allude to the fire-fly. Imagine thousands of flashing diamonds every night powdering the ground, the trees,
and the air, especially in the darkest places, and in the corn-
fields. They give at once a delicacy and brilliance to Italian
darkness, inconceivable. It is the glow-worm, winged, and
flying in crowds. In England it is the female alone that can
be said to give light; that of the male, who is the exclusive
possessor of the wings, is hardly perceptible. "Worm" is a
wrong word, the creature being a real insect. The Tuscan
name is *lucciola*, little-light. In Genoa they call them *cœe-
belle* (*chiare-belle*), clear and pretty. When held in the hand,
the little creature is discovered to be a dark-coloured beetle,
but without the hardness or sluggish look of the beetle tribe.
The light is contained in the under part of the extremity of
the abdomen, exhibiting a dull golden-coloured section by day,
and flashing occasionally by daylight, especially when the hand
is shaken. At night the flashing is that of the purest and most
lucid fire, spangling the vineyards and olive-trees, and their
dark avenues, with innumerable stars. Its use is not known.
In England, and I believe here, the supposition is that it is a
signal of love. It affords no perceptible heat, but is supposed
to be phosphoric. In a dark room, a single one is sufficient
to flash a light against the wall. I have read of a lady in the
West Indies who could see to read by the help of three under
a glass, as long as they chose to accommodate her. During
our abode in Genoa a few of them were commonly in our rooms

all night, going about like little sparkling elves. It is impossible not to think of something spiritual in seeing the progress of one of them through a dark room. You only know it by the flashing of its lamp which takes place every two or three feet apart, sometimes oftener, thus marking its track in and out of the apartment, or about it. It is like a little fairy taking its rounds. These insects remind us of the lines in Herrick, inviting his mistress to come to him at night-time, and they suit them still better than his English ones:—

> " Their lights the glow-worms lend thee ;
>   The shooting-stars attend thee ;
>   And the elves also,
>   Whose little eyes glow,
> Like the sparks of fire, befriend thee."

To me, who when I was in Italy passed more of my time, even than usual, in the ideal world, the spiritual-looking little creatures were more than commonly interesting. Shelley used to watch them for hours. I looked at them, and wondered whether any of the particles he left upon earth helped to animate their loving and lovely light. The last fragment he wrote, which was a welcome to me on my arrival from England, began with a simile taken from their dusk look and the fire underneath it, in which he found a likeness to his friend. They had then just made their appearance for the season.

There is one circumstance respecting these fire-flies, quite as extraordinary as any. There is no mention of them in the ancient poets. Now, of all insects, even southern, they are, perhaps, the most obvious to poetical notice. It is difficult to conceive how any poet, much more a pastoral or an amatory poet, could help speaking of them ; and yet they make their appearance neither in Greek nor Latin verse, neither in Homer, nor Virgil, nor Ovid, nor Anacreon, nor Theocritus. The earliest mention of them, with which I am acquainted, is in Dante (*Inferno*, canto 21), where he compares the spirits in the eighth circle of hell, who go about swathed in fire, to the "lucciole" in a rural valley of an evening. A truly saturnine perversion of a beautiful object. Does nature put forth a new production now and then, like an author? Or has the glow-worm been exalted into the fire-fly by the greater heat of the modern Italian soil, which appears indisputable? The supposition is, I believe, that the fire-fly was brought into Europe from the New World.

With respect to wood in Italy, olive-trees in particular, travellers hearing so much of the latter, and accustomed to their pickled fruit, are generally disappointed at sight of them. Whether my enthusiasm was borne out by judgment, I cannot say, but I liked them, at least in combination. An olive-tree by itself is hardly to be called handsome, unless it is young, in which state it is very much so, quite warranting Homer's comparison with it of the slain youth. It is then tender-looking and elegant. When old the leaves are stiff, hard, pointed, willow-like, dark above, and of a light leathern colour underneath; the trunk slight, dry-looking, crooked; and it almost always branches off into a double stem at a little distance from the ground. A wood of olive-trees looks like a huge hazy bush, more light than dark, and glimmering with innumerable specks, which are the darker sides of the leaves. When they are in fruit they seem powdered with myriads of little black balls. My wife said, that olive-trees looked as if they only grew by moonlight; which gives a better idea of their light, faded aspect, than a more prosaical description.

The pine-tree is tall, dark, and comparatively branchless, till it spreads at top into a noble, solid-looking head, wide and stately. It harmonizes as beautifully with extended landscape, as architectural towers, or as ships at sea.

The cypress is a poplar in shape, but more sombre, stately, and heavy; not to be moved by every flippant air. It is of a beautiful dark colour, and contrasts admirably with trees of a rounder figure. Two or three cypress-trees by the side of a white or yellow cottage, slated and windowed like our new cottage-houses near London, the windows often without glass, are alone sufficient to form a Tuscan picture, and constantly remind you that you are at a distance from home.

The consumption, by the way, of olive oil is immense. It is probably no mean exasperator of Italian bile. The author of an Italian *Art of Health* approves a moderate use of it, both in diet and medicine; but says, that as soon as it is cooked, fried, or otherwise abused, it inflames the blood, disturbs the humours, irritates the fibres, and produces other effects very superfluous in a stimulating climate. The notoriousness of the abuse makes him cry out, and ask how much better it would be to employ this pernicious quantity of oil in lighting the streets and roads. He thinks it necessary, however, to apologize to his countrymen for this apparent inattention to their pecuniary profits, adding, that he makes amends by diverting them into another channel. I fear the two ledgers would make a very different show of profit and loss: not to mention, that unless the oil were consecrated, or the lamps hung very high, it would assuredly be devoured. We had no little difficulty in keeping the servants from disputing its food with our lamp-light. Their lucubrations were of a more internal nature than ours.

> " The rather thou,
> Celestial *oil* shine inwards."

I was told that the olive-trees grew finer and finer as you went southwards.

The chestnut-trees are very beautiful; the spiky-looking branches of leaves, long, and of a noble green, make a glorious show as you look up against the intense blue of the sky. Is it a commonplace to say that the *castanets* used in dancing, evidently originated in the nuts of this tree, *castagnette?* They are made in general, I believe, of cockle-shells, or an imitation of them; but the name renders their vegetable descent unequivocal. It is pleasant to observe the simple origin of pleasant things. Some loving peasants, time immemorial, fall dancing under the trees: they pick up the nuts, rattle them in their hands; and behold (as the Frenchman says) the birth of the accompaniment of the fandango.

Thus much for insects and trees. Among the human novelties that impress a stranger in Italy, I have not before noticed the vivacity prevalent among all classes of people. The gesticulation is not French. It has an air of greater simplicity and sincerity, and has more to do with the eyes and expression of countenance. But after being used to it, the English must look like a nation of scorners and prudes. When serious, the women walk with a certain piquant stateliness, the same which impressed the ancient as well as modern poets of Italy, Virgil in particular; but it has no haughtiness. You might imagine them walking up to a dance, or priestesses of Venus approaching a temple. When lively, their manner out of doors is that of our liveliest women within. If they make a quicker movement than usual, if they recognize a friend, for instance, or call out to somebody, or despatch somebody with a message, they have all the life, simplicity, and unconsciousness of the happiest of our young women, who are at ease in their gardens or parks.

On becoming intimate with Genoa, I found that it possesses

multitudes of handsome women; and what surprised me, many of them with beautiful northern complexions. But an English lady told me, that for this latter discovery I was indebted to my short sight. This is probable. I have often, I confess, been in raptures at faces that have passed me in London, whose only faults were being very coarse and considerably bilious. It is not desirable, however, to have a Brobdignagian sight; and where the mouth is sweet and the eyes intelligent, there is always the look of beauty with a right observer. Now, I saw heaps of such faces in Genoa. The superiority of the women over the men was indeed remarkable, and is to be accounted for perhaps by the latter being wrapt and screwed up in money-getting. Yet it is just the reverse, I understand, at Naples; and the Neapolitans are accused of being as sharp at a bargain as anybody. What is certain, however, is, that in almost all parts of Italy, gentility of appearance is on the side of the females. The rarity of a gentlemanly look in the men is remarkable. The commonness of it among women of all classes is equally so. The former was certainly not the case in old times, if we are to trust the portraits handed down to us; nor, indeed, could it easily have been believed, if left upon record. What is the cause, then, of this extraordinary degeneracy? Is it, after all, an honourable one to the Italians? Is it that the men, thinking of the moral and political situation of their country, and so long habituated to feel themselves degraded, acquire a certain instinctive carelessness and contempt of appearance; while the women, on the other hand, more taken up with their own affairs, with the consciousness of beauty, and the flattery which is more or less paid them, have retained a greater portion of their self-possession and esteem? The alteration, whatever it is owing to, is of the worst kind. The want of gentility is not supplied, as it so often is with us, by a certain homely simplicity and manliness, quite as good in its way, and better, where the former does not include the better part of it. The appearance, to use a modern cant phrase, has a certain *raffishness* in it, like that of a suspicious-looking fellow in England, who lounges about with his hat on one side, and a flower in his mouth. Nor is it confined to men in trade, whether high or low; though at the same time I must observe, that all men, high or low (with the exceptions, of course, that take place in every case), are given to pinching and saving, keeping their servants upon the lowest possible allowance, and eating as little as need be themselves, with the exception of their favourite *minestra*, of which I will speak presently, and which being a cheap as well as favourite dish, they gobble in sufficient quantity to hinder their abstinence in other things from being regarded as the effect of temperance. In Pisa, the great good of life was a hot supper; but at Pisa and Genoa both, as in "the city" with us, if you overheard anything said in the streets, it was generally about money. *Quatrini*, *soldi*, and *lire*, were discussed at every step. A stranger, full of the Italian poets and romances, is surprised to find the southern sunshine teeming with this northern buzz. One thinks sometimes that men would not know what to do with their time, if it were not for that succession of hopes and fears, which constitutes the essence of trade. It looks like a good-humoured invention of nature to save the major part of mankind from getting tired to death with themselves; but, in truth, it is a necessity of progression. All mankind must be fused together, before they know how to treat one another properly, and to agree upon final good. Prince Albert's project for next year * is a great lift in this direction. It was a most happy thought for combining the ordinary and extraordinary interests of the world.

One of the greatest causes of the deterioration of the modern Italian character, has been the chicanery, sensuality, falsehood, worldliness, and petty feeling of all sorts, exhibited by the Court of Rome. Mazzini has denounced it in eloquence, of which the earth has not yet seen the result, however extraordinary its consequences have been already in the events at Rome. But the same things were talked of when I was in Italy, and the truth very freely uttered.

The Italians owned, that for centuries they had been accustomed to see the most exalted persons among them, and a *sacred* court, full of the pettiest and most selfish vices; that, while they had instinctively lost their respect for those persons, they had, nevertheless, beheld them the most flourishing of their countrymen; and that they had been taught, by their example, to make such a distinction between belief and practice, as would startle the saving grace of the most lawless of Calvinists. From what I saw myself (and I would not mention it, if it had not been corroborated by others who resided in

* The first Crystal Palace. [The remark was written in 1850, and it is difficult to correct it without altering the context.]

Italy for years) there was a prevailing contempt of truth in the
country, that would have astonished even an oppressed Irishman. It formed an awful comment upon those dangers of
catechizing people into insincerity, which Bentham pointed out
in his *Church-of-Englandism.* We in England are far enough,
God knows, from this universality of evil yet ; and some of the
most conscientious of our clergy themselves have lately been
giving remarkable indication of their disinterested horror on
the subject. May such writers, and such readers of them,
always be found to preserve us from it ! In Shelley's preface
to the tragedy of the *Cenci,* which was written at Rome, the
religious nature of this profanation of truth is pointed out with
equal acuteness and eloquence. I have heard instances of
falsehood, not merely in shops, but among " ladies and gentlemen," so extreme, so childish, and apparently so unconscious
of wrong, that the very excess of it, however shocking in one
respect, relieved one's feelings in another. It showed how
much might be done by proper institutions, to exalt the
character of a people who are by nature so ingenuous. But
received Italian virtues, under their present governments,
consist in being Catholic (that is to say, in going to confession),
in not being " taken in " by others, and in taking in everybody else. Persons employed to do the least or the greatest
jobs, will alike endeavour to cheat you through thick and
thin. Such, at least, was the case when I was in Italy. It
was a perpetual warfare, in which you were obliged to fight in
self-defence. If you paid anybody what he asked you, it never
entered into his imagination that you did it from anything but
folly. You were pronounced a *minchione* (a ninny), one of
their greatest terms of reproach. On the other hand, if you
battled well through the bargain, a perversion of the natural
principle of self-defence led to a feeling of respect for you.
Dispute might increase ; the man might grin, stare, threaten ;
might pour out torrents of argument and of " injured innocence," as they always do; but be firm, and he went away
equally angry and admiring. Did anybody condescend to
take them in, the admiration as well as the anger was still in
proportion, like that of the gallant knights of old when they
were beaten in single combat.

The famous order of things called *Cicisbeism* is the consequence of a state of society more inconsistent than itself,
though less startling to the habits of the world ; but it was
managed in a foolish manner ; and, strange to say, it was

almost as gross, more formal, and quite as hypocritical as what
it displaced. It is a stupid system. The poorer the people,
the less, of course, it takes place among them; but as the
husband, in all cases, has the most to do for his family, and
is the person least cared for, he is resolved to get what he can
before marriage; so a vile custom prevails among the poorest,
by which no girl can get married unless she brings a certain
dowry. Unmarried females are also watched with exceeding
strictness; and in order to obtain at once a husband and
freedom, every nerve is strained to get this important dowry.
Daughters scrape up, servants pilfer for it. If they were not
obliged to ornament themselves, as a help towards their object,
I do not know whether even the natural vanity of youth would
not be sacrificed, and girls hang out rags as a proof of their
hoard, instead of the " outward and visible sign " of crosses
and ear-rings. Dress, however, disputes the palm with saving;
and as a certain consciousness of their fine eyes and their
natural graces survives everything else among southern woman-
kind, English people have no conception of the high hand with
which the humblest females in Italy carry it at a dance or an
evening party. Hair dressed up, white gowns, satins, flowers,
fans, and gold ornaments, all form a part of the glitter of the
evening, and all, too, amidst as great, and perhaps as graceful
a profusion of compliments and love-making as takes place in
the most privileged ball-rooms. Yet it is twenty to one that
nine out of ten persons in the room have dirty stockings on,
and shoes out at heel. Nobody thinks of saving up articles
of that description; and they are too useful, and not showy
enough, to be cared for *en passant*. Therefore Italian girls
may often enough be well compared to flowers; with head
and bodies all ornament, their feet are in the earth; and thus
they go nodding forth for sale, " growing, blowing, and all
alive." A foolish English servant whom we brought out with
us, fell into an absolute rage of jealousy at seeing my wife
give a crown of flowers to a young Italian servant, who was
going to a dance. The latter, who was of the most respectable
sort, and looked as lady-like as you please when dressed,
received the flowers with gratitude, though without surprise;
but English and Italian both were struck speechless, when, in
addition to the crown, my wife presented the latter with a
pair of her own shoes and stockings. Doubtless, they were
the triumph of the evening. Next day we heard accounts of
the beautiful dancing;—of Signor F., the English valet, open-

ing the ball with the handsome chandler's-shopkeeper, &c.; and our poor countrywoman was ready to expire.

One anti-climax more. If Italy is famous at present for any two things, it is for political uneasiness and *minestra*.* Wherever you find shops, you see baskets full of a yellow stuff, made up in long stripes like tape, and tied up in bundles. This is the main compound of *minestra*, or, to use the Neapolitan term, it is our now growing acquaintance, *maccaroni*. Much of it is naturally of a yellowish colour, but the Genoese dye it deeper with saffron. When made into a soup it is called *minestra*, and mixed sometimes with meat, sometimes with oil and butter, but always, if it is to be had, with grated cheese. An Italian, reasonably to do in the world, has no notion of eating anything plain. If he cannot have his bit of roast and boiled, and, above all, his minestra and his oil, he is thrown out of all his calculations, physical and moral. He has a great abstract respect for fasting; but he struggles hard to be relieved from it. He gets, whenever he can, what is called an "indulgence." The Genoese in particular, being but Canaanites or borderers in Italy, and accustomed to profane intercourse by their maritime situation, as well as to an heterodox appetite by their industry and sea air, are extremely restive on the subject of fasting. They make pathetic representations to the Archbishop respecting beef and pudding, and allege their health and their household economies. Fish is luckily dear. I have seen in a Genoese Gazette, an extract from the circular of the Archbishop respecting the Lent indulgencies. "The Holiness of our Lord," he says (for so the Pope is styled), "has seen with the greatest displeasure, that the ardent desire which he has always cherished, of restoring the ancient rigour of Lent, is again rendered of no effect by representations which he finds it impossible to resist." He therefore permits the inhabitants of the Archbishop's diocese to make "one meal a day of eggs and white-meats (*latticini*) during Lent; and to such persons as have really need of it, he allows the use of flesh:" but he adds, that this latter permission "leaves a heavy load on his conscience," and that he positively forbids the promiscuous use of flesh and fish. I must add, for my part, I thought the Pope had reason in this roasting of eggs.

* I used to think that *cicisbeism* was its main distinction; but young Italy insists that it is going out of fashion; and, as Italians ought to know more about the subject than I do, I shall not let certain spectacles that were shown me in their country, pretend to refute it.

As to the political uneasiness, I should have so much to say about it, if I entered upon the subject, that I dare but occasionally allude to it in this volume. It would require a book to itself. The whole of this volume, however, may be said to be about it, inasmuch as it concerns the transition state of the human mind. I shall advert again to the religious part of the subject before I conclude.

Meantime, I shall only say that Italy is a wonderful nation, always at the head of the world in some respect, great or small, and equally full of life. Division among its children is its bane; and Mazzini's was the best note that has been struck in its favour in modern times, because he struck it at Rome, in the place of the very Pope, and thus gave it the best chance of rallying under one summons. Heaven forgive the French for the shameless vanity of their interference! for it has delayed, under the most unwarrantable circumstances, what must assuredly take place before long, as far as priests and priestly government are concerned. The poor good Pope can no more keep it down, than he could tread out a volcano with his embroidered slippers.

I differ with Mazzini, inasmuch as I prefer a republic under a limited monarch, to a republic without one. It seems to me to promise better for order and refinement, and for the security, against reactions, of progression itself. Still I should have rejoiced to see his noble experiment at Rome completed: for the throne which he and his compeers occupied, and from which, in accordance with his own awful words, he had made falsehood descend,* was occupied by justice and reason, and infamous was the intervention that broke it up. But if poor, divided, and still in great measure (as far as the uneducated classes are concerned) priest-ridden Italy is not yet strong enough or worthy enough to complete an experiment so noble, then the best thing to be desired is, that the gallant king of Sardinia should succeed with his constitutional experiment, which would end in something far better than absolutism of any kind, and might ultimately crown republicanism itself with the superior grace and security, of which mention has just been made.

* "YOU ARE A LIE: DESCEND!"—*Mazzini to the Papal Power.*

CHAPTER XXII.

RETURN TO ENGLAND.

On our return from Italy to England, we travelled not by
post, but by *vettura*, that is to say, by easy stages of thirty or
forty miles a-day, in a travelling carriage; the box of which
is turned into a chaise, with a calash over it. It is drawn by
three horses, occasionally assisted by mules. We paid about
eighty-two guineas English, for which some ten of us (counting as six, because of the children,) were to be taken to
Calais; to have a breakfast and dinner every day on the road;
to be provided with five beds at night, each containing two
persons; and to rest four days during the journey, without
further expense, in whatever places and portions of time we
thought fit. Our breakfast was to consist of coffee, bread,
fruit, milk, and eggs (plenty of each), and our dinner of the
four indispensable Italian dishes, something roast, something
boiled, something fried, and what they call an *umido*, which
is a hash, or something of that sort; together with vegetables,
wine, and fruit. Care, however, must be taken in these bar-
gains, that the vetturino does not crib from the allowance by
degrees, otherwise the dishes grow fewer and smaller; meat
disappears on a religious principle, it being *magro* day, on
which " nothing is to be had;" and the vegetables, adhering
to their friend the meat in his adversity, disappear likewise.
The reason of this is, that the vetturino has two conflicting
interests within him. It is his interest to please you in hope
of other custom; and it is his interest to make the most of
the sum of money which his master allows him for expenses.
Withstand, however, any change at first, and good behaviour
may be reckoned upon. We had as pleasant a little Tuscan
to drive us as I ever met with. He began very handsomely;
but finding us willing to make the best of any little deficiency, he could not resist the temptation of giving up the
remoter interest for the nearer one. We found our profusion
diminish accordingly; and at Turin, after cunningly asking
us whether we cared to have an inn not of the very highest
description, he brought us to one, of which it could only be
said that it was not of the very lowest. The landlord showed
us into sordid rooms on a second story. I found it necessary
to be base and make a noise; upon which little Gigi looked

frightened, and the landlord became slavish, and bowed us into his best apartments. We had no more of the same treatment.

Our rogue of a driver had an excellent temper, and was as honest a rogue, I will undertake to say, as ever puzzled a formalist. He made us laugh with his resemblance to Lamb, whose countenance, a little jovialized, he engrafted upon an active little body and sturdy pair of legs, walking about in his jack-boots as if they were pumps. But a man must have some great object in life, to carry him so many times over the Alps: and this, of necessity, is money. We could have dispensed easily enough with some of the fried and roasted; but to do this would have been to subject ourselves to other diminutions. Our bargain was reckoned a good one. Gigi's master said (believe him who will) that he could not have afforded it, had he not been sure, at that time of the year, that somebody would take his coach back again ; such is the multitude of persons that come to winter in Italy.

We were told to look for a barren road from Florence to Bologna, but were agreeably disappointed. The vines, indeed, and the olives disappeared ; but this was a relief to us. Instead of these, and the comparatively petty ascents about Florence, we had proper swelling Apennines, valley and mountain, with fine sloping meadows of green, interspersed with wood.

[Starting from Maiano at an early hour on the 10th of September, 1825,] we stopped to refresh ourselves at noon at an inn called Le Maschere, where there was an elegant prospect, a mixture of nature with garden ground; and we slept at Covigliaio, where three tall buxom damsels waited upon us, who romped during supper with the men-servants. One of them had a better tone in speaking than the others, upon the strength of which she stepped about with a jaunty air in a hat and feathers, and " did the amiable." A Greek came in with a long beard, which he poked into all the rooms by way of investigation, as he could speak no language but his own. I asked one of the girls why she looked so frightened ; upon which she shrugged her shoulders and said " *Oh Dio!* " as if Bluebeard had come to put her in his seraglio.

Our vile inn knocked us up ; and we were half starved. Little Gigi, on being remonstrated with, said that he was not aware till that moment of its being part of his duty, by the agreement, to pay expenses during our days of stopping. He had not looked into the agreement till then! The rogue ! So we lectured him, and forgave him for his good temper; and he was to be very honest and expensive for the rest of the journey.

Next morning we set off at five o'clock, and passed a volcanic part of the Apennines, where a flame issues from the ground. We thought we saw it. The place is called Pietra Mala (Evil Rock). Here we enter upon the Pope's territories; as if his Holiness were to be approached by an infernal door.

We refreshed at Poggioli, in sight of a church upon a hill, called the Monte dei Formicoli (Ant Hill). Sitting outside the inn-door on a stone, while the postilion sat on another, he told us of an opinion which prevailed among travellers respecting this place. They reported, that on a certain day in the year, all the ants in the neighbourhood come to church in the middle of the service, and die during the celebration of the mass. After giving me this information, I observed him glancing at me for some time with a very serious face, after which he said abruptly, "Do you believe this report, signore?" I told him, that I was loath to differ with what he or any one else might think it proper to believe; but if he put the question to me as one to be sincerely answered—

"Oh, certainly, signore."

"Well, then, I do not believe it."

"No more," said Little Gigi, "do I."

I subsequently found my postilion very sceptical on some highly Catholic points, and he accounted for it like a philosopher. Seeing that he made no sign of reverence in passing the images of the Virgin and Child, I asked him the reason.

"Sir," said he, "I have travelled."

These were literally his words. (Ho viaggiato, signore.) He manifested, however, no disrespect for opinions on which most believers are agreed; though whenever his horses vexed him, he poured forth a series of the most blasphemous execrations which I ever heard. Indeed, I had never heard any at all resembling them; though I was told they were not uncommon with persons unquestionably devout. He abused the Divine presence in the sacrament. He execrated the body and——but I must not repeat what he said, for fear of shocking the reader and myself. Nevertheless, I believe he did it all in positive innocence and want of thought, repeating the words as mere words which he heard from others all his life, and to which he attached none of the ideas which they expressed. When a person d—ns another in English, he has no real notion of what he condemns him to ; and I believe our postilion had as little when he devoted the objects of his worship to malediction. He was very kind to the children, and took leave of us at the end of our journey in tears.

The same evening we got to Bologna, where we finished for the present with mountains. The best streets in Bologna are furnished with arcades, very sensible things, which we are surprised to miss in any city in a hot country. They are to be found, more or less, as you travel northwards. The houses were all kept in good-looking order, owing, I believe, to a passion which the Bolognese have for a gorgeous anniversary, against which everything, animate and inanimate, puts on its best. I could not learn what it was. Besides tapestry and flowers, they bring out their pictures to hang in front of the houses. Many cities in Italy disappoint the eye of the traveller. The stucco and plaster outside the houses get worn, and, together with the open windows, gives them a squalid and deserted appearance. But the name is always something. If Bologna were nothing of a city, it would still be a fine sound and a sentiment; a thing recorded in art, in poetry, in stories of all sorts.

We passed next day over a flat country, and dined at Modena, which is neither so good-looking a city, nor so well sounding a recollection, as Bologna; but it is still Modena, the native place of Tassoni. I went to the cathedral to get sight of the *Bucket* (La Secchia) which is hung up there, but found the doors shut, and a very ugly pile of building. The lions before the doors looked as if some giant's children had made them in sport; wretchedly sculptured, and gaped as if in agony at their bad legs. It was a disappointment to me not to see the Bucket. The poem called the *Rape of the Bucket* (La Secchia Rapita), next to Metastasio's address to Venus, is my oldest Italian acquaintance ; and I reckoned upon saying to the subject of it, " Ha, ha ! There you are ! " Pope imitated the title of this poem in his *Rape of the Lock ;* and Dryden confessed to a young critic, that he himself knew the poem, and had made use of it. The bucket was a trophy taken by the Modenese from their rivals of Bologna, during one of the petty Italian wars.

There is something provoking, and yet something fine too, in flitting in this manner from city to city. You are vexed at not being able to stop and see pictures, &c. ; but you have a sort of royal taste of great pleasures in passing. The best

thing one can do to get at the interior of anything in this
hurry, is to watch the countenances of the people. I thought
that the aspects of the Bolognese and Modenese people singularly answered to their character in books. What is more
singular, is the extraordinary difference and nationality of
aspect in the people of two cities, at so little distance from
one another. The Bolognese have a broad steady look, not
without geniality and richness. You can imagine them to
give birth to painters. The Modenese are crusty-looking and
carking, with a narrow mouth, and a dry twinkle at the corner
of the eyes. They are critics and satirists on the face of them.
For my part, I never took very kindly to Tassoni, for all my
young acquaintance with him ; and in the war which he has
celebrated, I was henceforward, whatever I was before, de-
cidedly for the Bolognese.

On the 12th of September, after dining at Modena, we slept
at Reggio, where Ariosto was born. His father was captain
of the citadel. Boiardo, the poet's worthy precursor (in some
respects, I think, his surpasser), was born at Scandiano, not
far off. I ran, before the gates were shut, to get a look at the
citadel, and was much the better for not missing it. Poets
leave a greater charm than any men upon places they have
rendered famous, because they sympathise more than any other
men with localities, and identify themselves with the least
beauty of art or nature—a turret or an old tree. The river
Ilissus at Athens is found to be a sorry brook ; but it runs
talking for ever of Plato and Sophocles.

At Parma I tore my hair mentally at not being able to see
the Correggios. Piacenza pleased us to be in it, on account of
the name ; but a list of places in Italy is always like a set of
musical tones. Parma, Piacènza, Voghèra, Tortòna, Felizàna,
—sounds like these convert a road-book into a music-book.

At Asti, a pretty place, with a " west-end" full of fine
houses, I went to look at the Alfieri palace, and tried to remember the poet with pleasure ; but I could not like him.
To me, his austerity is only real in the unpleasantest part of
it. The rest seems affected. The human heart in his hands
is a tough business ; and he thumps and turns it about in his
short, violent, and pounding manner, as if it were an iron on
a blacksmith's anvil. Alfieri loved liberty like a tyrant, and
the Pretender's widow like a slave.

The first sight of the Po, of the mulberry-trees, the meadows, and the Alps, was at once classical, and Italian, and

northern. It made us feel that we were taking a great step nearer home. Poirino, a pretty little place, presented us with a sight like a passage in Boccaccio. This was a set of Dominican friars, with the chief at their head, issuing out of two coaches, and proceeding along the corridor of the inn to dinner, each holding a bottle of wine in his hand, with the exception of the abbot, who held two. The wine was doubtless their own, that upon the road not being sufficiently orthodox.

Turin is a noble city, like a set of Regent-streets, made twice as tall. We found here some of the most military-looking officers we ever saw, fine, tall, handsome fellows, whom the weather had beaten but not conquered, very gentlemanly, and combining the officer and soldier as completely as could be wished. They had served under Bonaparte. When I saw them, I could understand how it was that a Piedmontese revolution was more dreaded by the legitimates than any other movement in Italy. The one concocted at that time was betrayed by the heir-apparent, then Prince of Carignan, who undertook to make amends by his heading another, as King Charles Albert. A second was lost not long ago. Suspicion still clung to him during the vicissitudes of the war ; but a death, looking very much like a broken heart, appears to have restored his memory to respect, and his son has made great and promising moves in the right direction.*

* [In this passage there is a very grave mistake, and none the less serious for being apparently countenanced by so conscientious a writer. The allusion to a betrayal of a liberal movement by Charles Albert in his youth, is based on an entirely false report. Charles Albert had joined the party of the Carbonari, and had suddenly withdrawn from them, but it was on grounds frankly stated, consistent with his own professions, and with the avowedly monarchical principles of the present volume. The Carbonari originally formed their combination to free their race from tyranny, and to restore Italy to the Italians. Charles Albert went with them; but when they enlarged their project and planned the establishment of a republic, he declared that he could not adopt republican principles, and he withdrew from the movement. The movement was defeated, but there is not the slightest evidence that Charles Albert, by deed or word, suggestion or silence, ever betrayed his former comrades. He afterwards endured great trouble of mind and sickness of body from the disappointment of his hopes, and, it is understood, doubts whether he was perfectly justified in opposing the Church. When opportunity again offered itself, Charles Albert again stood forward, and staked his throne in the national cause. When he found that his presence embarrassed the endeavours of the constitutional party, he spontaneously surrendered his throne, and doomed himself to die in exile, leaving his son, his companion in the field and in council, to carry on the enter-

At Turin was the finest dancer I had ever seen, a girl of the name of De' Martini. She united the agility of the French school with all that you would expect from the Italian. Italian dancers are in general as mediocre as the French are celebrated ; but the French dancers, in spite of their high notions of the art and the severity of their studies (perhaps that is the reason), have no mind with their bodies. They are busts in barbers' shops, stuck upon legs full of vivacity. You wonder how any lower extremities so lively can leave such an absence of all expression in the upper. De' Martini was a dancer all over. Her countenance partook of the felicity of the limbs. When she came bounding on the stage, in two or three long leaps like a fawn, I should have thought she was a Frenchwoman ; but the style undeceived me. She came bounding in front, as if she would have pitched herself into the arms of the pit ; then made a sudden drop, and addressed three enthusiastic courtesies to the pit and boxes, with a rapidity and yet a grace, a self-abandonment yet a self-possession, quite extraordinary, and such as, to do justice to it, should be described by a poet combining the western ideas of the sex with eastern licence. She was beautiful, too, both in face and figure, and I thought was a proper dancer to appear before a pit full of those fine fellows I have just mentioned. She seemed as complete in her way as themselves. In short, I never saw anything like it before, and did not wonder that she had the reputation of turning peoples' heads wherever she went.

At Sant' Ambrogio, a little town between Turin and Susa, is a proper castle-topped mountain *à la Radcliffe*, the only one we had met with. Susa has some remains connected with Augustus ; but Augustus is nobody, or ought to be nobody, to a traveller in modern Italy. He, and twenty like him, never gave me one sensation all the time I was there ; and even the better part of the Romans it is difficult to think of. There is something formal and cold about their history, in spite of Virgil and Horace, and even in spite of their own violence, which does not harmonize with the south. They are men in northern iron, and their poets, even the best of them, were copiers of the Greek poets, not originals, like

prise with happier auspices. Charles Albert proved at once the bitterness of the sacrifice which he voluntarily incurred and his devotion to Italy, by ordering on his deathbed that his heart should be carried back to the beloved land.]

Dante and Petrarch. So we slept at Susa, not thinking of Augustus, but listening to waterfalls, and thinking of the Alps.

Next morning we beheld a sight worth living for. We were now ascending the Alps; and while yet in the darkness before dawn, we beheld the top of one of the mountains basking in the sunshine. We took it with delighted reverence into our souls, and there it is for ever. The passage of the Alps (thanks to Bonaparte, whom a mountaineer, with brightness in his eyes, called "Napoleon of happy memory,"—*Napoleone di felice memoria*) is now as easy as a road in England. You look up towards airy galleries and down upon villages that appear like toys, and feel somewhat disappointed at rolling over it all so easily.

The moment we passed the Alps, we found ourselves in France. At Lanslebourg, French was spoken, and amorous groups gesticulated on the papering and curtains. Savoy is a glorious country, a wonderful intermixture of savage precipices and pastoral meads; but the roads are still uneven and bad. The river ran and tumbled, as if in a race with our tumbling carriage. At one time you are in a road like a gigantic rut, deep down in a valley; and at another, up in the air, wheeling along a precipice I know not how many times as high as St. Paul's.

At Chambéry, I could not resist going to see the house of Rousseau and Madame de Warens, while the coach stopped. It is up a beautiful lane, where you have trees all the way, sloping fields, and a brook; as fit a scene as could be desired. I met some Germans coming away, who congratulated me on being bound, as they had been, to the house of " Jean Jacques." The house itself is of the humbler genteel class, but neat and white, with green blinds. The little chapel, that cost its mistress so much, is still remaining.

We proceeded, through Lyons and Auxerre, to Paris. Beyond Lyons, we met on the road the statue of Louis XIV. going to that city to overawe it with Bourbon memories. It was an equestrian statue, covered up, guarded with soldiers, and looking on that road like some mysterious heap. Don Quixote would have attacked it, and not been thought mad: so much has romance done for us. The natives would infallibly have looked quietly on. There was a riot about it at Lyons, soon after its arrival. I had bought in that city a volume of the songs of Béranger, and I thought to myself, as I met the statue, " I have a little book in my pocket, which will not suffer you to last long." And, surely enough, down it went; for down went King Charles.

Statues rise and fall; but, a little on the other side of Lyons, our postilion exclaimed, "Monte Bianco!" and turning round, I beheld, for the first time, Mont Blanc, which had been hidden from us, when near it, by a fog. It looked like a turret in the sky, amber-coloured, golden, belonging to the wall of some ethereal world. This, too, is in our memories for ever,—an addition to our stock,—a light for memory to turn to, when it wishes a beam upon its face.

At Paris we could stop but two days, and I had but two thoughts in my head; one of the Revolution, the other of the times of Molière and Boileau. Accordingly I looked about for the Sorbonne, and went to see the place where the guillotine stood;—the place where thousands of spirits underwent the last pang of mortality; many guilty, many innocent, but all the victims of a re-action against tyranny, such as will never let tyranny be what it was, unless a convulsion of nature should swallow up knowledge, and make the world begin over again. These are the thoughts that enable us to bear such sights, and that serve to secure what we hope for.

Paris, besides being a beautiful city in the quarter that strangers most look to, the Tuileries, Quai de Voltaire, &c., delights the eye of a man of letters by the multitude of its book-stalls. There seemed to be a want of old books; but the new were better than the shoal of *Missals* and *Lives of the Saints* that disappoint the lover of duodecimos on the stalls of Italy; and the Rousseaus and Voltaires were endless. I thought, if I were a bachelor, not an Englishman, and had no love for old friends and fields, and no decided religious opinions, I could live very well, for the rest of my life, in a lodging above one of the bookseller's shops on the Quai de Voltaire, where I should look over the water to the Tuileries, and have the Elysian fields in my eye for my evening walk.

I liked much what little I saw of the French people. They are accused of vanity; and doubtless they have it, and after a more obvious fashion than other nations; but their vanity, at least, includes the wish to please; other people are necessary to them; they are not wrapped up in themselves; not sulky; not too vain even to tolerate vanity. Their vanity is too much confounded with self-satisfaction. There is a good deal of touchiness, I suspect, among them—a good deal of ready-made heat, prepared to fire up in case the little commerce of flattery and sweetness is not properly carried on. But this is better than ill-temper, or than such egotism as is not to be appeased by anything short of subjection. On the other hand, there is more melancholy than one could expect, especially in old faces. Consciences in the south are frightened in their old age, perhaps for nothing. In the north, I suspect, they are frightened earlier, perhaps from equal want of knowledge. The worst in France is (at least, from all that I saw), that *fine* old faces are rare. There are multitudes of pretty girls; but the faces of both sexes fall off deplorably as they advance in life; which is not a good symptom. Nor do the pretty faces, while they last, appear to contain much depth, or sentiment, or firmness of purpose. They seem made like their toys, not to last, but to break up.

Fine faces in Italy are as abundant as cypresses. However, in both countries, the inhabitants appeared to us amiable, as well as intelligent; and without disparagement to the angel faces which you meet with in England, and some of which are perhaps finer than any you see anywhere else, I could not help thinking, that, as a race of females, the countenances both of the French and Italian women announced more pleasantness and reasonableness of intercourse, than those of my fair and serious countrywomen. The Frenchwoman looked as if she wished to please you at any rate, and to be pleased herself. She is too conscious; and her coquetry is said, and I believe with truth, to promise more than an Englishman would easily find her to perform : but at any rate she thinks of you somehow, and is smiling and good-humoured. An Italian woman appears to think of nothing, not even of herself. Existence seems enough for her. But she also is easy of intercourse, smiling when you speak to her, and very unaffected. Now, in simplicity of character the Italian appears to me to have the advantage of the English women, and in pleasantness of intercourse both Italian and French. When I came to England, after a residence of four years abroad, I was grieved at the succession of fair sulky faces which I met in the streets of London. They all appeared to come out of unhappy homes. In truth, our virtues, or our climate, or whatever it is, sit so uneasily upon us, that it is surely worth while for our philosophy to inquire whether, in some points of moral and political economy, we are not a little mistaken. Gipsies will hardly allow us to lay it to the climate.

It was a blessed moment, nevertheless, when we found our-

selves among those dear sulky faces, the countrywomen of
dearer ones, not sulky.   We set out from Calais in the steam-
boat, which carried us to London, energetically trembling all
the way under us, as if its burning body partook of the
fervour of our desire; [arriving on the 14th of October.]
Here (thought we), in the neighbourhood of London, we are;
and may we never be without our old fields again in this
world, or the old "familiar faces" in this world or in the
next.

CHAPTER XXIII.

AT HOME IN ENGLAND.

On returning to England, we lived a while at Highgate, where
I took possession of my old English scenery and my favourite
haunts, with a delight proportionate to the difference of their
beauty from that of beautiful Italy. For a true lover of nature
does not require the contrast of good and bad in order to be
delighted; he is better pleased with harmonious variety. He
is content to wander from beauty to beauty, not losing his
love for the one because he loves the other. A variation on
a fine theme of music is better still than a good song after a
bad one. It retains none of the bitterness of fault-finding.

I used to think in Italy that I was tired of vines and olives,
and the sharp outlines of things against indigo skies; and so
I was; but it was from old love, and not from new hatred.
I humoured my dislike because I knew it was ill-founded.   I
always loved the scenery at heart, as the cousin-german of all
other lovely scenery, especially of that which delighted me in
books.

But in England I was at home; and in English scenery I
found my old friend "pastoral" still more pastoral.   It was
like a breakfast of milk and cream after yesterday's wine.
The word itself was more verified : for pastoral comes from
pasture; it implies cattle feeding, rather than vines growing,
or even goats browsing on their tops; and here they were in
plenty, very different from the stall-fed and rarely seen cattle
of Tuscany.   The country around was almost all pasture;
and beloved Hampstead was near, with home in its church-

yard as well as in its meadows. Again I wandered with transport through

> " Each alley green,
> And every bosky bourn from side to side,—
> My daily walks and ancient neighbourhood."

Only for " bosky bourn" you must read the ponds in which Shelley used to sail his boats, and very little brooks unknown to all but the eyes of their lovers. The walk across the fields from Highgate to Hampstead, with ponds on one side, and Caen Wood on the other, used to be (and I hope is still, for I have not seen it for some years) one of the prettiest of England. *Poets'* (vulgarly called Millfield) *Lane* crossed it on the side next Highgate, at the foot of a beautiful slope, which in June was covered with daisies and buttercups; and at the other end it descended charmingly into the Vale of Health, out of which rose the highest ground in Hampstead. It was in this spot, and in relation to it and about this time (if I may quote my own verses in illustration of what I felt), that I wrote some lines to " Gipsy June," apostrophizing that brown and happy month on the delights which I found again in my native country, and on the wrongs done him by the pretension of the month of May.

*   *   *   *   *

> " May, the jade, with her fresh cheek,
> And the love the bards bespeak,—
> May, by coming first in sight,
> Half defrauds thee of thy right,
> For her best is shared by thee
> With a wealthier potency;
> So that thou dost bring us in
> A sort of May-time masculine,
> Fit for action or for rest,
> As the luxury seems the best,—
> Bearding now the morning breeze,
> Or in love with paths of trees,
> Or disposed full length to lie,
> With a hand-enshaded eye,
> On thy warm and golden slopes,
> Basker in the buttercups,
> List'ning with nice distant ears
> To the shepherd's clapping shears,
> Or the next field's laughing play
> In the happy wars of hay,
> While its perfume breathes all over,
> Or the bean comes fine, or clover.

" Oh! could I walk round the earth
    With a heart to share my mirth,
    With a look to love me ever,
    Thoughtful much, but sullen never,
    I could be content to see
    June and no variety,
    Loitering here, and living there,
    With a book and frugal fare,
    With a finer gipsy time,
    And a cuckoo in the clime,
    Work at morn and mirth at noon,
    And sleep beneath the sacred moon."

No offence, nevertheless, as John Buncle would have said,
to the " stationary domesticities." For fancy takes old habits
along with it in new shapes; domesticity itself can travel;
and I never desired any better heaven, in this world or the
next, than the old earth of my acquaintance put in its finest
condition, my own nature being improved, of course, along
with it. I have often envied the household waggon that one
meets with in sequestered lanes—a cottage on wheels—moving whithersoever it pleases, and halting for as long a time as
may suit it. So, at least, one fancies; ignoring all about
parish objections, inconvenient neighbourhoods, and want of
harmony in the vehicle itself. The pleasantest idea which I
can conceive of this world, as far as oneself and one's enjoyments are concerned, is to possess some favourite home in
one's native country, and then travel over all the rest of the
globe with those whom we love; always being able to return,
if we please; and ever meeting with new objects, as long as
we choose to stay away. And I suppose this is what the inhabitants of the world will come to, when they have arrived
at years of discretion, and railroads will have hastened the
maturity.*

I seemed more at home in England, even with Arcadian
idealisms, than I had been in the land nearer their birth-place;
for it was in England I first found them in books, and with
England even my Italian books were more associated than

* " There is a flock of pigeons at Maiano, which, as they go careering
in and out among the olive-trees, look like the gentle spirits of the
Decameron again assembled in another shape. Alas! admire all this
as I may, and thankful as I am, I would quit it all for a walk over
the fields from Hampstead, to one or two houses I could mention.
My imagination can travel a good way; but, like the Tartar, it must
carry its tents along with it. New pleasures must have old warrants.
I can gain much, but I can afford to lose nothing,"—Notes to *Bacchus
in Tuscany*, p. 174.

with Italy itself. When in prison, I had bought the collection of poetry called the *Parnaso Italiano*, a work in fifty-six duodecimo volumes, adorned with vignettes. The bookseller, by the way, charged me thirty pounds for it; though I could have got it, had I been wise, for a third part of the sum, albeit it was neatly bound. But I thought it cheap; and joyfully got rid of my thirty pounds for such a southern treasure; which, I must own, has repaid me a million times over, in the pleasure I have received from it. In prison it was truly a lump of sunshine on my shelves; and I have never since been without it. I even took it with me to its native land.

This book aided Spenser himself in filling my English walks with visions of gods and nymphs—of enchantresses and magicians; for the reader might be surprised to know to what a literal extent such was the case. I suspect I had far more sights of " Proteus coming from the sea," than Mr. Wordsworth himself; for he desired them only in despair of getting anything better out of the matter-of-fact state of the world about him; whereas, the world had never been able to deprive me, either of the best hopes for itself, or of any kind of vision, sacred or profane, which I thought suitable to heaven or earth. I saw fairies in every wood, as I did the advent of a nobler Christianity in the churches; and by the help of the beautiful universality which books had taught me, I found those two classes of things not less compatible than Chaucer and Boccaccio did, when they talked of " Holy Ovid," and invoked the saints and the gods in the same exordium. I found even a respectful corner in my imagination for those poetical grown children in Italy, who (literally) played at " Arcadians " in gardens made for the purpose, and assumed names from imaginary farms in old Greece. The " bays" upon poets' heads in old books had prepared me, when a boy, to like that image of literary success. I had myself played at it in dedications and household pastimes; and the names of Filicaia, Menzini, Guidi, and other grave and classical Italian poets, who had joined the masquerade in good faith, completed my willingness not to disesteem it.

The meaning of all this is, that at the time of my life in question, I know not in which I took more delight—the actual fields and woods of my native country, the talk of such things in books, or the belief which I entertained that I should one day be joined in remembrance with those who had talked it.

I used to stroll about the meadows half the day, with a book under my arm, generally a "Parnaso" or a Spenser, and wonder that I met nobody who seemed to like the fields as I did. The jests about Londoners and Cockneys did not affect me in the least, as far as my faith was concerned. They might as well have said that Hampstead was not beautiful, or Richmond lovely; or that Chaucer and Milton were Cockneys when they went out of London to lie on the grass and look at the daisies. The Cockney school of poetry is the most illustrious in England; for, to say nothing of Pope and Gray, who were both veritable Cockneys, "born within the sound of Bow Bell," Milton was so too; and Chaucer and Spenser were both natives of the city. Of the four greatest English poets, Shakspeare only was not a Londoner.

But the charge of Cockneyism frightened the booksellers. I could never understand till this moment, what it was, for instance, that made the editor of a magazine reject an article which I wrote, with the mock-heroical title of *The Graces and Anxieties of Pig Driving.* I used to think he found something vulgar in the title. He declared that it was not he who rejected it, but the proprietor of the magazine. The proprietor, on the other hand, declared that it was not he who rejected it, but the editor. I published it in a magazine of my own, the *Companion,* and found it hailed as one of my best pieces of writing. But the subject was a man inducting a pig into Smithfield through the intricacies of Cockney lanes and alleys; and the names of Smithfield, and Barbican, and Bell-alley, and Ducking Pond-row, were not to be ventured in the teeth of my friends the Tories under the signature of the quondam editor of the *Examiner.* I subsequently wrote a fictitious autobiography, of which I shall speak presently, under the title of *Sir Ralph Esher.* It was republished the other day with my name to it for the first time. The publisher in those days of Toryism and Tory jesting would not venture to print it. I was at length irritated by misrepresentations on the subject of Lord Byron to publish some autobiographical accounts of myself, and a refutation of matters relating to his lordship; and to this book, for obvious reasons, my name was suffered to be attached; but this only made matters worse; and it is inconceivable to what extent I suffered, in mind, body, and estate, because the tide of affairs was against me, and because the public (which is not the best trait in their character) are inclined to believe whatever is said of a man by the prosperous. I have since been lauded to the skies, on no other account, for productions which at that period fell dead from the press. People have thought I wrote them yesterday; and I have sometimes been at once mystified and relieved, to observe who the persons were that have so praised them, and what they have omitted to notice for no better reason. It is said, and I believe truly, that no man in the long run can be written down, or up, except by himself; but it is painful to think how much can be done to both purposes in the meantime, and for those who deserve neither the one nor the other. A secret history of criticism, for some twenty years at a time, with its favouritisms, its animosities, and its hesitations, would make a very curious book; but the subject would be so disagreeable, that it would require almost as disagreeable a person to write it.

But adieu to records of this kind for ever. It is not possible for many persons to have had greater friends than I have. I am not aware that I have now a single enemy; and I accept the fortunes which have occurred to me, bad and good, with the same disposition to believe them the best that could have happened, whether for the correction of what was wrong in me, or the improvement of what was right.

I struggled successfully with this state of things, as long as their causes lasted. It was not till Toryism began its declension with the rise of Louis Philippe, and the small stock of readers who never left me was increasing, that the consequences of what I had battled with, forced me almost to drop the pen for some years. I had never lost cheerfulness of tone, for I had never ceased to be cheerful in my opinions. I had now reason to be more hopeful than ever; but the wounds resulting from a long conflict, my old ignorance of business, and that very tendency to reap pleasure from every object in creation, which at once reconciled me to loss, retained me my few readers, and hindered me from competing with the more prudential lessons of writers who addressed the then state of society, conspired to set me at the mercy of wants and creditors. The ailment from which I suffered in Italy returned with double force; and I know not what would have happened to me for some time, short of what temperance and my opinions rendered impossible, if friends, with a delicacy as well as generosity which I have never been able to thank sufficiently to this day (for the names of some with whom I was not conversant eluded my gratitude) had not supplied the defects of fortune. Ought I to blush for stating my obligations thus publicly ? I do, if it be held fit that I should; for I am loth not to do what is expected of me, even by a respectable prejudice, when it is on the side of delicacy and self-respect. But far more, I conceive, should I have reason to blush, and upon those very accounts, first, if I could not dare to distinguish between an ordinary and an exceptional case; and secondly, and most of all, if I could not subordinate a prejudice, however respectable, to the first principles of social esteem, and justify by my gratitude the sympathies which my writings had excited.

The little periodical work to which I have alluded—the *Companion*—consisted partly of criticisms on theatres, authors, and public events, and partly of a series of essays in the manner of the *Indicator*. Some of the essays have since accompanied the republications of that older work. They contained some of what afterwards turned out to be my most popular writing. But I had no money to advertise the publication; it did not address itself to any existing influence; and in little more than half a year I was forced to bring it to a conclusion.

The *Companion* was written at Highgate; but the opening of the court scenes in *Sir Ralph Esher* was suggested by the locality of Epsom, to which place we had removed, and which saw the termination of what it had commenced.

Those who are not acquainted with the work, may be told that it is the fictitious autobiography of a gentleman of the court of Charles the Second, including the adventures of another, and notices of Cromwell, the Puritans, and the Catholics. It was given to the world anonymously, and, notwithstanding my wishes to the contrary, as a novel; but the publisher pleaded hard for the desirableness of so doing; and as he was a good-natured man, and had liberally enabled me to come from Italy, I could not say Nay. It is not destitute of adventure; and I took a world of pains to make it true to the times which it pictured; but whatever interest it may possess is so entirely owing, I conceive, to a certain reflecting exhibition of character, and to fac-simile imitations of the courts of Charles and Cromwell, that I can never present it to my mind in any other light than that of a veritable set of memoirs.

The reader may judge of the circumstances under which authors sometimes write, when I tell him that the publisher had entered into no regular agreement respecting this work; that he could decline receiving any more of it whenever it might please him to do so; that I had nothing else at the time to depend on for my family; that I was in very bad health, never writing a page that did not put my nerves into a state of excessive sensibility, starting at every sound; and that whenever I sent the copy up to London for payment, which I did every Saturday, I always expected, till I got a good way into the work, that he would send me word he had had enough. I waxed and waned in spirits accordingly, as the weeks opened and terminated; now being as full of them as my hero Sir Ralph, and now as much otherwise as his friend Sir Philip Herne; and these two extremes of mirth and melancholy, and the analogous thoughts which they fed, made a strange kind of harmony with the characters themselves; which characters, by the way, were wholly fictitious, and probably suggested by the circumstance. Merry or melancholy, my nerves equally suffered by the tensity occasioned them in composition. I could never (and I seldom ever could, or can) write a few hundred words without a certain degree of emotion, which in a little while suspends the breath, then produces a flushing in the face, and, if persevered in, makes me wake up, when I have finished, in a sort of surprise at the objects around me, and a necessity of composing myself by patience and exercise. When the health is at its worst, a dread is thus apt to be produced at the idea of recommencing; and work is delayed, only to aggravate the result. I have often tried, and sometimes been forced to write only a very little while at a time, and so escape the accumulation of excitement; but it is very difficult to do this; for you forget the intention in the excitement itself; and when you call it to mind, you continue writing, in the hope of concluding the task for the day. A few months ago, when I had occasion to look at *Sir Ralph Esher* again, after some lapse of time, I was not a little pleased to find how glibly and at their ease the words appeared to run on, as though I had suffered no more in writing it than Sir Ralph himself. But thus it is with authors who are in earnest. The propriety of what they are saying becomes a matter of as much nervous interest to them, as any other exciting cause; and I believe, that if a writer of this kind were summoned away from his work to be taken to the scaffold, he would not willingly leave his last sentence in erroneous condition.

The reader may be surprised to hear, after these remarks, that what I write with the greatest composure is verses. He may smile, and say that he does not wonder, since the more art the less nature, or the more artificiality the less earnestness. But it is not that; it is that I write verses only when I most like to write; that I write them slowly, with loving recurrence, and that the musical form is a perpetual solace and refreshment. The earnestness is not the less. In one respect it is greater, for it is more concentrated. It is forced, by a sweet necessity, to say more things in less compass. But then the necessity *is* sweet. The mode, and the sense of being able to meet its requirements, in however comparative a degree, are more than a sustainment: they are a charm. This is the reason why poetry, not of the highest order, is sometimes found so acceptable. The author feels so much happiness in his task, that he cannot but convey happiness to his reader.

CHAPTER XXIV.

LITERARY PROJECTS.

WE left Epsom to return to the neighbourhood of London, which was ever the natural abiding-place of men of letters, till railroads enlarged their bounds. We found a house in a sequestered corner of Old Brompton, and a landlord in the person of my friend Charles Knight, with whom an intercourse commenced, which I believe has been a pleasure on both sides. I am sure it has been a good to myself. If I had not a reverence of a peculiar sort for the inevitable past, I could wish that I had begun writing for Mr. Knight immediately, instead of attempting to set up another periodical work of my own, without either means to promulgate it, or health to render the failure of little consequence. I speak of a literary and theatrical paper called the *Tatler*, set up in 1830. It was a very little work, consisting but of four folio pages; but it was a daily publication: I did it all myself, except when too ill; and illness seldom hindered me either from supplying the review of a book, going every night to the play, or writing the notice of the play the same night at the printing-office. The consequence was, that the work, slight as it looked, nearly killed me; for it never prospered beyond the coterie of playgoing readers, to whom it was almost exclusively known; and I was sensible of becoming weaker and poorer every day. When I came home at night, often at morning, I used to feel as if I could hardly speak; and for a year and a half afterwards, a certain grain of fatigue seemed to pervade my limbs, which I thought would never go off. Such, nevertheless, is a habit of the mind, if it but be cultivated, that my spirits never seemed better, nor did I ever write theatricals so well, as in the pages of this most unremunerating speculation.

I had attempted, just before, to set up a little work called *Chat of the Week;* which was to talk, without scandal, of anything worth public notice. The Government put a stop to this speculation by insisting that it should have a stamp; which I could not afford. I was very angry, and tilted against governments, and aristocracies, and kings and princes in general; always excepting King William, for whom I had regard as a reformer, and Louis Philippe, whom I fancied to be a philosopher. I also got out of patience with my old antagonists the Tories, to whom I resolved to give as good as they brought; and I did so, and stopped every new assailant. A daily paper, however small, is a weapon that gives an immense advantage; you can make your attacks in it so often. However, I always ceased as soon as my antagonists did.

In a year or two after the cessation of the *Tatler* [*i. e.* in 1833], my collected verses were published by subscription; and as a reaction by this time had taken place in favour of political and other progress, and the honest portion of its opponents had not been unwilling to discover the honesty of those with whom they differed, a very handsome list of subscribers appeared in the *Times* newspaper, comprising names of all shades of opinion, some of my sharpest personal antagonists not excepted.

In this edition of my *Poetical Works* is to be found the only printed copy of a poem, the title of which (*The Gentle Armour*) has been a puzzle for guessers. It originated in curious notions of delicacy. The poem is founded on one of the French *fabliaux, Les Trois Chevaliers et la Chemise.* It is the story of a knight, who, to free himself from the imputation of cowardice, fights against three other knights in no stouter armour than a lady's garment thus indicated. The late Mr. Way, who first introduced the story to the British public, and who was as respectable and conventional a gentleman, I believe, in every point of view, as could be desired, had no hesitation, some years ago, in rendering the French title of the poem by its (then) corresponding English words, *The Three Knights and the Smock;* but so rapid are the changes that take place in people's notions of what is decorous, that not only has the word " smock" (of which it was impossible to see the indelicacy, till people were determined to find it) been displaced since that time by the word " shift ;" but even that harmless expression for the act of changing one garment for another, has been set aside in favour of the French word " chemise ;" and at length not even this word, it seems, is to be mentioned, nor the garment itself alluded to, by any decent writer! Such, at least, appears to have been the dictum of some customer, or customers, of the bookseller who published the poem. The title was altered to please these gentlemen ; and in a subsequent edition of the Works, the poem itself was withdrawn from their virgin eyes.

The terrible original title was the *Battle of the Shift;* and a more truly delicate story, I will venture to affirm, never was written. Charles Lamb thought the new title unworthy of its refinement, " because it seemed ashamed of the right one." He preferred the honest old word. But this was the author of *Rosamond Gray.*

We had found that the clay soil of St. John's Wood did not agree with us. Or, perhaps, it was only the melancholy state of our fortune : for the New Road, to which we again returned, agreed with us as little. It was there that I thought I should have died, in consequence of the long fatigue which succeeded the working of the *Tatler.*

While in this quarter I received an invitation to write in the new evening paper called *The True Sun.* I did so; but nothing of what I wrote has survived, I believe ; nor can I meet with the paper anywhere, to ascertain. Perhaps an essay or two originated in its pages, to which I cannot trace it. I was obliged for some time to be carried every morning to the *True Sun* office in a hackney-coach. I there became intimate with Laman Blanchard, whose death [about ten years back] was such a grief and astonishment to his friends. They had associated anything but such end with his witty, joyous, loving, and beloved nature. But the watch was over-wound, and it ran suddenly down. What bright eyes he had ! and what a kindly smile ! How happy he looked when he thought you were happy; or when he was admiring somebody ; or relating some happy story! If suicide, bad as it often is, and full of recklessness and resentment, had not been rescued from indiscriminate opprobrium, Laman Blanchard alone should have rescued it. I never think of him without feeling additional scorn for the hell of the scorner Dante, who has put all suicides into his truly infernal regions, both those who were unjust to others, and those who were unjust only to themselves.*

From the noise and dust of the New Road, my family removed to a corner in Chelsea, where the air of the neighbouring river was so refreshing, and the quiet of the "no-thoroughfare" so full of repose, that although our fortunes were at their worst, and my health almost of a piece with them, I felt for some weeks as if I could sit still for ever, embalmed in the silence. I got to like the very cries in the street, for making me the more aware of it by the contrast. I fancied they were unlike the cries in other quarters of the suburbs, and that they retained something of the old quaintness and melodiousness which procured them the reputation of having been composed by Purcell and others. Nor is this unlikely, when it is considered how fond those masters were of sporting with their art, and setting the most trivial words to music in their glees and catches. The primitive cries of cowslips, primroses, and hot cross-buns seemed never to have quitted this sequestered region. They were like daisies in a bit of surviving field. There was an old seller of fish, in particular, whose cry of "shrimps as large as prawns," was such a regular, long-drawn, and truly pleasing melody, that in spite of his hoarse and, I am afraid, drunken voice, I used to wish for it of an evening, and hail it when it came. It lasted for some years; then faded, and went out; I suppose, with the poor old weather-beaten fellow's existence.

This sense of quiet and repose may have been increased by an early association of Chelsea with something out of the pale; nay, remote. It may seem strange to hear a man who has crossed the Alps talk of one suburb as being remote from another. But the sense of distance is not in space only; it is in difference and discontinuance. A little back-room in a street in London is farther removed from the noise, than a front room in a country town. In childhood, the farthest local point which I reached anywhere, provided it was quiet,

* See the speech of the good Piero delle Vigne, who was driven to kill himself by the envy of those that hated him for fidelity to his master.—*Inferno*, canto xiii.

always seemed to me a sort of end of the world; and I remembered particularly feeling this, the only time when I had previously visited Chelsea, which was at that period of life. So the green rails of the gardens in Paddington seemed as remote as if they were a thousand miles off. They represented all green rails and all gardens, at whatever distance. I have a lively recollection, when a little boy, of having been with my mother one day walking out by Mile End, where there was a mound covering the remains of people who died in the Plague. The weather had been rainy; and there was a heavy mud in the road, rich with the colour of brown (I suppose Mr. West had put his thought in my head of finding colour in mud. Whoever it was, he did me a great deal of good). I remember to the present day looking at this rich mud colour and admiring it, and seeing the great broad wheels of some waggons go through it, and thinking awfully of the mound, and the plague, and the dead people; always feeling at the same time the delight of being abroad with my mother, with whom I could have walked through any peril, to say nothing of so many strange satisfactions. Now, this region also looked the remotest in the world. Even the name of " Mile End " had to do with the impression; for it seemed to be, not the end of one mile, but of many; the end of miles in general; of *all* miles. Measurement itself terminated at that spot. What there was beyond it, I did not conjecture.

I know not whether the corner I speak of remains as quiet as it was. I am afraid not; for steamboats have carried vicissitude into Chelsea, and Belgravia threatens it with her mighty advent. But to complete my sense of repose and distance, the house was of that old-fashioned sort which I have always loved best, familiar to the eyes of my parents, and associated with childhood. It had seats in the windows, a small third room on the first floor, of which I made a *sanctum*, into which no perturbation was to enter, except to calm itself with religious and cheerful thoughts (a room thus appropriated in a house appears to me an excellent thing); and there were a few lime-trees in front, which, in their due season diffused a fragrance.

In this house we remained seven years; in the course of which, besides contributing some articles to the *Edinburgh and Westminster Reviews*, and producing a good deal of the book since called *The Town*, I set up [in 1834] the *London Journal*, endeavoured to continue the *Monthly Repository*, and wrote the poem entitled *Captain Sword and Captain Pen*, the *Legend of Florence*, and three other plays which are yet unpublished. Here, also, I became acquainted with Thomas Carlyle, one of the kindest and best, as well as most eloquent of men; though in his zeal for what is best he sometimes thinks it incumbent on him to take not the kindest tone, and in his eloquent demands of some hearty uncompromising creed on our parts, he does not quite set the example of telling us the amount of his own. Mr. Carlyle sees that there is a good deal of rough work in the operations of nature : he seems to think himself bound to consider a good deal of it devilish, after the old Covenanter fashion, in order that he may find something angelical in giving it the proper quantity of vituperation and blows; and he calls upon us to prove our energies and our benevolence by acting the part of the wind rather than the sun, of warring rather than peace-making, of frightening and forcing rather than conciliating and persuading. Others regard this view of the one thing needful, however strikingly set forth, as an old and obsolete story, fit only to be finally done with, and not worth the repetition of the old series of reactions, even for the sake of those analogies with the physical economy of the world, which, in the impulse which nature herself gives us towards progression, we are not bound to suppose everlastingly applicable to its moral and spiritual development. If mankind are destined never to arrive at years of discretion, the admonition is equally well-founded and unnecessary; for the old strifes will be continued at all events, the admonition (at best) being a part of them. And even then, I should say that the world is still a fine, rich, strenuous, beautiful, and desirable thing, always excepting the poverty that starves, and one or two other evils which on no account must we consent to suppose irremediable. But if the case be otherwise, if the hopes which nature herself has put into our hearts be something better than incitements to hopeless action, merely for the action's sake, and this beautiful planet be destined to work itself into such a condition as we feel to be the only fit condition for that beauty, then, I say, with every possible respect for my admirable friend, who can never speak but he is worth hearing, that the tale which he condescends to tell is no better than our old nursery figment of the *Black Man and the Coal-hole*, and that the growing desire of mankind for the cessation of bitterness, and for the prevalence of the sweets of gentleness and persuasion, is an evidence that the time has arrived for dropping the thorns and husks of the old sourness and austerity, and showing ourselves worthy of "the goods the gods provide us."

Mr. Carlyle's antipathy to "shams," is highly estimable and salutary. I wish Heaven may prosper his denouncements of them, wherever they exist. But the danger of the habit of denouncing—of looking at things from the antipathetic instead of the sympathetic side—is, that a man gets such a love for the pleasure and exaltation of fault-finding, as tempts him, in spite of himself, to make what he finds; till at length he is himself charged with being a "sham;" that is to say, a pretender to perceptions and virtues which he does not prove, or at best a willing confounder of what differs from modes and appearances of his own, with violations of intrinsical wisdom and goodness. Upon this principle of judgment, nature herself and the universe might be found fault with; and the sun and the stars denounced for appearing no bigger than they do, or for not confining the measure of their operation to that of the taper we read by. Mr. Carlyle adopted a peculiar semi-German style, from the desire of putting thoughts on his paper instead of words, and perhaps of saving himself some trouble in the process. I feel certain that he does it from no other motive; and I am sure he has a right to help himself to every diminution of trouble, seeing how many thoughts and feelings he undergoes. He also strikes an additional blow with the peculiarity, rouses men's attention by it, and helps his rare and powerful understanding to produce double its effect. It would be hard not to dispense with a few verbs and nominative cases, in consideration of so great a result. Yet, if we were to judge him by one of his own summary processes, and deny him the benefit of his notions of what is expedient and advisable, how could he exculpate this style, in which he denounces so many "shams," of being itself a sham? of being affected, unnecessary, and ostentatious? a jargon got up to confound pretension with performance, and reproduce endless German talk under the guise of novelty?

Thus much in behalf of us dulcet signors of philanthropy, and conceders of good intention, whom Mr. Carlyle is always girding at, and who beg leave to say that they have not confined their lives to words, any more than the utterers of words more potential, but have had their "actions" too, and their sufferings, and even their thoughts, and have seen the faces of the gods of wonder and melancholy; albeit they end with believing them to be phantoms (however useful) of bad health, and think nothing finally potential but gentleness and persuasion.

It has been well said, that love money as people may, there is generally something which they love better: some whim, or hobby-horse; some enjoyment or recreation; some personal, or political, or poetical predilection; some good opinion of this or that class of men ; some club of one's fellows, or dictum of one's own;—with a thousand other *somes* and probabilities. I believe that what Mr. Carlyle loves better than his fault-finding, with all its eloquence, is the face of any human creature that looks suffering, and loving, and sincere; and I believe further, that if the fellow-creature were suffering only, and neither loving nor sincere, but had come to a pass of agony in this life, which put him at the mercies of some good man for some last help and consolation towards his grave, even at the risk of loss to repute, and a sure amount of pain and vexation, that man, if the groan reached him in its forlornness, would be Thomas Carlyle.

The *London Journal* was a miscellany of essays, criticism, and passages from books. Towards the close, it was joined by the *Printing Machine*, but the note which it had struck was of too æsthetical a nature for cheap readers in those days; and [in 1836], after attaining the size of a goodly folio double volume, it terminated. I have since had the pleasure of seeing the major part of the essays renew their life, and become accepted by the public, in a companion volume to the *Indicator*, entitled the *Seer*. But the reputation, as usual, was too late for the profit. Neither the *Seer* nor the *Indicator* are mine.—The *Seer* does not mean a prophet, or one gifted with second sight, but an observer of ordinary things about him, gifted by his admiration of nature with the power of discerning what everybody else may discern by a cultivation of the like secret of satisfaction. I have been also pleased to see that the *London Journal* maintains a good, steady price with my old friends, the bookstalls. It is in request, I understand, as a book for sea-voyages; and assuredly its large, triple-columned, eight hundred pages, full of cheerful ethics, of reviews, anecdotes, legends, table-talk, and romances of real life, make a reasonable sort of library for a voyage, and must look pleasant enough, lying among the bulky things upon deck. The *Romances of Real Life* were, themselves, collected into a separate volume. They contain the best things out of the *Lounger's Common-Place Book,* and other curious publications, with the addition of comments by the editor. These romances are as little my property as the books of essays just mentioned : but I venture to think that they are worth recommending for their own sakes, and that the comments contain some of my best reflections.

Alas ! whither am I going, thus talking about myself ? But I must finish what I have got so far with.

Among the contributors to the *London Journal* was a young friend, who, had he lived, would have been a very distinguished man. I allude to Egerton Webbe, a name well known in private circles of wit and scholarship. He was a wit of the first water, a scholar writing elegant Latin verse, a writer of the best English style, having philological reason for every word he uttered—a reasoner, a humorist, a politician, a cosmopolite, a good friend, brother, and son; and to add a new variety to all this, he inherited from his grandfather, the celebrated glee composer, a genius for musical composition, which in his person took a higher and wider range, being equally adapted for pathos and comedy. He wrote a most humorous farce, both words and music ; and he was the author of a strain of instrumental music in the funeral scene of the *Legend of Florence,* which was taken by accomplished ears for a dirge of some Italian master.

Unfortunately, like Beethoven, he was deaf ; but so delightful was his conversation, that I was glad to strain my voice for it the whole evening to such an extent, that, on his departure, my head would run round with dizziness, and I could not go to sleep.

Had he lived, he would have enriched a family too good and trusting for the ordinary course of the world. He died; and their hopes and their elder lives went with him, till they all meet somewhere again. Dear Egerton Webbe ! How astonished was Edward Holmes, the best musical critic which this nation has produced, to see him come into his house with his young and blooming face, after reading essays and metaphysics, which he took for those of some accomplished old gentleman !

I would not do my friend's memory such disservice as to give the following *jeux d'esprit* by way of specimens of his *powers.* They are samples only of his pastime and trifling. But I fear, that such entertainment as my book may contain has been growing less and less; and I put them in, that he may still do for me what he has done before—give my jaded spirits a lift.

Scholarly readers know Martial well enough; and therefore they know, that in pouring forth everything which came into his head, bad and good, he is sometimes bad indeed. He realizes his own jest about the would-be sly fellow, who, in order not to be thought poor, pretended a voluntary appearance of poverty. Martial, on these occasions, utters his nothings with an air as if they were something on that very account; as if they possessed a merit which stood in no need of display. Such are the "epigrams" which my friend bantered in the *London Journal* with the following exquisite imitations. He has not even forgotten (as the *Journal* observed) the solemn turn of the heads of the epigrams, "Concerning Flavius"—"On the same "—" To Antonius concerning Lepidus," &c., "nor the ingenious art with which Martial contrives to have a reason asked him, for what he is bent on explaining." The banters, it is true, "have this drawback; that being good jokes upon bad ones, they cannot possibly convey the same impression;" but the reader is willing to guess it through the wit.

> "CONCERNING JONES.
> Jones eats his lettuces undress'd;
> D' you ask the reason? 'Tis confess'd,—
> That is the way Jones likes them best."

> "TO SMITH, CONCERNING THOMSON.
> Smith, Thomson puts no claret on his board;
> D' you ask the reason?—Thomson can't afford."

> "TO GIBBS, CONCERNING HIS POEMS.
> You ask me if I think your poems good;
> If I could praise your poems, Gibbs,—I would."

> "CONCERNING THE SAME.
> Gibbs says, his poems a sensation make;—
> But Gibbs, perhaps, is under a mistake."

> "TO THOMSON, CONCERNING DIXON AND JACKSON.
> How Dixon can with Jackson bear,
> You ask me, Thomson, to declare;—
> Thomson, Dixon's Jackson's heir."

Were ever three patronymics jumbled so together! or with such a delightful importance? It is like the jingling of the money in Jackson's pocket.

How strange to sit laughing at my fireside over these epigrams, while he that wrote them, instead of coming to drink tea with me, is . . .

But we are all bound somewhere together, as the sun and the planets are bound in one direction towards another part of the heavens; and the intervals between the departures of the dead and the living are very small.

The *London Journal* was followed by the production of *Captain Sword and Captain Pen;*—a poem which, poem though it was, and one which gave me a sense of my advance in imaginative culture, and consequent power of expression, nothing but a sense of duty could have enabled me to persist in writing. I have implied this before; but I will now state, for reasons which may be of service, that I was several times forced to quit my task by accesses of wonder and horror so overwhelming, as to make me burst out in perspirations (a thing very difficult in me to produce), and that nothing but the physical relief thus afforded me, the early mother-taught lesson of subjecting the one to the many, and perhaps the habit of thinking the best in worst, and believing that everything would, somehow or other, come right at last, could have given me courage enough to face the subject again.

I remember three passages in particular, which tried me to a degree almost unbearable. One was that in which the shriek of the horse is noticed; another, the description of the bridegroom lying by the ditch, sabred, and calling for water; and the third, the close of the fourth canto, where the horriblest thing occurs, that maddens a taken city. Men of action are too apt to think that an author, and especially a poet, dares and undergoes nothing as he peacefully sits by his fireside "indulging his muse." But the muse is sometimes an awful divinity. With truest devotion, and with dreadful necessity for patience, followed by what it prayed for, were the last three lines of that canto written.* Not that the trusting belief, for which I owe an unceasing debt of gratitude to my parents, failed me then or ever; but all the horror of wonder (and in such visitations wonder is a very horrible thing) passed over me with its black burthen; and I looked back on it, as one might look upon the passage of some tremendous spirit, whose beneficence, though you still believed in it, had taken that astounding shape. Firmly do I believe, that all such sufferings,—and far worse, those under the very imagination of which they suffer,—are for the very best and hap-

* "O God! let me breathe, and look up at thy sky.
    Good is as hundreds, evil as one:
    Round about goeth the golden sun."

piest ends, whatever may be the darkness which they cast on one as they go.

It was in that persuasion, as well as from need of relief, and for the due variation of my theme, that I intermingled these frightful scenes with passages of military gaiety, of festive enjoyment, and even of pleasantry; such as the description of the soldier's march, of the entertainments given to Captain Sword, and of the various dances in the ball-room:—

> "The country-dance, small of taste;
> And the waltz, that loveth the lady's waist;
> And the gallopade, strange agreeable tramp,
> Made of a scrape, a hobble, and stamp," &c.

Gibbon said, that his having been a captain of militia was of use to him in writing his great work. With due feelings of subordination to the captain, I can say, that my having been a private in a regiment of volunteers was of use to me in performing this painful duty.

> "Steady   steady!—the masses of men
> Wheel, and fall in, and wheel again,
> Softly as circles drawn with pen."

I had been a part of the movement, and felt how soft and orderly it was.

> "Now for the flint, and the cartridge bite;
> Darkly gathers the breath of the fight,
> Salt to the palate, and stinging to sight."

Many a cartridge had I bitten, and thus learned the salt to that dreadful dinner.

It was about this time that I projected a poem of a very different sort, which was to be called *A Day with the Reader*.

I proposed to invite the reader to breakfast, dine, and sup with me, partly at home, and partly at a country inn, in order to vary the circumstances. It was to be written both gravely and gaily, in an exalted or in a lowly strain, according to the topics of which it treated. The fragment on Paganini was a part of the exordium:

> "So play'd of late to every passing thought
> With finest change (might I but half as well
> So write!) the pale magician of the bow," &c.

I wished to write in the same manner, because Paganini, with his violin, could move both the tears and the laughter of his audience, and (as I have described him doing in the verses) would now give you the notes of birds in trees, and even hens feeding in a farm-yard (which was a corner into which I meant

25

to take my companion), and now melt you into grief and pity,
or mystify you with witchcraft, or put you into a state of
lofty triumph like a conqueror. That phrase of "smiting"
the chords,—

> "He smote;—and clinging to the serious chords
> With godlike ravishment," &c.—

was no classical commonplace; nor, in respect to impression
on the mind, was it exaggeration to say, that from a single
chord he would fetch out

> "The voice of quires, and weight
> Of the built organ."

Paganini, the first time I saw and heard him, and the first
moment he struck a note, seemed literally to strike it; to give
it a blow. The house was so crammed, that, being among
the squeezers in "standing room" at the side of the pit, I
happened to catch the first sight of his face through the arm
akimbo of a man who was perched up before me, which
made a kind of frame for it; and there, on the stage, in that
frame, as through a perspective glass, were the face, bust, and
raised hand, of the wonderful musician, with his instrument
at his chin, just going to commence, and looking exactly as I
have described him.

> "His hand,
> Loading the air with dumb expectancy,
> Suspended, ere it fell, a nation's breath.
>
> "He *smote;*—and clinging to the serious chords
> With godlike ravishment, drew forth a breath,—
> So deep, so strong, so fervid thick with love,—
> Blissful, yet laden as with twenty prayers,
> That Juno yearn'd with no diviner soul
> To the first burthen of the lips of Jove.
>
> "The exceeding mystery of the loveliness
> Sadden'd delight; and with his mournful look,
> Dreary and gaunt, hanging his pallid face
> 'Twixt his dark flowing locks, he almost seem'd,
> To feeble or to melancholy eyes,
> One that had parted with his soul for pride,
> And in the sable secret liv'd forlorn."

To show the depth and identicalness of the impression
which he made on everybody, foreign or native, an Italian who
stood near me, said to himself, after a sigh, "O Dio!" and
this had not been said long, when another person in the same
manner uttered the words, "O Christ!" Musicians pressed
forward from behind the scenes, to get as close to him as possible; and they could not sleep at night for thinking of him.

I have mentioned the *Monthly Repository*. It was originally a magazine in the Unitarian interest, and contained admirable papers by Mr. William Johnson Fox, the present member for Oldham, Mr. John Mill, and others; but it appeared, so to speak, in one of the least though most respectable corners of influence, and never obtained the repute it deserved. Nor, if such writers as these failed to counteract the drawback, could it be expected that others would help it better. The author of *Orion* made the attempt in vain; and so did the last of its editors, the present writer, though Landor assisted him. [The transfer of editorship took place in 1837.] In this publication, like better things before it, was sunk *Blue-Stocking Revels*, or the *Feast of the Violets*—a kind of female *Feast of the Poets*, which nobody took any notice of; though I had the pleasure of hearing that Mr. Rogers said it would have been sufficient " to set up half a dozen young men about town in a reputation for wit and fancy."

As Apollo in the *Feast of the Poets* gave a dinner to those gentlemen, in *Blue-Stocking Revels* he gives a ball and supper to literary ladies. The guests were so numerous as to call forth a pleasant remark from Lord Holland, who, in a letter in which he acknowledged the receipt of the poem, said, that "the inspector of blue ankles under Phœbus" had, he perceived, "no sinecure." I believe the fair guests were not dissatisfied with their entertainment. It was thought by somebody, that objection was intended to Mrs. Somerville, because it was said of her, that

"Instead of the little Loves, laughing at colleges,
    Round her, in doctors' caps, flew little Knowledges."

But I did not mean to imply, either that the lady's knowledge was little, or that she was not a very amiable person. It was only a commonplace jest in a new shape. Perhaps it ought to have been followed by a recommendation to look into the faces of the " little Knowledges;" who are apt to have more love in them, than people suspect.

A bookseller objected to publishing this poem on a very different account. He thought that Lady Blessington would take offence at the mention of her " shoulders," and at being called a " Venus grown fat."

"'Lady Blessington!' cried the glad usher aloud,
    As she swam through the doorway, like moon from a cloud.
I know not which most her face beam'd with,—fine creature !
    Enjoyment, or judgment, or wit, or good-nature.

Perhaps you have known what it is to feel longings
    To pat buxom shoulders at routs and such throngings;—
    Well,—think what it was, at a vision like that!
    A Grace after dinner!—a Venus grown fat!"

It would be strange if any lady, grown stout, would object to
being thought a Venus notwithstanding: and it would be still
stranger, if, after having her face lauded for so many fine
qualities, she should object to having her shoulders admired.
Lady Blessington, at all events, had too much understanding to
make such a mistake; and, though I had not the pleasure of
her acquaintance, I had good reason to know that she took the
passage in anything but an offensive light. Let me take this
opportunity of saying that her ladyship's account of Lord
Byron is by far the best and most sensible I am acquainted
with. Her writings, indeed, throughout, though not of a
nature qualified to endure, were remarkable for a judgment
as well as benevolence for which many would not give credit
to an envied beauty.

CHAPTER XXV.

PLAY-WRITING.—CONCLUSION.

POEMS of the kind just mentioned were great solaces to care;
but the care was great notwithstanding. I felt age coming
on me, and difficulties not lessened by failing projects : nor
was I able, had I been never so inclined, to render my faculties profitable " in the market." It is easy to say to a man
—Write such and such a thing, and it is sure to sell. Watch
the public taste, and act accordingly. Care not for original
composition ; for inventions or theories of your own ; for
æsthetics, which the many will be slow to apprehend. Stick
to the works of others. Write only in magazines and reviews.
Or if you must write things of your own, compile. Tell
anecdotes. Reproduce memoirs and topographies. Repeat,
in as many words of your own as you can, other men's criticisms. Do anything but write to the few, and you may get
rich.

There is a great deal of truth in all this. But a man can
only do what he can, or as others will let him. Suppose he
has a conscience that will not suffer him to reproduce the
works of other people, or even to speak what he thinks commonplace enough to have become common property. Suppose

this conscience will not allow him to accommodate himself to the opinion of editors and reviewers. Suppose the editors and reviewers themselves will not encourage him to write on the subjects he understands best, perhaps do not understand the subjects themselves; or suppose, at best, that they play with him, postpone him, and keep him only as a resource when their ordinary circle fails them. Suppose he has had to work his way up through animosities, political and religious, and through such clouds of adversity as, even when they have passed away, leave a chill of misfortune round his repute, and make "prosperity" slow to encourage him. Suppose, in addition to all this, he is in bad health, and of fluctuating, as well as peculiar powers; of a temperament easily solaced in mind, and as easily drowsed in body; quick to enjoy every object in creation, everything in nature and in art, every sight, every sound, every book, picture, and flower, and at the same time really qualified to do nothing, but either to preach the enjoyment of those objects in modes derived from his own particular nature and breeding, or to suffer with mingled cheerfulness and poverty the consequences of advocating some theory on the side of human progress. Great may sometimes be the misery of that man under the necessity of requesting forbearance or undergoing obligation; and terrible will be his doubts, whether some of his friends may not think he had better have had a conscience less nice, or an activity less at the mercy of his *physique*. He will probably find himself carelessly, over-familiarly, or even superciliously treated, pitied, or patronized, by his inferiors; possibly will be counted inferior, even in moral worth, to the grossest and most mercenary men of the world; and he will be forced to seek his consolation in what can be the only final consolation of any one who needs a charitable construction; namely, that he has given, hundreds of times, the construction which he would receive once for all.

I did not understand markets; I could not command editors and reviewers; I therefore obeyed an inclination which had never forsaken me, and wrote a play. The propensity to dramatic writing had been strong in me from boyhood. I began to indulge in it long before my youthful criticisms on the theatre. The pieces which I then wrote have been mentioned in the earlier part of this volume. They were all failures, even in my own opinion; so that there can be little doubt of their having been actually such:

but the propensity remained, and the present consequence was the *Legend of Florence.*

I wrote this play in six weeks, in a state of delightful absorption, notwithstanding the nature of the story and of the cares which beset me; and now, for the first time, I thought I had done something dramatic, which might be put forth to the world without misgiving. It was declined by the principal manager then reigning. I wrote another blank-verse play in five acts, thinking to please better by adapting it to his taste, but I succeeded as little by this innocent artifice; and thus seemed closed upon me the prospect of any bettering of my fortunes, the most needed.

I have reasons of a very special and justifiable kind for saying thus much, and showing how my labours were lost; and I subsequently lost more; but not without an interval of refreshment and hope. How pleasant it was, long afterwards, to find my rejected *Legend* welcomed and successful at another theatre [Covent Garden, in February, 1840]. Here I became acquainted, for the first time, with a green-room, and surrounded with a congratulating and cordial press of actors and actresses. But every step which I took into Covent Garden Theatre was pleasant from the first. One of the company, as excellent a woman as she was an actress, the late Mrs. Orger, whom I had the pleasure of knowing, brought me acquainted with the management; an old and esteemed friend was there to second her, in the person of the late Mr. Henry Robertson, the treasurer, brother too of our quondam young society of "Elders," and every way harmonious associate of many a musical party afterwards at the Novellos', and at Hampstead. Mr. Charles Mathews welcomed me with a cordiality like his own: Mr. Planché, the wit and fairy poet of the house, whom envy accused of being jealous of the approach of new dramatists, not only contributed everything in his power to assist in making me feel at home in it, but added the applause of his tears on my first reading of the play. To conclude my triumph in the green-room, when I read the play afterwards to its heroine, Miss Tree (now Mrs. Charles Kean), I had the pleasure of seeing the tears pour down her glowing cheeks, and of being told by her afterwards, that she considered her representation of the character her best performance. And finally, to crown all, in every sense of the word, loyal as well as metaphorical, the Queen did the play the honour of coming to see it twice (to my knowledge)

—four times, according to that of Madame Vestris, who ought to have known. Furthermore, when her Majesty saw it first, she was gracious and good-natured enough to express her approbation of it to the manager in words which she gave him permission to repeat to me; and furthermost of all, some years afterwards she ordered it to be repeated before her at Windsor Castle, thus giving me a local memory in the place, which Surrey himself might have envied, and which Warton would certainly have hung, as a piece of its tapestry, with a sonnet.

The four other blank-verse plays of which I have spoken, and one or two of which would have also come out at Covent Garden, had the management prospered, were called *The Secret Marriage*, since called *The Prince's Marriage*, which is the play I have mentioned as having endeavoured to propitiate my first manager's good-will. *Lovers' Amazements*, in three acts; *The Double*, the piece of mixed prose and verse in two; and *Look to your Morals*, the prose afterpiece, or petty comedy. *Lovers' Amazements* has since made its appearance, as late as the year 1858, with a success equal to that of the *Legend*. I shall have occasion to speak of it once again, before I conclude.

The *Secret Marriage* is the story of a prince of Navarre, whose marriage with a lady not of blood royal is resented by an envious nobility. It is founded on the celebrated history of Ines de Castro, of which, indeed, I first intended it to consist; but in these effeminate days of the drama, I found that its tragical termination would not be endured. At least the actors told me so. I said, that I had not intended to crown her dead body (which was what her husband actually did, forcing the nobles who assassinated her to attend the ceremony); my design was to crown her coffin; which is done in the *Secret Marriage*; though matters in that play, in deference to modern requirement, are still brought happily about. I confess that, both as a critic and an Englishman, I am ashamed of this alleged weakness on the part of the British public; this charge of not being able to endure a strong sensation, however salutary. Nor do I believe it. The strong Saxon people, who have carried the world before them, are not the audiences to quail before a tragedy. The only point is how to set it truly and nobly before them; and not in that gratuitous and vulgar style of horror, which it becomes manhood to repudiate. How is it that they endure *Othello* and *Lear?* "Oh!" but say the

actors, "that is Shakspeare's writing." Yes; and thus, like
the cunning priests of a faith which they dishonour, they make
a bugbear as well as a business of their idol; as if all worship
of the true and beautiful were to fail in its effects with others,
because they are without it themselves. I have heard actors
themselves say, notwithstanding this esoterical religion of
theirs, that Shakspeare himself would be damned to-morrow
if he were to write now. The *Secret Marriage* was rejected
by the same manager that rejected the *Legend of Florence;*
which is perhaps a good omen, if I could get it performed.
But then it "costs money," pathetically say these caterers for
the public amusement.

Lovers' Amazements is an imbroglio of two ladies and two
gentlemen, who are constantly undergoing surprises, which
make them doubt the fidelity or the regard of one another.
But then, in this beautiful modern state of the British theatres,
I was asked, with the like pathos, where were two gentleman
actors and two lady actresses to be found, who could, or, if
they could, would perform a play in which they are all four
put on a level perhaps in point of intellectual pretension.
Nevertheless, after a lapse of many years, the piece, as I have
just stated, has been brought out with success. Some other
particulars respecting it will be given in order of time. In
vain I answered that one charming actress took singular pains
to get it performed, and that another would have had it performed, but for the closing of her theatre. I was defied to
get four gentlefolks of the stage together, or any four together,
competent to perform the parts. How different from what I
had seen in former days !

The *Double* is founded on a story, from the Italian novelists,
of a clever fisherman, who bears so strong a resemblance to a
gentleman who is drowned, while bathing in his company,
that he is tempted to personate the deceased, and to take
possession of his house. To render the personation more probable, I turned the fisherman into an actor. But this piece
also was objected to on the score of its not being thoroughly
"pleasant." That, according to the actors, is the great requisite
now with the robust British public. You must make everything "pleasant" to them ;—give them nothing but sops and
honey. At least, in polite theatres. You may frighten the
people in the Borough ; but you must not think of startling
the nerves at the West End.

The two principal characters in *Look to your Morals,* are

an English valet, and a French damsel whom he has married. He is very jealous; and in order to keep down the attractiveness of her animal spirits, he has told her that there is nothing but the most rigid propriety in England, both in morals and demeanour, and that she is to regulate her behaviour accordingly. The girl, who is a very innocent girl, believes him; and the consequence is, that she has to undergo a series of attentions, which very much open her French eyes. I know not how far the impression of this is to rank with the "*unpleasant*" things that are not to be risked with the British public. The stage, to be sure, is so much in the habit of pampering the national self-love, especially on the side of its virtues and respectability, and this, too, at the expense of our lively neighbours, that I can suppose it possible for a theatre to see some danger in it. At all events, the manager in whose hands it has been put, kept it by him as safe as gunpowder:—so safe indeed, Hibernically speaking, that on a late inquiry for it, it appeared to be lost; and I have no complete copy. He is old and ailing, however; and I shall not turn gunpowder myself, and blow him up. [It was found after the author's death, and returned to the family.]

About a dozen years ago, in consequence of disappointments of this kind, and of those before mentioned, some friends renewed an application to Lord Melbourne, which they had made in the reign previous. It was thought that my sufferings in the cause of reform, and my career as a man of letters, rendered me not undeserving a pension. His lordship received both the applications with courtesy; which he does not appear to have shown in quarters where the interest might have been thought greater; but the pension was not granted. Perhaps the courtesy was on that account. Perhaps he gave my friends these and other evidences of his good-will towards me, knowing that he should advise nothing further; for I had twice during his administration received grants from the Royal Bounty Fund, of two hundred pounds each; once during the reign of King William, and the second after the accession of her Majesty. It subsequently turned out, that Lord Melbourne considered it proper for no man to have a pension given him by one sovereign, who had been condemned in a court of law for opposing another.

Simultaneous with the latest movement about the pension, was one on the part of my admirable friend Dickens and other distinguished men,—Forsters and Jerrolds,—who, combining kindly purpose with an amateur inclination for the stage, had condescended to show to the public what excellent actors they could have been, had they so pleased,—what excellent actors, indeed, some of them were. They were of opinion that a benefit for myself at one of the metropolitan theatres would be a dishonour on neither side. A testimonial of a different sort, which had been proposed by some other friends, was superseded by this form of one; and preparations were being accordingly made, when the grant of the pension seemed to render it advisable that the locality of the benefit should be transferred from London to a provincial stage, in acknowledgment to the superior boon, and for the avoidance of all appearance of competing with it. The result was still of great use to me, and my name was honoured in a manner I shall never forget by an address from the pens of Mr. Serjeant (late Justice) Talfourd and Sir Edward Bulwer, and the plaudits of Birmingham and Liverpool. Talfourd had always been one of my best and dearest friends; and Sir Edward, with whom I became acquainted much later, had, before I knew him, and when it was a bold thing to praise me in the circles, done me, nevertheless, that handsome and valuable service. The pieces performed on this occasion were Ben Jonson's *Every Man in his Humour*, and the farce of—I forget what, in the country, for I was not there; but the play had been repeated before in town, as it was afterwards, and several farces came after it.

If anything had been needed to show how men of letters include actors, on the common principle of the greater including the less, these gentlemen would have furnished it. Mr. Dickens's "Bobadil" had a spirit in it of intellectual apprehension beyond anything the existing stage has shown: his farce throughout was always admirable,—quite rich and filled up; so were the tragical parts in which he subsequently appeared; and Mr. Forster delivered the verses of Ben Jonson and Fletcher with a musical flow and a sense of their grace and beauty unknown, I believe, to the recitation of actors at present. At least I have never heard anything like it since Edmund Kean's. The lines came out of his lips as if he loved them. I allude particularly, in this instance, to his performance of the "Younger Brother." But he did it always, when sweet verse required it.

Meantime, I had removed with my family from Chelsea to Kensington; and although my health was not bettered, as I hoped it would have been by the change, but, on the contrary, was made worse in respect to body than I ever experienced, and showed me the formidable line that is drawn between being elderly and being old (for we unfortunately got into a part which had been denounced in the books of the Sanitary Commissioners), yet I loved Kensington for many reasons, and do still, even for one more of a melancholy description, hereafter to be noticed, nay, love it the more on that account, though I can never pass the spot without a pang.

Here, sometimes in the Gardens, sometimes in the quondam Nightingale-lane of Holland House (now partially diverted), I had the pleasure of composing the *Palfrey*, the scenes of which are partly laid in the place. Here (with the exception of a short interval at Wimbledon) I wrote, besides reviews and shorter articles, one of the dramatic pieces above mentioned, the criticism in *Imagination and Fancy*, and *Wit and Humour*; the *Stories from the Italian Poets*; the *Jar of Honey*; the criticism in the *Book for a Corner*; a portion of the *Town* (most of which had been produced long before); and lastly, the greater part of the work which the reader is now perusing. At the close of the second volume of the *Italian Stories* I had a severe illness. I had opposed a lethargic tendency to which I am subject, the consequence of hepatitis, with too free a use of coffee, which ended in a dangerous attack of the loins, the effects of which appeared for a good while to be irrecoverable; but they were not. A friend, the late estimable Mr. Stritch, who had often looked in upon me and found me sitting with cold feet, and with a bust, as it were, on fire, repeatedly warned me of what would happen ; but I was sanguine, was foolish, and down I went. I used to envy my friend for his being able to walk leisurely in and out, and thought how sure he was of living beyond me. And now he is gone. Too many of such surprises have I had ; but there is always good of some kind in evil. My friend's last moments were as brief as they were unlooked for. I had also another consolation during my illness. It has so happened that several of my illnesses have taken place after I had been writing on matters connected with religion, and in those cases I have always had the comfort of knowing that I had been doing my best to diminish superstition. In the present instance, I had been attacking the infernal opinions of Dante—a task which no respect for his genius, or false considerations for the times in which he lived (for others who lived in them were above them), can ever make me regard but as a duty and a glory ;

for though I acknowledge the true part of might to be right, yet might of any sort never so much astonished me as that I could not discern in it what was not might ; and Dante's venturing on his ghastly visions did not blind me to that false support and intoxicating spirit of vindictiveness, which enabled him to do it. Dante (alas ! that such a conjunction should be possible) was one of the greatest poets and most childishly mistaken men that ever existed; and if it requires an audacity like his own to say it—here it is.

One more book I wrote partly at Kensington, which I can take no pride in,—which I desire to take no pride in,—and yet which I hold dearer than all the rest. I have mentioned a book called *Christianism, or Belief and Unbelief Reconciled*, which I wrote in Italy. The contents of that book, modified, were added to the one I speak of ; and the latter (of which more, when I speak of its completion) had the same object as the former, with better provision for practical result ; that is to say, it proposed to supply, not thoughts and aspirations only, but a definite faith, and a daily set of duties, to such humble, yet un-abject, and truly religious souls, as cannot accept unintelligible and unworthy ties of conscience, and yet feel both their weakness and their earnestness with sufficient self-knowledge to desire ties of conscience, both as bonds and encouragements. My family, some other friends, and myself, were in accord upon the principles of the book ; it did us good for a sufficient length of time to make us think it would do good to others ; and its publication, which has since taken place, was contemplated accordingly.

With the occasional growth of this book, with the production of others from necessity, with the solace of verse, and with my usual experience of sorrows and enjoyments, of sanguine hopes and bitter disappointments, of bad health and almost unconquerable spirits (for though my old hypochondria never returned, I sometimes underwent pangs of unspeakable will and longing, on matters which eluded my grasp), I passed in this and another spot of the same suburb by no means the worst part of these my latter days, till one terrible loss befell me. The same unvaried day saw me reading or writing, ailing, jesting, reflecting, rarely stirring from home but to walk, interested in public events, in the progress of society, in the "New Reformation" (most deeply), in things great and small, in a print, in a plaster-cast, in a hand-organ, in the stars, in the sun to which the sun was hastening, in the flower on my table, in the fly on my paper while I wrote. (He crossed words, of which he knew nothing ; and perhaps we all do as much every moment, over things of divinest meaning.) I read everything that was readable, old and new, particularly fiction, and philosophy, and natural history ; was always returning to something Italian, or in Spenser, or in the themes of the East; lost no particle of Dickens, of Thackeray, of Mrs. Gaskell (whose *Mary Barton* gave me emotions that required, more and more, the consideration of the good which it must do); called out every week for my *Family Herald*, a little penny publication, at that time qualified to inform the best of its contemporaries ; rejoiced in republications of wise and witty Mrs. Gore, especially seeing she only made us wait for something newer ; delighted in the inexhaustible wit of Douglas Jerrold, Thackeray, and his coadjutors, Tom Taylor, Percival Leigh, and others, in *Punch*, the best-humoured and best-hearted satirical publication that ever existed; wondered when Bulwer Lytton would give us more of his potent romances and prospective philosophies; and hailed every fresh publication of James, though I knew half what he was going to do with his lady, and his gentleman, and his landscape, and his mystery, and his orthodoxy, and his criminal trial. But I was charmed with the new amusement which he brought out of old materials. I looked on him as I should look upon a musician, famous for " variations." I was grateful for his vein of cheerfulness, for his singularly varied and vivid landscapes, for his power of painting women at once lady-like and loving (a rare talent), for his making lovers to match, at once beautiful and well-bred, and for the solace which all this has afforded me, sometimes over and over again, in illness and in convalescence, when I required interest without violence, and entertainment at once animated and mild.

Yet I could at any time quit these writers, or any other, for men, who, in their own persons, and in a spirit at once the boldest and most loving, dared to face the most trying and awful questions of the time,—the Lamennais and Robert Owens, the Parkers, the Foxtons, and the Newmans,—noble souls, who, in these times, when Christianity is coming into flower, are what the first Christians were when it was only in the root,—brave and good hearts, and self-sacrificing consciences, prepared to carry it as high as it can go, and thinking no earthly consideration paramount to the attainment of its heavenly ends. I may differ with one of them in this or that respect; I may differ with a second in another; but difference with such men, provided we differ in their own spirit, is more harmonious than accord with others; nay, would form a part of the highest music of our sphere, being founded on the very principle of the beautiful, which combines diversity with sameness, and whose "service is perfect freedom." Nobody desires an insipid, languid, and monotonous world, but a world of animated moral beauty equal to its physical beauty, and a universal church, embracing many folds.

I admire and love all hearty, and earnest, and sympathizing men, whatever may be their creed—the admirable Berkeleys and Whichcotes, the Father Matthews and Geddeses, the Mendelssohns, the Lavaters, the Herders, the Williamses and the Priestleys, the Channings, Adam Clarkes, Halls, Carlyles and Emersons, the Hares, Maurices, Kingsleys, Whatelys, Foxes, and Vaughans; but, of course, I must admire most those who have given the greatest proofs of self-sacrifice, equal to them as the others may be, and prepared to do the like if their conclusions demand it.

Alas! how poor it seems, and how painfully against the grain it is, to resume talk about oneself after adverting to people like these. But my book must be finished; and of such talk must autobiographies be made. I assure the reader, that, apart from emotions forced upon me, and unless I am self-deluded indeed, I take no more interest in the subject of my own history, no, nor a twentieth part so much as I do in that of any other autobiography that comes before me. The present work originated in necessity, was commenced with unwillingness, has taken several years of illness and interruption to write, repeatedly moved me to ask the publisher to let me change it for another (which, out of what he was pleased to consider good for everybody, he would not allow), and I now send it a second time, and with additional matter, into the world, under the sure and certain conviction, that every autobiographer must of necessity be better known to his readers than to himself, let him have written as he may, and that that better knowledge is not likely to lead to his advantage. So be it. The best will judge me kindliest; and I shall be more than content with their conclusions.

Among the verses with which I solaced myself in the course of these prose writings, were those which from time to time appeared in the *Morning Chronicle*, on occasions connected with the happiness of the Queen, such as the celebration of her Majesty's birthday, the births of the royal children, &c. I have mentioned the train of ideas which circumstances had led me to associate with my thoughts of the Queen.

I consider myself always a royalist of the only right English sort; that is to say, as a republican, with royalty for his safe-guard and ornament. I can conceive no condition of society in which some form of that tranquil, ornamental, and most useful thing called monarchy, will not be the final refuge of political dispute and vicissitude; and this being my opinion, and loving the Queen as I do, I wish with all my heart that her family may govern us in peace and security to the end of time. But though I reverence the past, and can imagine that aristocracies, like all other great facts, may have rendered great and necessary service in its time, and though I would have no change from past to future take place by any but the softest and most respectful degrees, yet, inasmuch as I am for seeing no paupers in the land, I am for seeing no ultra rich. I love individuals among the aristocracy, and bless and reve-rence the good they do with their riches; but for their own sakes, as well as for that of the poor, I wish the poor did not give so much trouble to their riches, nor the riches of their less worthy brethren so many miserable thoughts to the poor. I feel just the same with respect to great cotton-spinners, or to any other amassers of treasure, by the side, and by the means, of the half-starved. And I do not hold myself at all answered by any reference to the ordinations of Providence; for Providence, by the like reasoning, ordinates dreadful revenges and retributions; and I think that in the instinctive efforts of humanity to advance, and to advance quietly, Pro-vidence clearly ordinates that we are to dispense with any such references in either direction.

These opinions of mine would have been seen fully ex-pressed in many a previous publication, nor had they been intimated even courtwards for the first time. They were implied in the following passage from the lines on the birth-day of the Princess Alice:

> "What a world, were human-kind
> All of one instructed mind!
> What a world to rule, to please;—
> To share 'twixt enterprise and ease!
> *Graceful manners flowing round*
> *From the court's enchanted ground;*
> Comfort keeping all secure,—
> *None too rich, and none too poor.*"

I never addressed any congratulation to the Queen without implying something in this spirit; something in behalf of progress and the poor:

> *" May she every day*
> *See some new good winning its gentle way*
> *By means of mild and unforbidden men!*
> *And when the sword hath bow'd beneath the pen,*
> *May her own line a patriarch scene unfold,*
> *As far surpassing what these days behold,*
> *E'en in the thunderous gods, iron and steam,*
> *As they the sceptic's doubt, or wild man's dream!"*

(The benediction here passes from the political to the religious future.)

> *"And to this end,—oh! to this Christian end,*
> *And the sure coming of its next great friend,*
> *May her own soul, this instant, while I sing,*
> *Be smiling, as beneath some angel's wing,*
> *O'er the dear life in life,—the small, sweet, new,*
> *Unselfish self,—the filial self of two;*
> *Bliss of her future eyes, her pillow'd gaze,*
> *On whom a mother's heart thinks close, and prays."*
>
> Lines on Her Majesty's Birthday.

In this passage I meant to express a hope that the next reigning sovereign would see a great advance in Christianity itself, and be its friend accordingly. But I did not state what I expected that advance to be. I now feel it my duty to be explicit on the subject; and the reader will see at once how "unorthodox" is my version of Christianity, when I declare that I do not believe one single dogma, which the reason that God has put in our heads, or the heart that he has put in our bosoms, revolts at. For though reason cannot settle many undeniable mysteries that perplex us, and though the heart must acknowledge the existence of others from which it cannot but receive pain, yet that is no reason why mysteries should be palmed upon reason of which it sees no evidences whatever, or why pain should be forced upon the heart, for which it sees grounds as little. On the contrary, the more mysteries there are with which I cannot help being perplexed, the less number of them will I gratuitously admit for the purpose of perplexing my brain further; and the greater the number of the pains that are forced upon my heart, the fewer will I be absurd enough to invite out of the regions of the unproveable, to afflict me in addition. What evils there are, I find, for the most part, relieved with many consolations: some I find to be necessary to the requisite amount of good;

and every one of them I find to come to a termination; for the sufferers either are cured and live, or are killed and die ; and in the latter case I see no evidence to prove, that a little finger of them aches any more. This palpable revelation, then, of God, which is called the universe, contains no evidence whatsoever of the thing called eternal punishment ; and why should I admit any assertion of it that is not at all palpable? If an angel were to tell me to believe in eternal punishment, I would not do it, for it would better become me to believe the angel a delusion than God monstrous; and we make him monstrous when we make him the author of eternal punishment, though we have not the courage to think so. For God's sake, let us have piety enough to believe him better. I speak thus boldly, not in order to shock anybody, which it would distress me to think I did, but because opinions so shocking distress myself, and because they ought, I think, to distress everybody else, and so be put an end to. Of any readers whom I may shock, I beg forgiveness. Only I would entreat them to reflect how far that creed can be in the right which renders it shocking in God's children to think the best of their Father.

I respect all churches which are practically good. I respect the Church of England in particular, for its moderate exercise of power, and because I think it has been a blessed medium of transition from superstition to a right faith. Yet, inasmuch as I am of opinion that the " letter killeth and the spirit giveth life," I am looking to see the letter itself killed, and the spirit giving life, for the first time, to a religion which need revolt and shock nobody.

But it becomes me, before I close my book, to make a greater avowal; for I think it may assist, in however small a degree, towards smoothing the advent of a great and inevitable change.

It seems clear to me, from all which is occurring in Europe at this moment, from the signs in the papal church, in our own church, in the universal talk and minds of men, whether for it or against it, that the knell of the letter of Christianity itself has struck, and that it is time for us to inaugurate and enthrone the spirit. I was in hopes, when Pius the Ninth first made his appearance in Europe, that a great as well as good man had arisen, competent to so noble a task. Young Italy, let loose from prison, fell at his feet; and I think, that had he persevered in what made it do so, all Europe would

have fallen at his feet, and the papal power have thus profited
by its greatest and only remaining chance of retaining the
sceptre of the Christian world. But the new Pope was frightened at being thought one of the "New Christians" (as
Lamartine called them); he hastened to issue a bull declaring
the unalterableness of every papal dogma; and the moment
he did that, he signed the death-warrant of his church.
Dogma, whatever may be the convulsive appearances to the
contrary in certain feeble quarters, has ceased to be a vital
European principle; and nothing again will ever be uni-
versally taken for Christianity, but the religion of Loving
Duty to God and Man ;—to God, as the Divine Mind which
brings good and beauty out of blind-working matter ; and to
Man, as God's instrument for advancing the world we live in,
and as partaker with his fellow-men of suffering, and endea-
deavour, and enjoyment. "Reason," says Milton, "is choice;"
and where is to be found a religion better to choose than this?
Immortality is a hope for all, which it is not just to make a
blessing for any less number, or a misery for a single soul.
Faith depends for its credibility on its worthiness; and without "works" is "dead." But charity, by which lovely Greek
word is not to be understood any single form of moral grace
and kindness, but every possible form of it conducive to love
on earth, and its link with heaven, is the only *sine quâ non*
of all final opinions of God and man.

"Behold I give unto you a new commandment,—Love one
another." "In this ye fulfil the law and the prophets." "By
their fruits ye shall know them." "God is Love."

Such, and such only, are the texts upon which sermons will
be preached, to the exclusion of whatsoever is infernal and
unintelligible. No hell. No unfatherliness. No monstrous
exactions of assent to the incredible. No impious Athanasian
Creed. No creed of any kind but such as proves its divineness by the wish of all good hearts to believe it if they might,
and by the encouragement that would be given them to believe
it, in the acclamations of the earth. The world has outgrown
the terrors of its childhood, and no spurious mistake of a
saturnine spleen for a masculine necessity will induce a return
to them. Mankind have become too intelligent; too brave ;
too impatient of being cheated, and threatened, and "put off;"
too hungry and thirsty for a better state of things in the
beautiful planet in which they live, and the beauty of which
has been an unceasing exhortation and preface to the result.

By that divine doctrine will all men gradually come to know in how many quarters the Divine Spirit has appeared among them, and what sufficing lessons for their guidance they have possessed in almost every creed, when the true portions of it shall hail one another from nation to nation, and the mixture of error through which it worked has become unnecessary. For God is not honoured by supposing him a niggard of his bounty. Jesus himself was not divine because he was Jesus, but because he had a divine and loving heart; and wherever such greatness has appeared, there has divineness appeared also, as surely as the same sunshine of heaven is on the mountain tops of east and west.

Such are the doctrines, and such only, accompanied by expositions of the beauties and wonders of God's great book of the universe, which will be preached in the temples of the earth, including those of our beloved country, England, its beautiful old ivied turrets and their green neighbourhoods, then, for the first time, thoroughly uncontradicted and heavenly; with not a sound in them more terrible than the stormy yet sweet organ, analogous to the beneficent winds and tempests; and no thought of here or hereafter, that can disturb the quiet aspect of the graves, or the welcome of the new-born darling.

And that such a consummation may come slowly but surely, without intermission in its advance, and with not an injury to a living soul, will be the last prayer, as it must needs be among the latest words, of the author of this book.

CHAPTER XXVI.

LIFE DRAWING TOWARDS ITS CLOSE.

When I closed the preceding chapter, which terminated the first edition of this biography, I did not think it would be followed by one like the present. I fancied I should go on, living as I did before, reading and writing as usual, working placidly rather than otherwise to the last, reckoning confidently on my being survived by every one of my family, old as well as young, and closing my days, if with no great applause from such of my fellow-creatures as had read me or heard of me, yet with no reproach from any of them, and something like regret from all.

This latter portion of my life, trying soever as much of the rest of it had been, has turned out to be the most trying of the whole. It has had at the same time some sweets as well as bitters, and I have never been without the comforts of a hopeful and unembittered religion.

Fortunately, the necessity of squaring the size of the new edition of this biography to that of the series of publications in which it is to appear, has required, that what I have to say, in continuation and completion of it up to the present moment, should be put into as brief a compass as possible; and with the comforts of this inexpressible relief (for I had been given to understand otherwise) I proceed.

The first disquiet I experienced was owing to mistakes respecting the book itself; some of which greatly surprised me. One was, that I had mentioned a friend in a disparaging, nay, in an ironical manner, when I intended him a positive compliment, and one of no little amount. Another, I fear (for I could construe the intimation in no other manner), consisted in supposing that I had undervalued a friend for one of his very accomplishments, when I never dreamt of such a thing, nor in fact thought of the accomplishment at all, but as a matter in which it pleased his great genius to interest itself. A third mistake, still more extraordinary, gave out that I had not mentioned another friend at all, whom I expressly and honourably recorded. And not to mention mistakes of critics, equally proveable by the simple statement of facts (though most of those gentlemen were very kind to the book, and expressed so much personal good-will as to warrant me in thinking my thanks would please them), one of them, who had got into a position of authority which he was not equal to, and whom I had unfortunately met a little while before at a dinner-party, when I had occasion to differ with him in almost all he said, took me to task for having written books at all, and not stuck to a prudent clerkship in the War Office. I thought this at first a singular objection for a Jew (for such, I was told, he was), seeing that I had been a friend of the Jews all my life, and an advocate for their emancipation from all uncivic restrictions. But then, to say nothing of the dinner, I found that he was a converted Jew.

These things disturbed me, and did me disservice; but the mistakes respecting friends were all cleared up, and the most uncomfortable of my feelings had lain in those—so I had nothing remaining at heart to complain of. Among the many pleasant letters, too, which I received about the book from readers old and new, two in particular would have made me amends for much worse treatment than I received from my bilious quitter of the synagogue; one from a man of lofty genius, whom I hesitate to name, because I have no right, perhaps, to boast of what may have been a mere impulse of his good-nature at the moment, congratulating me on having been victorious in my struggles with the perplexities of good and evil; and another from my dear friend the late Duke of Devonshire, whom I do name because it gives me an opportunity for saying how grateful I am to his memory for acts of kindness never to be forgotten.

Towards the close of the year 1849, a proposition was made to me for the revival, in another form, of the *London Journal*, which had been published under my name. It was revived accordingly, and had to boast of contributions from distinguished friends; but it failed—partly, perhaps, for want of accordance with other pens concerned; but chiefly from the smallness of the means which the proposers had thought sufficient for its establishment.

I had scarcely become reconciled to this disappointment, when the impending danger was disclosed to me of a domestic calamity of which I had not had the least suspicion. It was the consumption of a beloved son, my youngest, the same who has been mentioned as having been born during my sojourn in Italy, and of whom it was added in the first edition, that from that hour to the one in which I was writing he had been a comfort to his parents. Let the reader judge with what feelings I write of him now. He was just reaching his thirtieth year. He had not lived away from home during the whole time, with the exception of some nine or ten months. He was one of the most amiable, interesting, and sympathising of human beings, a musician by nature, modulating sweet voluntaries on the pianoforte—a born poet of the tender domestic sort, though in his modesty he had taken too late to the cultivation of the art, and left little that was finished to show for it; and he was ever so ready to do good offices for others at his own expense, that I am not sure the first seeds of his distemper were not produced by an act almost identical with that which was the death of my mother, and aggravated by his first undergoing fatigue in assisting the wayfaring and the poor. For nearly two years I saw him fading before my eyes; and a like time elapsed before he ceased to be the chief occupation of my thoughts. For nine months it was all but a monomania with me ; and I devoutly thanked Heaven for having twice in the course of my life undergone the like haunting of one idea, and so learnt to hope that it might terminate. I mention this to comfort such persons as have experienced the like suffering. My son's Christian name was Vincent. This is only the second time I have dared to write it. He died at the close of October, in the year 1852, and was buried in beautiful Kensal Green, my own final bed-chamber, I trust, in this world, towards which I often look in my solitary walks, with eyes at once most melancholy, yet consoled.

I add a sonnet of his writing, not because, though very good, it was the best thing he could do, as verses which he left unfinished bear witness; but because it shows the sweetness of his nature. For his whole life was of a piece with it, though it was not called upon to act in that particular manner.

THE DEFORMED CHILD.

An angel, prison'd in an infant frame
      Of mortal sickness and deformity,
      Looks patiently from out that languid eye,
Matured, and seeming large, with pain. The name
Of "happy childhood" mocks his movements tame,
      So propp'd with piteous crutch; or forced to lie
      Rather than sit, in its frail chair, and try
To taste the pleasure of the unshared game.

He does; and faintly claps his wither'd hands
      To see how brother Willie caught the ball;
      Kind brother Willie, strong, yet gentle all:
'Twas he that placed him, where his chair now stands,
      In that warm corner 'gainst the sunny wall,—
God, in that brother, gave him more than lands.

It was a colder break of dawn than usual, but equally beautiful, as if, in both respects, it came to take him away, when my son died. His last words were poetry itself. A glass of water had been given him at his request; and on feeling the refreshment of it, he said, " I drink the morning."

And there are those who would persuade us, that this beautiful soul will never be seen by us more ! Could space then be filled? so that there should nowhere be any room for the soul? That is impossible. And must not beauty exist, as long as there are stars, and their orderly movements anywhere? That is certain. Why then should any such portions of beauty perish, when there is no need of their perishing? And why should they not live on, and drink up those tears as they did the morning, since God has so made us long for it, when he need not have done so? As the tendency to sleep is the augury and harbinger of sleep, so desire like this—let us be sure of it—is the augury and harbinger of what it has been made to desire. Do we suppose that God makes manifest halves of anything, without intending the remainders?

I took what refuge I could from this and other afflictions in a task which I had long been anxious to execute, and which, as I was now verging on the time of life usually allotted to human existence, I thought I might not live to perform at all, if I did not hasten it. This was the completion of the work which I have alluded to before under its first title of *Christianism, or Belief and Unbelief Reconciled*, and which I now enlarged and finished, and entitled the *Religion of the Heart.* I knew it could produce me no money; was ashamed indeed of being under the necessity of letting it pay such of its expenses as it could; and to a sense of this waste of precious time (as my friend, the converted Jew, would have called it), I had to add the uneasiness arising from a fear, lest, in spite of all my endeavours to the contrary, and my wish to offend nobody more than it could help, I should displease some of the friends whose attachment and adherence to me under all other trials I most valued. I wish, for many reasons, that I could here say more of the book, than from the limits assigned me I find possible. I had hoped to say much, and to enlarge on that remarkable state of existing religious uneasiness, which I cannot but regard as one of the last phases of transition from inconsistent and embittered modes of faith to one more at peace with itself, ultimately destined to be wholly so with God, man, and futurity. In the first, faintest, and even turbid dawn of the advent of that time, I see the tops of our church steeples, old and new, touched by a light long looked for, long announced, long in spirit against letter prepared for and produced by the divinest hearts that have appeared on earth, very different from polemical prelates or the threatening mistakes of many men; and it was by the sincerity of my belief in the sufficiency of those hearts, and of what they have done for the coming ages (which it was only my humble business to collect and record, as a help towards better services), that I found myself happily relieved from the anxiety alluded to respecting the feelings of friends; not one of whom, from their highest to humblest quarters, gave me the least reason to suppose that I had done anything but even increase their good-will. For which good issue God and their good hearts be thanked. Perhaps it is better, upon the whole, that the book in question, the *Religion of the Heart*, should be left to stand apart for consideration from the present book, and so speak for itself to those who choose to consult it ; for my creed, however as serious upon serious points as eternity itself, being, nevertheless, as cheerful as its freedom from cruel terrors gives it a right to be, I have never yet been able to free myself from the perplexity caused to me as a furtherer of it, between the professional, and as it were exemplary kind of gravity expected of the inculcators of any creed, and the natural spirits, and old cheerful style of intercourse with my readers in ordinary, which the very nature of my religious convictions tends not only to warrant but to increase. Heaven, we may be assured, which has been pleased to gift us with smiles as well as tears, and with hearty laughter itself, does not weigh our levity, no, nor our gravity either, in any such scale of narrowness, as the dulness or dictatorialness of the would-be exclusively pious assume the privilege of determining.

<blockquote>
"Alas!
Like smiles and tears upon an infant's face,
Who wonders at himself, and at such things
In others' faces, my swift thoughts are mixed."
</blockquote>

One of the last things that was said to me by my dying son expressed his adhesion to the religion in that book ; and the first adherent which it had, and who was the strongest in expressing to me the comfort which it gave her — I keep putting off the mention of what I must say, but time and necessity press me — was the partner of my life for more than half a century; for I was married nearly as long ago, and I knew her some years before marriage. She followed her son at the beginning of 1857, and lies near him in the same ground. I dare to say little more. I now seemed—and it has become a consolation to me—to belong as much to the next world as to this, and think I know exactly how I shall feel when I die; more than half, perhaps, unwilling to go, inasmuch as pangs may attend the process, and life, by its nature, is not made willingly to be parted with ; but as far as affections are concerned, half sorrowing to leave those that still remain to be loved, and half solaced—I think I could even say rejoicing, if it were not for them—in the hope of meeting with those that are gone. My wife was a woman of great generosity, great freedom from every kind of jealousy, great superiority to illusions from the ordinary shows of prosperity.   In all the hazards to which I put our little means in the pursuit of what I thought it my duty to do in furtherance of social advancements, and all the injury which really resulted to them, she never uttered a word of objection.   She was as uncomplaining during the worst storms of our adversity, as she was during those at sea in our Italian voyage. She had a fine eye for art, as she showed early in life, when wholly untaught, by cutting a little head of Homer in clay, which Mr. West pronounced to be of " extraordinary promise ;" and she subsequently surprised everybody with her facility in cutting profiles of our friends in paper, so true to spirit as well as letter, as to make them laugh at the instantaneous recognition of the likeness.   Wilkie (afterwards Sir David) was among their admirers, and (to use his own words), he said he " couldn't but wonder to think how *the hard scissors* could treat the lips in particular with so much expression."   She then took some lessons from a sculptor ; and fortune seemed in her hands, when the worms, that a modeller cannot avoid in manipulating the fresh clay, sickened her so with her crushing them, that, being in a delicate state of health, she was obliged to give up the practice.   A well-intended but ill-advised treatment of her constitution in girlhood had brought on a life-long spitting of blood, which was only lessened by the years of acute rheumatism, that in depriving her of all power of locomotion ultimately killed her ; though such is the strength given to weakness itself by a quiet domestic life, and the care of a good physician (Dr. Southwood Smith, famous for keeping friends in delicate health alive), that she outlived many another physician who had augured her a brief existence, and she died at the age of sixty-nine.   I wonder how I can talk of these things as calmly as I do ; but I myself am in my seventy-fifth year, and I seem to be speaking more of those whom I am to join again shortly than of such as have left me at a distance. Like them too, though alive I decay; and when I go to bed, and lie awhile on my back before turning to sleep, I often seem to be rehearsing, not without complacency or something better, the companionship of the grave.

May all of us who desire to meet elsewhere do so, and be then shown the secret of the great, the awful, yet, it is to be trusted, the beautiful riddle ; for why (let it be asked again so much half-beauty here, and such need for completing it, if complete it is not to be? I do not think that enough has been made of that argument from analogy, divine as was the mind of Plato that suggested it. Oh, why did any kind of religious creed ever put such injustice into its better portion, as to render it possible for any of the Maker's infirm creatures to wish it might not be true, even for others' sakes? For my part, infirm as I am, I fear it not for myself or for my body, trusting, as I do, to that only kind of divineness which it is possible for me to believe in; which has *itself* made it impossible for me to believe otherwise. As to the fulfilment of these yearnings on earth to be made entire in a future state, I can no more believe in the existence of regions in space where God has made half-orbs in their heavens, or half-oranges on their trees, than I can believe He will fail to make these anxious half-satisfied natures of ours which thus crave for completeness, as entire and rounded in that which they crave for, as any other fruits of his hands.

To return to the business of the brief portion of life that remains to me:—I have only two more circumstances to particularize; both very pleasant in themselves, though occurring amidst a multitude of anxieties caused by vicissitudes in the fortunes, and bereavements in the homes, of dear friends and connections; the worst of which is, as far as one's self is concerned, that one cannot make little means fill up large wishes.

But to return to the circumstances alluded to. The first was the publication of an American edition of my collected poems, proposed to me and carried out in Boston by my friend Mr. Lee, one of the illustrious family of the Lees of Virginia, connections of Washington, and brother founders with him of the Republic; and the other (which sounds like an anti-climax; but is not so, for a reason which I shall presently mention), the appearance at last of a second of my plays at a London theatre, the one entitled *Lovers' Amazements*, of the nature of which an account has been given on a previous occasion.

Both these circumstances of late occurrence have been very precious to me; the first because of the universal burst of good-will towards me which it called forth from the American press, showing the heartiness with which the nation met the regrets of their kinsman at having in a moment of impatience with their booksellers confounded the feelings of the nation with a mistake in its ordinances; and the second circumstance, first, because the play brought forth a like manifestation of regard from the whole of the London press, showing an increase rather than a loss of old sympathies; and secondly, because, on the first night of its performance, the audience called for me with the same fervour as on the appearance of the *Legend of Florence*, and I felt myself again, as it were, in the warm arms of my fellow-creatures, unmistaken, and never to be morbidized more.

I cannot sufficiently express to either country the joy which these circumstances gave me, and the good which they have done me. They would have been more than a set-off against the most painful portion of my life, if those whom I have lost had survived to partake the pleasure, and those who remain to me had not had trials of their own. But the pleasure is great still, and is shared still, to the comfort of us all; and the approach of my night-time is even yet adorned with a break in the clouds, and a parting smile of the sunset.

May we all meet on some future day among the vortex of living multitudes, the souls of the dead, where "all tears shall be wiped off from all faces;" or, in another view of futurity, before that time arrives, may we all meet in one of Plato's vast cycles of re-existence, experiencing the sum-total of all that we have ever experienced and enjoyed before, only under those circumstances of amelioration in the amount which progressive man has been made to look for, and with no necessity for the qualification of *errors excepted*.

POSTSCRIPT.

THE event which was anticipated in the last chapter was not long delayed. Leigh Hunt died on the 28th August, 1859; and he was buried in the place of his choice, Kensall Green Cemetery. He had for about two years been manifestly declining in strength. Although well aware of the grand cause, and more than content to meet the will of his Creator, he still retained a keen interest in life, and with characteristic cheerfulness constantly hoped that some new plan—some change of diet, or of place—would restore him for a few years more of companionship with surviving friends. Just two months before completing his seventy-fifth year, he quietly sank to rest. He had come to the end of the chapter which the reader has just perused; but the volumes were still awaiting one or two finishing touches, and it was left for other hands to close.

For some months before the end he had been planning a removal from his cottage at Hammersmith to London, in order to be nearer to his eldest son and some of his most valued friends; for he felt a renewed appetite for intercourse with other minds. In the interval, he was to visit some few friends out of town, especially Southwood Smith, and Charles Reynell, who lived near at hand. It is an interesting incident, that his very last efforts were devoted to aid the relatives of Shelley in vindicating the memory of the friend who had gone so many years before him. Among the passing visits of these later days was one to his old friend Charles Ollier, who contributed such important materials to the *Shelley Memorials;* a valued companion being Charles Ollier's son, Edmund, who was engaged in the same congenial task. Another of his latest visits was paid on purpose to see, and solace, an admirable friend whose excellence he had learned but lately to appreciate at its full. The sense of beauty and gentleness, of moral beauty and faithful gentleness, grew upon him as the clear evening closed in.

When he went to visit his relative at Putney, he still carried with him his work and the books he more immediately wanted. Although his bodily powers had been giving way, his most conspicuous qualities—his memory for books, and his affection—remained ; and when his hair was white, when his ample chest had grown slender, when the very proportion of his height had visibly lessened, his step was still ready, and his dark eyes brightened at every happy expression and at every thought of kindness. His death was simply exhaustion : he broke off his work to lie down and repose. So gentle was the final approach, that he scarcely recognized it till the very last, and then it came without terrors. His physical suffering had not been severe; at the latest hour he said that his only "uneasiness" was failing breath. And that failing breath was used to express his sense of the inexhaustible kindnesses he had received from the family who had been so unexpectedly made his nurses,—to draw from one of his sons, by minute, eager, and searching questions, all that he could learn about the latest vicissitudes and growing hopes of Italy,—to ask the friends and children around him for news of those whom he loved,—and to send love and messages to the absent who loved him.

Printed by SMITH, ELDER and Co., Little Green Arbour Court, Old Bailey, E.C.